Case Studies in Defence Procurement and Logistics

Volume II: From Ancient Rome to the Astute Class Submarine

Cambridge
Academic

Case Studies in Defence Procurement and Logistics

Volume II: From Ancient Rome to the Astute Class Submarine

David Moore and Peter Antill (eds)

Printed and bound in the United Kingdom by
4edge Ltd, 7a Eldon Way Industrial Estate, Hockley, Essex, SS5 4AD.

Contents

Foreword

David Moore and Peter Antill have provided a tremendous service to many involved in defence, including the Armed Forces, industry and those who analyse and comment on defence policy, by compiling another fascinating volume of case studies in procurement and logistics.

The demands of austerity are driving a restructuring of the Armed Forces and have also helped to spur a fundamental look at the processes for acquisition of equipment and provision of support for our Armed Forces. This path does not necessarily run smoothly, as the Government's experiences in looking to reform DE&S testify. Public expectations that, what is after all, their money will be spent efficiently and effectively have quite rightly grown. Whilst the public demonstrate high levels of support for the Armed Forces and are ready to voice concern when they believe that they are not provided with the right kit, they are unforgiving when money is not spent well. The hoped-for return to a more positive economic outlook will certainly not turn the clock back in this respect.

A re-structured Armed Forces and the anticipated return from enduring operations to contingency throw up a new set of challenges in acquisition and logistics. This volume provides a fascinating combination of historical case studies and analysis from the Ancient World through to the Gulf War and also includes analysis of contemporary challenges in acquisition and logistics. What better place to start in mapping out our response to the new challenges that we are facing than to consider how our predecessors approached theirs?

Rt. Hon. James Arbuthnot MP
Chairman, House of Commons Defence Committee

Contributors

Editors

Dr David M. Moore is currently Director of the Centre for Defence Acquisition within Cranfield University at the Defence Academy of the United Kingdom in Shrivenham. His varied career has included managerial positions in both the public and private sector. He finished his final tour in the Royal Logistic Corps (RLC) at the rank of Lt. Colonel. David has also developed and implemented Purchasing and Logistics courses for a range of major clients as well as MBA programmes whilst at the University of Glamorgan.

Peter D. Antill is currently a research assistant working for Cranfield University at the Centre for Defence Acquisition. Peter has practical experience in the service industry as well as the civil service. A degree holder from both Staffordshire University and the University College of Wales, Aberystwyth he also holds a PGCE (Post Compulsory Education) from Oxford Brooks University. A published author, he is currently conducting post-graduate research into defence acquisition and logistics, British defence policy and expeditionary operations.

Authors

Dr. Jeffrey P. Bradford a trans-Atlantic defence and national security consultant, formerly with Babcock International Group PLC and prior to that, a specialist with Arthur D. Little Inc. in corporate strategy within the aerospace and defence sector. In addition, Jeffrey holds degrees from Staffordshire, Aberystwyth and Cranfield University at the Royal College of Military Science, Shrivenham.

Jon T. Hoffman is deputy director of the Office of the Secretary of Defense Historical Office. A retired Marine Corps Reserve colonel, he has a MA in military history from Ohio State University and a law degree from Duke University. He is the author of *Chesty: The Story of Lieutenant General Lewis B. Puller* (2001), *Once a Legend: 'Red Mike' Edson of the Marine Raiders* (1994), and *USMC: A Complete History* (2002).

Pete Ito has served as a lecturer and researcher in defence acquisition since September 2008. He serves as the academic leader on the Acquisition Employment Training course, runs the Financial Military Capability (Advanced) course, and delivers the International Dimensions of Defence Acquisition and Research Methodology courses in the Defence Acquisition Management MSc. He has undertaken various research projects in the area of defence acquisition. After earning a BA in Political Science from the University of

California at Berkeley, and a Juris Doctor (law) degree and a MA in International Affairs from George Washington University in Washington, D.C. He worked for twenty-five years as a Foreign Service Officer for the US State Department. He joined Cranfield University in September 2007.

Dr Thomas M. Kane is a Senior Lecturer at the University of Hull, specialising in Strategic Studies and International Relations. He has published over eight books on these topics, notably Military Logistics and Strategic Performance (Frank Cass, 2001), Ancient China on Postmodern War (Routledge, 2007) and Understanding Contemporary Strategy (co-authored with Dr. David J. Lonsdale, Routledge, 2012). His book Strategy: Key Thinkers was published by Polity Press in November 2013.

Professor David Kirkpatrick was trained as an aeronautical engineer and later as an economist. During his career in the Scientific Civil Service (1962-1995), he undertook aeronautical research (in aerodynamics and aircraft design) in the Royal Aircraft Establishment at Farnborough, military operational analysis and project cost forecasting in the Ministry of Defence (MoD), and attaché duties on the British Defence Staff in Washington DC. He retired from the MoD after service in two Grade 5 (1 star) posts. Later (1995-2004) he worked in the Defence Engineering Group (DEG) at University College London, which then was MoD's designated centre of excellence for education and research in defence equipment acquisition. In 1999, he was awarded a Personal Chair of Defence Analysis, and was later appointed Head of the DEG. He has been, from 1995 to 2011, an independent member of the Defence Science Advisory Council, and was a specialist advisor to successive House of Commons Defence Committees between 1998 and 2011. He was a Fellow of the Royal Aeronautical Society and is an Associate Fellow of the Royal United Services Institute for Defence Studies. Apart from numerous papers printed within the MoD, he has written many published papers on various aspects of aeronautics, defence acquisition, defence economics and military history. He has written booklets on cost-effectiveness analysis (1996) and on the UK's Strategic Defence and Security Review (2010). He was also one of the principal authors of a book 'Conquering Complexity – Lessons for Defence Systems Acquisition' (2005) and lead author of Chapter 25 'Integrated Logistic Support and all that; a review of through-life project management' in the Wiley Guide to Project Management, edited by P. W. G. Morris and J. K. Pinto, published by Wiley in 2004. He frequently gives lectures on these topics at the Defence Academy of the UK and elsewhere.

Lt Col Randy McCanne (USAF), LTC Greg D. Olsen (US Army) and **Cdr Dario E. Teicher** were students in Class 02-3S, Joint and Combined Warfighting Course, Joint Forces Staff College, Norfolk, VA from 2001 – 2002.

David R. Rabaut was a master's degree student, studying at the University of Illinois, from 1961 to 1962.

Steve Robinson is a professional project manager with extensive experience in managing military equipment projects, developing HR policy and implementing HR programmes centred on the development of knowledge and skills. He has well developed management consultancy skills and has lectured on project & risk management in the UK, France, Germany, Norway & South East Asia in additional to acting as a Cranfield University visiting lecturer over a number of years. Qualified to Masters level in Electrical & Electronic Engineering, he is also a Managing Successful Programmes (MSP) Practitioner, Association for Project Management Professional (APMP), Fellow of the APM and Member of the Institute of Engineering Technology. He was a previous Chairman of the UK Engineering Project Management Forum and has had articles on Developing a Project Management Culture and Project Management in Schools published in the national media. He established The Learning Project in July 2012 to provide business learning and consultancy services. This followed employment within the MOD DE&S as Team Leader of the BAES Terms of Business Agreement (ToBA) Joint Project Office. Prior to this he was Deputy Head of Civilian Skills with responsibility on behalf of the Permanent Under Secretary for developing the first MOD Skills Strategy. Earlier appointments included the team leader role for the Smart Acquisition People, Skills & Behaviour Workstream and Head of the Acquisition Training Cell at the Defence Academy. Steve was a Project Management Course Manager at Portsmouth University following an appointment as a Project Management Consultant in DERA. Earlier roles included Deputy Project Manager Type 23 Frigate Combat System, Missile Performance Engineer for Harpoon & Exocet and Commissioning Engineer for the MOD Weapon Systems Tuning Group. This latter role exploited experience gained as a Graduate Engineer and since joining the MOD as a Technician Apprentice.

Jeremy C. Smith spent twenty-five years of his working life as an Army logistician and Ammunition Technical Officer. During his time in uniform he commanded a variety of supply and transport units in UK, Germany, and on operations in Northern Ireland, the Balkans and the Middle East. He served on the staff of the Quartermaster General and the Defence Logistics Organisation, managing support to a variety of weapon systems and developing through life support policy. He left the Army in 2008 and took up an appointment with Cranfield Defence and Security, based in Shrivenham, Wiltshire. He now lectures in Logistics and Supply Chain Management, in which he has an MSc, and in Through Life Support.

Dr Peter Tatham joined the Royal Navy in 1970 and served in a variety of appointments during his career of some 35 years. Highlights include Logistics Officer of the aircraft carrier HMS Invincible in 1994/5 during Operations in Bosnia against the Former Republic of Yugoslavia, and Chief Staff Officer responsible for all high level Personnel and Logistics issues emanating from the 10,000 sailors and 30 surface ships in the Royal Navy (1999-2000). His final three years in the Service were spent in the UK's Defence Logistics Organisation where he was responsible for key elements of the internal programme of Change Management (2000-2004). During this period, he also gained an MSc in Defence Logistic Management. Following his retirement from the RN, he joined the staff of Cranfield University where he lectured in Human Systems and Humanitarian Logistics. He was awarded his PhD for research into the issues surrounding the role of shared values within military supply networks. He now works at Griffith University in Queensland, Australia.

Major David F. Tosch was a student at the School of Advanced Military Studies, US Army Command and General Staff College, Fort Leavenworth, Kansas from 1986 – 1987.

Prof. Trevor Taylor was formerly Head of the Department of Defence Management and Security Analysis at Cranfield University's faculty at the Royal Military College of Science in the UK. He was previously Professor of International Relations at Staffordshire University and between 1990 and 1993 was Head of the International Security Programme at the Royal Institute of International Affairs in London. He is also a past Chairman of the British International Studies Association and has been Visiting Professor at the National Defence Academy in Tokyo. He was educated at the London School of Economics (B.Sc(Econ) and PhD) and Lehigh University (MA) in Pennsylvania. He has published extensively on European security and defence industrial issues, and is currently working on the political and defence implications of defence restructuring in Europe.

Anthony G. Williams is an independent consultant specialising in small arms and automatic cannon. He has written many magazine articles and has authored or co-authored the following books: "Rapid Fire" (2000); "Flying Guns" (three volumes, 2003-4); "Assault Rifle" (2004) and "Machine Gun" (2008). He is also Co-editor (since 2005) of "Jane's Ammunition Handbook" and Editor (since 2004) of "The Cartridge Researcher", the bulletin of the European Cartridge Research Association. He maintains a website on military guns and ammunition at www.quarry.nildram.co.uk.

Stuart Young joined Cranfield University in 2008 as a Deputy Director in the Centre for Defence Acquisition where he has a particular interest in the relationship between the MoD and Industry across the supply chain and the development of strategies for major acquisition programmes. Stuart joined the Royal Navy in 1977 as a Maritime Engineer Officer, doing a post-graduate level qualification at the Royal Naval Engineering College in Plymouth. He has served in a variety of operational posts at sea but also a number of acquisition-related appointments in the Ministry of Defence. This has included spending three years as the Defence Equipment Marine Engineer with the Defence Staff at the British Embassy in Washington DC and serving as the Electric Ship Programme Manager in the Defence Procurement Agency with direct responsibility for a major UK-France technology development programme. He has also been involved in the selection of innovative technologies for the Type 45 destroyer and CVF programmes and served in the DLO, the Defence Electronic Commerce Service and in the Defence Management and Leadership Centre in Shrivenham.

Acknowledgements

The Editors would like to thank the following for their kind permission to include the mentioned material:

Jon T. Hoffman and Marine Corps Gazette for being able to use the *Downfall* article.

Anthony Williams for his *'Future Small Arms'* paper.

Prof. Trevor Taylor and Dr. Peter Tatham for the *Challenger II* case study.

Prof. David Kirkpatrick for his two cases on the American Civil War and land warfare.

Dr Jeffrey Bradford for the case studies on the Options-for-Change Defence Review and updating his de-classified case study on the Bowman communication system.

Simon Mitchell and the RUSI Defence Systems journal for being able to use previously published material.

Anita Hauser and the Defence Procurement International journal for being able to use previously published material.

All the photos used in this volume were obtained from publically available sources, such as Flickr, Wikimedia Commons and defenceimagery.mod.uk and came with licenses that permitted their re-use, commercially, such as the Open Government License. In most instances this was at the behest of the author/uploader who only required an acknowledgement as to their source.

Where the photo originated from an employee of the US Federal Government, any image produced by that person during the performance of their duties is considered to be in the public domain. Any photographs from defenceimagery.mod.uk are made available to use freely under the OGL (Open Government License) so long as the source is acknowledged. The images of Morning of the Battle of Agincourt, the Duke of Marlborough at Blenheim and Sherman's men destroying railroad track are considered to be in the public domain (as their copyright has expired) as per the copyright laws within the European Union and Australia, which consider copyright to run for the life of the author plus seventy years. The image of Napoleon retreating from Moscow is considered to be in the public domain (as its copyright has expired) within the United States and those countries that have a copyright term of the life of the author plus 100 years or less, which includes the European Union and Australia.

The photographs of the 5-inch howitzer during the Second Boer War, the aircraft carriers during the Suez Crisis and the panzers in the desert are considered to be in the public domain as they are photographs created or obtained by the UK Government prior to 1 June 1957. The photograph of Admiral Isoroku Yamamoto is considered to be in the public domain as it comes under the jurisdiction of the Government of Japan and was published before 31 December 1956 or taken before 1946 and thus falls under Article 23 of the old copyright law of Japan and Article 2 of the supplemental provision of the copyright law of Japan.

Preface

This second volume contains seventeen cases focusing on defence procurement and logistics issues that will provide an excellent learning opportunity to a variety of readers. This wide-ranging audience will include military personnel, those on defence education and training programmes, employees of the defence industry, those in defence agencies and those engaged in defence and security-related research (an example being under- and postgraduate students on international politics and strategic studies courses). It will also be of relevance to students undertaking procurement and supply chain management courses that are not necessarily intended for military or defence careers. This is because many of the cases focus upon fundamental aspects which pervade all the relevant areas of, for example, logistics. An example of this is in the very first case where we discuss the mechanics of logistics. Hence, this is also of relevance to students on MBA, MSc, MA and professional qualification courses.

As well as featuring seventeen cases, there is a foreword, notes on contributors, acknowledgements, preface and an overview. There will also be an introductory chapter on the contemporary nature of defence acquisition, logistics and supply chain management and in particular the current issues surrounding austerity that faces the UK. The majority of the cases presented will provide a useful source of reference as they are factual, albeit often in a précised form. Others, are based on fact, but are produced in such a manner as to prompt the reader's thinking, conceptualisation and application of concepts into practise.

A key feature of the first part is the chronological nature of the cases; although the date and the contextual setting for each case may change, and indeed the scale involved may differ, the overarching theme is that there is much to be learnt from studying experiences from the past and considering them in a contemporary environment. However, part two identifies, within particular defence procurement projects, the central challenges faced by a number of contemporary defence projects. These cases are progressive, and build towards a comprehensive appreciation of major issues and challenges that have presented themselves in the way that the UK and other countries have undertaken defence procurement and logistics.

The intention is that the reader should be able to shape his or her thinking in respect of defence procurement and logistics. They should be taking into account not only the factual details of each case, but developing conceptual perspectives in order to influence contemporary ideas, doctrine and their implementation. The chronological nature of the cases and the broad spectrum of operating environments covered, permit a consideration of existing and emergent theories and practice.

Book Overview

Building from the approach taken in our first volume, we are very grateful to colleagues, both within the Centre for Defence Acquisition (CFDA) and around the globe for their contributions to this second volume.

Similarly, we are extremely grateful the Rt Hon James Arbuthnot MP (Chairman of the House of Commons Defence Committee), who has taken time out from his busy schedule to consider our work and make pertinent comment.

We commence with a perspective on austerity and although this significantly focuses on the UK, it also provides an insight into both the European and US positions which can be seen as applicable, given the current global economic situation. As such, it will provide the reader with valuable perspectives on the challenges that have to be faced, frequently involving difficult decisions. This is a volatile socio-economic situation, heavily influenced by political input, as can be seen by the postscript to this introduction whereby a considerable change to the intended strategic approach to the reform of the Ministry of Defence's procurement and logistics organisation took place just as the book was being finalised.

The first case considers logistics and the Roman Army and it identifies that the mechanics of logistics are still the same today, as they were all those centuries ago. However, it also identifies the critical role that logistics does play in successful military campaigns. In this abridged version of David Rabaut's dissertation, fundamental logistics principles regarding storage, transport and having the right goods in the right place at the right time are brought to the fore. It also introduces the concept of 'commoditisation' and the need for individual logistic support skills.

Continuing the importance of logistics theme, Professor David Kirkpatrick provides an informative and fascinating overview of the comparative approaches used in the American Civil War by Union and Confederate armies. In particular it brings out the importance of transport, especially the widespread use of railways to move men and munitions around. This conflict has significance, as it can be seen as a portent of future large-scale war (such as the Franco-Prussian War, Boer War and the First World War).

Moving on in chronological terms, we feature four cases from the Second World War. The first being Operation Sealion by Lt Col Randy McCanne, Lt Col Olsen and Cdr Dario Teicher, who take a retrospective view on the planning for and logistics of, the planned German invasion of the UK in the autumn of 1940. They identify critical issues that if handled differently, could have brought about a situation where the Germans may have been in a position to launch said invasion with a chance of success. This is valuable for contemporary thinking and should be seen through a 'capability management' lens that encompasses a range of factors, including the use of allies. The second case by Major David Tosch looks at the North African campaign from the perspective of the Germans and whilst identifying 'traditional' logistic themes, adds the key feature of sustainability. He identifies the importance of infrastructure and long-term support over a series of changing scenarios. This has great resonance with current and potential future operational campaigns. The third case identifies the sheer scale of logistic support to particular campaigns, which was certainly the case in the Pacific War. Whilst very few countries could have sustained the logistics effort to both the European and Pacific Theatres of War in the way the USA did, this case, by Peter Antill and Dr Tom Kane, also identifies the importance of integration and joint planning, processes and procedures. The last of the Second World War cases examines what had the potential to be the largest amphibious invasion ever attempted – the planned Allied invasion of Japan, codenamed Operation Downfall, which consisted of two subsidiary operations, Olympic and Coronet, scheduled for November 1945 and March 1946 respectively. While it may seem a little strange looking for lessons in an operation that never actually took place, the planning and organisation that did happen does provide lessons for future planners, which includes that there is sometimes danger inherent in choosing what appears to be (superficially at least) the best course of action and the importance of unity of command.

The final case of part one by Professor David Kirkpatrick, is an overarching view of logistics in land warfare, progressing from the Middle Ages through to the Gulf War and uses mini-case studies to identify key themes. He focuses upon supply and re-supply while examining a range of approaches from foraging through supply by wagon, by rail, truck and air. He then discusses supply lines and the importance of transport in enabling adequate provisioning. His final point is telling . . . assessing any new weapon system must take into account its associated logistic requirements.

Part two takes a slightly different approach, where we seek to identify important challenges that need to be overcome in the procurement of modern weapon systems. The first case study by Steve Robinson looks at the latest addition to the UK's nuclear submarine fleet, the Astute-class hunter killer. This is probably one of the most complex procurement programmes that has been undertaken by the MoD in recent years (with the possible exception of the new carriers). Above all, it has been complicated by two maritime portfolio issues, the first being the maintenance of the UK's submarine building capability and the second, is the protection of the UK's nuclear deterrent. Nevertheless, it provides a wealth of learning examples that can only be of benefit to this and other such complex projects.

The second case by Peter Tatham and Professor Trevor Taylor concerns the procurement of the British Army's current main battle tank (MBT). It is set against a backdrop of considerable change in doctrine, production and procurement methods. Whilst the final result was a success in terms of both the weapon system and the production approach, it ultimately led to the demise of company involved. The third case, by Peter Antill and Jeremy Smith, brings the procurement of land equipment up-to-date again by examining the Urgent Operational Requirements (UORs) that have bought into service a wide-range of Protected Patrol Vehicles (PPVs). These have come about because of the threat posed by Improvised Explosive Devices (IEDs) in both Iraq and Afghanistan. The case identifies the challenges of Through-Life Support (TLS) in both planning for, and undertaking the overall management of the fleet including spares and maintenance.

The fourth case, by Peter Antill, focuses on the British Army's assault rifle (the SA80) providing a historical backdrop followed by key issues in its design, manufacture, introduction into, and support in-service. Over a period of time and a number of different operations, the rifle has undergone various modifications and updates. It is now, arguably, the weapon the British Army should have received when it was first introduced into service in 1985. For the reader, this case brings out many issues that need to be considered in any contemporaneous procurement project. For optimal understanding, this case should be read in conjunction with the EM-2 case study, which is featured in the first volume.

Jeffrey Bradford provides the next case, which looks at the Bowman project. This concerns a major IT / communications procurement project that was to be used on a tri-service basis. The case identifies key aspects of project management for a programme of considerable complexity that takes place over a long period of time. It highlights the technological, political and economic pressures upon such a project, and how these in turn impact upon the way the project is managed.

The final case in part two, by Peter Antill, concerns what was initially an ambitious collaborative European project to build a light, wheeled armoured personnel carrier. This case is indicative of many such potential collaborative ventures; on the one hand considerable benefits could be gained by pooling requirements, on the other hand, it often transpires that the countries involved cannot agree upon the compromises necessary for progress (another example being the Horizon Common New Generation Frigate, which is covered in the first volume of the series). For the UK, whilst multi-national collaboration has often offered considerable potential benefits, there is now a greater focus upon bi-lateral arrangements with the USA and France.

Part three changes emphasis once again to consider challenges within the context of the wider defence *acquisition* environment. In the first case, Jeffrey Bradford takes an academic perspective and considers the 'Options for Change' defence review twenty-five years on within initially, the hypothesis of rationality. This is followed by a model based on organisational process and then by a third that considers bureaucratic politics as the overarching model.

Having earlier identified that the UK is increasingly moving from multi-lateral collaboration to bi-lateral collaboration, the next case study by Pete Ito, Peter Antill and Steve Robinson examines the potential UK-France collaborative approach. It covers past activities, current policy and rationale and then takes into account political aspects as well as contemporary operations, such as Libya. It moves on to consider industrial participation and development, technological progress and the wider European perspective. It is a study of recent issues that may well set the scene for future collaborative programmes.

History has a habit of repeating itself, and arguably, this is exactly the case with small arms. In this penultimate case, Anthony Williams draws upon experience in Afghanistan to identify that after this major undertaking, the British Army (as well as other NATO countries) will end the campaign with a variety of weapons and ammunition of varying calibre. He argues that if we are not careful we will be in exactly the same position as in the past, where we seek to rationalise existing weapons and ammunition inventories instead of taking a more strategic view of the long-term future.

The final case study, by Peter Antill and Stuart Young, identifies opportunities for naval procurement in Asia. It brings out the drivers and geo-strategic imperatives that underlie the continued expansion in defence budgets that has characterised the region. For most countries, there are considerable challenges in maintaining the security of their national boundaries, an issue that is complicated by the continued development of blue-water naval capability by both India and China. The case also identifies the current and future procurement requirements of a number of countries, hence bringing the case studies to a conclusion with a focus upon an environment in a different region of the globe.

Introduction

Austerity and the Current Challenges in the Defence Environment

Dr David M. Moore, Peter D. Antill, Jeremy C. D. Smith and Pete Ito
Centre for Defence Acquisition, Cranfield University, Defence Academy of the UK.

Introduction

The defence and security environment has continued to evolve since 2011 when we published the first volume of our series, as has the economic environment. Despite the advanced industrialised countries starting to see their economies recover[1] after the recession of the last few years, the impact of that recession, the squeeze it has had on public sector finances and the methods used to bring public sector spending under control all continue to affect the provision of defence and security. Many governments have had to make difficult decisions in order to bring public sector spending into line, including those in the Eurozone who have had an especially difficult task. This has included making cuts to budgets and the numbers of personnel employed in both the civil service and armed forces as exemplified by the UK's Strategic Defence and Security Review (SDSR) of 2010[2] but also seen right across Europe. This chapter will look in detail as to what has happened in recent years with the UK in relation to the defence budget and reforming the Ministry of Defence (MoD), the way it acquires equipment and services as well as the armed forces but also more generally, Europe and the USA.

United Kingdom[3]

The financial crisis of 2008 and subsequent economic recession once again cast the spotlight on the Ministry of Defence's track record of future planning and in using the resources available to it to obtain the best value for UK taxpayers. Numerous reports from the National Audit Office (NAO)[4] and the House of Commons Public Accounts Committee (HCPAC)[5] as well as the SDSR and Lord Levene's 'Defence Reform' report of 2011[6] all underlined the situation and highlighted the reasons behind the Department's poor performance as well as ways to rectify the situation. The MoD currently faces a critical period, having to juggle the need to conduct a major transformation of the MoD itself, changing the way in which it acquires defence capability and services (in other words, reforming Defence Equipment and

Support (DE&S)), restructuring the armed forces and all the while managing a huge portfolio of activity. The Government however deems it necessary and so in order for defence to play its part in bringing Government spending under control and tackling the UK's budgetary deficit, defence has been required to make £4.3bn worth of savings[7] by 2015, a figure that was increased by £875m during Spending Round 2013.[8]

Restructuring the MoD

It is encouraging that the MoD has recognised the need for change, and not only produced a new defence vision in its most recent business plan[9] but has instituted a transformation package that consists of a portfolio of thirty-seven programmes with an additional ten deliverables. These are split into three tiers:[10]

- Tier 1 – the most critical programmes which are subject to detailed oversight by the Defence Operating Board (Transformation);
- Tier 2 – all other change programmes;
- Tier 3 – additional security and defence commitments.

The Defence Operating Board (Transformation) meets once a week and includes the 2nd Permanent under Secretary, Vice Chief of the Defence Staff and Director General Finance as permanent members, with the Director General Transformation and Director Corporate Strategy attending regularly. The Board is supported by the Defence Transformation Unit which holds to account those responsible for delivering change as well as looking at portfolio risks, issues and dependencies.[11]

With frontline costs due to come down after the UK begins its withdrawal from Afghanistan next year (2014), the drive to reduce costs has meant an emphasis on short-term cost reduction in non-frontline expenditure. The defence budget, unlike most departmental budgets, has a relatively high proportion of fixed costs in the short-term, with a significant proportion (in both operational expenditure terms and procurement terms) being committed in advance. As a consequence, the MoD was left with very little room to manoeuvre when it came to reducing its spending in the short-term. With personnel costs making up over a third of the budget, a high proportion of the savings that the MoD is going to make will come from a reduction in the number of people who work for it, both civilian and military. The numbers in the SDSR were subsequently revised upwards in the spring of 2011 to 29,000 civilians (thirty-four per cent of the total) and 25,000 military (fourteen per cent of the total).[12]

With the MoD still developing the details associated with Lord Levene's new operating model[13], the reductions in the Department's personnel numbers will be well advanced by the time they're worked out, which means they will have been implemented before there is clarity as to what exactly the MoD's requirements will be with regard to its future workforce, in terms of both numbers of personnel and their exact makeup. There is a risk therefore, that a significant skills gap will open up, meaning that the MoD will have to rely even more (in the short-to-medium term at least) on external expertise, the cost of which rose from £6m in 2006-07 to £270m in 2010-11. In reality, the pressure on the MoD to reduce costs in the short-term combined with its only real course of action being to reduce numbers of both military and civilian personnel, means that the MoD will have to deal with not only the impact on morale but in addition the very real risk of critical skill shortages with its consequent effects on consultancy expenditure.[14]

Restructuring DE&S

The reform of DE&S was a key component in Lord Levine's report about reforming the MoD[15] but was also featured in the Defence Materiel Strategy[16] and both Bernard Gray's and Charles Haddon-Cave's 2009 reports.[17] Indeed, reforming the way the MoD has bought and supported equipment (and services) has a long history. The Gibb-Zuckermann report of 1961 recommended a five-stage process be introduced into the way defence procurement is carried out and which still forms the basis of how it operates today. These stages were:[18]

1. Produce a Staff Target to define the required capability;
2. Conduct a feasibility study to identify risk (especially technical risk);
3. Formulate a Staff Requirement to define the project's key performance criteria;
4. Undertake a Project Study to resolve risks, define development and forecast the cost and time; and
5. Initiate a full Development Phase leading to Full Production.

This process was formally introduced as the 'Downey Cycle' in 1968. This was as a result of a report issued by the Steering Group on Development Cost Estimates, chaired by William Downey, and replaced the 'Project Study' stage with a more detailed 'Project Definition' stage and stated that each stage must be complete before the project can move on to the next. It also recommended that the 'Feasibility Study' and 'Project Definition' stages absorb around fifteen percent of the total development cost. The Procurement Executive (PE) was formed in April 1971 from the separate Service ministries as a procurement 'agency' covering defence as a whole. It followed a report by Sir Derek Rayner (later Lord Rayner) who also became its first Chief Executive, followed by Sir Michael Cary. Its aim was to create clearer customer-supplier relationships. In 1985, Peter Levene became the new Chief of Defence Procurement, and brought with him a much more commercial approach in an attempt to bring about cost savings from the use of competition for contracts, fixed price contracts and the use of prime contractors from industry. In 1987, a report on Managing Major Projects in the Procurement Executive by Jordan, Lee and Cawsey recommended the MoD take a more incremental approach to procurement and that dedicated project managers be appointed to each project. In 1994, the Front Line First: Defence Costs Study recommended that the entire PE apparatus be collocated at the site at Filton, Bristol which was subsequently done.[19] In 1999, following the introduction of Smart Procurement the previous year, both the Defence Procurement Agency (out of the PE) and Defence Logistics Organisation (out of the separate Service logistics branches)[20] were created, eventually followed by the amalgamation of the two to form DE&S on 2 April 2007.[21] Additional initiatives have also been put in place such as the Defence Change Portfolio (2002), Defence Logistics Transformation Programme (2004), Defence Acquisition Change Programme (2006) and PACE (Performance, Agility, Confidence and Efficiency – 2008).[22]

While some reforms have been implemented, such as having the Chief of Defence Materiel (CDM) now on the Defence Board and having the lead for commercial and industrial policy across defence, as well as it now being mandatory for the independent costings from the Cost Assurance and Analysis Service (CAAS) to be used in the Deputy Chief of Defence Staff, Capability (DCDS (Cap)) area – something that will be extended to the Frontline Commands as part of the wider reforms of financial management – there is still much work to be done. There are still significant time and cost overruns being encountered in defence acquisition, with an average forty percent increase in the projected cost and an eighty percent increase in the time taken to bring an item of equipment into service. Further analysis identified three main causes:[23]

- The overheated programme;
- A weak interface between DE&S and the wider MoD resulting in poor discipline and change control (which contributed towards the 'conspiracy of optimism' and 'specification creep');
- Insufficient levels of business capability in DE&S for the size and complexity of the programmes it handles (in other words, a lack of commercial skills).

Ministers were then presented with three options for the restructuring of DE&S in December 2011:[24]

- A trading fund (TF);
- An executive, non-departmental public body with a strategic partner (ENDPB/SP); and
- A government-owned, contractor-operated (GOCO) entity.

Since then the Government has been moving steadily towards favouring the GOCO option.[25] Originally, it advocated the Atomic Weapons Establishment (AWE), outsourced under a GOCO arrangement, as a successful model for possible reform, but it is difficult to ascertain how successful this project has been, given its security sensitive nature and the resultant lack of public scrutiny. The failure of security contractor G4S to provide enough security guards at the London Olympic Games in 2012 (they fell short by almost 5,000 personnel) forced a brief period of reconsideration, with the Defence Secretary Philip Hammond "rethinking his attitude to private sector procurement".[26] However, the Defence Secretary then announced in May 2013, that an assessment would be undertaken over the coming year of two possible options for DE&S: 1) A private sector led GOCO model and 2) 'DE&S+' which would be a fully funded, restructured version of the existing organisation, thus staying in the public sector.

The MoD has noted that during this assessment phase, there will be coordination with the Treasury and the Cabinet Office to examine the possible outcomes of DE&S+. At the same time, a commercial competition will be initiated to assess how a GOCO would work in practice. The Defence Secretary emphasised that there would be an objective assessment of the two options, stating that

> "No decisions have yet been made. At the end of this 12-month Assessment Phase we will have a comprehensive set of qualitative and quantitative data for both possible operating Models which will enable us critically to evaluate the two options and make a final decision about the future of DE&S."[27]

However, it is notable that the 2013 MoD statement contains the comment that in July 2012, the GOCO model was already provisionally announced as the preferred option with regard to transforming DE&S – something that had been reported in The Times on 22 June 2012.[28] This, despite significant questions still being raised about how exactly it would operate and how it would report[29] with one commentator saying

"Think about the political gamble here: the Defence Secretary, Philip Hammond, and Mr Osborne are willing to let one of the most sensitive aspects of national security be run by business, most likely overseas behemoths. This is extraordinary – even more so if this unparalleled, globally unproven idea actually works."[30]

Indeed, the Defence Secretary conceded in the 2013 announcement that:

"We have made no secret of our expectation that the GOCO option is likely to prove better value for money, but we need to test this assumption with the market, to see what can be delivered and at what cost."[31]

The MoD followed this up with the release of the White Paper entitled 'Better Defence Acquisition' in June 2013.[32] Despite the Defence Secretary's May 2013 statement that no decision had been made as regards the future structure of DE&S, the document sets out proposals for two changes to DE&S, the first being the creation of a new GOCO operating model to "manage the procurement and support of defence equipment by the Defence Equipment and Support organisation as the agent of the MoD, subject to demonstrating affordability and value for money."[33] It asserts that this step would attract "incentivised private sector expertise" to improve the MoD's acquisition process by introducing processes and procedures that would "provide staff with the best access to the necessary skills, processes and tools to enable them to do their jobs better" driving "value for money in equipment projects".[34] The second change is the adoption of a "new statutory framework to ensure transparency and to encourage efficiency in single-source procurement contracts".[35] The White Paper also notes that analysis "carried out to date suggests that the establishment of a 'GOCO' operating model would realise significant benefits over those that could be achieved from a wholly public sector model for reform".[36]

Restructuring the Armed Forces

The SDSR of 2010 put forward the model towards which the UK Armed Forces will gradually transform over the next few years, which was entitled 'Future Force 2020'. Underpinning this vision is a new set of Defence Planning Assumptions which include the armed forces being able to conduct:[37]

- An enduring[38] stabilisation operation at approximately brigade level (up to 6,500 personnel) with maritime and air support as required, while also conducting . . .

One non-enduring[39] complex intervention (of up to 2,000 personnel), and . . .
One non-enduring simple intervention (of up to 1,000 personnel).

or alternatively . . .

- three non-enduring operations if the UK is not already engaged in an enduring operation.

or for a limited time (and with sufficient warning) . . .

- a one-off intervention of up to three brigades, with maritime and air support (around 30,000 personnel, two-thirds of the force deployed to Iraq in 2003).

This will mean that in future, forces will generally be in one of three readiness states at any one time:[40]

1. The Deployed Force – forces currently engaged in operations;
2. The High Readiness Force – forces kept at a high state of readiness so as to be able to respond to a crisis or threat;
3. The Lower Readiness Force – all other forces, which would include forces that have recently returned from operations or have recently been stepped down from high readiness.

However, it must be remembered that all these changes are being carried out by a department that has been under a great deal of pressure to find budgetary savings in order to contribute towards the overall reduction in Government spending. Despite being couched in terms of making the UK Armed Forces more 'relevant' and 'effective' for the 21st Century, this restructure represents a major reduction in defence capability with:

- The Royal Navy[41] having to maintain the maritime defence of the UK and its overseas territories, maintain a continuous-at-sea deterrence posture (with the Vanguard class submarines due to be replaced after 2028), continue to play a major role in British foreign policy and maintain 3rd Commando Brigade as a rapid deployment force, with a commando group of 1,800 personnel ready to go at very short notice. The Service is reducing its personnel by over 5,000 to 30,000 and its frigate and destroyer force from twenty-three to nineteen, losing a Bay class amphibious ship, reducing its carrier force from three to two (admittedly they are much bigger carriers but only one will be at sea at any one time) and after converting HMS Illustrious into a helicopter carrier[42] as well as scrapping the Sea Harriers, HMS Ark Royal[43] and HMS Invincible[44] have no fixed wing capability until the F-35 enters service in around 2020.

- The Royal Air Force[45] having to maintain the air defence of the UK and its overseas territories, an expeditionary capability to support enduring land operations, tactical and strategic airlift and specialist support such as ISTAR and the RAF Regiment. The Service is reducing its personnel by 5,000 to 33,000 and has lost the Harrier force, will not now receive the Nimrod MR4 aircraft (despite the programme being almost complete and some £4bn having been spent[46]), will lose the VC10 / Tristar fleet, and lose the Hercules fleet ten years earlier than planned (in anticipation of the much-delayed A400-M).

- The British Army[47] having to maintain forces for the UK's standing commitments and provide light / specialist forces for any short-term interventions and multi-role forces for more complex operations, as well as retain the ability to command UK and allied forces up to theatre level. It is restructuring around two elements – the Reaction Force (comprising a divisional headquarters, three armoured infantry brigades and 16th Air Assault Brigade) and the Adaptable Force (a divisional headquarters with seven regionally-based brigade headquarters). However, it is also downsizing to 82,000 personnel – half the size it was in 1978 during the Cold War and the smallest it's been since the Boer War – effectively losing five infantry battalions, forty percent of the Challenger II fleet and thirty-five percent of its heavy artillery.[48]

In addition to restructuring the regular forces, the MoD is looking to change the way the various components of defence interact with each other. The Whole Force Concept (WFC) was one of a range of ideas and initiatives to emerge from the Strategic Defence and Security Review (SDSR) of 2010.[49] It was subsequently formalized in Key Recommendation Eleven of Lord Levene's report which stated that:

"In line with the overall capability planning and financial management model, the Department should afford greater priority to managing its 'human capability' as a strategic resource, to ensure a better balance with its consideration of equipment capability. Specifically, it should develop the 'Whole Force Concept,' which seeks to ensure that Defence is supported by the most cost-effective balance of regular military personnel, reservists, MOD civilians and contractors." [50]

The WFC consists, therefore, of three components: the UK Armed Forces (both regular and reservist); the civil servants who work alongside them; and the contractors who support them on operations. It is, as its name suggests, conceptual and, as was emphasized by the Independent Commission to Review the UK's Reserve Forces[51], should not be thought of as representing a rigid structure. The Commission stressed the dynamic nature of the WFC: that at any given time the contributions the three components make to the Whole Force should aggregate up to represent what is most operationally relevant and cost effective.

In addition to a review of reserve forces, a number of other enabling studies and initiatives underpin the WFC. Amongst them are a review of the implications for the defence estates, a review of existing terms and conditions of service, and how a new employment model could be structured. This will be based on "...flexible structures, segmented careers, categories of readiness, and the mix of Regulars and Reserves with graduated commitment, set within a tri-Service structure, with options for full and part time working".[52] Other reviews have focused on strategic force development and on force generation. An important subset of the WFC is the Total Support Force (TSF – explained below) and it is worth noting that to turn the concepts of both the TSF and the WFC into concrete reality will require that the mix of Armed Forces Regulars and Reservists, MoD civil servants, and contractors, is optimized. To achieve this optimization will demand the balancing of affordability and operational risk.

The Independent Commission reviewing the Reserve Forces recognized the critical contribution of the reserves to the WFC but also the need for their quality and availability to be guaranteed. This would, they said, require an improvement in the proposition (prospects, responsibilities and rewards of reserve service) to the reservists, a change to legislation to enable more routine mobilization, better employer support and employment protection, and better methods to achieve the integration of Regulars and Reservists. Within the UK MoD, the Defence Medical Services are considered to be leading practitioners of the WFC but work done by the Commission suggested that the UK could also learn much from the experience of its ABCA[53] partners who employ a whole force approach.

The Total Support Force (TSF) on the other hand, was proposed by SDSR Support Study 3.4. The MoD's vision for the TSF is of an end-to-end support force "...capable of deploying and operating with fully integrated support capabilities derived from a pre-planned mix of military and civilian individuals and organisations".[54] The TSF requires that Reservists and contractors from industry be integrated into Regular force structures against readiness assumptions and agile force generation requirements. It envisages "... the greater planned use of contractors on operations, in functions that are commensurate with the category of threat level in order to accommodate force protection and duty of care responsibilities, normally with an increasingly higher proportion of contractors on successive roulements for enduring operations".[55]

The UK MoD has outsourced much of its support capability and moved the support given to many of its major platforms and equipment assets over to long-term contracts for availability (CfA) while securing the provision of commodities and services through a range of other, often shorter duration contracts. One obvious manifestation of the extent of this outsourcing activity has been the number of contractors deployed in support of UK operations – approximately 6,000 in Afghanistan currently, representing a ratio of two contractors for every three uniformed military personnel.[56] These contractors provide vital support to UK operations in logistics, infrastructure support, and the maintenance and operation of battle-winning equipment. However, the provision of this support, whilst vital to operational success, has not been as coherent as the MoD, and in particular operational commanders, would wish it to have been. The intent behind the TSF is that it brings this coherence to the integration of Regulars, Reservists and industry personnel into a single support force.

A successful TSF should deliver assured support for the operational commander, a safe and secure working environment for industry personnel, good value for Defence, and an acceptable reward for industry. It should be pre-planned and work end-to-end. The TSF vision sees industry and the MoD working together to deliver assured support from an established home base, along the Joint Support Chain and into the theatre of operations. The scale and scope of industry commitment to operations will be shaped by their attitude to risk and what they deem to be an acceptable balance between risk and reward. Such informed assessment will require the sharing of information, including that associated with the physical risk associated with deployed operations. This will require a change of mindset, based on the principle of 'need to share' rather than 'need to know', and it will also demand greater integration of MoD and industry information systems.

It is envisaged that the TSF will comprise several categories of personnel, amongst them:[57]

- Regular Servicemen and women, trained and available to deploy at short notice, to provide immediate support to operations;
- Reservists, mobilized and trained to deliver support at longer notice;
- Contractors from industry who will provide equipment and logistic support under CfA arrangements;
- Civilian workers, who may be recruited locally to provide unskilled labour.

Industry personnel are envisaged to fit into three broad categories:

- Integrated Partners, who will be part of the military force structure and who will plan, train and deliver together;
- Essential Contractors, who the MoD needs to deliver operational effect but who require limited support from the MoD, and who deliver a specific service such as freight distribution;
- Ancillary Contractors, who will provide generic services which are probably freely available on the commercial market and may be sourced locally.

Categorizing support personnel in this fashion is expected to bring the greater coherence to the planning and delivery of support, both in the home base and in the theatre of operations that the MoD requires.[58]

Currently, the Frontline Commands are engaged in a range of TSF feasibility studies and implementation initiatives. Inevitably, financial pressures are influencing where the Commands are focusing their work as well as constraining them. Successful implementation of the TSF will be dependent on the new employment model referred to above, '... underpinned by the appropriate legal framework, and a basing strategy that enables a strong link between the Home Base and the operational area'.[59] The ability of Industry to contribute to force generation and then sustain a cost-effective, enduring capability, noting political and legal constraints that might apply in the build-up to conflict, is key. The associated risks must be understood and clearly stated.[60]

The Inventory Problem

In its June 2012 report on the Defence Inventory[61], the National Audit Office (NAO) observed that the Department's inventory holdings are increasing, the result of a number of factors:

- An increase in operational activity over the past decade;
- The procurement of new equipment to prosecute operations, including capabilities procured against an accelerated timescale via the urgent operational requirements process;
- A failure to dispose of inventory it no longer requires;
- The purchase of more inventory than it uses;
- The creation of greater visibility of its stock levels by recording more inventory on its IT systems.

Amyas Morse, the Head of the NAO, observed that "In the current economic climate where the Department is striving to make savings, it can ill-afford to use resources to buy and hold unnecessary levels of stock, and it clearly does so. The root cause of excess stock, which the Department is seeking to address, is that management and accountability structures currently fail to provide the incentives for cost-effective inventory management".[62] The Gross Book Value (GBV) of the Defence inventory[63], at the time of the Report's publication, was £40.3 billion, a value which continues to increase at a rate of approximately £200 million per month.

The MoD has been aware for some time of the financial value tied up in its inventory, of its inherent complexity, and of the shortfalls in its inventory management (IM) processes across the Maritime, Land and Air domains. It has instigated a number of initiatives aimed at improving its inventory position, amongst them the Defence Inventory Effectiveness Transformation (DIET) project which originated in the IM Diagnostic Study and ran from January to July 2007, and the Stock Transition Programme (STRAP) which followed DIET and which has become the Defence Stock Transition Programme (DSTP) in March 2010. Both DIET and DSTP focused on the classification and segmentation of the inventory, with the aim of implementing more appropriate and cost-effective management systems, and on disposal of surplus inventory. DIET, in particular, also directed attention to the paucity of qualified and experienced inventory managers and put in place an up-skilling programme to address the shortfall.[64]

In responding to the NAO report, and to its own recognition of the need to manage its inventory more efficiently and effectively, in 2012/13 the MoD commissioned the development of a departmental IM strategy. It vested 'ownership' of the defence inventory in the three-star appointment of Director General Resources in DE&S who issued direction to the DE&S Operating Centres aimed at improving the scrutiny of equipment support solutions, including their provision for inventory management. In 2014 the MoD will add further substance to its IM Strategy by launching the Inventory Management Operating Centre which will be created from the current two-star Director Joint Support Chain organisation. A number of other studies and research projects are underway; some of them focusing on what has been an enduring problem for the MoD – the disjointed nature of its logistics information systems and the quality and availability of its spares demand and consumption data. Supply chain theory has long recognized that to enable the efficient and effective flow of materiel downstream from the supplier to the ultimate user, there must be an accurate and timely flow of demand and consumption data upstream.[65] As the NAO observed in its 2011 report[66] the MoD has not been able to achieve this effective information flow because its information systems have been disjointed and lacking in required functionality. The NAO concluded that the "...Department's use of information to manage its supply chain falls short of general logistics industry best practice".[67] The NAO also reported on the new logistics information systems being developed under the Logistics Network Enabled Capability Programme, and their deployment should make a significant contribution to improving the flow of logistics information as they are rolled out. The MoD will continue to manage its stock within its broad accounting categories: raw materials and consumables, capital spares, and guided weapons, missiles and bombs. It is also expected to continue the work done in DIET and DSTP to segment the inventory, using appropriate measures such as the rate at which it turns over (slow-mover, non-mover etc.), financial value, procurement lead-time, or other criticality measures, in order to develop and apply stock management regimes which make sense. In many cases these will be automated, in others they will require a higher level of manual intervention, ideally by a more appropriate number of qualified and experienced inventory managers.

Europe

The financial crisis of 2008 and subsequent economic recession also hit Europe hard. In essence, the individual defence policies of Europe's major powers were finally caught up by economic reality. Since the end of the Cold War, economic globalisation and increasing financial problems related to their welfare systems gradually led to a worsening fiscal situation and a concern for any loss of jobs domestically. This in turn led to an over-reliance on old defence structures to maintain jobs, which stymied any move to reform defence and military structures in line with the changing security environment. In one sense therefore, the financial crisis has proven to be an opportunity for member states to undertake painful, but necessary reforms. This is in addition to the much deeper political challenge which has occurred at the same time – that the European Union is faced with a strategic coming-of-age that has been fuelled since 2005 by the changing strategic priorities in Washington DC and the USA's focus moving away from Europe onto Asia. However, declarations related to the Common Foreign and Security Policy (CFSP) and the Common Security and Defence Policy (CSDP) have usually fallen short in their implementation which has eroded Europe's credibility.[68]

The recession has continued to put pressure on defence budgets, with the trouble in the Eurozone merely adding fuel to the fire, with budgets being squeezed in order to deal with Europe's sovereign debt crisis. Greater emphasis has been placed on NATO's 'Smart Defence' and 'Connected Forces Initiative', along with the 'pooling and sharing' initiative by the European Union, to try and curtail the potential loss of military capability that hangs over the decline in defence spending, as several programmes have either been cut back or cancelled.[69] 'Smart Defence' originated with the May 2012 NATO summit in Chicago whose agenda had largely been defined by the Lisbon summit, two years earlier. NATO leaders committed themselves to creating "modern, tightly connected forces equipped, trained, exercised and commanded so that they can operate together and with partners in any environment"[70] as part of a move towards *NATO Forces 2020* – forces generated through prioritisation, cooperation and specialisation – building blocks of 'Smart Defence'. All this represents a "changed outlook, the opportunity for a culture of cooperation in which mutual collaboration is given new prominence as an effective option for delivering critical capability".[71] The summit adopted a package of some twenty 'Smart Defence' related projects, including the pooling of maritime patrol aircraft and improving the availability of precision weapons. Each project will be taken forward by a volunteer member state and the list of active projects is expected to grow into a wider pool of around 150. Such a development may also provide an answer to the worry regarding the maintenance of interoperability once combat operations start to draw down in Afghanistan, which for many European states is a major commitment. The 'Connected Forces Initiative' is a little sketchier but appears to be designed as a framework to ensure that NATO forces and the forces of its partners maintain the coherence built up through working together in an operational environment and so is likely to concentrate on combat effectiveness through a focus on joint training and exercising.[72]

The continued implementation of the CSDP will depend on the progress made in developing military capability. The European Union has a similar agenda to NATO's 'Smart Defence' with its 'pooling and sharing' initiative. The idea actually goes back a couple of years, with the NATO Secretary General, Anders Fogh Rasmussen, warning that 'there is a point where you are no longer cutting fat; you're cutting into muscle, and then into bone … Cuts can go too far" and that Europe needs to "look at pooling scarcer resources together, so we can buy and do things together that individually we couldn't afford."[73] It was also articulated by the European Union's Foreign Affairs Council in March 2012 which said that ". . . cooperation on pooling and sharing military capabilities represents a common response to European capability shortfalls, aiming at enhancing operational effectiveness in a context of financial austerity and a changing security environment"[74] and given added impetus by General Håkan Syrén, then Chairman of the EU Military Committee in September 2012 who said that as well as defence becoming more and more costly, Europe's efforts were "spread too thinly to be really efficient and most important that our decisions are taken in 27 different national contexts. The potential for generating a greater capability output is substantial if we are able to coordinate our efforts better."[75]

Indeed, a look at defence spending highlights the concern felt in many European capitals, as well as by the NATO Secretary General. With rising debt-to-GDP ratios across Europe, defence budget austerity has, since 2008, mirrored European growth rates. Despite a nominal increase in early 2011 from $293.16bn to $304.02bn due to exchange rate movements (the Euro appreciated relative to the US dollar by an average of 4.8% across 2011) the general trajectory was down, and continued that way in 2012, with spending falling by 7.01%, helped again by exchange rate movements, this time in the opposite direction (the Euro depreciated by around 9.9% relative to its 2011 average). After adjusting for those exchange rate effects and factoring in inflation, real defence spending in Europe (as a whole) fell by 2.52% in 2011 and 1.62% in 2012 (using constant 2010 prices and exchange rates). Defence spending has fallen faster than the European economies have contracted, with a result that defence spending, as a percentage of GDP, fell from 1.63% in 2010 to 1.53% in 2012. These figures however, seem to indicate that the rate of decrease in European defence spending is decelerating, given that real defence spending fell by an average of 3.7% between 2008 and 2010. It is worth remembering at this point that defence spending in the European part of NATO accounts for about 93% of the regional total, with defence spending in these countries increasing from $273.04bn in 2010 to $281.96bn in 2011 (up by 3.27%). However, after accounting for exchange rate movements and inflation, real defence spending in NATO Europe actually declined by 2.6% in 2011 and 1.54% in 2012. The top ten defence spenders in the region accounted for 85% of planned expenditure, while the top five spenders (UK, France, Germany, Italy and Turkey) accounted for approximately 70% of the regional total. Real defence spending fell in almost two-thirds of European countries, with the largest reductions happening in Spain (-17.6%), Hungary (-16.7%) and Slovenia (-16.1%), as governments sought to reduce their budget deficits and the burden of public debt. There were however notable increases, such as Estonia, Croatia and Albania (+17.8%, +12.6% and +11.8% respectively), along with Poland, who increased defence spending by 6.1% in 2011 and 4.7% in 2012. As far as sub-regions are concerned, defence spending fell most rapidly in Southern Europe (-11.19%), with the Balkans coming next (-5.6%), followed by Western Europe (-3.28%), Central Europe (-2.45%) and Northern Europe (-0.07%). Only South-eastern Europe showed an increase in real terms of 1.06%.[76]

As regards changes in individual country's budgets and force structure / personnel counts, France announced in the White Paper of 2008 that it was looking to cut its military personnel by 54,000 and its defence spending would remain fixed (so falling as a percentage of GDP).[77] Germany's defence spending is in the process of being cut by €8.3bn by 2015 (although it has to spend slightly more in the short term to realise those savings) and the Bundeswehr will reduce in size from 220,000 to 185,000 by 2019.[78] Italy's defence spending is being cut by around 10% as part of the Italian Government's attempts to reign in public spending and reduce its debt, along with a reduction in the armed forces from 179,000 to 141,000.[79] Spain's MoD has already suffered three rounds of cuts to its budget (3% in 2009, 6.2% in 2010 and 14% in 2012) with its total personnel due to fall by 6,000.[80] Greece has cut spending by 16% with changes to its force structure, although further cuts are envisaged.[81] The Netherlands will be instituting widespread reductions, with 15,600 personnel being cut by 2015 and defence spending being reduced by 13%.[82] This is by no means the complete story however, as some European countries have managed to sustain or even increase defence spending and personnel counts. As well as Estonia, Croatia, Albania and Poland which were noted above, Sweden has reversed a slow decline in the defence budget and numbers of personnel and committed to spending a de facto budget of €4.8bn until at least 2015[83] while Norway has increased its defence budget from Kr39.2bn in 2011 to Kr42.2bn in 2013.[84]

The one thing that still seems to differentiate the European Defence Industrial Base (DIB) from the American one is the degree to which is has been consolidated. The US DIB went through a period of consolidation during the mid-1990s where

"Boeing merged with McDonald Douglas in August 1997 after acquiring Rockwell's aerospace and defence concerns the year before. Lockheed and Martin Marietta merged in March 1995 and then acquired the defence electronics and systems integration businesses of the Loral Corporation in 1996 as well as elements of General Dynamics, while Northrop Aircraft merged with Grumman Aerospace in April 1994 and acquired a number of smaller companies such as Teledyne Ryan, Litton Industries, Newport News Shipbuilding, Federal Data Corporation and Sterling Software Inc."[85]

What would have an been an important consolidation for the European DIB was revealed in September 2012 when it became known that EADS and BAE Systems were discussing the possibility of a merger between the two companies. Such a group would have probably centred on Airbus, the world's largest builder of civil aircraft, but one that possessed a substantial defence arm – a structure similar to that of Boeing in the USA – one that would have had a strong foundation and been more resilient to budgetary and economic cycles. Of course, such a merger involved sensitive technologies and despite the companies arguing that the idea was based on strong commercial principles, the move provoked strong reaction, much of it political and centred on the idea of sovereignty and the role of national governments. EADS had around 133,000 employees while BAE had 93,500 employees. A group containing 226,500 employees would have been a sizeable one and one that would have been important for both manufacturing and R&D, but not a 'monster' as some have described it. The group's combined annual sales revenues of $100bn would have been larger than both Boeing and Lockheed Martin in the US but smaller than many companies in the energy, automotive and electronics industries.[86]

In the end, the merger failed to materialise as Germany, France and the UK all had sensitivities to it, and while the talks brought some uncomfortable realities about the European DIB out into the open, it is worth noting that all three governments had, fifteen years earlier, all demanded that such a merger take place. The then leaders of the three countries (President Jacques Chirac, Prime Minister Tony Blair and Chancellor Helmut Kohl) issued a statement in December 1997 encouraging the restructuring of the European DIB. They had seen the rapid restructuring that had taken place in the US DIB (as outlined above) and worried that this would lower the American corporations' cost base to the point where European governments would have no choice but to buy from US companies rather than the much smaller ones in Europe. The writing was on the wall – the end of the Cold War had meant a sharp drop in defence spending and the European DIB was still organised along national lines, something which was unsustainable. However things did not go as planned. While British Aerospace started merger talks with DaimlerChrysler Aerospace (aka DASA) with the hope of incorporating France's Aérospatiale and Matra at a later date, GEC-Marconi had started talks with Thomson-CSF of France. In a sudden change of heart, GEC decided to exit the market, while selling their Marconi defence business to British Aerospace which became BAE Systems in November 1999. This upset the continental companies and so DASA and their Spanish counterpart Construcciones Aeronáuticas SA (aka CASA) announced they were merging in June 1999, which was followed by DASA and the now Aérospatiale-Matra (who had merged in February 1999) merging in June 2000 to form EADS. Thomson-CSF, now renamed Thales, bought Racal while Finmeccanica of Italy bought Westland. With few adjustments (mainly in the realm of naval shipbuilding), it has been this structure that has prevailed in Europe for over a decade. BAE has expanded its US arm with the acquisition of second-tier defence systems suppliers, as well as its armoured vehicle and shipbuilding operations but sold its shareholding in Airbus and the subsidiary Astrium. EADS has sought to expanding its defence business but failed to gain critical mass.[87]

The talks between BAE Systems and EADS may be a signal that this quiet period will be coming to an end, especially as some of the factors that were in play in the mid-1990s have reappeared. Chief among these is the on-going reduction in defence spending (as outlined above) right across Europe. Although the European DIB is busy with contracts won some years ago, the prospects for major new projects seem fairly limited. Presently, there are no plans for any future manned aircraft after production of the current generation of aircraft (Typhoon, Rafale and Gripen) has concluded and many European companies will be employed as subcontractors on the US F-35 programme which is being bought by several European governments. The failure to build on the consolidations of the late 1990s means that many companies (bar the big 'four' – BAE, EADS, Finmeccanica and Thales) will be poorly placed to withstand the continued reductions in defence spending by European governments. In fact, looking at the number of defence procurement projects that were underway in Europe with a value that exceeded €1bn, the period between 2008 and 2012 saw a decline from forty-one projects to thirty-one. Added to that, there has been little progress with regard to the harmonisation and coordination of governmental requirements, meaning that companies will find it hard to achieve economies of scale (and hence better value for taxpayers) by operating across borders. Collaborative projects may be a key to securing future business in the long term (and those projects that offer the greatest scope for retaining and building a skills base usually involve the development of new technologies) but between 2008 and 2012, no new projects of this scale were started. Indeed, European governments seemed to move towards favouring 'Off-The-Shelf' purchases in an effort to limit risk and cost growth. It is this seeming absence of future orders, the limited prospects for new technology development and for many, an over-reliance on defence which has signalled that a new round of consolidation in the European DIB is needed and prompted the talks between BAE and EADS, a move eventually vetoed by Berlin. However, the pressures that prompted this have not gone away and it is very probable that while the first move was checked, future consolidation will indeed happen, despite political constraints.[88]

North America

For Canada, the economic recession has meant a scaling back of the defence budget and capabilities. Although not affected immediately, the

> ". . . defence budget is now to be reduced by 13% over three years. Although withdrawal from a combat role in Afghanistan will produce savings, capability reductions have already begun, with the elimination of anti-air and anti-armour missiles from the army and withdrawal from NATO surveillance programmes."[89]

In addition, there has been a major revision in the Canadian command structure with "the creation of a single command, the Canadian Joint Operations Command (CJOC), to be implemented over a period of months. Ottawa has said that the move was prompted by a 'logical evolution' of the 2006 transformation initiative that saw the creation of Canada Command, Canadian Expeditionary Force Command, Canadian Special Operations Forces Command and Canadian Operational Support Command. It was also prompted by the lessons of domestic and overseas operations, including in Afghanistan. According to DND, 'the revised structure will reduce the number of CF Officers in strategic headquarters by up to 25 per cent and will make more efficient use of administrative resources'."[90]

As far as the US is concerned, defence spending still dwarfs that of any other country, although a strong case can be made that the fundamental challenge facing the Pentagon in the next few years involves the budget. Such a claim may generate little sympathy from other defence establishments, as the Department of Defense (DoD) budget (without the sequester, outlined below) for Fiscal Year (FY) 2013 is $525 billion, rising to $567 billion in 2017.[91] However, a number of steps, culminating with the implementation of the sequester in 2013, will force the Pentagon to make tough decisions due to dramatic reductions in its budget.

It is important to note that major efforts to change the way in which the Pentagon does business were initiated well before the sequester came into effect. Former Secretary of Defense Gates began the process with an announcement in 2010 of a plan to achieve $100 billion of savings over five years.[92] The cost containment proposal affected $400 billion of DoD acquisition, with $200 billion involving contracts for goods (weapons, fuel, etc.) and $200 billion involving contracts for services (IT, maintenance, etc.).[93] This was also exemplified by the termination of a number of critical acquisition programmes: C-17 Globemaster, F-22 Raptor fighter, a combat search and rescue helicopter, a multiple kill vehicle and a kinetic energy interceptor.[94]

Subsequently, the 2011 Budget Control Act (BCA) required a reduction of future DoD expenditures by $487 billion over 10 years, a cut of almost 9%.[95] Combined with a reduction of the account to pay for war costs, total US defence spending was estimated to drop by 22% from its peak in 2010, after accounting for inflation.[96]

Finally, provisions of the BCA and failure to reach agreement on a deficit reduction package in 2011 have generated additional cuts in the BCA caps, which are the 'sequester– level' caps.[97] Sequestration came into effect in March 2013. As noted by Secretary of Defense Hagel in a 10 July 2013 letter to the Senate Armed Services Committee, "The sequester-level BCA cap reduction for FY 2014 would result in a cut of $52 billion in funding in FY 2014 compared with the President's budget."[98]

While an extensive discussion of the sequester is beyond the scope of this article, it is worthwhile to highlight why such a dramatic step was taken. There are two types of spending in the US budget. Mandatory spending includes Social Security and Medicare. Discretionary spending includes areas such as defence. Social Security, Medicare and Medicaid alone are expected to account for 55% of federal expenditure, or some 12.2% of GDP by 2022, even if the sequester is fully enacted.[99] The result of such extensive growth in mandatory spending is even more drastic cuts in discretionary spending. Indeed, defence and non-defence discretionary spending were expected to fall by 2012 by 4% before the sequester while mandatory spending was expected to increase by 1%.[100]

While there are uncertainties with regard to the actual impact of the sequester due to questions about what action Congress might take,[101] it would appear that full implementation of the sequester on the Pentagon budget would have a significant impact. With regard to personnel, Hagel notes in his letter that in FY 2014, DoD "would, for the second year in a row, impose hiring freezes and sharply reduce facilities maintenance."[102] He goes on to write that DoD "hopes to avoid a second year of furloughs of civilian personnel, but DoD will have to consider involuntary reductions-in-force to reduce civilian personnel costs" adding the point that "these actions alone would not be sufficient."[103]

Highlighting the fact that cuts in military personnel do not generate immediate savings, Hagel stresses that "the inability to reduce military personnel costs quickly would put additional downward pressure on other portions of the FY 2014 budget."[104] He notes that if a sequester-level cut occurred in FY 2014 "most services conclude that military training and readiness would remain at currently degraded levels or, in some cases, would even continue to decline".[105] Hagel then cites specifics: "two Navy air wings might not be able to achieve full flight hours and special operations units, which are key to counter terrorism activities, would experience declining readiness."[106] The Army had "cancelled many of the culminating training events at its combat training centres" and "would have difficulty avoiding similar cutbacks in FY 2014."[107] The Air Force, which had to "stop all flying at about one third of its combat-coded active squadrons, would significantly reduce training at more than half of its active flying units," and "maintenance cutbacks would continue or worsen, threatening future readiness levels."[108]

The impact on Pentagon acquisition, research, development test and evaluation (RDT&E) and military construction would be significant, and Hagel's warning to the Senate Armed Services Committee regarding these areas is worth citing in its entirety

Indeed, cuts of 15 percent to 20 percent might well be necessary, even though the total budget is reduced by only 10 percent. The services would seek to protect most or all funding for a few programs that are most critical to the President's DSG (Defense Strategic Guidance). However, funding for hundreds of program line items, large and small, would have to be cut significantly. We would be forced to buy fewer ships, planes, ground vehicles, satellites, and other weapons. Modification programs would be cut sharply, even though these programs maintain the effectiveness of older weapons. Nor would cuts be limited to buys of weapons. Research funding represents more than 10 percent of the defense budget, and many research projects – including those performed by universities and small companies – would inevitably have to be scaled back.

Marked cuts in investment funding, especially if they continue for several years, would slow future technology improvements and may erode the technological superiority enjoyed by U.S. forces. In some future conflict, less capable weapons could mean a less desirable military outcome and more casualties. Investment cutbacks are of particular concern because they would occur during a period when many categories of U.S. weapons are aging sharply.

Slowing investment would also adversely affect DoD's efforts to improve its acquisition practices and become a better buyer. Hundreds of weapon and support program line items, which are now being bought based on stable and efficient acquisition plans, would be disrupted. Unit costs would rise, reversing successful efforts in recent years to hold down unit cost growth or even reverse it. The disruption would spill over to defense industry. Defense industry jobs would be lost and, as prime contractors pull back work to protect their internal work forces, small businesses may experience disproportionately large job losses.[109]

The sequester is also having a major impact on U.S. defence industry. Dennis Muilenburg, the president and CEO of Boeing's Defense, Space and Security unit, has said that "The combination of the sequester and the [recent] government shutdown is causing chaos for the aerospace industry."[110] Muilenburg emphasizes that

"The inability to do consistent, long-term planning also causes difficulty for the industry as we think about capital outlays and equipment. It's a destructive force, and we really need an alternative solution to the nation's budget situation before it causes irreparable damage. We're seeing damage every day with facility closures, job reductions and impact on the supply chain."[111]

In short, the Pentagon was facing challenging times even before the inability of the political leadership in Washington to reach agreement on a deficit reduction plan. The imposition of the sequester has generated the prospect of devastating cuts in DoD spending and significant impact on U.S. defense industry. The glimmers of hope centre on the fact that the impact of these purely political decisions can be ameliorated, or even completely removed, by agreement in Washington. However, the inability of the US political leadership to avoid a shutdown of the Federal government in October 2013 and the constant wrangling over raising the US debt ceiling indicates the extent to which a political agreement, at least in the near term, appears unlikely. As a result, the Pentagon will face daunting challenges in the near-to-medium term in coming to grips with what will in all likelihood be a sharply reduced level of funding.

Conclusion

This chapter has primarily focused on the issues facing the UK MoD in order to play its part in the Government's attempts to control public spending and therefore the deficit and sovereign debt, which includes reform of the MoD itself, reform of the agency tasked with undertaking defence acquisition (DE&S) and reform of the armed forces themselves. It has also looked at what is happening more broadly with both Europe and North America to show that the UK's problems are shared by many, but no means all, countries in NATO and the EU. The actions taken by many European Governments has prompted both the head of NATO[112] and the US Defense Secretary[113] to urge them to increase defence spending in order to maintain current defence capabilities, but the slowness of the economic recovery in the EU, especially in those countries in the Eurozone means that is unlikely that there will be any turnaround in the near future, which could potentially lead to a straining of relations with the USA.

Postscript: As this book was being finalised, the Defence Secretary Philip Hammond announced on 10 December 2013 that the GOCO option for the reform of DE&S was no longer an option, as one of the two bidding consortia had withdrawn, leaving Bechtel-led *Material Acquisition Partners* as the sole interested party. The Government will thus follow the option of turning DE&S into a "bespoke government trading entity" (an enhanced version of 'DE&S Plus') with an additional injection of private sector skills, keeping the option to revisit the GOCO option at a later date.[114]

Endnotes

[1] BBC. (2013) 'UK GDP: Fastest Growth for Three Years' on the *BBC News* website, dated 25 October 2013, located at http://www.bbc.co.uk/news/business-24668687 as of 11 November 2013; BBC. (2013) 'Eurozone Data Shows Fragile Economic Recovery' on the BBC News website, dated 6 November 2013, located at http://www.bbc.co.uk/news/business-24835547 as of 11 November 2013; BBC. (2013) 'US Job Creation Stronger in October' on the *BBC News* website, dated 8 November 2013, located at http://www.bbc.co.uk/news/business-24870322 as of 11 November 2013.

[2] HM Government. (2010) *Securing Britain in an Age of Uncertainty: The Strategic Defence and Security Review*, Cm7948, October 2010, located at http://www.direct.gov.uk/prod_consum_dg/groups/dg_digitalassets/@dg/@en/documents/digitalasset/dg_191634.pdf as of 19 August 2013.

[3] Much of this section is based on material that was published in: Antill, P D and Smith, J C D. (2012) 'United Kingdom Defence Acquisition in the Age of Austerity' in *RUSI Defence Systems*, Volume 15, No. 2 (Autumn / Winter 2012), pp. 14-21 and Antill, P D and Ito, P. (2013) 'Reforming DE&S and the GOCO Option' in *Defence Procurement International*, Summer 2013, pp. 9-13.

[4] See for example National Audit Office. (2013) *Ministry of Defence – The Major Projects Report 2012*, HC684, 10 January 2013, at http://www.nao.org.uk/report/ministry-of-defence-the-major-projects-report-2012/ as of 19 August 2013.

[5] See for example House of Commons Public Accounts Committee. (2013) *Ministry of Defence: Equipment Plan 2012-2022 and Major Projects Report 2012*, HC53, 14 May 2013, located at http://www.publications.parliament.uk/pa/cm201314/cmselect/cmpubacc/53/53.pdf as of 19 August 2013.

[6] Lord Levene. (2011) *Defence Reform – An Independent Report into the Structure and Management of the Ministry of Defence*, June 2011, at https://www.gov.uk/government/uploads/system/uploads/attachment_data/file/27408/defence_reform_report_struct_mgt_mod_27june2011.pdf as of 19 August 2013.

[7] National Audit Office. (2013) *A Summery of the NAO's Work on the Ministry of Defence 2011-2012*, March 2013, at http://www.nao.org.uk/wp-content/uploads/2013/04/009964-001-MOD-Departmental-Overview_2011-12.pdf, p. 15. Accessed: 19 August 2013.

[8] Kirkup, J. (2013) 'Britain's debt interest payments will be double the defence budget' in *The Telegraph*, 26 June 2013, at http://www.telegraph.co.uk/news/politics/spending-review/10144686/Britains-debt-interest-payments-will-be-double-the-defence-budget.html as of 19 August 2013.

[9] Ministry of Defence. (2012) *Business Plan 2012-2015*, 31 May 2012, at https://www.gov.uk/government/uploads/system/uploads/attachment_data/file/27185/mod_plan_final_11_06_12_P1.pdf as of 19 August 2013.

[10] National Audit Office (2012) *Reforming the Ministry of Defence*, Briefing for the Committee of Public Accounts, February 2012, at http://www.nao.org/publications/1213/reforming_the_mod.aspx, p. 8. Accessed: 16 August 2013.

[11] *Ibid.*

[12] National Audit Office. (2012) *Managing Change in the Defence Workforce*, HC1791, 9 February 2012, at http://www.nao.org.uk/wp-content/uploads/2012/02/10121791.pdf, p. 5. Accessed: 19 August 2013.

[13] Ministry of Defence. (2011) *Defence Reform – Blueprint for the Future Department*, December 2011, at https://whitehall-frontend-production.s3.amazonaws.com/system/uploads/attachment/file/425/85_20111216_Departmental_Blueprint_Dec_11_final_for_circulation-U.pdf as of 19 August 2013.

[14] House of Commons Committee of Public Accounts. (2012) *Ministry of Defence: Managing Change in the Defence Workforce*, HC1905, 25 May 2012, at http://www.parliament.uk/documents/TSO-PDF/committee-reports/1905.pdf, pp. 3-5. Accessed: 19 August 2013.

[15] *Op Cit.* Lord Levene, 2011.

[16] Ministry of Defence. (2011) 'New defence materiel strategy announced' webpage, 31 May 2011, located at https://www.gov.uk/government/news/new-defence-materiel-strategy-announced as of 19 August 2013.

[17] Bernard Gray. (2009) *Review of Acquisition for the Secretary State of Defence – An Independent Report by Bernard Gray*, October 2009, at http://www.bipsolutions.com/docstore/ReviewAcquisitionGrayreport.pdf as of 19 August 2013; Haddon-Cave QC, C. (2009) *The Nimrod Review – An Independent Review into the Broader Issues Surrounding the Loss of the RAF Nimrod MR2 Aircraft XV230 in Afghanistan in 2006*, HC1025, 28 October 2009, at http://www.official-documents.gov.uk/document/hc0809/hc10/1025/1025.pdf as of 19 August 2013.

[18] *Op Cit.* Gray, 2009, pp. 239-240.

[19] Wragg, D. (1973) 'Hunting defence bargains' in *Flight International*, 31 May 1971 at http://www.flightglobal.com/pdfarchive/view/1973/1973%20-%201531.html as of 22 August 2013; *Op Cit.* Gray, 2009, pp. 239-240.

[20] Defence Logistics Organisation. (2002) 'New Chief of Defence Logistics takes up Post', 2 September 2002, located at http://webarchive.nationalarchives.gov.uk/+/http://mod.uk/dlo/press/2002/cdlstart.htm as of 22 August 2013.

[21] House of Commons Defence Committee. (2008) 'Current and Future Issues' webpage, currently located at http://www.publications.parliament.uk/pa/cm200708/cmselect/cmdfence/295/29506.htm as of 22 August 2013.

[22] *Op Cit.* Gray, 2009, pp. 239-240.

[23] House of Commons Defence Committee. (2012) *Defence Acquisition: Written Evidence from the Ministry of Defence*, DAQ001, dated 21 May 2012, located at http://www.publications.parliament.uk/pa/cm201213/cmselect/cmdefence/writev/aquisition/m01.htm as of 23 August 2013.

[24] *Ibid.*

[25] Editorial. (2013) 'MoD contemplates going for GoCo' in *The Financial Times*, 7 May 2013, located at http://www.ft.com/cms/s/0/8bd9173e-b713-11e2-841e-00144feabdc0.html#axzz2dCHTIz1B as of 27 August 2013.

[26] Editorial. (2012) 'Hammond: G4S issues force private sector rethink' on *defencemanagement.com*, 14 August 2012, at http://www.defencemanagement.com/news_story.asp?id=20586 as of 27 August 2013.

[27] Defence Contracts Online. (2013) 'Assessment Phase Begins: GOCO or DE&S+', dated 13 May 2013, at http://www.contracts.MoD.uk/assessment-phase-begins-GOCO-or-des/ as of 28 August 2013.

[28] RUSI Acquisition Focus Group. (2012) 'The Defence Material Strategy and the GOCO Proposal for Abbey Wood', July 2012, at http://www.rusi.org/downloads/assets/GOCO_Briefing.pdf as of 28 August 2013.

[29] Pannu, Amman. (2012) 'How would GOCO procurement work in practice?', defencemanagement.com, dated 17 August 2012, located at http://www.defencemanagement.com/feature_story.asp?id=20517 as of 28 August 2013; *Op Cit.* RUSI Acquisition Focus Group, 2012.

[30] Leftly, M. (2013) 'Mark Leftly: Osbornism – one small step for the man, one giant leap for the economy . . . ideally' in *The Independent*, dated 27 June 2013, currently located at http://www.independent.co.uk/news/business/comment/mark-leftly-osbornism--one-small-step-for-the-man-one-giant-leap-for-the-economy-ideally-8675821.html as of 28 August 2013.

[31] *Op Cit.* Defence Contracts Online, 13 May 2013.

[32] Ministry of Defence. (2013) *Better Defence Acquisition – Improving How We Procure and Support Defence Equipment*, Cm8626, June 2013, currently located at https://www.gov.uk/government/uploads/system/uploads/attachment_data/file/206032/20130610_WP_Better_Def_Acquisition_screen_final.pdf as of 9 July 2013.

[33] *Ibid.* pp. 4-5.

[34] *Ibid.* p. 5.

[35] *Ibid.*

[36] *Ibid.* p. 6.

[37] *Op Cit.* HM Government, 2010, p. 19.

[38] Enduring is defined as an operation that lasts more than six months and requires units to undertake a tour of duty after which they are replaced by another unit. *Op Cit.* HM Government, 2010, p. 18.

[39] Non-enduring is defined as an operation that lasts less than six months where units deploy, conduct the operation and then withdraw without the need for replacement. *Op Cit.* HM Government, 2010, p. 18.

[40] *Op Cit.* HM Government, 2010, p. 19.

[41] HM Government. (2010) *Fact Sheet 6: Future Force 2020 – Royal Navy*, located at https://www.gov.uk/government/uploads/system/uploads/attachment_data/file/62488/Factsheet6-Royal-Navy.pdf, as of 2 September2013.

[42] BBC. (2013) 'HMS Illustrious sets sail amid Gibraltar row', dated 12 August 2013, located at http://www.bbc.co.uk/news/uk-23663262 as of 2 September 2013.

[43] BBC. (2013) 'Ark Royal makes final journey to scrapyard', dated 20 May 2013, located at http://www.bbc.co.uk/news/uk-22600299, as of 2 September 2013.

[44] BBC. (2011) 'HMS Invincible makes final journey to Turkish scrapyard', dated 24 March 2011, located at http://www.bbc.co.uk/news/uk-12848226, as of 2 September 2013.

[45] HM Government. (2010) *Fact Sheet 8: Future Force 2020 – Royal Air Force*, located at https://www.gov.uk/government/uploads/system/uploads/attachment_data/file/62490/Factsheet8-RoyalAirForce.pdf, as of 2 September 2013.

[46] Gordon, L. (2011) 'Sadness as scrapping of £4bn Nimrods gets underway', dated 27 January 2011, located at http://www.bbc.co.uk/news/uk-12297139, as of 2 September 2013.

[47] HM Government. (2010) *Fact Sheet 7: Future Force 2020 – British Army*, located at https://www.gov.uk/government/uploads/system/uploads/attachment_data/file/62489/Factsheet7-British-Army.pdf, as of 2 September 2013.

[48] British Army. (2012) *Transforming the British Army*, July 2012, located at http://www.army.mod.uk/documents/general/Army2020_brochure.pdf, as of 2 September 2013; BBC. (2013) 'Q&A: Army 2020 reorganisation', dated 3 July 2013, located at http://www.bbc.co.uk/news/uk-18710936, as of 2 September 2013; Rayment, S. (2012) 'Territorial Army not fit for new role, warn Generals' in *The Telegraph*, 11 February 2012, located at http://www.telegraph.co.uk/news/uknews/defence/9076527/Territorial-Army-not-fit-for-new-role-warn-Generals.html, as of 2 September 2013.

[49] Chris Mace, (D DSR). *A Strategic Vision for Defence Support*, DSR/VP/001, 15 November 2010.

[50] *Op Cit*. Levene, 2011.

[51] Ministry of Defence. (2011) *The Independent Commission to Review the United Kingdom's Reserve Forces*, July 2011, located at http://www.mod.uk/NR/rdonlyres/263D5F71-30CE-45BC-9442-398B1DC12C93/0/futurereserves_2020.pdf as of 3 September 2013.

[52] DCDS (Personnel). (2010) *Service Personnel New Employment Model (A Report by DCDS(Pers))*, SDSR Study 1.1, 16 July 2011, D/DCDS(Pers)/40.

[53] America, Britain, Canada, Australia, and New Zealand.

[54] ACDS (Log Ops). (2011) *Total Support Force - What it means for Defence and Industry*, Presentation to RUSI, 21 March 2011.

[55] *Op Cit*. Mace, 2010.

[56] SO2 Force Policy, ACDS (Logs Ops). (2012) *Contractor Support to Operations and the Total Support Force*, Presentation to the MoD Acquisition Employment Training Course, UK Defence Academy, 19 September 2012.

[57] Op Cit. Antill and Smith, 2012.

[58] *Ibid*.

[59] *Op Cit*. Mace, 2010.

[60] *Ibid*.

[61] National Audit Office. (2012) *Managing the Defence Inventory*, HC 190, 28 June 2012, available here: http://www.nao.org.uk/publications/1213/managing_the_defence_inventory.aspx as of 3 September 2013.

[62] *Ibid*.

[63] GBV is the gross value without adjustment for depreciation.

[64] *Op Cit*. National Audit Office, 2012, HC190; House of Commons Defence Committee. (2012) *Ministry of Defence Supplementary Estimate 2011-12*, dated April 2012, located at http://www.publications.parliament.uk/pa/cm201213/cmselect/cmdfence/99/99we03.htm, as of 3 September 2013.

[65] Klein, R & Rai, A. (2009) 'Interfirm Strategic Information Flows in Logistics Supply Chain Relationships' in *MIS Quarterly*, Vol. 33, Issue 4, pp. 735-762; Christopher, M. (2005) *Logistics and Supply Chain Management: Creating Value-Adding Networks*, Harlow: Pearson Education / Prentice-Hall, pp. 180-3; Prajogo, D & Olhager, J. (2012) 'Supply chain integration and performance: The effects of long-term relationships, information technology and sharing, and logistics integration' in *International Journal of Production Economics*, Vol. 135, Issue 1, pp. 514-522.

[66] National Audit Office. (2011) *Ministry of Defence: The Use of Information to Manage*

the Logistics Supply Chain, HC 827, 31 March 2011,available here: http://www.nao.org. uk/publications/1011/logistics_supply_chain.aspx as of 3 September 2013.

67 Editorial. (2011) 'Military could save millions with better supply chain IT', *logisticsmanager.com*, 31 March 2011, http://www.logisticsmanager.com/liChannelID/2/ Articles/15850/Military+could+save+millions+with+better+supply+chain.html, as of 3 September 2013.

68 Brune, S., Cameron, A., Maulny, J. and Terlikowski, M. (2010) *Restructuring Europe's Armed Forces in Times of Austerity*, SWP Comments No. 28, November 2010, located at http://www.swp-berlin.org/fileadmin/contents/products/comments/2010C28_brn_ua_ ks.pdf, as of 10 September 2013.

69 De Larrinaga, N. (2012) 'JDW 2012 Annual Defence Report: Europe', *Jane's Defence Weekly*, posted 7 December 2012 at ihm.janes.com, as of 8 September 2013.

70 NATO. (2012) *Summit Declaration of Defence Capabilities: Toward NATO Forces 2020*, Press Release (2012) 064, located at http://www.nato.int/cps/en/natolive/official_ texts_87594.htm?mode=pressrelease, as of 12 September2013.

71 *Ibid*.

72 IISS. (2013) *The Military Balance 2013*, Routledge: London, 14 March 2013, pp.89-90, also located at http://dx.doi.org/10.1080/04597222.2013.756999 as of 9 September 2013.

73 NATO. (2010) *The New Strategic Concept: Active Engagement, Modern Defence – Speech by NATO Secretary General Anders Fogh Rasmussen at the German Marshall Fund of the United States (GMF), Brussels*, 8 October 2010, located at http://www.nato. int/cps/en/natolive/opinions_66727.htm, as of 12 September 2013.

74 Council of the European Union. (2012) *Council conclusions on pooling and sharing of military capabilities*, 3157th Foreign Affairs Council Meeting, Brussels, 22-23 March 2012, located at http://www.consilium.europa.eu/uedocs/cms_Data/docs/pressdata/en/ esdp/129162.pdf, as of 12 September 2013.

75 European Union Military Committee. (2012) *Keynote Speech – General Håkan Syrén*, Cyprus EU Presidency High Level Seminar - ''Innovative European Defence Cooperation - Pooling and Consolidating Demand'', Brussels, 19 September 2012, located at http://consilium.europa.eu/media/1749978/ceumc_keynote_speech_cyprus_presid_ seminar_19_sep2012_2012.pdf , as of 12 September 2013.

76 *Op Cit*. IISS, 2013, pp. 92-94.

77 Larrabee, S et al. (2012) *NATO and the Challenges of Austerity*, RAND (Santa Monica), located at http://www.rand.org/content/dam/rand/pubs/monographs/2012/RAND_ MG1196.pdf, as of 12 November 2013, p. 19.

78 O'Donnell, C. (2012) *The Implications of Military Spending Cuts for NATO's Largest*

Members, Brookings Institute, Analysis Paper, July 2012, located at http://www.brookings. edu/~/media/research/files/papers/2012/7/military%20spending%20nato%20odonnell/ military%20spending%20nato%20odonnell%20pdf, as of 12 November 2013.

[79] European Parliament. (2011) *The Impact of the Financial Crisis on European Defence – Annex*, April 2011, located at http://www.europarl.europa.eu/document/activities/cont/ 201106/20110623ATT22406/20110623ATT22406EN.pdf, as of 12 November 2013, pp. 19-20

[80] *Op Cit*. Larrabee, 2013, pp. 45-47.

[81] Gobbi, F. (2013) *NATO in the Aftermath of the Financial Crisis*, European Parliament, 3 April 2013, at http://www.europarl.europa.eu/RegData/bibliotheque/briefing/2013/130453/ LDM_BRI(2013)130453_REV1_EN.pdf, as of 13 November 2013, p. 2.

[82] *Op Cit*. Larrabee, 2013, p. 53.

[83] *Op Cit*. European Parliament, 2011, p. 28.

[84] *Op Cit*. IISS, 2013, p. 160.

[85] Antill, P D and Ito, P. (2011) 'Multi-National Collaborative Procurement – The Joint Strike Fighter Programme' in Moore, D M. (Ed) (2011) *Case Studies in Defence Procurement and Logistics: Volume I – From World War II to the Post-Cold War World*, Cambridge: Cambridge Academic, p. 177.

[86] *Op Cit*. IISS, 2013, p. 37.

[87] Wikipedia. (2013) 'EADS' webpage, located at http://en.wikipedia.org/wiki/EADS as of 15 October 2013; *Op Cit*. IISS, 2013, pp. 37-38.

[88] Giegerich, B and Nicoll, A. (2012) 'The Struggle for Value in European Defence', *Survival*, Volume 54, Issue 1 (February-March 2012), pp. 53-82; *Op Cit*. IISS, 2013, pp. 38-40.

[89] *Op Cit*. IISS, 2013, p. 68.

[90] *Ibid*. p. 67.

[91] Corsdesman, A. (2013) *Tracking the Defense Budget- US Defense Budget Cuts, Sequestration, the FY2014 Budget and the FY2014-FY2022 Forecast*, Centre for Strategic and International Studies, located at https://csis.org/publication/tracking-defense-budget-us-defense-budget-cuts-sequestration-fy2014-budget-and-fy2014-fy, as of 13 November 2013, p. 10.

[92] *Ibid*, p. 7.

[93] Ibid.

[94] Ibid, p. 8.

[95] Ibid, p. 10.

[96] Ibid.

[97] Ibid, p. 61.

[98] Ibid.

[99] Ibid, p. 29.

[100] Ibid.

[101] Ibid, p. 45.

[102] Ibid, p. 63.

[103] Ibid.

[104] Ibid, p. 64.

[105] Ibid, p. 65.

[106] Ibid.

[107] Ibid.

[108] Ibid.

[109] Ibid, p. 69.

[110] Anselmo, J. (2013) 'Boeing's Muilenburg on Defense, Space Challenges' in *Aviation Week*, dated 4 November 2013, located at http://www.aviationweek.com/Article.aspx?id=/article-xml/AW_11_04_2013_p42-629094.xml as of 15 November 2013.

[111] *Ibid.*

[112] Vandiver, J. (2013) 'NATO chief urges Europe to spend more on defense' on *Stars and Stripes* website, 13 September 2013, located at http://www.stripes.com/news/europe/nato-chief-urges-europe-to-spend-more-on-defense-1.242159, as of 13 November 2013.

[113] Shanker, T. (2011) 'Defense Secretary warns NATO of 'Dim' Future' in *The New York Times*, dated 10 June 2011, located at http://www.nytimes.com/2011/06/11/world/europe/11gates.html?_r=0 as of 13 November 2013.

[114] Hammond, Rt Hon P. (2013) 'Oral Statement to Parliament: Defence Procurement', dated 10 December 2013, located at https://www.gov.uk/government/speeches/defence-procurement, as of 19 December 2013.

Part One // Defence Logistics & Support Chain Strategy

Logistics and the Roman Army of the Late Republic

David R. Rabaut
University of Illinois, 1962

[Editor's Note – the following case study features elements taken from the author's MA History dissertation, hence the use of 'chapters'. The text has been left 'as written' as far as possible, with only minor corrections applied, mainly to conform to the series style.]

Introduction

Throughout the course of history, logistics, that is, the supply, transport, and movement of troops, has been of extreme importance in military affairs. In the modern era advances in the methods of transport and communications appear to have solved many of the problems and limitations that logistics formerly imposed. But because of the peculiar conditions existing in the ancient world and its lack of these advantages, logistics played a much larger and much more visible role in the formation of military policy than is perhaps true today. It is therefore the purpose of this study not only to show the methods and organization of logistics in the late Roman Republic, but also to indicate the role it played in ancient warfare.

The Mechanics of Logistics

The purpose of this first chapter is to describe the mechanics of the Roman logistical system. In other words we shall try and show how goods were shipped to the armies, where the means of transport and the supplies themselves came from, the nature of organization, and so forth. From the many small bits of information available in ancient sources it is difficult to construct a complete picture, for in fact, there was no one logistical system. The methods of supply changed as times, generals, politics, and greed demanded.

Therefore, in any description of the methods of transport and supply, these variations and exceptions must be taken into account. This chapter is divided into three general sections. The first deals with transport by sea and land, and the influence of geography. The second takes up the problem of supplies, including their sources and types; and the third is a discussion of the Roman Logistical Office - the quaestor. I have also added a fourth section on the logistical problems of the Roman forts, properly a tactical question, as its consideration seems more appropriate here than in the following chapters.

The first requirement of any logistical system is to put the desired supplies in the proper place at the proper time. In modern times the use of railroads, airplanes or other mechanical means of transportation allows man to overcome geographic features, but this was not true in the ancient world. Men were forced to live with their geography, and this made the Mediterranean region more of a hindrance than a help.

The basin is ringed with mountains of various sizes and descriptions, Spain, with the exception of the small coastal plain, is a high table-land broken by the Cantabrian, Pyrenees, and Betic Mountains. In Gaul the Massif Central and the Alps cause transport difficulties, as do the Apennines of Italy, the mountains of the Balkans and the Asia Minor plateau. The relative flatness of Palestine, Egypt, and the African coast ease the problem, only to be recreated by the desert and the Atlas Mountains. At best, then, the Mediterranean can be described as circumscribed by close-set barriers of mountains having been erected by a rolling-up movement of the Earth. But this mountain system can be surmounted by a series of relatively low altitude passes, and river carved valleys. The passes and valleys, of course, are favorable to supply movement, but the rivers, generally speaking, are useless for transportation. In their upper reaches they plummet from lofty heights and in their lower sections are difficult for consistent navigation because of the variable amount of water. Few of the rivers attain width, but even narrow streams may lack convenient fords. In some areas, because of great quantities of limestone, rivers cut their valleys and gorges in deep V-shaped troughs, requiring the construction of bridges for convenient crossing. Often when Mediterranean rivers reach the coast they become slow and sluggish, forming marshes, forever meandering over the plain, and silting up one river channel after another.[1]

Geographically, the position of Italy is both good and bad. By land, to the west, there are good features, a small narrow coastal plain extends from Naples in south Italy, along the western Italian coast, skirting the Gulf of Lions and the eastern edge of the Iberian Peninsula. This coastal plain could, and did, provide a natural highway for the march of Roman armies and civilization into Spain. As part of this same system the Rhone valley could be considered as a side road, providing passage between the French Alps and the Massif Central from the Mediterranean into central and northwest France. As a secondary route Roman armies could take the Toulouse passage between the Massif Central and the Pyrenees.

There was however, no such natural road system leading to the east. A dry, stony plateau called the Karst begins about ten to twenty miles inward from the Adriatic Sea, and with its porous limestone deposits and sinkholes, forms a formidable barrier for transport from Italy east. The land of Greece, although providing good harbors, is also extremely difficult to traverse overland and just about completes a barrier to overland transport from Italy.

In any war to the east, therefore, geography dictates the use of the sea as an avenue for transport. Italy's physical position in the center of the Mediterranean was a great asset, for it was only about 100 miles from the chief ports of Brundisium in Italy or Lilybaeum in Sicily to points in Greece or North Africa. The sea itself was also helpful. In the summer tradewinds blew in a constant north or northeast direction and the lack of tides made the sea easy to navigate. In the winter however, it was a different story. The Mediterranean is a cyclone factory, frequently swept by gales which have little sense of direction. Irregular coasts, although a blessing when giving shelter, are a curse as they cause cross seas and eddies which provide little encouragement for the would be mariners. With storms, cyclones, and other disturbances Father Neptune is able to keep intruding ships off his sea for the winter months.[2]

For any large military operation from Italy to the East, Africa, and to a lesser extent .Spain, large numbers of ships were required for supply purposes. Rome faced this problem for the first time during the Second Punic War, when supplies were needed for operations in Spain, Sicily and Africa. In this early period the military operations were under the control of the Roman government which made contracts with private groups for the transport of supplies[3], but during the later Republic when military operations slipped out of the control of the central government and into the hands of various "heroes", the collection of needed transport became more unofficial.

Basically the needed ships appear to have been procured in two ways. They were built by the military themselves on the scene, or as in modern times, requisitioned from private persons or companies, probably with some type of compensation given. In that simpler age the construction of a. ship did not present the overwhelming constructional and engineering problems that such a task does today. In an emergency three Roman legions could throw together twelve warships and have them fully equipped within 30 days.[4] Transports are usually larger than warships, but we can be confident that a similar feat could take place if conditions demanded. Simpler still were the barges and light boats that were often built to ford rivers or collect supplies locally by using the river. There was practically no constructional problem as they were of light construction (wood frame .with hide hulls) and could easily be transported to their destination overland by horse or mule.[5] Construction of a ship, especially a transport, took time and work. Even though this could always be done, it was much simpler to requisition those at hand. These ships could come directly from private persons or companies[6], who owned most of the ships, or as when Caesar was faced with a transport shortage in his pursuit of Pompey, from local towns. In most cases, since the general might want or need ships again in some future campaign, and because he would have little use for a large fleet of transports when the campaign was over, at the end of the war the ships were sent back to their owners.[7] In the east, which had a rich maritime tradition, the Roman allies were able to furnish needed transports[8], but these ships also probably came from private owners.

It should hardly need be noted that the major advantage of a sea supply system for the Roman armies was the tremendous quantity of material that a ship could carry over the minute amounts that could be transported by the slow and cumbersome land transport. A second advantage is that the sea offers great flexibility in transport lines. Men, and especially food, could, with little increased difficulty, be shipped to about any point on the Mediterranean coast. But even this second advantage would be negligible if it was not for the relatively huge quantities that these ships could carry.

The size of these ancient transports is estimated by various scholars to be from 250 to 1,500 tons[9], but in general the consensus of the sources seems to indicate that 10,000 talents was about the average transport ship. At a quarter of a ton to each talent, such transports would average about 250 tons.[10] Although this might have been the average, smaller ships of 60 tons are recorded by Cicero[11], and a huge Egyptian grain ship of an estimated 1,228 tons is recorded by Lucian.[12] Whatever the size of these ships, the point is clear that one ship could carry much more than a whole train of overland carts and pack animals, at much less the cost. (It would take over 600 mules to equal the carrying capacity of only one sixty-ton ship.) By use of the sea, Roman armies could be supplied quickly and in large quantities, something which would be impossible to do by land. In fact, I do not think that it would be an exaggeration to say that Roman armies depended on sea transport to such an extent that without it the conquest of the Mediterranean would have been extremely more difficult if not impossible.

The first job of the transport service was to move men and their battle equipment to the theatre of war. Normally the requisitioned merchant ships would be used. Caesar in the invasion of Britain calculated eighty transports for two legions (10,000 men) and their equipment and retinues. Caesar also had a special, broadened, flatter, transport built to carry pack animals and bulk supplies.[13] In the Mediterranean the port of Brundisium served the Roman Republic in its eastern theatre of war as San Diego and San Francisco served the United States in World War II. Through this port poured Roman men and arms to fight in the eastern wars and back either to be discharged or fight a civil war in Italy. In 83 BC Sulla returned from the east through Brundisium with a force of 40,000 men in 1,600 ships.[14] Acilius Manius Glabrio left the same port in 66 BC with 2,000 cavalry, 20,000 foot, and a few elephants[15], as did Pompey and Caesar with their armies. Brundisium thus served as a staging area for the assemblage of men and materials heading east.

Once Roman troops left Italy and were in the war theatre they continued to be moved from place to place by sea, generally by merchant transport.[16] In campaigns in the Aegean and off the coast of Asia Minor, supplies and men were borne by sea, as they were in military operations off the African coast.[17] In the Balkans and Asia Minor some areas were so prohibitive to land transport that sea movement of armies was not only the quickest but the safest and easiest as well. In such areas the hot sun made marching more difficult and the packs heavier, the roads were narrow and special precautions were needed to protect the baggage. Under such conditions one who used the land instead of the sea was thought to be a fool indeed.[18]

The second category of cargo was the basic supplies of the army which were necessary to keep the war machine well functioning. As with troop transports, supply ships were almost exclusively merchant ships, although there was a type of ship called a Phaselus, which was a combination warship and merchant vessel.[19] Most of the ships carried grain, but armor, clothing, and artillery would also be carried. Once the army had been put on shore, it was up to the supply fleet to keep the army supplied with at least some of its wheat, daily military supplies, and at times its water.[20]

A large supply fleet generally accompanied any military expedition,, During the Civil Wars, it is recorded that Lepidus left Africa with 1,000 supply ships and seventy warships, the fleet containing twelve legions, 500 cavalry, and assorted war apparatus and supplies.[21] As these figures indicate a supply fleet was sent under the protection of a fleet of war ships in a type of convoy method. These escort ships prevented the supplies and equipment from falling into enemy hands[22], and could search for supply ships which might get blown off course. These large square-rigged ships were more subject to whims of the weather than the smaller, sleek and oared warships. In time of war, for example, a lightly protected supply fleet caught in a calm could meet disaster before a strong enemy war fleet.[23] But under good weather conditions, a strong and favorable wind would make the merchant ships far superior to the smaller warships.[24]

These convoyed supply ships formed the basic arteries of the supply system. But we should not think that this system was an easy system to maintain. The loaded merchant ships could be attacked in their harbors, disrupting supply operations[25], or an enemy might kidnap the fleet and use the supplies himself.[26] There were navigational troubles and problems of the sea which had to be net. When outside the Mediterranean tides could cause bewilderment[27], and within the Mediterranean there was always the possibility of a storm or ship wreck on some forlorn island. One of the most dangerous areas to navigate was the tip of the Peloponnesos. The usual Roman practice was to land in Greece, travel overland, then into the Aegean Sea; but at times it must have seemed desirable to avoid this trans-shipment. This problem was recognized by the Greeks long before the Romans burst on the scene, as they had built a land ford across the neck of land which separates the Gulf of Corinth from the Aegean.[28] Over this road (diolkos) ships were dragged by animal power. It is true that these were mostly warships, but the evidence indicates that fairly large vessels, possibly merchant ships, were pulled across. The Romans made use of this system at least once, for in 102 BC the Roman general Marcus Antonius put his fleet over the ford and into the Aegean. Obviously this ship ford was not a vital link in the supply system, but it does ably demonstrate the importance placed on sea transport and the methods that could be used to keep the sea lanes open.

The sea transport service formed the backbone of the Roman supply system, but when an army was in the field or the sea was dominated by an enemy, there was no choice but to use land supply. This presented problems. With no modern Merlin to blast away mountains, change the flow of rivers, span caverns, lay great super highways, or perform any of the other miracles of modern transport, the Romans had to take the physical earth as they found it and could make only very minor changes. The basic development of overland travel had been completed by Hellenistic times. The succeeding ages, although making new applications, added no new principles. Three basic motive forces were used for land movement, the horse, the mule, and the camel. The camel was well suited for the eastern deserts, but little else. The horse was used for rapid communication and travel of high personages, but being dependent on good roads, was limited in use for long-range and large scale transportation. The mule was the all-purpose motive power for land transport.[29]

Land transport was especially dominant in the large continental areas of the empire - Spain and Gaul. Much of these areas are inaccessible to direct sea supply which could be used in most of the sea-centered empire, so land supply lines had to be established. Supplies coming from Italy into Spain could use the roads that Rome built in the narrow coastal plain. Supplies for Gaul came by way of the same coastal plain or from Province, but Gaul's internal supply system was greatly assisted by the excellent river system. Unlike the narrow and shallow rivers characteristic of the rest of the Mediterranean, the rivers of Gaul are deep, wide, and also generally free of ice, perfect for barge traffic.[30] The principal entrance into Gaul from the Mediterranean was the Rhone valley.[31] The mouth of this river, however, has a tendency to silt up, which prevented it from being used as a receiving harbor for supplies from Italy. Marius corrected this temporarily by building a canal and artificial harbour to avoid the mouth.[32] Even so, the Rhone becomes very swift above its mouth so that heavy cargo was sent by a road along the river bank, until it reached Lugdunume and the quiet waters of the Saome, then was shipped by barge.[33] The Rhine, Loire, Seine, and other rivers completed the inland water system. Accompanying this system was the natural system of roads which Gaul possessed in the form of river valleys or intermediate uplands. These "roads" allowed the use of pack animals and wheeled carts long before the Romans built their roads and of course greatly facilitated Roman transport.[34]

For overland transport, be it in the western empire of Spain and Gaul or the eastern empire of the Balkans or Asia Minor, roads were needed to pave the way for armies and supplies. Some of the large eastern armies had road-makers go before them to clear a path for the army and its train.[35] In the case of Rome however, it was up to the allies to ease the way, escorting and scouting, repairing the bridges and existing roads, bridging the unfordable streams, and furnishing some of the supplies.[36] When such precautions were not taken the army could be put in serious military and logistical embarrassment.[37] In some areas there were no roads at all, so the Romans had their allies build them, but under the direction of Roman engineers.[38]

The only power of overland transport available to the ancient world was the pack horse or mule. Carts and wagons, because they are dependent on good roads, were rarely used by the Roman Republican Armies. But where there were good roads, these carts made of wood and drawn by pairs of mules were a common sight.[39] Thus we hear of carts being used by the army in Italy, Spain, and Gaul[40], and used everywhere by the sutlers who followed the armies. The basic method of carrying goods overland was by pack animal, so each legion had between 400-500 such animals[41] and a corps of men to handle them.[42] This division handled the baggage of the Roman army, transporting it from place to place. If there happened to be a shortage of mules, some of the local natives could be pressed into service as carriers.[43]

Many of the carts, wagons, mules and horses needed by the Roman Army for its supply train came from Italy, purchased by the army, but if the army was in the field, they were often requisitioned. Sulla, for example, in his siege of Athens, collected 20,000 mules and handlers from the surrounding country to handle some of his supply.[44] At other times the allies and towns of the area would be required to turn over carts and draft animals to the army[45], or detachments of the legion might be sent out on a scorch for the earth expedition and seize what animals they could find.[46] Transporting goods is always a headache so the army might try to solve it by shoving the entire problem off on someone else. This someone else was generally the towns or allies, who at times, would not only have to supply the animals, but also ship the supplies themselves to the army. The whole supply problem could be dumped on these towns, either in whole or in part.[47]

A system of overland supply and transport required the maintenance of lines of communication that sea supply did not entail. If control over the road was broken the army could be put in a militarily dangerous position. In sea transport there are many alternative routes to bring supplies to any one point, and unless control of the sea is lost, it was almost impossible to stop a supply fleet. Even where the enemy controlled the sea, the limitations of ancient naval sea power often allowed a supply force to get through. Witness Caesar's crossing of the Adriatic in spite of the fact that Pompey's forces supposedly controlled this sea. Because of the danger in the cutting of land supply lines, steps had to be taken to avoid this break in communications. Even in the east, where sea supply tended to override land supply this problem had to be faced with regard to supply lines leading from the army to the sea.[48] The most obvious answer to this problem is to guard the roads, and several steps could be taken. A detachment of the legion could be sent with the supplies to beat off an attack on the supply convoy itself.[49] An alternative method would be to set up a system of forts along the supply route. A division of infantry would be used to protect the fort and control the surrounding territory, while a detachment of cavalry would be used to patrol the roads and protect the supplies.[50] By this method, it appears that the roads could be kept open. However, these methods present several problems. First, the road or convoy garrisons take valuable men away from the regular military forces, and secondly, as the army advances the supply line grows longer and longer and either requires more men to guard, or the guard grows weaker. If the line grows weak it is more liable to attack,[51] or the increased guard causes a decrease in the strength of the main army. These dangers are especially prevalent where the army would have to pass through hostile territory. In sea transport, because the army and transport service are separate, the guarding of the lines does not draw forces from the army, and as noted above, it is almost impossible to break sea lines.

An intrical and essential part of the land-transport supply system was the baggage train of the legion which transported the daily needs of the legion. In spite of what may appear to be a cumbersome method, the Roman baggage train was efficient and made for a great deal of mobility. The use of pack animals instead of carts allowed the baggage to go anywhere a man could go,[52] and although carts were used to stockpile supplies and by the sutlers, they were almost never used by the army in field operations.

The baggage train carried the basic equipment of the legion. First of all, to protect the soldiers from the weather, the pack train carried the tents. With about ten men to each, adding additional tents for Centurions and other officials about 500 tents would supply one legion. The leather tents were estimated to weigh about forty pounds, including the poles. If each pack animal could carry 200 pounds, 100 mules (five tents each) would carry the tents.[53] Along with the tents, the train would also have to carry the everyday equipment of the legion as shovels, axes, saws, spades, pick-axes, and baskets, for use in digging and transporting earth, cutting wood, clearing road ways, and constructing war machines.[54] The supply train did not carry war machinery or artillery, which could have made the supply train unmanageable. These apparatus were simple enough that an ordinary legionary could build one, but even so the legion had a corps of carpenters to handle actual construction and an engineer to direct construction. The metal parts could be procured from allies and the wood at the scene.[55] Smaller materials of war such as rope, sulphur, hemp and pitch for purposes of fire, might also be carried by the legion.[56] The supply train also carried the arms and armour of the soldiers[57] – swords, helmets, shields, graves – as well as changes of clothing, blankets, cooking utensils, and other such items.

Since in any period of time an army marches on its stomach, the most important cargo of the baggage train was food. As a system of supply depots had been established, the legion did not have to carry huge quantities of grain, but only enough to last a single campaign or trip. The basic ration of the army was wheat; barley was used as a punishment food, and cattle meat in emergencies.[58] The estimated wheat ration for one day was about 1 2/3 pounds, and on a short expedition the soldier's ration would probably amount to a two-week supply, or about twenty-five pounds.[59] This, the solder might carry himself, but on longer campaigns the ration was issued for thirty days[60] and it seems unlikely that he would carry sixty pounds of food. Along with the grain, wine, oil, salt, and water was also taken.[61] Unless the legion was travelling by sea, in which case pre-cooked rations were issued,[62] the grain was not ground or cooked so grinding mills were needed along with various other cooking and carrying utensils.[63]

As to what the soldier personally carried the sources are contradictory, but it can probably be safely said that he carried some of his food, his personal effects, and perhaps his shield, sword, and helmet.[64] We know he carried some of the baggage because the army, in order to maintain its mobility, had to limit the number of pack animals. This limitation would have increased the size of the soldier's pack had it not been for the invention of the Marius Mule. This piece of equipment was a forked pole, upon which the soldier carried his utensils, food, and personal effects tied to the top. On the march the pole was carried on the shoulder, at rest it could be set on the ground.[65]

With the lack of mechanized equipment to lighten the work and duties of a legionary it was natural that many of the personal tasks – cooking, cleaning weapons – would fall to their personal slaves.[66] The source of these servants were the captives made during

41

the war, and although the soldier could easily ransom his captive to a nearby relative or sell him to one of the slave dealers that followed any legion, it was natural that he keep at least one to help out around the camp. Their presence could be a corrupting influence, and although Marius tried to reform the use of slaves[67] it is quite evident that he did not succeed, for in Caesar's day they are called a "normal" comfort. In spite of this danger, the slaves contributed to the smooth functioning of the legion by handling of the baggage train[68] and assisting in other jobs which left the soldiers free for other tasks.

The last thing we should note about the baggage train are the methods used to protect it. The loss of so many vital supplies and equipment could be disastrous. Under most circumstances the army did not march under arms, the weapons being kept in the baggage thus making the legion very vulnerable to attack and ambush, especially by cavalry. In such an event some of the men would have to collect their arms from the baggage while the scouts and cavalry escort would try to hold off the attack.[69] Another dangerous situation arose from the length of the legion and its supply train. When we estimate 500 pack animals on a twenty-foot road, the train would extend about 1,300 feet and the legion and train about 3,900 feet; on a forty-foot road about 2,050 feet.[70] An increase in the number of legions would increase the distance accordingly. To stretch a legion, with the baggage following, out such a distance is only to invite disaster when travelling through enemy territory. To combat these threats the legion would first of all march under arms, and secondly, place the baggage of the legion within a square; a formation by which the baggage was surrounded by columns of centuries, front, rear, and on both flanks.[71]

After transport, a second part of logistics concerns the supplies which keeps the army functioning. The first category includes the arms, weapons, and other war equipment or tools which allow the army to fulfil its purpose.

The complexity of the Roman war equipment could advance no further than the state of ancient industrial technology. Both were simple. There were no great steel mills, no mass production, and no great industrial complexes in the ancient world. Muscle power was the only useful power, and through the years there was a broadening of industrial application but no technical progress.[72] This means that the Romans would use essentially the same weapons as their distant ancestors. It also means that a wealthy state held no military - technological advantage in the production of arms and war equipment. The furnaces of the ancient world could not produce molten ore in large quantities, no matter how civilized or wealthy the state was. Cast-iron, steel weapons or tools could not be mass produced. Each weapon was produced by repeated heatings and forgings on individual anvils.[73] The Germans, or any other group of people, could produce a sword just as well as a Roman. The different types of arms were limited and their basic simplicity allowed anyone with any mechanical ability to produce them if they so desired. A barbaric group of Germans could over night easily produce equipment to storm Roman fortifications[74] or a city in revolt could quickly establish arms factories.[75] But if the enemy had an advantage in ease of production, Rome had the same advantage; weapons could be made overnight and siege machinery built on the scene.[76]

Although the technology and production of war equipment might be simple, we should not be under the mistaken idea that there was no industrial development to supply the needs of the army. Industry always seems to flourish on war, and the ancient world was no exception. During the Republic, Italy itself served as a giant factory for the production of war goods, but this industry served civilian life as well. The city of Rome produced tunics, togas, blankets, smocks, and shoes; iron tools – scythes, spades, and axes – harnesses, and chains could be found at Cales and Minturnae; Rome also produced iron bars and nails, while Capua could supply pulleys and rope.[77] The city of Arretium produced more specialized equipment in the form of shields, helmets, and javelins.[78]

The 'arsenal of Roman democracy', if it can be called that, was located in Campania at the city of Puteoli, near modern Naples. The island of Aethaleia (Elba) off the western Italian coast, because of its extensive deposits of iron ore, supported a large iron industry. The iron ingots produced here were purchased by the merchants of Puteoli, who with their large workshops transformed the metal into tools and weapons. From the city's fine harbor the weapons were shipped abroad to the Roman armies. But along with the arms industry, the city produced tools for the prosperous agriculture which surrounded it. Other centers of industrial concentration and military production were located at Syracuse, Rhegium, Venafrum, Populonia, and Volterra.[79]

Most of this production was in private hands, individually owned and operated workshops. But in order to secure a completely dependable supply of arms, Rome set up state arsenals during the later Republic. These institutions, under the control of public officials, not only produced arms and war equipment, but stockpiled the weapons against future need.[80] In no sense of the word can these arsenals, or the industrial concentration at Puteoli be compared to the mass production facilities of the Ford River Rouge Plant. At best they were a collection of individual shops and craftsmen, all working on individual anvils and producing similar products.

The day-to-day metal products of the ancient world did not come from the large workshops of the cities, but from small, local smiths and artisans. The local farmers, thus most of the population, depended on these individual craftsmen for their need,[81] as did the armies and arsenals. From their small, but many workshops came the helmets, breastplates and the standard sword and spear.[82] These small businessmen also followed the legion as it conquered, not only replacing broken weapons, but also supplying the finer types of equipment that a plunder burdened soldier might wish to buy. Evidence also indicates that some of these smiths were discharged soldiers who had gone into the business of selling armor and war goods to their former comrads.[83] The local smiths also formed the manpower for emergency arsenals that the Roman array might set up to supply its immediate needs in the local theatre of war. If the army should find itself short of armaments of some kind, or need a new type of machine or additional artillery, the general could send out a 'drag-net' for the local metal and wood smiths. After he had collected them, they would be interned in a public workhouse, given the raw materials, and told to produce the needed equipment.[84]

To take care of daily needs and to allow the legion to be an independent unit, the legion had a division of carpenters, engineers, smiths, and armors.[85] The individual men of the legion were probably capable of making minor repairs on their own equipment, building crude bridges and siege machines, but major armor repairs, construction of field artillery, or something like 'Agrippa's Grip'[86] required a little more imagination and skill. To handle these special projects, construction of artillery and the direction of building forts and roads, members of this special and skilled division could be used.

If these normal production methods failed to meet the legion's demand, it had other methods to procure needed equipment. In the field the army could call upon client kings and allies to furnish arms and equipment. The weapons of private citizens could be seized, or when an enemy surrendered a supply of arms could easily be made part of the armistice agreement. Lastly, as noted previously, when the Roman needed siege machines, the wood could be found near by and allies could supply the metal parts.[87]

The second category of supplies is food. The best equipped army can do nothing without men, and men do nothing without food. Much of the army's grain came from Sicily, Sardinia and Corsica.[88] These Roman tributary provinces paid their tithes in grain. In the later Republic this amounted to about 3,000,000 modii, other crops pushing the total up to 4,000,000.[89] The supply of pork came from north Italy and south France,[90] while cattle and lamb meat came from south Italy. Smoking or salting would make these products suitable for shipping to the army.

When the army was operating away from regular supply points, other sources of grain and food could be found. The towns and cities of the ancient world were great storehouses, not only to enable the city to withstand a siege, but also to deny supplies to the enemy. With countless numbers of such cities supplies were always at hand, either to be taken by force[91] or purchased from the occupants.[92] Another source of grain was from the allies. In the great campaign of the civil war the allies of Pompey furnished large supplies of corn,[93] as allies did in other times and in other wars (i.e. Philip of Macedonia in 190). Local political considerations would also help the Romans out. Local kings who wanted Roman help in furthering their own ambitions might offer to furnish supplies,[94] as might various states who desired Roman protection against rivals.[95] Even some local, private persons, who were financially able, might furnish grain, if they were appealed to,[96] as would states that wanted to avoid war and Roman plundering.

If the collection of food through organized channels failed, the army could collect the needed grain and meat by sending a detachment of troops and cavalry on a ravaging expedition of the country side. This method was best used only in enemy territory, but in the case of need it would be used anywhere. Of course the local population knew about this characteristic habit of armies, so took measures to prevent it. Grain in Africa for example, was hidden in underground vaults[97] or if the people knew the army was coming they might collect their possessions into cities or forts.[98] The raiding of sea commerce and the enemy's sea supply lines or the extortion of merchants was far from an unheard of practice.[99] In a severe shortage, severe measures were needed. Meat, although always a grumbled second to grain was readily at hand in the form of the pack animals which could be slaughtered,[100] not the best food perhaps, but good enough to prevent starvation. In place of grain, a substitute sometimes could be found. A root called Chara, for example, when mixed with milk, could be made up into a bread-like substance. Such experiments did not always end successfully however. Antony's men once found roots to eat, but the effect was to make the eaters sick and mad.[101]

The majority of legionaries came off the farm, and at times their experiences could be put into practical use. For if there was no grain to collect, the Roman army became an army of farmers. The supply train carried tools that could easily be turned to agricultural use. If the population, fleeing before the army, left an unharvested grain crop, the legion could harvest it and put it to good use.[102] If they had the time, or were forced to, they could plant a crop, harvest it, and thrash it, to obtain the needed food.[103]

Other supplies are necessary of course. Water does not appear to have been a great problem unless the army was besieged in a circumscribed location or travelling through desert areas. Salt is an absolute necessity, but it could easily have been taken from the sea or from one of the numerous salt works scattered around the Mediterranean. Wood was also plentiful unless enemy action caused a shortage. How such things as oil and wine were procured we do not know, but they probably came by way of the sutlers who followed the legion, or were bought at local markets. One important item, which normally causes logistical headaches, is fodder for the cavalry. Rome found its asprin by simply limiting the cavalry to the absolute minimum. But even these horses had to eat like their riders, and such demands could cancel their military advantages. As in collecting grain or wood, detachments were sent out to secure fodder, but the horses were not as temperamental in their tastes as their legionary masters, so everything from swamp plants to sea weed would serve.[104]

The supplying of a legion in winter is in some respects less complicated than the same job in other seasons of the year. In the west, as in Gaul, the legion could be scattered over the land. Placed in forts, the troops could garrison the country to prevent disorders and solve the supply problem at the same time. Each group of troops would have a relatively large area of territory to draw its food from preventing the devastation that would result if the whole army was quartered in one area. In the east the billeting of an army on the population proved to be the least expensive (from the Roman standpoint) way of wintering the troops. Some areas could buy the privilege of not having a winter visit. Cyprus regularly paid 200 Attic talents. Cicero brags that during his administration of the island there was no billeting, no requisitions, and no money paid to avoid billeting.[105] Evidently the opposite was the common practice. We can also appreciate Cicero's statement: "Which do you think have been more frequently destroyed during the late years – the cities of your enemies by your soldiers' arms or the territory of your friends by their winter quarters?"[106] when we consider the regulations of Sulla. His troops were billeted in Asia Minor during the winter of 84 or 83 under the following requirements. Each soldier was sent to a private home. Each "host" gave his "guest" four tetradarchmue every day, for pocket money, and furnished him and his invited friends with supper. The military tribunes received fifty drachmas a day and two changes of clothing, one for the house, one for the outside.[107] This type of quartering may not have been pleasant for the natives, but it solved a supply problem for Rome.

The sources on the organization of logistics are practically non-existent and those we do have are confused. There is no consistency in the officials who handled logistical problems, problems of purchase and records are not discussed at all. In spite of this however, I believe it is possible to draw what might be termed the paper organization of logistics, keeping in mind that in practice the organization varied tremendously.

The Roman Senate, either in advance, or during the war, would vote for pay of the soldiers and the money for supplies.[108] If the army was already operating in the field the Roman general would requisition the needed supplies and it would be up to the representatives of that country in Rome to settle the question of payment with the Senate.[109] If the requisitions were made in enemy territory payment was no problem, but it seemed that Rome tried to pay for what it took. The money appropriated for contracts would be handled by the quaestor's office, which would let out contracts for the equipment and supplies that was thought to be needed. The various companies which secured the contracts would collect or manufacture the required supplies and ship them to the needed theatre of action.[110] When the supplies arrived they were turned over to the quaestor's organization in the legion, which was in charge of army supplies and pay.

The quaestor was the chief logistical officer of the legion,[111] although there are references to praetors, military tribunes, and prefects acting in this capacity.[112] In the civilian government the quaestor was, of course, the treasury office, but he also served in this capacity in the army.[113] We thus have combined in one office the men who were responsible for paying the soldiers their wages and supplying their basic material needs. Within the camp the quaestor had tents to hold the supplies and an open court for a market place.[114]

Before we consider the role of the quaestor in greater detail we must discuss legionary pay. Polybius (IV. 39) records that the ordinary foot soldier received two obols a day in pay, centurions receiving twice as much. From this pay the quaestor deducts the price fixed for their wheat (2/3 of an Attic mendemmus per month) clothing, and any additional arms and weapons they required. Although the pay of the legion increased over that of the Punic War period, (Caesar doubled the pay) the basic principle that soldiers paid for their grain and equipment seems to have continued. Tacitus (Ann.I. 17) records the legionaries as buying clothing, weapons, tents, and the good will of the centurion. In 123 BCG. Gracchus' reform gave the legionaries free clothing and grain,[115] but in 109 BC the provision for free grain was abolished[116] and it would appear that free clothing did not last much longer. The basic principle, then, was that the soldier paid for his own food and equipment.

Polybius also says that the quaestor deducted from the pay of the soldier the cost of corn and other items that he needed. What was the nature of this deduction? Was it a set amount? Was each soldier's pay deducted the same amount? What was the purpose of the quaestors market? To understand the nature of the quaestor's office in the army these questions must be answered. The deduction, at least for wheat, was not a set amount. This is clearly indicated by the great fluctuations in the price of food. When the army had plenty of booty or was in a wealthy country the price of food would fall to almost nothing. The price of an ox once dropped to one drachma.[117] But if there was a breakdown in the supply system or a severe shortage of grain the price would sky-rocket. It might rise to as much as fifty denarrii (200 sesterces) a peck, when the ordinary price was 3½ - 4 sesterces.[118] When prices rose this high they wiped out the savings of the soldiers.[119] Such fluctuations in the price of grain and thus the amount of deductions puts a new light on the operations of the quaestors office. It appears that the quaestor operated like a merchant. He bought local grain at local prices from merchants or towns, or received contracted grain sent from elsewhere in the empire.[120] The grain, or other supplies, was sold to the soldiers, in the quaestorfs market, at a price allowing him to cover expenses. The individual soldier bought and paid for only what he wanted and needed. These purchases were kept on record by the quaestorfs office staff in a type of charge account process, with the soldier as the purchaser and the quaestor as the retailer. Since the soldier was paid his wages by the same organization from which he made his purchases, before the soldier received his pay the office would check his account, deduct the appropriate amount from the pay and turn the rest over to the soldier. This system amounts to a company store type of operation, but is the most logical explanation of Polybius' remarks.[121] (For an additional remark on the quaestor see Note I at end of chapter)

Because whatever supplies the quaestor has must be transported by the army, it is unlikely that he carried any superfluous items. Anything other than basic supplies would be carried by the sutlers who followed the army. With their wares Piled in carts and wagons, these merchants followed in the wake of every Roman army as it plundered its way around the Mediterranean.[122] The Roman soldier had little use for an art object he might have knocked off some Greek temple, and about one slave was all he could use. The merchants could buy these items of plunder and supply the members of the legion with other goods they might want, such as the finer types of arms and military clothing, foreign wines,[123] personal effects, and various luxury items. This trade at the merchants markets that were inevitably set up near the forts,[124] provided an outlet for the booty collected by the legion, gave the soldiers a few "extras", and allowed the legionaries to build up savings for when they were discharged. These sutlers also supplied the quaestor with some of the goods his office needed to supply the troops[125] and could act as scouts and sources of information for the army.[126]

A third, but even more unofficial branch of the Roman supply system were the Roman and Italian traders that were scattered around the Mediterranean world. Cicero complains that Narbonese Gaul is packed with Roman traders.[127] Mithridates is said to have killed 80,000 Romans and Italians in Asia Minor, and large numbers are known to have been living in Africa. These traders had a strong attachment to Rome, so the Roman Army could count on their support. Their presence in the area was valuable militarily since they knew the local area, and logistically valuable because as merchants they would know where to get what, and so could help the Romans collect supplies. These traders, with their valuable information and Roman sympathies, amounted to a fifth column in favor of Rome so it is little wonder that Mithridates wanted to get rid of them. Several examples of their logistic help to Roman armies might be noted. When Metellus was fighting in Africa he found that the center of trade was the Numidian town of Vaga. This city happened to be populated by large numbers of Romans and Italians who Metellus knew would not only help collect supplies, but protect them as well.[128] Caesar also found the merchants willing to help. In Africa the merchants at Thysdra collected 71,000 bushels of wheat for his use and in his Gallic campaign the large supply depots are generally staffed by Italians or Romans.[129] This evidence seems to indicate the active assistance of the non-military merchants was an important factor in Roman logistics. In effect then, long before a Roman army reached an area its logistical agents-the Italian-Roman merchants were on the scene, lining up possible supplies.

Before turning to the logistical operations and influence on strategy we should consider the implications of the Roman fort. This custom caused logistic problems. First of all the legion would have to carry in its supply train the necessary tools for construction, enough wood had to be present for fortifications, and there must be a source of water for drinking and sanitary purposes. The camp must also be in a military defensible position. Securing the timber was not ordinarily a problem except when the enemy decided to make things difficult. When Caesar was fighting against the Pompian forces in Spain, for example, he found he had an acute shortage of timber when he arrived at one town. It seems that in order to prevent the building of Caesar's fort and war equipment his enemies had collected all the wood for six miles around and dumped it into their own fort![130] But just the collection of wood could be dangerous as the foragers could be attacked by the enemy cavalry.[131] Unless the water was poisoned, this also was generally plentiful and easily maintained. If water was scarce in the area, an advance scouting party would be sent out and a site which had a good supply of water would be secured for that night's camp.[132] Even in the more plentiful areas however, the Romans took great pains to secure their water supply so as to have easy access to it from the camp. At times they went to the extreme of building fortifications to the water source so the supply might be had without danger of cut-off or attack.[133] If the camp was placed under siege a shortage of water could result if the opposing forces diverted or cut the supplying rivers and streams.[134] In such cases the sanitary and thirst problems would be equally serious.

Any camp intended for a period of time longer than a night or two had to be placed in reference to the supply lines that were established. In Caesar's Gallic campaign, where the supply lines depended on the rivers, the camp was placed near or on a major river bank.[135] In the rest of the Mediterranean an access to the sea was needed. Pompey's camp at Petra during the Civil wars was well suited for the arrival of sea supplies.[136] The camps at Philippi however, are probably classic examples in the logistical placement of camps. Cassius had the best position by far. His camp was on a hill, wood was supplied from the nearby mountains, water from rivers and supplies from Thasos with a cartage of only a few stades. Antony, on the other hand, was in a bad logistical position. His camp was on plain, which could give drainage problems, his fuel came from a swamp which could give disease problems, and his supplies came overland from Amphipolis, 350 stades away.[137]

Note I

In reference to the role of the quaestor as 'merchant' it is interesting to note that he may also have handled the sale of the booty taken in war. In Plautus' play, *The Captives*(34), a son is taken captive in a war among Greeks. Although the play is of Greeks in a Greek setting, it is written in Latin, and the word used to designate the officials that sold the young men taken captive is quaestoribus. "So in the hope of getting that son back home more readily he bought both of these prisoners from the commissioners (quaestoribus) who were disposing of the spoils".

Conclusions

As one carefully considers the evidence bearing on the military history of the late Roman Republic, one cannot but be impressed by the critical role that logistics played in these wars. Not that it was an unimportant consideration before, but during this period it seems to have become a dominating rather than an influencing factor.

In the early Republic, Rome was not as dependent on logistics as she later became. There were many alternatives to a highly organized system. The armies were small and worked in close proximity to Rome or friendly territory. Supplies could be shipped a short distance overland from allied city's which dotted Italy, or the small numbers of men allowed the army to live off the land. In any case, however, large amounts were not needed. But the day soon passed when Rome could fight all its wars within easy reach of home. Begun during the Second Punic War, when armies in Africa and Spain as well as those in Italy needed supplies, a trend toward distant wars continued through the Republican period. Distant places in Asia Minor, Armenia, Britain, and Gaul, as well as the closer areas of Africa, Greece, and Spain saw the presence of Roman arms. As the scope of Rome's military operations drew further and further away from the center of the empire, Italy, the armies tended to become larger and larger. The number of men under arms constantly grew, until by the end of the Republic armies of 100,000 were a common occurrence. To distance and numbers was added the obvious problem that the theatre of war was not chosen for its logistic possibilities, but for strategic reasons. Greece, although very poor in food, was often chosen as a battle ground during the civil wars. Media, also poor in supplies, was Antony's roadway for the invasion of Parthia. Of course, some areas were logistically rich and strategically sound - Spain and Gaul for example - but this was more of a coincidence than plan. Thus during the late Republic, three logistic problems presented themselves: the size of armies, the distance needed to transport supplies, and the condition of the theatre of war.

It was, however, these very problems which increased the dependence of the Roman army on its supply system. The larger the army, the less able it was to live off the land, and the more supplies it required. The poorer the theatre of war, the more outside supplies the army needed. As the amount of supplies increased so did the size of the supply base and the distance of transport. But as these complications set in, the solutions grew more and more limited. First, with the exception of the cavalry, foraging became impracticable and an insufficient means of meeting the army»s supply needs. As the army continued to grow in size, whole districts could no longer supply the needs, and even if they could the system of land transports was so inefficient that it could not have transported it. Also, for military reasons, the cavalry had become increasingly importand and was able to disrupt any supply system by land which had been established. In effect, therefore, by the end of the Roman Republic it had become impossible effectively to supply the army by land. Under such pressure the sea became the dominant element in the supply system. It became the only way to solve the logistical problems, and as such, the Roman armies became dependent upon it. With large cargo holds, distance became of little consequence so long as ships could reach the army. The logistical condition of the war theatre need not bother the commander as supplies could reach him from the whole empire, and with the large quantities the fleet could bring almost any sized army could be supported. The sea, therefore, made the army logistically independent of the land in which it operated, minimized transport difficulties, and was capable of supporting the largest army.

Within the framework of these general problems, changes took place within the idea of war. The wars of the early Republic were national in character, their purpose being to crush an enemy of the state. The late Republic saw civil wars. This change, along with military and political expediency, called for the "winning over", not the destruction of the opposing army. Military strategy was thus reoriented. The object was to force surrender en masse of the whole army. This purpose could be accomplished by propaganda or military defeat, but there was no reason why this defeat had to be made at the cost of destroying the army. If it could be forced into surrender by means other than battle - and this is where logistical strangulation played such an important part – a general would remove his opponent, win over the army intact, and be ready for the next challenge. This frame of mind, added to the excellence of the generalship, tended to lead to wars of strategic movement and position-seeking, rather than to attacks which sought the destruction of the enemy. Each campaign is different, of course, but the connecting theme in all is a strategy of this type.

To carry out such a strategy required a highly mobile fighting force, a requirement that could be met only by cavalry on land and a fleet on the sea. If the supply system was based on the land, as was true in the Parthian expedition, the cavalry could destroy the supply system and force the army into defeat, or as in this case, into retreat. Agrippa, at Actium, demonstrated the same principle on the sea. Of course, one cavalry force could cancel another, one fleet another, and both sides knew this. A campaign, therefore, may not be decided by the infantry, but by the side which holds, and continues to hold, land and sea superiority; that is, freedom of movement. Not because of this superiority per se, but by its use the enemy supply lines could be cut and forced to surrender. The use of the fleets at Actium and the cavalry in Media are perfect examples of this principle at work.

A secondary, but equally important problem that each civil war general had to face, was the recruitment of his troops. The fighting elements of the Roman armies were made up of Italians, and each general had to keep this in mind. At all times, but more especially if he went east, he had to keep, or plan on regaining control of the recruiting areas. We see this factor most at work in the case of Antony, but it must also have been of concern to Pompey.

The importance of Logistics rests on these two interacting factors. Militarily, the distances covered by the army and the resulting transport difficulties, the condition of the war theatre and the size of the army, forced the army to place great dependence on its logistical system for survival. Strategically, the growth of the idea of logistic strangulation gave logistics a tremendous importance as the central means of winning military campaigns.

Bibliography

Modern Works

Adcock, F E. *Roman Art of War Under the Republic*, New York, 1960.

Gary, Max. *The Geographic Background of Greek and Roman History*, London, 1949.

Casson, Lionel. 'The Isis and Her Voyage', *Transactions of the American Philological Association*, LXXXI (1950).

Craven, Lucile. 'Antony's Oriental Policy Until the Defeat of the Parthian Expedition', University of Missouri Studies, III No. 2 (1920).

Debevoise, N C. *A Political History of Parthia*, Chicago, 1938.

Ferrero, Guglielrao. *The Greatness and Decline of Rome*(translated by H J Chaytor), New York, 1909.

Forbes, R J. *Metallurgy in Antiquity*, Leiden, 1950.

Frank, Tenney. *An Economic History of Rome to the End of the Republic*, Baltimore, 1920; *An Economic Survey of Ancient Rome*, Baltimore, 1940.

Gomme, A. W. 'A Forgotten Factor in Greek Naval Strategy', *Essays in Greek History and Literature*, Oxford, 1937.

Heitland, W E. *The Roman Republic*, Cambridge, 1909.

Holmes, T. Rice. *The Roman Republic and Founder of the Empire*, Oxford, 1923; *Architect of the Roman Empire*, Oxford, 1928.

Judson, Harry P. *Caesar's Army*, Boston, 1888.

Lepper, F A. *Trajan's Parthian War*, Oxford, 1948.

Lucas, F L. 'The Battlefield of Pharsalos', *Annual of the British School in Athens*, XXIV (1929).

Marsh, Frank B. *A History of the Roman World 146-30 BC.*, London, 1935.

Mommsen, Theodor. *The History of Rome* (translated by William Dickson), New York, 1895.

MacMullen, Ramsay. 'Inscriptions on Armor and the Supply of Arms in the Roman Empire', *American Journal of Archaeology*, LXVII (1960).

Oliver, Edmund H. *Economic Conditions at the End of the Republic*, Toronto, 1907.

Rawlinson, H C. 'Memoir on the Site of the Atropatenian Ecbatana', *Journal of the Royal Geographic Society*, X (1841).

Rawlinson, George. *The Sixth Great Oriental Monarchy*, London, 1873.

Reinhold, Meyer. *Marcus Agrippa*, Geneva (N.Y.), 1933.

Richardson, G W. 'Actium', *Journal of Roman Studies*, XXVII (1937).

Rodgers, W L. *Greek and Roman Naval Warfare from Salamis to Actium*, Annapolis, 1937.

Starr, Chester G. *The Roman Imperial Navy*, Ithaca, 1941.

Syme, Ronald. *The Roman Revolution*, Oxford, 1952.

Tarn, W W. 'Antony's Legions', *Classical Quarterly*, XXVI (1932); 'Actium: A Note', *Journal of Roman Studies*, XXVIII (1938); 'The Battle of Actium', *Journal of Roman Studies*, XXI (1931); *Cambridge Ancient History*, X, New York, 1928.

Torr, Cecil. *Ancient Ships*, Cambridge, 1895.

Westermann, William L. 'On Inland Transportation and Communication in Antiquity', *Political Science Quarterly*, XLIII (1929).

Woodhouse, W J. *Aetolia*, Oxford, 1897.

Primary Sources (All of the Loeb Classical Library)

Appian
  Civil Wars
  Macedonian Wars
  Mithridatic War
  Syrian War

Caesar
  African War
  Alexandrian War
  Civil Wars
  Gallic War
  Spanish War

Cicero
  Letters to Atticus
  Letters to His Friends
  Pro Fonteio
  Pro Lege Manilia
  In Pisonem
  Pro Rabirio
  De Republica
  Tusculan Disputations

Dio Cassius

Diodorus Siculus

Florus

Livy

Lucian
  Navigium

Orosius

Plautus
  Captivi

Pliny
  Natural History

Plutarch
  Antony
  Caesar
  Cato Minor
  Crassus
  Lucullus
  Marius
  Pompey
  Sulla

Polybius

Sallust
  Bellum Iugurthinum

Strabo

Tacitus

Annals

Varro

Endnotes

[1] Cary, Max. *The Geographic Background of Greek and Roman History*, London, 1949, pp. 29-300.

[2] *Ibid*, p. 26.

[3] Livy, XXV, 10.

[4] Caesar, *B. Civ.* I. 36.

[5] Caesar, *B. Civ.* I. 54.

[6] Caesar, *B. Civ.* I. 34.

[7] Caesar, *B. Civ.* I. 30.

[8] Appian, *B. Civ.* V. xii. 127.

[9] Casson, Lionel. 'The Isis and Her Voyage', *Transactions of the American Philological Association*, LXXXI (1950), 51.

[10] Torr, Cecil. *Ancient Ships*, Cambridge, 1895, p. 25.

[11] Cicero, *Fam.* XII. xv. 2.

[12] Lucian, *Navigum*5; Casson, pp. 51-56.

[13] Caesar, *B. Gall.* IV. 22; V. 1.

[14] Appian, *B. Civ.* I. ix. 79.

[15] Appian, *Syr.* IV. 17.

[16] Appian, *B. Civ.*V. xi. 104.

[17] Appian, *B. Civ.* III. ix. 72; Caesar, *B. Afr.* 8.

[18] Appian, *Syr.* VII. 43.

[19] Appian, *B. Civ.* V. xi. 95.

[20] Caesar, *B. Afr.* 8; <u>B. Alex</u>. 8.

[21] Appian, *B. Civ.* V. xi. 98.

[22] Appian, *B. Civ.* II. viii. 54.

[23] Appian, *B. Civ.* IV. xi. 86.

[24] Appian, *B. Civ.* IV. xv. 115.

[25] Caesar, *B. Civ.* III. 41.

[26] Caesar, *B. Civ.* II. 33.

[27] Caesar, *B. Gall.* IV. 29.

[28] Westermann, William L. 'On Inland Transportation and Communication in Antiquity' in *Political Science Quarterly*, XLIII (1929), 383.

[29] *Ibid*, p. 367 ff.

[30] Caesar, *B. Gall.* VII. 65; for barge traffic see Caesar, *B. Gall.* I. 16.

[31] Cary, *Geographic Background*, p. 250.

[32] Plutarch, *Marius.* XV.

[33] Cary, *Geographic Background*, p. 251.

[34] *Ibid*, p. 250.

[35] Appian, <u>*Mith*</u>. IX. 69.

[36] Appian, *Mac.* IX. 5; <u>Syr</u>. V. 23.

[37] Appian, *Syr.* VL 43.

[38] Cicero, *Pro Font.* 17; Teney, F. *An Economic Survey of Ancient Rome*, Baltimore, 1940, I, 227.

[39] Varro, *Rust.* II. viii. 5.

[40] Plutarch, *Pompey.* 6; Caesar, *B. Hisp.* 6; *B. Gall.* I. 6.

[41] Judson, H P. *Caesar's Army*, Boston, 1888, p. 17; Frank, *Economic Survey*, p. 42.

[42] Caesar, *B. Gall.* VII. 45.

[43] Plutarch, *Lucullus.* XIV.

[44] Plutarch, *Sulla.* XII.

[45] Caesar, *B. Afr.* 8.

[46] Caesar, *B. Gall.* VI. 43,

[47] Sallust, *Iug.* XLVI.

[48] Appian, *B. Civ.* LV. xvi. 12.

[49] Appian, *B. Civ.* III. ii. 11.

[50] Caesar, *B. Gall.* VII. 34.

[51] Appian, *B. Civ.* V. xiv. 140.

[52] Adcock, F E. *Roman Art of War Under The Republic*, New York, 1949, p. 69.

[53] Judon, *Caesar's Army*, pp. 16 – 17.

[54] Caesar, *B. Gall.* V. 42; Tacitus, *Ann.* I. 65.

[55] Appian, *Mith.* V. 30; Caesar, *B. Gall.* V. 11; Appian, *B. Civ.* I. 24.

[56] Sall, *Iug.* 57; Appian, *Mith.* V. 36.

[57] Caesar, *B. Gall.* II. 21.

[58] Plutarch, *Antony.* XXXIX.

[59] Judson, *Caesar's Army*, p. 36.

[60] Livy, *XLIII.* 1.

[61] Caesar, *B. Afr.* 43; Plutarch, *Crassus.* 19; Sallust, *Iug.* LXXV.

[62] Livy, *XLIV.* 35.

[63] Plutarch, *Antony.* XV; Sallust, *Iug.* LXXV.

[64] Cicero, *Tusc.* 37.

[65] Front, *Strat.* IV. i. 7.

[66] Plutarch, *Marius.* XIII.

[67] Plutarch, *Marius.* XII.

[68] Caesar, *B. Gall.* III. 29.

[69] Caesar, *B. Gall.* II. 21; Sall, *Iug.* LXXV.

[70] Judson, *Caesar's Army*, p. 49.

[71] Sallust, *Iug.* C; Caesar, *B. Gall.* VII. 67; II. 19.

[72] Forbes, R J. *Metallurgy in Antiquity*, Leiden, 1950, p. 450.

[73] Tenney, F. *An Economic History of Rome to the End of the Republic*, Baltimore, 1920, p. 179.

[74] Caesar, *B. Gall*. V. 40.

[75] Caesar, *B. Alex*. 2.

[76] Caesar, *B. Gall*. V. 40; Appian, *Mith*. V. 30.

[77] Cato, *Agr*. 135.

[78] Oliver, E H. *Roman Economic Conditions at the End of the Republic*, Toronto, 1907, p. 137.

[79] Diod, V. 13; Pliny, *N. H.* XIV. xiv. 139; Forbes, *Metallurgy in Antiquity*, p. 461.

[80] Cicero, *Rab. Post*. 20; Pis. 87.

[81] Varro, *Rust*. I. xvi. 3-4.

[82] Frank, *Economic History*, p. 181.

[83] MacMullen, R. "Inscriptions on Armor and the Supply of Arms in the Roman Empire", *American Journal of Archaeology*, LXIV (January 1960), 25.

[84] Livy, XXVI. 51; XXXIX. 35,

[85] Cicero, *Rep*. II. 395; Caesar, *B. Gall*. V. 11; *B. Civ*. I. 24.

[86] Appian, *B. Civ*. V. xv. 118-119.

[87] Appian, *B. Civ*. II. viii. 51; Caesar, *B. Civ*. II. 18; Sallust, *Iug*. LXII; Appian, *Mith*. V. 30.

[88] Appian, *B. Civ*. V. vii. 72.

[89] Frank, *Economic Survey*, p. 140.

[90] Polybius, II. 15.

[91] Caesar, *B. Gall*. I. 23, 38.

[92] Appian, *B. Civ*. III. iii. 26.

[93] Caesar, *B. Civ*. III. 5.

[94] Plutarch, Crassus XIX.

[95] Caesar, *B. Civ*. I. 48; *B. Gall*. I. 16.

[96] Caesar, *B. Afr*. 21.

[97] Caesar, *B. Afr*. 65.

[98] Sallust, *Iug*. LXXXVI; Caesar, *B. Gall*. VI. 10.

[99] Caesar, *B. Civ*. III. 23.

[100] Appian, *Mith*. 97.

[101] Caesar, *B. Civ*. III. 48; Appian. *B. Civ*. II. ix. 61.

[102] Caesar, *B. Gall*. IV. 32; VI. 36.

[103] Caesar, *B. Civ*. III. 58; Appian, *Mac*. 13.

[104] Caesar, *B. Alex*. 1; *B. Afr*. 24.

[105] Cicero, *Att*. V. 21.

[106] Cicero, *Leg. Man.* 38.

[107] Plutarch, *Sulla* XXV.

[108] Sallust, *Iug.* XXXVIII.

[109] Livy, XLIV. XVI.

[110] Livy, XXII. 48, 49; XXV. 3; Caesar, *B. Civ.* II. 18; Oliver, *Economic Conditions*, p. 117.

[111] Polybius, VI. 31: Sallust, *Iug.* XXIX; Caesar, *B. Afr.* 34.

[112] Caesar, *B. Afr.* 8; *B. Gall.* III. 7; Livy, XXIX. 36.

[113] Sallust, *Iug.* CV.

[114] Polybius, VI. 31.

[115] Plutarch, *G. Gracch.* V.

[116] Frank, *Economic Survey*, p. 25.

[117] Plutarch, *Lucullus* XIV.

[118] Caesar, *B. Civ.* I. 52.

[119] Caesar, *B. Afr.* 47.

[120] Livy XXXIV. 9; Appian, *B. Civ.* III. iii. 26.

[121] For an additional remark on the quaestor see note I at the end of chapter.

[122] Caesar, *B. Afr.* 75.

[123] Sallust, *Iug.* XLIV.

[124] Caesar, *B. Gall.* VI. 37.

[125] Caesar, *B. Gall.* I. 52.

[126] Caesar, *B. Gall.* II. 26.

[127] Cicero, *Pro Font.* 11-12.

[128] Sallust, *Iug.* XLVIII.

[129] Caesar, *B. Afr.* 36; *B. Gall.* III. 38, 55.

[130] Caesar, *B. Hisp.* 41.

[131] Dio Cass. XLIX. 27.

[132] Sallust. *Iug.* L.

[133] Caesar, *B. Civ.* I. 73; III. 66.

[134] Caesar, *B. Civ.* III. 44.

[135] Caesar, *B. Civ.* II. 5.

[136] Caesar, *B. Civ.* III. 42.

[137] Appian, *B. Civ.* IV. xiv. 107.

Supplying Johnny Reb and Billy Yank: Logistics in the War Between the States

David Kirkpatrick

Visiting Professor, Cranfield Defence and Security, Defence Academy of the UK.

Introduction

The American Civil War (ACW) was a bitter struggle between twenty-five Union states in the north and west and eleven Confederates states in the south, and it remains one of the most important and formative events in American history. More Americans died in that war than in all of the other wars in the history of the US, and the death rate in the defeated Confederacy was three times the rate suffered by Britain in World War I. By the end of the war the Confederacy had been fought over, devastated and occupied to an extent that Britain has not experienced since the Norman Conquest, and in the Southern states resentment at defeat lasted for decades (in the South 'damnyankee' was, until very recently, a single word). Interest in the ACW continues to be strong because it was the first war in which the soldiers were mostly literate and left voluminous memoirs, correspondence and diaries, because it was the first war which was extensively photographed, and because Hollywood has made many films and TV series which have communicated its legends.

This paper briefly reviews the origins and the course of the war, and then considers the challenges which it presented in the supply and transport of troops, using the alternative modes of transport available in that period. It then considers the influence of logistics on the operations of Union and Confederate forces. Finally the paper discusses how some of the logistic features of the ACW were reflected in later wars.

Origins of the War

After the thirteen American colonies won their independence from Britain, different economic systems arose in north and south. In the north the climate favoured European-style agriculture by independent farmers, supplemented by fishing and trade. The availability of 'free' land on the frontier required established farmers to pay their hired labourers good wages (otherwise they would leave for an independent life settling farther west) and thus encouraged high productivity. In the early 19th Century canals and railways stimulated markets and specialisation in production, and encouraged the development of industry which attracted many immigrants from Europe.

The southern climate favoured cash crops of cotton, rice and indigo which could only be cultivated by Negro slaves, who were not permitted to leave and could easily be detected if they ran away. In a slave society improved productivity would be dangerous if it created idle hands, so innovation was not encouraged. Only a minority of Southern whites were rich plantation owners, but that minority was sufficiently powerful to dominate local society and politics.

The northern states made slavery illegal after independence and an increasing body of opinion, led by the Quakers of Pennsylvania, regarded slavery as an abhorrent institution which ought to be abolished. The northern states also wanted tariffs on imported goods to protect their infant industries. Southern leaders resented both the tariffs on the manufactured goods they imported from Europe, and the threat which the potential abolition of slavery presented to their economy and lifestyle. When Abraham Lincoln was elected President in 1860, southerners suspected that he could not be trusted to withstand the pressure from abolitionists in his Republican Party, and eleven Southern states seceded from the Union to form an independent Confederacy. The legality of secession remains debatable, and the Confederacy was never formally recognised by any foreign powers.

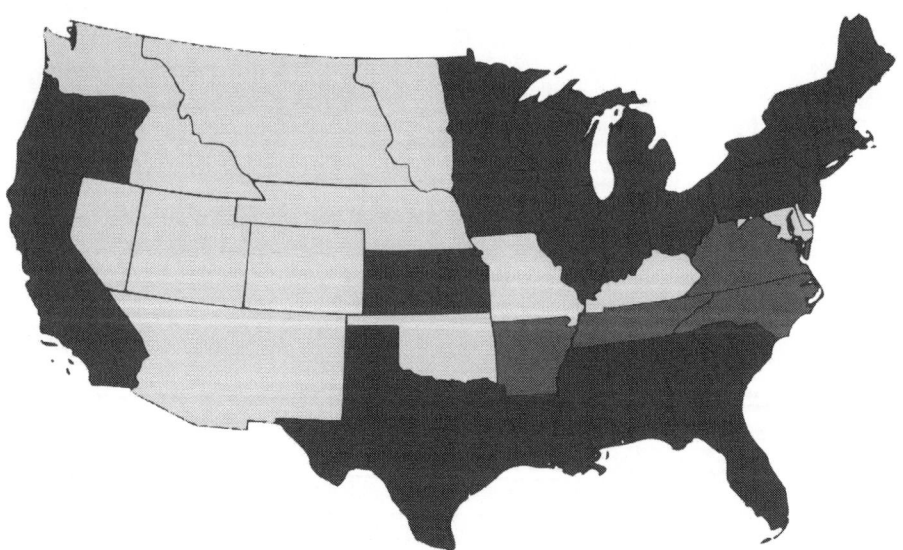

A map showing the results of secession in 1861 with states being divided into: Those that remained in the Union and forbade slavery (blue); those that remained in the Union and permitted slavery (yellow); those that seceded before 15 April 1861 (dark red); those that seceded after 15 April 1861 (light red); and unaffiliated territories (grey). (Source: Júlio Reis via Wikipedia)

A Review of Operations

To subdue the Confederacy, the Union adopted an 'Anaconda' strategy of advance on many fronts:

- Successive advances on the Confederate capital at Richmond from the north and/or up the James River; thwarted by a series of victories won by General Robert E. Lee's Confederate army.
- The invasion of Tennessee and Georgia along an axis of operations from Nashville through Chattanooga to Atlanta; this Union advance was almost uniformly successful, and ultimately extended to Savannah and the Carolinas.
- Amphibious war in the Mississippi valley to cut the Confederacy in two, and to make the river available for commercial traffic from the Union states in the Mid-West; in this theatre more troops and better gunboats enabled Union forces to capture Vicksburg and Port Hudson in 1863, achieving both Union objectives.
- Naval blockade of southern ports by Union warships, facilitated by amphibious operations along the Confederacy's coastline to plug estuaries and establish naval bases; southern entrepreneurs operated blockade-runners and privateers, but the blockade progressively strangled the southern economy.

All of these campaigns affected, and were affected by, the problems of logistics.

The Armies

The opposing Confederate and Union armies, at least near the start of the ACW, closely resembled the armies which had fought at Waterloo, except that most of the latter were veterans while the ACW armies were almost all inexperienced volunteers. Most of the ACW infantry were initially armed with 0.69" muzzle-loading smoothbore muskets and bayonets, and they manoeuvred in Napoleonic lines and columns. As the war continued the infantry were re-equipped with 0.58" muzzle-loading rifles which had a much-longer effective range, and later some had breech-loading magazine rifles with a much higher rate of fire.[1]

Weapon	Effective range, yards	Shots fired per min, max.
Smoothbore musket	50	3
Muzzle-loading rifle	200	3
Repeating rifle	200	20

In face of this increased firepower, infantry adopted more-dispersed formations for manoeuvre and attack and constructed field fortifications which presaged those of the First World War.

A Springfield Model 1863 rifled percussion musket (Source: 19th Century Firearms via Wikimedia Commons)

ACW cavalrymen fought in mounted melees using sabres, though some preferred shotguns or revolvers, and they also fought dismounted using carbines. The increased firepower of infantry and artillery, relative to the Napoleonic period, made it highly dangerous to attempt mounted charges on the battlefield, so cavalry in the ACW were used largely for reconnaissance and raiding.

ACW artillery used horse-drawn smoothbore cannon, which were an improved version of the guns used by Napoleon. These guns fired solid shot and explosive shell at ranges of up to 800 yards; at short ranges below 350 yards they fired canister – a container filled with musket balls or scrap metal – which burst on firing to create a shotgun-like spray of shot which was very effective against charging enemy cavalry or infantry. Artillery also used rifled guns which could fire more accurately and at longer ranges (out to 2,000 yards) whenever the terrain was sufficiently open for the artillerymen to see their targets.

Theatre of Operations

The ACW was fought over a vast area. The fifteen states in which slavery was legal in 1860, and which could potentially have joined the Confederacy to preserve that 'peculiar institution', extended 1,000 miles southward from the Mason-Dixon Line, and 1,500 miles westward from the Atlantic coast. Excluding the remote and scarcely-populated areas of Florida and west Texas, the territory of the slave states measured some 700 by 1,000 miles. Because Kentucky and Missouri did not secede, the Confederacy's actual heartland was 200 miles (on average) less deep west of the Appalachians, but was still more than twice the area of France.[2] Since Great Britain had found it impractical to re-conquer the rebellious thirteen American colonies (which then formed a strip no more than 200 mile deep along the Atlantic coast), and since Napoleon had failed in his 1812 campaign to conquer Russia when its centres of power were 600 miles from his bases in Poland, the leaders of the Confederacy considered that their new state was virtually invulnerable (a decade earlier, before the railways were built, they might have been right).[3]

The theatres of operation included some fertile and prosperous areas like the Shenandoah Valley, and also some rugged and undeveloped areas like the Appalachians and the Ozarks which offered no subsistence to the men or animals of an army marching through. The country was intersected by ranges of hills and mountains which armies could cross only at a limited number of passes, and by bridgeless rivers which could be crossed only at ferries or at fords which were sometimes passable and sometimes not. In some areas armies needed to have bridging trains (typically of about seventy-five large wagons carrying pontoons, roadway timber, tools, etc.) so that they could construct bridges when required.[4] Even relatively-small rivers could flood at inconvenient moments, sweeping away temporary bridges and disrupting the best-laid plans of commanders.

Only a very few of the roads across this vast landscape were suitable for a marching army. These 'turnpike' roads had stone foundations and gravel top dressing, and accordingly could be used by wagons at all seasons of the year. Accordingly these turnpikes, where they existed, strongly influenced military operations (for example, the Valley Pike facilitated Stonewall Jackson's campaign in the Shenandoah Valley). Most other roads were dirt roads, some no wider than a farm cart, which degenerated to bottomless mud in wet weather. When the Union Army of the Potomac tried to manoeuvre inland from Fredericksburg in January 1863, its wheeled vehicles and draft animals became immovably bogged down – guns sank to their axles and mules to their chins – and the march had to be abandoned after days of fruitless struggle.

Some of the dirt roads were upgraded to 'plank' roads by adding layers of timber cut from the surrounding forest; this provided a firmer albeit uneven surface, but it rapidly rotted into dangerous ruts and pitfalls unless it was regularly renewed. Sherman's veteran Union troops crossed the Carolina swamps in the winter of 1864-65 by building simpler 'corduroy' roads, of split logs laid perpendicular to a track, at a rate of twelve miles/day.[5]

Logistics Requirements

The motive power of armies in the American Civil War was provided by horses and mules – carrying cavalrymen and senior officers, and pulling guns, ambulances and wagons full of ammunition and other supplies. An army of 100,000 men needed between a third and a half of that number of horses, and it was the latter which presented the greatest problem in logistics.

American Civil War soldiers were entitled to a daily ration of 3lbs of food[6] (though Confederate soldiers rarely received full rations, and Union soldiers suffered intermittent shortages) which might be supplemented by plundering if and only if the army was marching through a rich agricultural area. Part of the daily ration might be provided by butchering some of the cattle from the herds (roughly 50 cattle per 1,000 men, representing two weeks rations[7]) accompanying the army on the hoof, but these cattle had to be given sufficient time and sufficient pasture to graze or they would become too emaciated to provide much nourishment.

Working horses needed a daily ration of 12lbs of grain and 14lbs of hay or other dry fodder, depending on their size and weight; smaller mules needed rather less. Whenever grass was available and the animals had time to graze it, their rations of hay could be reduced in proportion. Horses and mules also need to drink about ten gallons of reasonably clean water each day, which could present problems for an army concentrated in an area where the springs and streams were few and limited in volume. They also needed a steady supply of horseshoes, nails and replacement harness, but their food, like that of the soldiers, presented the greatest logistics problem.[8]

The rigours of campaigning, incompetent riders and drivers, and pandemic diseases in the crowded Army horse lines reduced the life expectancy of serviceable horses and mules to a few months, and frequent replacements were required. Some incompetent army agents bought horses which were already diseased or otherwise unfit for service from unscrupulous dealers. Both sides established animal infirmaries, where sick animals could rest and recover in quarantine and where veterinary science was developed by trial and error (and by killing some sick animals prematurely to study the characteristics and spread of various diseases). During the ACW, the Union army procured 650,000 horses and 450,000 mules, and 70 million horseshoes.[9]

In addition to the food needed to sustain soldiers and their animals, ACW armies needed continuous supplies of shoes, clothing and camp equipment. Some US army shoes, procured in haste from fraudulent contractors, fell apart within four days on the march. After a major battle the armies needed lots of ambulances and less-comfortable wagons to evacuate wounded soldiers to rear areas for treatment, and simultaneously needed to replenish their stocks of ammunition for small arms and artillery. Both of these requirements depended on the scale and intensity of the battle. After the particularly-severe battle of Gettysburg, for example, the Union army needed to evacuate 15,000 wounded soldiers (of both armies) from field hospitals to the nearest railhead and onward in special trains to an adequate hospital.[10] Simultaneously, the Union army would have needed about 200 wagon loads of ammunition from an ordnance depot to replace the amount fired during the battle.[11] Given the limited resources available for evacuation and replenishment, both of these processes took many days. However, food formed the lion's share of the armies' requirements.

The soldiers' cartridge boxes held some 40 rounds[12] and could be rapidly depleted in a protracted firefight, so the regimental ammunition wagon had to stay sufficiently close to the firing line to allow rapid and regular resupply. In the early years of the ACW, this resupply process was complicated because regiments had been raised in haste and equipped with whatever firearms were available, so many regiments carried a variety of smoothbore and rifled muskets of different calibres.

Modes of Transport

Wagons

A wagon train of the Military Telegraph Corps near Richmond, Virginia (Source: US Government via The American Civil War Photo Gallery)

In the ACW, as in the Napoleonic wars, supplies for an army in the field were provided by wagons travelling between the army and its base depot (or magazine). In America the standard army wagon was 10ft x 3.5ft and was drawn by four horses or six mules; the load which they could pull varied between 1,800 and 4,500lbs depending on the condition of the roads and on the weather.[13] The average load in good conditions was 3,000lbs and the driver and his draught animals would together eat about 140lbs per day (or less if lush grass were available en route and if the draught animals could be given time to graze).

An army of 80,000 men and 35,000 horses, similar to the opposing armies at Gettysburg, would need about 1,150,000lbs (510 tons) of food per day, and if the army was engaged in active operations in an undeveloped area, very little of this food could be collected along the line of march. If the army were close to its base, the food could be delivered by (1,150,000/3,000 =) 380 wagons, but if the army advanced into enemy territory its requirement for wagons would increase exponentially because each wagon's load of deliverables would be decreased by the need to carry enough food to sustain its driver and draught animals through the round trip from the depot to the army and back. If the roads were good enough for the wagons to carry 3,000lbs each and to cover twenty miles per day (two fairly optimistic assumptions), the wagons supplying the army, when it was 100 road miles into enemy territory, would each have to carry 1,400lbs of food for the divers and draught animals, reducing their deliverables by half. The army would then need a veritable fleet (10 x 1,150,000/1600 = 7,200) of wagons shuttling to and fro between the army and its base in order to avoid starvation.

The scale of the wagon train might be larger or smaller according to the condition of the roads and the army's access to grazing. It could be reduced by establishing intermediate depots where the wagons could replenish their supplies of grain and fodder, and it would be increased by any escorts required for the wagon trains or by the need for garrisons to protect the intermediate depots. It follows that any army relying on wagons could not move far from its main supply base (or from a railhead) without creating an exorbitant demand for wagons, drivers, horses and mules, and the army could not be supplied at all unless the roads were reasonably dry.

Supply by wagon could not sustain any army which was advancing faster than its wagons could follow. The troops could carry a few days' rations for themselves and their horses, but when these were consumed the army would have to pause to allow the wagons to catch up and deliver additional supplies.

Railways

The capability to supply an army far from its base was vastly increased by the construction on railways in the first half of the 19th Century. By 1860, the US has 31,000 miles of track, including 9,000 miles in those states which joined the Confederacy.[14] Railways could operate in almost all weathers, and was powered by wood and water which was both obtainable almost everywhere. In parts of America the railway tracks met European standards but in other parts they were relatively crude, sometimes no more than a strip of iron on top of a wooden rail fixed to oak sleepers, laid directly on the dirt rather than on a ballasted roadbed; accordingly speeds were limited to between fifteen and twenty-five miles per hour. A single train could carry 130 tons of freight (in sixteen freight cars carrying about 8 tons each) but the average load was often smaller because some of the cargo (such as hay) was bulky rather than heavy.[15] Nevertheless the army considered above (80,000 men with 35,000 horses at 100 miles from its base) could have been supplied by four trains shuttling daily between the army and its base 100 miles away and requiring some twelve hours for the round trip including unloading. However, this was only possible if the army was located close to an operational railway; whenever the army moved away from a railway, it was forced to rely on wagons.

Railways could also carry fifty infantry (or more in extremis) per passenger car[16], so a single train of between ten and fifteen cars could carry a regiment as far in an hour as it could march in a day, and deliver it to its destination free from fatigue or straggling. For strategic re-deployments, larger numbers of troops could be carried on longer trains.

Railways were vulnerable to destructive raiding by hostile cavalry, but both track and bridges could be rapidly rebuilt (in the 1864 Atlanta campaign, Sherman's engineers could repair three miles of track per day whenever it was ravaged by Confederate raiders[17]). In the latter years of the war, Union cavalry devised methods of bending and twisting rails which Confederate engineers could not quickly repair or replace, thus accelerating the collapse of the Confederate railway system.

A locomotive on a steel girder bridge (Source: US Government via The American Civil War Photo Gallery)

Steamboats and Steamships

The exploitation of steam power by railways on land was paralleled by the development of steamboats designed to carry passengers and freight on the mighty Mississippi and its tributaries. In favourable conditions these steamboats could travel as fast as a railway train, but because rivers bend and meander the steamboats point-to-point speed was rather slower and their speed was inevitably rather faster going downstream than upstream. A typical river steamboat could travel downstream at about eighty miles per day[18], and half as far upstream, and could carry 500 tons[19], enough to supply the daily requirements of the army considered above provided that it was operating on a navigable river. Supply by steamboat was thus constrained by geography, and it could also be interrupted by fog and ice in winter and by low water in summer.

Similarly, ocean-going steamships could be used to carry supplies for amphibious operations, though these ships were at risk of destruction and delay from stormy weather and there were often difficulties in getting soldiers and their equipment on to a tidal foreshore.

River steamboats and ocean-going steamships could also carry troops. Their capacity depended on the size of the ship and the duration of the voyage, but on short trips both types could hold 400-1,000 men (depending on the amount of accompanying horses, guns, baggage, etc.). The large steamboat 'Sultana' was carrying over 1,900 US troops home for demobilisation in 1865 when its boiler exploded killing three-quarters of those on board.[20] Large USN warships could carry 3,000 troops.[21]

Interfaces

American Civil War armies were supplied by a combination of foraging, wagons, railways, steamboats and steamships depending on where they operated. Where the three latter modes were used, it was vitally important to organise effectively the railheads and ports at which supplies were offloaded into wagons for distribution to the troops in forward areas. Inexperienced officers often tried to retain railway wagons as de facto warehouses, cluttering the tracks and depleting the railway's capacity; in other cases supplies were offloaded hastily, and were spoilt by decay or weather before being distributed.

The Impact of Logistics on Operations

Union

The ability of Union forces to conquer the Confederacy depended on achieving both a superiority of force and the ability to supply advancing armies. In the Eastern theatre, Union forces proved unable to advance the 100 miles (as the crow flies) between the Union capital in Washington DC and the Confederate capital in Richmond without relying on seaborne supplies. Union forces were able to quickly conquer most of Tennessee during 1862 using the Tennessee and Cumberland rivers as supply lines. However, their subsequent advance south-eastward towards Chattanooga in 1863 was much slower, characterised by successive short advances followed by pauses of several weeks while the Nashville & Chattanooga RR was reconstructed. By 1864, the Union railway repair organisation was streamlined so that the railhead moved forward closely behind the Union General Sherman's advancing army – even while the Union troops were still skirmishing with Confederate rearguards, they heard the whistle of locomotives bringing up fresh supplies. Exceptionally General Grant, in his 1863 Vicksburg campaign, abandoned his supply line for two weeks trusting that he could obtain sufficient subsistence from the rich Mississippi countryside and that he could re-establish a supply line (via Haines Bluff) before shortages of ammunition etc. became critical.

In the autumn of 1864, the Union commanders realised that the continued survival of the Confederacy depended as much on the products of its farms and factories as on its remaining veteran armies in the field. So they targeted the Confederacy's civilian economy, inaugurating a new phase of total warfare such as Europe had abandoned two centuries before. General Sherman burned Atlanta and marched through Georgia to the sea, destroying all the crops, railways, bridges and public buildings along his route. General Sheridan directed his troops to ravage the Shenandoah Valley so that 'a crow flying over it would have to carry its own rations'.

The Union railway system allowed reinforcements to be transferred quickly from one theatre of operations to another. In 1863, the Union XI and XII Corps of 20,000 men and sixty guns with appropriate horses and baggage were carried 1,200 miles from Culpeper in Virginia to Bridgeport in Tennessee. The leading troops began to move on the 25 September and the whole force was assembled near Bridgeport by the 2 October.[22] The superior Union capability for strategic re-deployments by railway gave its forces a significant operational advantage.

The movement of Union armies in the field was impeded by their accompanying wagon trains and herds of cattle, which clogged the roads and fords. When the Union Army of the Potomac moved south across the Rapidan River in May 1864, its 127,000 men were accompanied by 4,000 wagons occupying about fifty miles of roadway.[23] The army crossed the river quickly and without opposition but then had to wait through an afternoon for the slower wagons to manage the river crossing, and consequently engaged the Confederates on the following day in thick second-growth forest (the Wilderness) where the Union superiority in artillery was valueless, rather than in the open country farther south.

Confederate

Logistic constraints presented much greater problems for the Confederate armies because their railway system was utterly unsuited to war. The network was incomplete, long-distance travel demanded several changes, and there was a shortage of rolling stock and infrastructure.

A significant part of the Confederacy's railroad mileage in 1861 (in Florida and the three states west of the Mississippi) was not linked to the main railway network serving the other seven Confederate states. Even within the main network, there were inconvenient strategic gaps which necessitated another mode of transport or a long detour. The Danville-Greenboro gap in NC forced all traffic coming to Virginia from the south to use the Petersburg RR through Weldon, which was vulnerable to Union forces pushing inland from the coast. At the start of the war the Confederacy had only one continuous lateral line – the Memphis & Charleston RR – linking the Mississippi valley and the Atlantic coast, and this line was cut early in the war by the Union capture of Corinth in May 1862. By contrast the Union had four east-west railways, and of these only the Baltimore & Ohio RR was ever interrupted by hostile forces. There was no east-west line across Alabama so that, after the Union captured Corinth, Confederate troops en route from the Atlantic coast to the Mississippi valley had to travel by steamboat from Montgomery to Selma and march west to Meridian using a ferry across the Tombigbee River, or alternatively take a long railway detour south to Tensas (a small harbour on Mobile Bay), followed by a ferry across Mobile Bay and another long train ride northward to their intended area of operations. During the war, some new track was laid between Selma and Meridian, and the Danville-Greenboro gap was finally closed in May 1864, but Confederate construction was hampered by chronic shortages of labour and materials.

The main Confederate railway network was divided between a multitude of independent railway companies, some of which used 4ft 8.5in gauge track and some used 5ft. Even where two adjacent companies used the same gauge there was generally no union station, and passengers had to detrain at one end of town, walk through the streets and entrain at the other end. Some of the better-disciplined Confederate regiments were able to accomplish this manoeuvre without excessive straggling, but even they would have had trouble persuading their horse and mules to board another train soon after being released after their previous train journey. The delay associated with changing trains was greater if a ferry crossing was involved, or if the operations of the adjacent companies were not well synchronised.

Although the railway companies appreciated the inconvenience to their passengers (and the Confederate government deplored the delays inflicted on its troops and supplies) any proposals for union stations were vigorously resisted by local interests, led by the teamsters and hoteliers. Even where Petersburg, for example, agreed to track being laid to link its stations, it stipulated that this track must be removed when victory was won which discouraged the railway companies from funding the work.

Sherman's men destroying railroad track near Atlanta, Georgia (Source: George N. Barnard via Wikimedia Commons)

Furthermore, Confederate railways were undercapitalised relative to railways in the North, with an average of $27,000 invested per mile of track relative to $42,000.[24] This

Confederate average concealed a wide variation from the railways of Virginia, which were equipped to Northern standards, down to the apocryphal 'right of way with two streaks of rust' in less-developed areas. It followed that the Confederate railways had less double track, fewer locomotives and weaker track, and hence less carrying capacity than the overall track mileage implied (in 1860 northern railways carried 600 tons of freight per mile of track while the southern railways carried 80[25]). The Confederate states lacked an adequate industrial base – in 1860 they produced 19 locomotives while the Union states produced 451 – and as the war continued the rolling stock and track suffered progressive deterioration, leading to accidents which accelerated the decline in the network's capability. This problem was only partially alleviated by the Confederate 'Stonewall' Jackson's raid on the Baltimore & Ohio RR in June 1861 when he captured 14 locomotives near Harper's Ferry and hauled them 40 miles overland to Strasburg in Virginia to augment the Confederacy's rolling stock.[26] Since these locomotives each weighed up to thirty tons[27], their relocation was a notable engineering achievement. In the same raid he destroyed forty-two Union locomotives and 386 cars, but this loss had only a limited and temporary effect on Union logistics.

Despite these disadvantages, the Confederates were sometimes able to use their railways to move reinforcements urgently from one theatre of operations to another. In July 1861, they moved 8,400 infantrymen from Piedmont Station to Manassas Junction to play a crucial role in achieving victory at First Bull Run.[28] A year later the Confederate railways carried 25,000 infantrymen the 776 miles from Tupelo to Chattanooga over a route involving six different railway companies, two gauge changes and two ferry trips.[29] In September 1864, two divisions of 12,000 men were moved 965 miles from Virginia to northern Georgia[30], and the leading five brigades arrived in time to win the battle of Chickamauga. From an analysis of these and other Confederate movements[31], it appears that after movement orders were issued it took one or two days to assemble the troops and trains, after which the leading troops could set off. Thereafter, infantry could be transported about 250 miles per day through the Atlantic states and at perhaps half that speed in the less-developed states further west. Artillery and supply units, with their heavy guns and wagons and their increasingly-fractious horses, could not be transferred as quickly from train to train and from train to ferry, and accordingly travelled more slowly. Infantry could be delivered to their destination at about 3,000 men per day, or less if they were accompanied by horses, guns and wagons.

But these strategic troop movements represented unsustainable efforts which could not be matched by regular deliveries of sufficient supplies to the Confederate armies in the field, which were often hungry, ragged and barefoot even when supplies were available in rear areas. After the Confederates' victory at First Bull Run in 1861, their decision not to exploit the victory by an advance on the Union capital was at least partly driven by the difficulty of supplying their army at Manassas Junction. In the winter of 1862-63 the Richmond, Fredericksburg & Potomac RR could run only two short trains per day[32] to the Confederate army at Fredericksburg, supplying about half of its requirements, so General Lee therefore had to detach two of his eight infantry divisions and most of his cavalry and artillery units southward into better-provided areas of Virginia; he therefore had to fight the battle of Chancellorsville at a 2:1 disadvantage. His subsequent decision to advance into Pennsylvania was at least partly motivated by the prospect of obtaining provisions and draught animals in the rich Cumberland Valley, and the (ultimately disastrous) battle of Gettysburg was initiated by one of his brigades seeking shoes.

Logistics after the ACW

Many of the logistic problems of the ACW recurred in later wars. In South Africa, in the Second Boer War (1899-1902), there were fewer railways and virtually no roads, so ox wagons found their own routes point to point across the open veldt. These wagons were even slower than those in the American Civil War, their load never exceeded one ton, and if the wagon's full complement of sixteen oxen had to be fed from the wagon's own load, they could consume it all within a week.[33] Draught oxen died from hunger, disease and overwork even more rapidly than horses and mules in the American Civil War.

In the Russo-Japanese war (1904-05), the Russians again demonstrated the enormous logistic capabilities of a railway, using the 5,400 mile Trans-Siberian railway to assemble and support an army of 310,000 men in Manchuria.

In August 1914, the Germany sought a decisive victory by an outflanking march through Belgium. Its railways deployed the armies for this manoeuvre but when the armies marched away from the railheads its horse-drawn supply wagons could not sustain supplies to the leading troops.

In the Second World War, the Wehrmacht initially had sufficient lorry transport (190 tons capacity per division) to sustain supplies for short-range offensives in Poland, the Low Countries and France – none more than 200 miles – but it was unable to sustain a continuous offensive over poor roads to the Russian centres of power, all over 600 miles from the frontier. Similarly General Rommel was given enough trucks to support two mechanised divisions 290 miles east of Tripoli, which predictably proved insufficient to support those divisions around Tobruk, 670 miles further east.

Conclusion

During the last century and a half, the supply requirements of an army division have increased from thirty tons per day (including fodder) in the American Civil War to 2,000-6,000 tons (depending on the intensity of combat) in the 1991 Gulf War. But all of these later wars reflect the lessons of the ACW in that

1. The number of supply vehicles required to meet a particular requirement depends on their capacity, speed and consumption/load ratio, as well as on their vulnerability to enemy action and to disease/breakdown;
2. Different modes of transport can be used in different circumstances, but the interfaces between them often cause confusion and delay;
3. The capacity of a multi-mode supply line from 'factory to foxhole' is limited by its worst bottleneck, which might be a shortage of resources in one of the modes or constraints at an interface between modes.

Epilogue – An Unintended Consequence

When the principal remaining Confederate army surrendered at Appomattox in April 1865, General Lee asked that paroled Confederate soldiers be allowed to take home any horses which were their personal property, to help restore their blighted farms; it was usual for Confederate cavalrymen and artillerymen to bring their own horses to war. General Grant was sympathetic and agreed. Neither general appreciated that this well-intended agreement would allow the diseased army horses to spread their diseases (notably glanders) throughout the length and breadth of the former Confederacy, and thus actually retarded the recovery of the devastated South.[34]

Notes and References

The author is grateful to Lt. Colonel Joe Whitehorne US Army (retired) for a private communication providing some of the information used in this paper. In addition to the publications cited in the endnotes, other information was drawn from:

Badeau, A. (1881) *Military History of Ulysses S. Grant from April 1861 to April 1865*, Appleton: New York.

Bowden, S. and Ward, B. (2001) *Last Chance for Victory – Robert E. Lee and the*

Gettysburg Campaign, Cambridge, MA: Da Capo Press.

Catton, B. (1962) *Centennial History of the Civil War*, London: Victor Gollanz.

McPherson, J. (1988) *Battle Cry of Freedom*, New York: Oxford University Press.

Nevins, A. (1959) *The War for the Union*, New York: Charles Scribner & Sons.

Weigley, R. (2000) *A Great Civil War*, Bloomington, IN: Indiana University Press.

Wiley, B. (1986) *The Life of Billy Yank*, Baton Rouge, LA: LSU Press.

Wiley, B. (1986) *The Life of Johnny Reb*, Baton Rouge, LA: LSU Press.

Endnotes

[1] The accuracy and rate of fire of these weapons varied with the skill and fatigue of the soldier; these values are derived from: Coggins, J. (1962) *Arms and Equipment of the Civil War*, New York: Fairfax Press, pp. 26-39; Griffith, P. (1986) *Battle in the Civil War*, Fieldbooks, UK, pp. 24 and 39; Adkin, M. (2008) *The Gettysburg Companion*, London: Aurum Press, pp. 92-102.

[2] The slave states of Maryland and tiny Delaware did not secede, and the trans-Appalachian counties of Virginia stayed loyal to the Union, but these decisions did not significantly affect the overall dimensions of the eastern part of the Confederacy.

[3] Weber, T. (1952) *The Northern Railroads in the Civil War*, New York: King's Crown Press, p. 3.

[4] *Op Cit.* Coggins, p. 104.

[5] Bacon, B. (1997) *Sinews of War*, Novato, CA: Presido Press, p. 216.

[6] Weigley, R. (1959) *Quartermaster General of the Union Army*, New York: Columbia Union Press, p. 3.

[7] Private communication with J. W. A Whitehorne.

[8] Whitehorne, J. 'Issues of animal logistics in the Civil War', *Crossfire*, December 2004, p. 17.

[9] Private communication with J. W. A Whitehorne.

[10] *Op Cit.* Adkin, p. 513.

[11] *Ibid.* pp. 103, 106, 169.

[12] *Op Cit.* Griffith, p. 39.

[13] Rogers, H. (1993) *The Confederates and Federals at War*, London: Ian Allen, p. 111.

[14] Drury, I et al. (1993) *The US Civil War Military Machine*, Limpsfield, Surrey: Dragon's World, p. 82.

[15] Rogers, H. (1993) *The Confederates and Federals at War*, London: Ian Allen, p. 91.

[16] *Ibid.* p. 99.

[17] Abdill, G. (1956) *Civil War Railroads*, New York: Bonanza Books, p. 159.

[18] Cornwall, J. (1970) *Grant as Military Commander*, London: Batsford, p. 104.

[19] Risch, E. (1989) *Quartermaster Support of the Army*, US Army, Washington DC, p. 406.

[20] *Op Cit*. Bacon, p. 228.

[21] Huston, J. (1966) *The Sinews of War: Army Logistics 1775 - 1953*, Washington DC: US Printing Office, p. 149.

[22] Foote, S. (1963) *The Civil War: A Narrative (Volume II)*, New York: Random House, p. 765.

[23] *Op Cit*. Whitehorne, p. 18.

[24] Black III, R. (1987) *The Railroads of the Confederacy*, Wilmington, NC: Broadfoot Publishing, pp. 1-11.

[25] Heidler, D. S. & J. T. (2000) Encyclopedia of the ACW, ABC- CLIO California.

[26] *Op Cit*. Abdill, p. 61.

[27] *Op Cit*. Black III, p. 16.

[28] Jones, V. (1980) *First Manassas*, Harrisburg, PA: Eastern Acorn Press, p. 22.

[29] *Op Cit*. Black III, p. 182.

[30] *Op Cit*. Foote, p. 709.

[31] Kirkpatrick, D. (1997) 'Slow train to Vicksburg', *RUSI Journal*, August 1997, pp. 76-81.

[32] Sears, S. (1996) *Chancellorsville*, New York: Houghton Mifflin Company, p. 34.

[33] Morris, D. (1973) *The Washing of the Spears*, London: Sphere Books, pp. 313-318.

[34] *Op Cit*. Whitehorne, p. 20.

Operation SEA LION: A Joint Critical Analysis

Lt Col Randy McCanne, LTC Greg Olson and Cdr Dario E. Teicher
Class 02-3S, Joint & Combined Warfighting Course, Joint Forces Staff College.

[Editor's Note: This paper was the students' joint dissertation as part of their course at the Joint Forces Staff College, Norfolk, VA, submitted on 30 August 2002 and as far as possible has been left 'as written']

Introduction

Military history contains many lessons from which the warfighting doctrine of the individual services, as well as joint doctrine, is derived. World War II stands as one of the major contributors of valuable lessons learned. From a joint and combined warfighting perspective, Germany's planning and preparatory military actions to the invasion of Great Britain after the fall of France are instructive. Their plan, called Operation SEA LION by the Germans, was never carried out, as certain prerequisite conditions were never achieved, and Hitler elected to move on to other operations. But Germany could have been successful in invading and, if necessary, occupying Great Britain had they exercised joint and combined operations to achieve better unity of effort within the German military, remained focused on key British operational centres of gravity, and exploited the capabilities of friendly nations such as Spain, Italy, and the Vichy government of France.

Background

Political Situation

World War II began with the German invasion of Poland on 1 September 1939. The German dictator, Adolf Hitler, advised his armed forces in *Fuehrer Directive No. 1:* "political means having been exhausted to correct in a peaceful manner the unbearable situation on Germany's eastern border, I have decided upon a solution by force" (9, 49).

The "unbearable situation" was the separation of East Prussia from Germany by the creation of Poland following World War I. Cleverly, Hitler had isolated Poland through "political means" and shaped the battlefield in his favour. He secured Germany's eastern borders when on 23 August 1939 Germany signed a nonaggression pact with the Soviet Union in which both secretly agreed to dismember Poland (21). Great Britain and France had offered Poland defence guarantees, and both declared war on Germany two days after the invasion; but with the Soviet Union in the German camp, the guarantees proved worthless. Trapped between Germany and the Soviet Union, a surrounded Poland ceased to exist in less than one month.

Meanwhile, to the south, Hitler had forged a close alliance with fellow Fascist dictator Benito Mussolini of Italy. In 1936, Italy had entered into a formal alliance with Germany known as the Rome-Berlin Axis. The Axis would later include Japan in September 1940 (2). Overseas in the United States, isolationist sentiments were strong, and in any case France and Britain appeared to have the balance of power in their favour. Hence, Americans hoped to remain on the sidelines and out of the trenches of yet another European war (1, 55).

However, on 10 May 1940, the Germans invaded the West, and by 19 June the German High Command of the Armed Forces (*Oberkommando der Wehrmacht*) announced, "The Fuehrer intends to stage a big parade in Paris" (9, 104). Three days later, after a short 43-day campaign, France surrendered and the Germans paraded under the *Arc de Triomphe* (1, 5). The redistribution of power on the European continent meant those minor powers not yet conquered by Germany, such as Switzerland and Hungary, were quickly cowed into pro-German neutrality or aligned with the Axis powers (2). Across the English Channel, Great Britain stood alone refusing to yield to German peace overtures and clinging to the hope that America would awaken from its isolationist stupor (1, 5).

Military Situation

In the summer of 1940, Germany became the hegemon of Europe. The rapid defeat of Poland showed the world a new combat doctrine called *blitzkrieg* (lightning-war) that combined the effects of infantry, armour, and aircraft in a massive display of firepower and mobility. All doubts regarding mechanized warfare were eliminated when Germany defeated France. "On the evening of 20 May, (German General) Guderian's panzer divisions reached the Channel coast at the mouth of the Somme. The French northern armies and the BEF (British Expeditionary Forces) had been cut off" (17, 23). The campaign continued into June, but the outcome was already decided in the first ten days. France, the best-equipped army in the world, had fallen victim to blitzkrieg, and the BEF had to flee by sea abandoning all its equipment on the beaches of Dunkirk (1, 15).

The brilliance of the operational and tactical plans to defeat France was not fully appreciated or anticipated by Germany's strategic commanders. No plan existed to follow up a decisive victory. Even after the panzers reached the English Channel, no serious consideration was given to the need for a campaign plan that called for the invasion of England. For example, the Germans needed ships, yet in the euphoria of victory they made no demands regarding the disposition of the powerful French fleet in the surrender terms, nor were there considerations to seize any of these naval units (1, 106). The German Commander in Chief of the Navy (Kriegsmarine), Admiral Raeder, recalled after the war, "Our mental as well as materiel preparations before the war had not been aimed at an armed conflict with England" (17, 82). Therefore, Hitler hoped the rapid defeat of France would be enough to encourage Britain to agree to peace terms.

By July 1940 it was apparent that Britain had no intentions of surrendering. Indeed, Prime Minister Churchill, in reference to a possible German invasion, had declared, "If the long history of our island is to come to an end, then it shall only end when every last one of us is beaten to the ground and lies choking in his blood" (17, 70). In the face of British stubbornness, the Oberkommando der Wehrmacht (OKW) on 2 July 1940 issued orders to commence planning Operation SEA LION; the cross-channel amphibious assault on the beaches of England (9, 105).

Centres of Gravity

> "The first task, then, in planning for war is to identify the enemy's centres of gravity, and if possible trace them back to a single one." Carl von Clausewitz

Centres of Gravity Defined

According to Joint Publication 1, *Joint Warfare of the Armed Forces of the United States*, of the enemy is one of the fundamentals of joint warfare (12, III-13). Success in warfare on understanding the adversary's critical vulnerabilities, capabilities, limitations, of gravity, and potential courses of action. Without such knowledge, or with only an incomplete of these aspects of the enemy, the probability of success is diminished.these characteristics, perhaps the most important to the success of a campaign or invasion is to understand the enemy's centres of gravity.

Centres of gravity (COGs) ought to be the focus of campaign planning at both the strategic and operational levels. Clausewitz described COGs in the military context as "the hub of all power and movement, on which everything depends." Joint doctrine defines COGs as "Those characteristics, capabilities, or localities from which a military force derives its freedom of action, physical strength, or will to fight" (12, III-13). Therefore, improper COG analysis can lead to expending limited military forces against enemy targets of little importance to the final outcome. Attacking COGs means concentrating against capabilities whose destruction or overthrow is most likely to yield success with the minimum of effort.

Enemy Centres of Gravity

An analysis of Hitler's *Fuehrer Directive No. 16*, which directed the General Staff and the service commanders in chief to begin planning Operation SEA LION, quickly reveals the British operational centres of gravity. The directive defined a number of prerequisites that the Kriegsmarine and Luftwaffe had to achieve before a cross-channel invasion could be attempted:

a. The British air force must be subdued....
b. Mine-free passages are to be created.
c. The Strait of Dover, as well as the western entrance of the Channel is to be tightly sealed off with minefields...
d. The coast is to be dominated and sealed off by...coastal artillery.
e. It is desirable to tie down the British naval forces...in the North Sea as well as in the Mediterranean (the latter by the Italians)... (9, 108)

Effectively, according to *Directive 16*, Operation SEA LION to succeed the mighty Royal Navy had to be deterred and the full strength of a Royal Air Force had to be defeated for the Germans to be able to support ground operations across the English Channel. *Directive 16*hardly mentions the British Army, perhaps because it was severely degraded during the evacuation from Dunkirk and posed no immediate threat. But it is clear that a German invasion would have to deal with what was left of the British ground forces upon landing, and they should thus be considered a centre of gravity. Ultimately, all would rest on who commanded the air and sea on both sides of the English Channel; thus, the RAF and Royal Navy would be the two centres of gravity posing the biggest challenge.

The British Army

Even though some 215,000 British troops escaped in the near-miracle of the Dunkirk evacuation, much of their equipment, particularly the heavy weaponry, was necessarily left behind (3, 121). The British Army desperately needed time—time to reorganize, reequip, and prepare defensive positions.

Hitler missed a golden opportunity at Dunkirk to largely destroy the BEF. On 24 May 1940, German General Guderian's Panzers were within 15 miles of Dunkirk while four motorized divisions and at least six infantry divisions were closing in as well. Dunkirk, and with it more than 300,000 British and French troops, was "ripe for the taking" when the panzers were ordered to halt and stand fast (3, 55).

If Hitler had recognized the British Army as a COG for the invasion of England, perhaps he would have done more to prevent their evacuation from Dunkirk. In consequence, Operation SEA LION called for a much larger invasion force than might otherwise have been necessary, further complicating invasion plans and endangering chances of success.

The Royal Navy

While the British Army was in disarray after the evacuation from Dunkirk, the Royal Navy outmatched German naval forces. The Kriegsmarine lost nearly half its surface fleet during the invasion of Norway in April 1940 and would have to rely heavily upon the Luftwaffe to turn any major naval engagement in Germany's favour (23, 111).

In addition to the Luftwaffe, Hitler and his staff were forced to place a lot of faith in coastal artillery (8, 32) and maritime minefields (8, 45) as "antidotes" to the Royal Navy. Ultimately, it was not a reassessment of the naval risks but the failure to establish air supremacy that made Hitler call off the invasion. All the evidence suggests that, had Germany won the air battle, Hitler's armies would have embarked and sailed according to plan. (8, 150)

The Royal Air Force

The most important centre of gravity and hence the British "hub of all power and movement" was the RAF. For an invasion to be successful, German strategy required air supremacy and not simply superiority in the air over southern England, the Channel, and the Continental ports from which the invasion was to be launched (8, 235). Perhaps more than any other aspect of the period, from Dunkirk to the end of the summer, German air strategy reflects the flaws in their understanding of this centre of gravity (8, 213). In particular, German failure to press successful strategies for degrading RAF radar, command and control, and other critical air defence systems indicates impatience in dealing with this key COG.

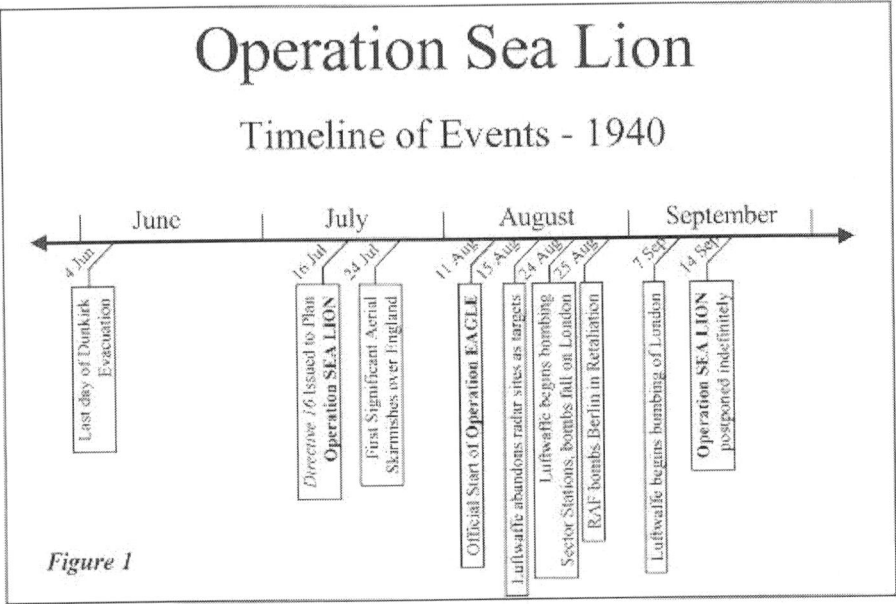

Figure 1

Figure 1 above shows significant events in the Battle of Britain (Operation EAGLE) and reinforces the view that Germany did not remain focused on any one set of targets long enough to effectively suppress the objective and achieve the operational task. The result was the indefinite postponement of Operation SEA LION.

Operation EAGLE focused initially on three tasks until 24 August 1940 as follows:

1. The main effort was to overwhelm the frontline of British air defences in southern England by drawing Fighter Command into battle and eliminating it through attrition. The RAF had the upper hand, at least in terms of loss ratios, because of a remarkably effective early warning and C2 system that often gave Fighter Command the initiative when engaging the enemy. Even so, British losses between 8 and 18 August included 154 pilots, with only 63 new pilots accessioned, and 213 aircraft, with only 150 replaced (8, 234). Evidence suggests that if Germany had kept up the pressure long enough, the RAF would have been forced to disengage from the fight or be destroyed.

2. As a supporting effort, the plan called for probing the left (northeast) flank of the island. Luftwaffe forces operating from Scandinavia were ordered to bomb targets in northeast England on 15 August 1940. The German bombers, escorted by long-range

but inferior ME-110 fighters, were intercepted well out to sea and the force suffered losses so great that Germany never again attempted daylight operations over England from that approach (8, 228). England's left flank was found to be adequately defended.

3. Finally, the plan required the bombing of aircraft production factories (8, 233). An important feature of the German air war plan was night attacks against aircraft plants. Daylight raids tended to suffer greater losses. The poor level of accuracy of the night bombing generally hampered the effectiveness of such attacks. Even so, the Germans were right to attack those targets but wrong to defer the attacks to the last moment (8, 227). If attacks against those targets had begun shortly after the fall of France, the effects would have been much more significant and possibly hadn't an impact on the final outcome.

On 12 August 1940, the Germans attacked and damaged five radar stations, one of which was not put back into operation for 11 days (8, 223). This was a significant achievement and would have been even more so if the Germans had continued to attack this set of targets. However, German commanders did not know "the role that radar played in the system.... It was assumed that Fighter Command fought a decentralized battle, with squadrons tied to the radio range of their individual stations, attacks on radar were not given high enough priority" (20, 79). Just three days after their successful attack the Luftwaffe largely abandoned radar targets.

After 24 August, the Luftwaffe began attacks on the sector stations, which performed an important command and control function for Fighter Command: group HQ launched the squadrons based on early warning information, then the sector stations passed by radio the latest combat intelligence from radar and forward observers, guiding the pilots into battle on advantageous terms (8, 233). By 6 September 1940, severe and cumulative damage to the sector stations was having a clear impact on the effectiveness of the RAF in repelling air attacks. The Luftwaffe was achieving the most favourable loss ratios of the war. Churchill wrote afterwards, "The scales had tilted against Fighter Command" (8, 236).

On 24 August 1940, the Germans made a fateful mistake that changed the course of the battle. German bombers with orders to attack British aircraft factories and oil installations on the extreme perimeter of London missed their mark and instead the bombs fell on residential districts in northern and eastern London, resulting in heavy casualties and leaving many Londoners homeless. Churchill subsequently ordered the bombing of Berlin on the following night. That bombing caused little real damage, but Hitler had often implied to his people that no bombs would ever fall on Berlin. Hitler lost face and promised devastating reprisals, which began on 7 September 1940. This switch in priorities undoubtedly saved Fighter Command (8, 276-278).

In retrospect, the factors that undermined the effectiveness of the German air campaign were largely self-inflicted. Many of the targets attacked were of secondary importance, and no target set, "whether airfields, communications, ports or industry, was attacked repeatedly, systematically, or accurately" (20, 115). Failure of the Luftwaffe to press attacks against these targets allowed the RAF to recover and continue the fight.

Unity of Effort

According to the *Doctrine for Joint Operations*, "unity of effort…requires coordination and cooperation among all forces toward a commonly recognized objective" (13, A-2). Following the defeat of France, instead of unity, the Wehrmacht found themselves in confusion without a plan to prosecute the war against Great Britain. In fact, the High Command of the Army (OKH), the Luftwaffe, and Kriegsmarine believed the war was over. For example, "OKH actually began to send 40 divisions home, because it did not know what to do…. (The service commanders)…were unable to imagine that the Fuhrer did not have a clearly defined objective" (17, 92).

In the confusion, the Germans failed in at least three joint planning facets that made Operation SEA LION an impossible mission. First, *unity of command* to be maintained to properly focus German military power on its last remaining enemy. Also, a new *commander's intent* had to be announced to the armed forces in view of the unanticipated early fall of France. Consequently, a new *concept of operations* to be drafted to achieve the revised end-state.

Unity of Command

During the Second World War, Hitler was both the political and military leader of Germany. He often blurred the strategic, operational, and even tactical levels of command, usually becoming involved in all aspects of a military campaign. He forced unity of effort using OKW to coordinate the Army, Kriegsmarine and Luftwaffe, providing them strategic and operational direction. The German military was not a well-oiled joint system, and Hitler's involvement was usually necessary to overcome service rivalries (18, 51).

Throughout the war, there was friction between OKW, OKH, and the Luftwaffe. This was due to the establishment of OKW to oversee the service branches and the creation of the Luftwaffe, which was led by the politically powerful Reich Marshal Goring. Both deprived

OKH of its previously elevated position. In earlier wars, OKH had been predominant with the Kriegsmarine as a supporting command. The revised organization had the three branches under OKW and OKW under Hitler (18, 58).

Normally, Hitler was able to create unity among the three service branches by becoming personally involved. This was not the case for SEA LION. He allowed the three branches to flounder in inter-service squabbles and seldom interfered. Without Hitler's involvement, OKW did not have sufficient stature to force unity of effort among the services. Instead, decisions regarding SEA LION became the product of compromise and not necessarily the best solutions (17, 265).

Furthermore, *Directive 16* not attempt to compensate for Hitler's lack of involvement by designating an overall SEA LION commander, thus establishing unity of command and perhaps leading to unity of effort. Instead, *Directive 16* inter-service confusion by ordering "each (Service) Commander in Chief will lead those belonging to his particular branch, under my orders and according to my general directives" (9, 108). However, as already stated, Hitler remained aloof; without him there was no unity of command, and the concept of operations for SEA LION began to suffer. One is left to agree with Kieser, who writes in *Hitler on the Doorstep*, "Left to themselves, the three commanders in chief would certainly never have reached agreement, only a Fuhrer order could have forced them to do so" (17, 265).

The Commander's Intent

The unexpected rapid demise of France and Britain's refusal to yield forced Hitler to revise his "commander's intent." According to the *Doctrine for Joint Operations*: "The commander's intent describes the desired end-state. It is a concise expression of the purpose of the operation….(The commander's intent) is the initial impetus for the entire planning process" (13, III-26).

Initially, the German intent was to subdue Britain through slow, "long term economic warfare…using the Luftwaffe and Kriegsmarine to cut her supply lines" (7, 218). No serious consideration was given to an amphibious assault on the English coast, and the end-state against Britain was nebulous. In fact, immediately following the defeat of France, Hitler's desired end state "was for [Britain] to acknowledge Germany's position on the Continent [and]…to make peace…on a basis that…[Britain] would regard as compatible with her honor to accept" (7, 218).

Under that end-state, it was up to Britain to decide whether or not economic warfare and generous peace overtures would make her succumb and thus bring the war to an end.

Perhaps aware of this dilemma and following Britain's rejection of several peace overtures, Hitler at last proposed to force a decision by taking advantage of the apparent window of opportunity caused by the fall of France and the disorganized hasty retreat of the BEF. On 16 July 1940, he finally provided the "impetus" for Operation SEA LION issuing *Directive No. 16*, which he redefined the end-state, calling for the occupation of English soil "to eliminate the British homeland as a base for continuing the war against Germany" (9, 107). Arguably, the window of opportunity was rapidly closing, but Operation SEA LION required slow meticulous planning because an opposed amphibious operation was a novel concept for the German military and the required resources had to be gathered.

The British high command including Prime Minister Churchill was certain the Germans would cross immediately after the French surrender and doubted a successful beachhead could be prevented. They did not expect an opportunity to rearm the BEF to provide adequate force-on-force opposition. Instead, it was the British intent to make the German breakout from the beaches costly by conducting conventional operations when possible and guerrilla warfare always (17, 263). It was best expressed by Churchill on 4 June 1940 before the House of Commons when he said, "We shall fight on the beaches, we shall fight on the landing grounds, we shall fight in the fields and in the streets, we shall fight in the hills; we shall never surrender" (5). Consequently, with all their equipment lost in France, poorly armed British troops awaited throughout 1940 what initially appeared to be certain invasion.

Concept of Operations

The British and Germans recalled that on 9 April 1940, with airborne troops in the vanguard, a German ground force had been successfully transported by sea to conquer Norway (17, 29). The Royal Navy was initially surprised but eventually punished the smaller Kriegsmarine. The German surface fleet lost nearly half its strength in vessels sunk or seriously damaged, but accomplished its mission of delivering troops into poorly defended Norwegian harbours; no beach assaults were conducted. Ultimately, lack of adequate Norwegian defences and the unchallenged powerful Luftwaffe decided the battle in Germany's favour (23, 111).

The lesson drawn by both the British and Germans was that amphibious operations were possible when under an air force umbrella and despite a weak navy (10, 27). In addition, the Kriegsmarine's after-action reports indicate that in the Norwegian campaign there was "smooth cooperation between the three services" (10, 26). That was one lesson the Germans did not incorporate as they prepared for SEA LION.

Notwithstanding the poor materiel condition of the British Army, the Germans faced a much tougher task in Operation SEA LION. Without amphibious assault experience, the planning resembled a large river crossing. In fact, 1,910 river barges to be towed by 419 tugs were gathered in preparation to ferry troops to the beaches. The plan envisioned soldiers moving from the barges into fast riverine assault craft for the initial assault wave. Later waves would have the barges move heavy equipment directly onto the beach, although the hope was for the early capture of a functioning port. Airborne troops would be employed for this task and once again be the vanguard of the invasion force. Above all, the crossing was dependent on calm weather. The flat bottoms of the barges would be swamped and risk sinking in anything beyond sea state 3. Furthermore, the Germans knew that unlike Norway, England would thoroughly oppose this undertaking (19, 155).

Despite Norway, Hitler appeared to have "no stomach for amphibious operations" (19, 159). He allowed dubious compromises to be made between the service branches. For example, in order to deter the Royal Navy, the Kriegsmarine proposed landings on a narrow front. This would allow better concentration of their submarines, torpedo boats, and defensive mine fields to guard the flanks of the ground assault waves, crossing from Calais to Dover (the shortest distance), against the expected Royal Navy onslaught. On the contrary, the German Army preferred to assault on a broad front (the whole length of the English southern coast) to avoid giving the British the opportunity to contain a narrow beachhead (17, 92).

The German Army was concerned that the 200.000-man BEF that had escaped from Dunkirk and possibly additional ground forces from Britain's vast empire would bottle up the beachhead. However, the Kriegsmarine knew the Royal Navy would sortie into the channel and, if not properly defended, the length of the beachfront would be purely academic. The debate raged with Hitler vacillating, and instead of a best decision, he allowed an uncomfortable compromise (17, 93). The initial landings would take place between Bognor and Ramsgate on the coast of England, east of the Isle of Wight; half of the beachfront desired by the Army and probably more than the Kriegsmarine could protect (7, 221).

The one issue where there was absolute agreement among the branches of the Wehrmacht was in the air. The Luftwaffe had to achieve command of the air to then be able to concentrate against the Royal Navy's attempts to interfere with the crossing of troops and supplies. Otherwise, a successful German landing would eventually wither through British interdiction of the sea lines of communication leading to the beachheads (17, 86).

Elstein in "Operation SEA LION: The Plan to Invade England," argues "that SEA LION was impossible without air supremacy, and superfluous if air supremacy were achieved" (7, 220). The statement is simplistic, but the British in 1940 seem to have echoed his sentiments. According to the British Admiralty, to oppose SEA LION, "the action of the navy's light forces (patrol boats, destroyers, and some cruisers) against enemy transports would be limited to the range of air cover provided by Fighter Command." The battleships and heavy cruisers would remain out of the range of German aircraft, 24 hours away in northern ports, until the actual beach assault had commenced. (19, 148). Clearly, the British too understood that it all depended on who commanded the air.

Therefore, one can argue that in fact Operation SEA LION was launched on 13 August 1940. The first phase was the Luftwaffe's effort to achieve air supremacy over England, Operation EAGLE.

On 1 August 1940, *Fuehrer Directive No. 17* , "The Luftwaffe is to overcome the British Air Force with all means at its disposal and in the shortest possible time. The attacks are to be directed primarily against the planes themselves, their ground installations, and their supply organizations, also against aircraft industry" (9, 110).

By 6 September 1940, British Fighter Command was close to the breaking point. During the previous two weeks, Fighter Command had suffered 295 fighters destroyed and 171 seriously damaged with only 269 new aircraft produced. Also, 300 pilots had been lost and only 260 replacement pilots generated by the flying schools. Air Chief Marshal Dowding of Fighter Command was on the verge of withdrawing the remainder of his forces to northern England to be recommitted when the actual amphibious landings occurred. In fact, the British Armed Forces were placed on highest alert in early September 1940 believing command of the air was about to be lost and the invasion was imminent (19, 150).

Suddenly, the situation changed when an insignificant British bombing raid on Berlin led Hitler to lose sight of the objective (the defeat of the RAF) (19, 153). He ordered at this crucial moment retaliatory air strikes against London. "From 7 September 1940, London was bombed for a total of fifty-seven consecutive nights" (22). The London Blitz had won a reprieve for Fighter Command. The people of London suffered, but Operation EAGLE failed and with it any hope for Operation SEA LION.

Friendly Nations

In August 1939, as Germany prepared for war, Hitler clearly understood the need for allies and friendly governments to secure the German position in the coming war. Defining the German geopolitical position to his commanders in chief, he said:

There are many factors in our favour at present and they may not last.... Probably no one will ever again have the confidence of the whole German people, as I do....

Mussolini's existence is also vital. If something happens to him, Italy's loyalty will be no longer certain.... A third personal factor favourable to us is Franco. We can only ask benevolent neutrality from Spain. But even that depends on Franco's personality. All these fortunate circumstances will no longer prevail in two or three years. No one knows how long I shall live.... We have no choice; we must act.... Therefore conflict is better now.... (11, 24)

This positive state of affairs was even more in favour of Germany upon the conclusion of the dramatically successful campaign in France. This event coupled to the Nazi-Soviet Non-Aggression Pact, which had secured Germany's eastern borders, shifted the military balance of power decisively in Germany's favour vis-à-vis Great Britain.

Although Britain stood alone in the summer of 1940, it still held a superior geostrategic position anchored by a vast empire defended by a powerful navy and strong air force. In preparation for SEA LION, Germany toyed with the notion of using allies to challenge the Royal Navy and perhaps sever British lines of communication within the empire. For example, *Directive 16*mentions the use of the Italian fleet to fix British naval forces in the Mediterranean to facilitate the SEA LION crossing.

In the end, Germany's allies were not part of the SEA LION planning process. In fact, there was very little coordination between the Axis powers. For example, Italy invaded Greece, disrupting German plans against Russia; Spain stonewalled German invitations to enter the war; and Japan never opened a second front against Russia and attacked the United States without consulting its Axis partners (16, 131).

According to the *Doctrine for Planning Joint Operations,* "an alliance is the result of formal agreements (i.e., treaties) between two or more nations for broad, long-term objectives that further the common interests of the members" (14, II-21). The Axis nations had signed the agreement, but the extent of their common interest was limited. One must wonder if a combined Axis campaign plan against Britain might have perhaps identified British vulnerabilities that would have contributed towards a successful Operation SEA LION.

Italy

Shortly before the fall of France, Italy entered World War II, opening possibilities in the Mediterranean for the Axis powers. Although comparatively weak, Italy could have contributed to the success of Operation SEA LION, but the Germans and Italians had to engage in early consultation, establish a common policy, and generate combined plans. However, German efforts to assist Italy in overcoming its material weakness and poor staff work were "frustrated by Mussolini's reluctance to accept help" (16, 149). Hitler blamed the Italians for being "jealous and childish" (16, 149).

Perhaps plans should have been in place for an Axis offensive along the Mediterranean periphery to support German operations against Great Britain following the defeat of France. The Central Mediterranean position of Italy and its modern navy were a threat to the nearby British Island of Malta, a key base on the British Mediterranean sea line of communication (SLOC). The early fall of Malta would have severed this vital SLOC, forcing the British to rely solely on the much longer SLOC around South Africa for resources coming from her Middle Eastern and Asian colonies. Also, the Italian SLOC to its colony in Libya would have been secured (11, 99).

Furthermore, early on, the Germans should have identified the Suez Canal as the gateway to the British East African, Middle Eastern, and Far Eastern colonies and therefore a vital objective to unhinge British economic power. Hence, the Germans could have combined with Italy in the failed Italian offensive into Egypt of September 1940 and probably changed that outcome. One should recall that in February 1941, after the threat of SEA LION, the Germans belatedly introduced two armoured divisions (the fabled Afrika Korps) to reinforce the much-weakened Italians in Libya and almost won in the Western Desert. An earlier arrival, while SEA LION was still a threat, and Britain would have been on the horns of a dilemma considering the risk of reinforcing Egypt with the imminent threat of Operation SEA LION (16, 149).

Spain

Hitler identified the Rock of Gibraltar as an important objective in Germany's war against Britain, but he waited until after the cancellation of SEA LION to approach Spain to discuss the possibility of a combined attack against the British fortress. On 23 October 1940, he met with the Spanish Fascist dictator, General Francisco Franco, to discuss terms for Spanish belligerency against Britain. Franco declared himself ready under the following conditions: that the Axis powers reward him with Gibraltar, French Morocco, and Western Algeria; and make available military and economic aid, particularly petroleum and wheat (4). Hitler agreed but was concerned about committing French colonial interests to the Spanish camp, not wanting to upset the Vichy French. He hoped to persuade the Vichy government by promising it parts of British West Africa. Ultimately, Spain continued to drag its heels and never served as a base against Gibraltar, but did contribute "volunteer" ground forces to the German Eastern Front (16, 131).

If Spain had been part of an overall campaign plan against Britain, then perhaps early in 1940, and almost certainly following the euphoric victory over France, Germany could have at least won access to Spain for an assault on Gibraltar. A successful seizure of Gibraltar would have made the Mediterranean an Axis lake protecting the Axis from enemy incursions into Europe from that direction. Simultaneously, Gibraltar's fall would have allowed the numerically significant Italian fleet to sail to French Channel ports and be available for Operation SEA LION (16, 131).

Vichy France

The government of France had moved to the town of Vichy as part of the armistice agreement reached with Germany following the French military's defeat. Also, the Vichy government still exercised control over the many French colonies and the French Navy. Surprisingly, during the invasion of France, the Germans never tried to forcibly seize any of the French naval units. Instead, the bulk of the French fleet sailed to ports in the French colonies of North Africa. Furthermore, Article 8 of the armistice with Germany confirmed lack of German foresight regarding the need for reflagged French warships for an invasion of England. Article 8 promised, "The German government solemnly undertook to refrain from using the French fleet for its own purposes" (6, 206).

Churchill was not ready to trust the defeated French and German guarantees. On 1 July 1940, he ordered Operation CATAPULT, in which the Royal Navy was to seek and destroy the French fleet. By 18.00 on that same afternoon, British warships opened fire on French ships moored in the Algerian ports of Oran and Mers El Kebir. Despite the British effort, a heavy cruiser, six cruisers, a seaplane carrier, and five destroyers escaped safely and returned to Toulon, France (6, 207).

Following this outrageous act and with the planning for SEA LION about to commence, Hitler should have engaged Marshal Petain, leader of Vichy France, to explore the possibility of using these ships against Britain, or perhaps he should have used force to capture the vessels in Toulon. He took neither action. It was not until 24 October 1940, one month after the indefinite postponement of SEA LION, that Hitler met Petain to discuss matters of "common interest" that would possibly lead to Vichy participation in the war on the German side (16, 131).

Conclusions

Three days after he ranted to an audience of thousands "I am coming! I am coming!" Hitler concentrated his air offensive on the city of London, saving the Royal Air Force from mortal attrition and undermining German air strategy (8, 132). Hitler would never again seriously contemplate an invasion. What caused Germany to abandon its plans to invade? As is shown in the preceding analysis, Operation SEA LION failed before it even started due to Germany's inability to achieve unity of effort, failure to remain focused on key operational centres of gravity, and unwillingness to exploit the capabilities of friendly nations.

Failure to Achieve Unity of Effort

Despite the brilliance of Blitzkrieg warfare, as already discussed, the German military had serious shortcomings regarding joint operations. *Directive 16* that independent service planning was doctrinal, and it was up to Hitler through OKW to bring the three services into compliance regarding a common plan. However, when Hitler chose to avoid the planning process as he did for SEA LION, OKW did not have the power to force unity. Therefore, it appears that no one was jointly planning the war long-term, but instead the services did so crisis to crisis.

In fact, one sees that SEA LION was crisis action planning due to a short-sighted desired end-state against Britain. While Germany forced a decision through force of arms on France, Hitler based his end-state against Britain on the "hope" that Britain would sue for peace. This may be why he allowed the BEF to escape from France. No one had the foresight to see in the BEF an obstacle to a future invasion of Britain because at that instant none was planned. Thus, when the British chose to continue the war, the Wehrmacht was unprepared for amphibious operations, yet was tasked to carry them out.

Lost Focus on the Centre of Gravity

Germany's approach to attacking the British centres of gravity suffered from both indecision and impatience. It may never be known if a more concerted effort to destroy the BEF at Dunkirk, or Germany's plans to deter the Royal Navy using coastal artillery, maritime minefields, and air power would have led to a successful invasion. But the risks posed by the British Army and Navy, while significant, paled in comparison to those posed by the Royal Air Force, and Germany's failure to defeat that COG and achieve air supremacy forced Hitler to call off the operation.

In this regard, evidence suggests that Germany correctly identified the RAF as the most critical COG, and in fact identified and attacked many of the operational centres of gravity that could have led to the defeat of the RAF, including the aircraft factories, radar and sector stations, and other supporting infrastructure that sustained or supported the RAF's warfighting capability. But bombing of aircraft production plants and support installations should have begun much earlier to have a significant impact during the planned invasion; and bombing of the radar stations, sector stations and other operational COGs that were crucial to day-to-day employment of the RAF was not sustained long enough to effectively degrade those systems. As a result, the RAF was able to recover from the attacks, continue the fight, and eventually win the Battle of Britain.

Failure to Include Allies

When Italy entered the war, Mediterranean opportunities became available to the Axis powers, but their failure to achieve unity of effort led to eventual defeat in the Western Desert without ever affecting Operation EAGLE or planning for Operation SEA LION. In addition, the German geopolitical position was undermined by Hitler's failure to engage friendly nations early enough to exploit their assets such as naval units or to gain geostrategic advantage through acquisition of bases against the British in preparation for Operation SEA LION.

Hitler approached both Spain and Vichy France in October 1940, but SEA LION had already been "indefinitely postponed" in September. Clearly, he missed more opportune moments to broach the topic of Spain's and Vichy's active collaboration in the war effort against Britain. For example, after the defeat of France and before Operation EAGLE, Hitler should have discussed Spanish entry into the war. Clearly, German political capital was at its highest immediately following the brilliant victory over the French. Also, in the case of the Vichy government, Hitler should have encouraged Vichy belligerency against Britain immediately following the British Operation CATAPULT of July 1940. Belatedly, by the end of October 1940, when Hitler decided to find additional allies, he had to meet with them knowing that Britain remained unconquered and had withstood the mighty Luftwaffe's best effort. Consequently, nations considering joining the Axis may have concluded that a German victory was no longer inevitable.

A Winning Concept of Operations

In summary, one must respond directly to the question of whether Germany could have succeeded in Operation SEA LION. The answer is yes, although a few key outcomes within the capabilities of the Wehrmacht and Hitler had to be performed differently to guarantee the greatest possibility of success.

First, once Hitler had redefined the end-state, then OKW and the service CinCs should have proceeded to plan SEA LION from a tactical, operational, and strategic perspective. The evidence discussed previously indicates that thorough strategic planning was not conducted for SEA LION. The Germans conducted their military operations oblivious to the possibility of including other friendly nations such as Italy in their war plans. They should have supported and coordinated operations with the Italians to encourage the possibility of stretching British military resources by engaging in a simultaneous offensive in the Mediterranean to support Operation EAGLE and later Operation SEA LION. The British were able through the summer of 1940 to concentrate the bulk of their armed forces in homeland defence without fearing a threat to their economic resources across the Suez Canal and beyond.

Furthermore, the Germans started World War II with an insignificant Navy, and it became even more so following their losses in the conquest of Norway. However, the strategic outlines of SEA LION never included possibilities of other countries providing naval forces. For example, an operation through Fascist Spain to seize Gibraltar, thus opening the Atlantic to the significant Italian Navy, was well within the realm of possibilities. Also, opportunities were missed to capture French warships following their surrender and certainly after the British attack on the French fleet. These warships would have been available to defend against the Royal Navy and for vital sea escort missions of supplies and troops to the beachheads.

If the end-state had initially been to occupy England, then an operational objective of the Wehrmacht would have been to capture the BEF. Instead, these troops escaped to fight another day. The existence of the under-equipped BEF defending the British beaches was enough to complicate planning. Without the BEF, German landings could have safely occurred on a narrow front. The Kriegsmarine could then adequately defend and support it against the Royal Navy.

Ultimately, Operation SEA LION was lost over the skies of England. The British centre of gravity was clearly the RAF, and a sustained air campaign against aircraft factories, radar and sector stations, airfields, and other support facilities could have led to the defeat of Fighter Command and paved the way for a German invasion from the sea. As it was, German numerical superiority was such that by mid-September 1940 command of the air was within grasp. Had Hitler and the Luftwaffe remained focused on these targets instead of redirecting the effort to a militarily insignificant terror bombing of London, the outcome of the Battle of Britain, and consequently also Operation SEA LION, might well have been very different.

Bibliography

1. Agar, Herbert, *The Darkest Year: Britain Alone (June 1940 – June 1941)*, York: Doubleday & Company, Inc., 1973.

2. "Axis Powers," On-line. Internet, 27 July 2002, Available from: Encarta, http://encarta. msn.com/index/conciseindex/5D/05D60000.htm?z=1&pg=2&br=1.

3. Barker, A.J., *Dunkirk: The Great Escape*, York: David McKay Company, Inc., 1977.

4. Burdick, Charles B, *Germany's Military Strategy and Spain in World War II*, York: Syracuse University Press, 1968.

5. Churchill, Winston, "We Shall Fight on the Beaches," On-line. Internet, 3 August 2002, Available from: The Winston Churchill Web Page, The Churchill Center, www. winstonchurchill.org/speeches.htm.

6. Elstein, David, "Operation SEA LION: The Plan to Invade England," *History of the Second World War*, . Pitt, Barrie, Marshall Cavendish Corp., 1978.

7. Fleming, Peter, *Operation SEA LION*, York: Simon and Schuster, 1957.

8. *Fuehrer Directives and Other Top-level Directives of the Wehrmacht*, , D.C., 1948.

9. *Germany, Naval Historical, German Staff Planning, World War II:* Office of Chief of Naval Operations, 1949.

10. Hinsley, Francis Harry, *Hitler's Strategy*, Cambridge: The University Press, 1951.

11. Joint Pub 1, *Joint Warfare of the Armed Forces of the United States:* Joint Chiefs of Staff, 2000.

12. Joint Pub 3-0, *Doctrine for Joint Operations*: Joint Chiefs of Staff, 2001.

13. Joint Pub 5-0, *Doctrine for Planning Joint Operations:* Joint Chiefs of Staff, 1995.

14. Kecskemeti, Paul, *Strategic Surrender*, California: Stanford University Press, 1958.

15. Keegan, John, *The Second World War*: Penguin Books, 1989.

16. Kieser, Egbert, *Hitler on the Doorstep: Operation 'SEA LION' the German Plan to Invade Britain, 1940:* Naval Institute Press, 1997.

17. Leach, Barry, *German General Staff, Weapons Book No. 32, .*, Mason, David, New York: Ballantine Books, Inc., 1973.

18. *Operation SEA LION, .*, Cox, Richard, San Rafael: Presidio Press, 1977.

19. Overy, Richard, *The Battle of Britain: The Myth and the Reality*, York: W.W. Norton & Company, 2000.

20. Saunders, Commander Malcolm G., "Operation Catapult: Britain Attacks the Vichy Fleet," *History of the Second World War*, . Pitt, Barrie, Marshall Cavendish Corp, 1978.

21. "Text of the Nazi-Soviet Pact," On-line. Internet, 27 July 2002, Available from: The History Place, www.historyplace.com/worldwar2/timeline/pact.htm.

22. "The Blitz Begins," On-line. Internet, 8 August 2002, Available from: Historical Society Online, www.battleofbritain.net/section-6/blitz-p01.html.

23. Von der Porten, Edward, *Pictorial History of the Kriegsmarine in World War II,* York: Thomas Y. Crowell Company, 1976.

24. Wilmont, Chester, *The Struggle for Europe,* York: Harper & Brothers Publishers, 1952.

German Operations in North Africa: A Case Study of the Link between Operational Design and Sustainment

Major David F. Tosch

School of Advanced Military Studies, US Army CGSC, Fort Leavenworth, Kansas

[Editor's Note – This case study was the monograph written by the author when a student at the School of Advanced Military Studies, US Army Command and General Staff College, Fort Leavenworth, Kansas in 1987. The text has been left 'as written' as far as possible, with only minor corrections applied, mainly to conform to the series style.]

Introduction

One of the most significant challenges facing U.S. Army operational planners is preparing for major operations and campaigns in undeveloped theaters of operation. This is due largely to the lack of readily accessible supplies and local resources in an austere environment. Everything an army consumes must be transported to such a theater and then distributed. It is critical to the success of operations in such a theater that logistical needs are thoroughly planned for and supplies are provided when called for by the plan or required by the force.

The purpose of this paper is to examine the tension between operational planning and sustainment in remote areas. Although adequate sustainment in and of itself may not win a campaign, history is replete with examples in which ineffective sustainment has lost a major operation or campaign. It is imperative that operational plans and logistical arrangements be synchronized – particularly in an austere environment. Otherwise a commander may reach or exceed his culminating point without realizing his predicament. A better understanding of this relationship between operational planning and sustainment will allow commanders and their planners to conduct more synchronized operations.

Before discussing operational sustainment an adequate definition must be provided so that it can be distinguished from tactical sustainment. "Operational sustainment comprises those logistical and support activities required to sustain campaigns and major operations within a theater of operations."[1] The operational or theater of operations sustaining base links strategic support with Combat Service Support (CSS) units organic to tactical forces. By contrast, "tactical sustainment includes all the CSS activities necessary to support battles and engagements and the tactical activities which precede and follow them."[2] In short, operational sustainment is concerned with providing the resources required to conduct major operations and campaigns. Tactical sustainment is designed to meet immediate support requirements. Operational sustainment capability, therefore, determines the bounds within which operations can succeed – if it does not provide a solid foundation, the outcome of the operation is placed in jeopardy. Throughout the remainder of this paper the term sustainment will refer only to operational sustainment.

Alexander the Great was extremely successful in sustaining his Macedonian Army in an austere environment characterized by limited agriculture.[3] Because Alexander's army was designed for speed and mobility it possessed fewer pack animals than other contemporary armies. As a result of the limited transport capability, his army could not remain self-sufficient for long distances when separated from navigable rivers or seaports. He found unique solutions to solve the provisioning problem for each area he encountered. Alexander's superior abilities in gathering intelligence and his thorough planning permitted him to overcome the obstacles that thwarted other armies. For example, he would obtain intelligence concerning the routes, climate, and resources of the country and then operate with a small, light force while the main army remained behind at a base – well supplied. Alternatively, he would divide the army into smaller units so that their diminished requirements could be provisioned more easily during their advance through the countryside. It is entirely possible that "Alexander better understood the capabilities and limitations of his logistic system than perhaps any other commander, before or since."[4] The level of synchronization Alexander achieved between operations and sustainment should be the same sought today – little has changed in its significance. On the other hand, warfare and armies have changed extensively since the days of Alexander. Planning has become much more complex because of added variables with which one must contend. Commanders also must grasp the capabilities and limitations of more sophisticated logistics means.

In order to uncover the linkage between operational planning and sustainment in an austere theater, German operations conducted in the World War II North African theater will be examined. The North African case study provides a unique example of the relationship between operations and sustainment because Erwin Rommel achieved both operational success and suffered operational failure in this remote area.

The enormity of the task facing Rommel was compounded by the characteristics of the theater of operations. Because it was a secondary theatre, Rommel was often unable to get the priority for resources he desired. The lines of communication (LOCs) were interdicted continuously by the enemy because German forces seldom possessed air superiority within the theater of operations. The ports of debarkation in North Africa were constrained in both number and capacity, a constraint which was further compounded by the lack of air superiority. Useful railroads were unavailable to Rommel and only one good hard surface road existed—along the coastline. Lastly, because Rommel was dependent upon motor transport to sustain his force, he required large numbers of cargo vehicles which were also in short supply. However, even after considering these constraints, Rommel achieved tremendous tactical successes. It was at the operational level that Rommel encountered serious shortcomings.

This paper about Rommel's campaign in North Africa provides a vehicle that will contribute to an improved understanding of the tension between operational design and sustainment. The results Rommel achieved can, in large part; be linked to his sustainment capability. This paper will conduct an analysis of Rommel's major operations between early 1941 and the fall of 1942 in order to determine how he integrated sustainment capability into his conduct of and planning for operations in North Africa. Next, the operational sustainment options available to Rommel will be analyzed. Then the paper will speculate about how Rommel might have improved the linkage between operational planning and sustainment. Finally, based upon this analysis, the implications of logistics for operational planning will be addressed.

Analysis of Rommel's Major Operations

In preparation for operations in North Africa Rommel undertook several key initiatives to smooth the transition of his force onto the continent. First, knowing that the British advance against crumbling Italian resistance had to be slowed, he ordered that the port of Benghazi be interdicted by the German Air Force. He also recognized that once the British realized they would be opposed with a defense in the vicinity of Sirte they would be forced to observe an operational pause to bring up supplies over their extended LOCs.[5] This would gain time for him to strengthen his forces and aid him in withstanding further enemy attacks. He was acutely aware of the importance of sustainment in the theater he was about to enter.

Because the Italians were forced to retire from Cyrenaica, the Axis were constrained to the use of one harbor – Tripoli – which was classified easily as the largest Libyan port.[6] Realizing the importance of establishing an adequate defense, Rommel challenged his logistics staff to displace immediately the German units arriving at Tripoli. They were to be moved forward to Sirte – over 300 miles to the east. Rommel's Quartermaster (Major Otto) readily recognized one hurdle that would persist throughout the campaign in North Africa.[7] This was a severe shortage of ground transportation assets. As there was no railway running eastward from Tripoli, the Afrika Korps had to operate at a distance from its base half again as large as that normally considered the limit for the sustainment of a force by surface transportation.[8] In this instance it was overcome by moving supplies along the coastline with small ships from Tripoli to Buerat and Ras el Ali, partially easing the burden on motorized transportation means.[9]

Initially Rommel was well supplied due to his relatively short LOCs but they rapidly lengthened to 400 miles, within a month, up to El Agheila. Consequently, the British felt he was in a precarious position which would allow them time to prepare for an Axis advance. They felt that their defensive positions, west of El Agheila, were almost beyond their support capabilities which stretched 300 miles from Tobruk. In contrast, Rommel considered his positions at El Agheila well within his sustainment capabilities.[10] The British estimated that it would take Rommel at least thirty days to move the necessary supplies forward in order to sustain a drive eastwards. At this early stage of operations in North Africa, the British clearly underestimated Rommel's capabilities. "Time for the moment, appeared to be on the British side; however imaginative, aggressive or daring the enemy commander might be, he could not ignore the iron laws of logistics. But Wavell did not yet know Rommel."[11]

Even at this early stage of operations in North Africa one factor that would have a later impact stands out. There was continual bickering between the administrative staff who were primarily interested in clearing the port at Tripoli and the staff of the German 5th Light Division who, just recently arrived, were concerned with building up stocks in the forward area. Rommel refused to devote attention to resolving these administrative matters. This is the first indication that Rommel appeared not to concern himself with logistics questions while always expecting his staff to have supplies available where and when they were required.[12] Because the Italian *Commando Supremo* was responsible for getting supplies to North Africa and discharged at the ports, Rommel was to later suffer the consequences for not concerning himself with sustainment matters in the planning stage.

Rommel's First Offensive

By the middle of March, Rommel realized that the British were not contemplating offensive operations because they were in a weakened state which he felt he could exploit. When he travelled to Berlin to make a case for undertaking an offensive earlier than planned, he was told to remain cautious because of constraints in transportation and supply. Nevertheless, in late March, Rommel authorized a raid on El Agheila which possessed a much needed water supply. Rommel believed that the British were momentarily weak, a vulnerability which had to be exploited in order to gain the initiative. However, he could expect no reinforcements until the end of May when the 15th Panzer Division was to arrive. At that time he was to attack Agedabia and perhaps Benghazi. Rommel felt strongly that he could not limit his efforts to Agedabia and Benghazi. Instead he felt he would have to occupy the whole of Cyrenaica because the Benghazi area could not be held by itself. However, the addition of the 15th Panzer Division would double the German motor-transport requirement to 6,000 tons per day – proportionally ten times as much as the forces preparing for operations in Russia.[13] Compounding his sustainment problem was the fact that coastal shipping could not alleviate the transportation shortfall. Finally, Tripoli's port capacity was exceeded by these new requirements.[14] Again, there is little evidence Rommel concerned himself with how his operations in North Africa would be sustained. Although he was aware of his logistic shortfalls, what he saw as a unique opportunity to gain the initiative was an overriding factor in his decision to press eastward.

The last day of March, Rommel began an operation against Mersa el Brega. In part he justified this action because it provided access to improved water supplies and a good jump-off point for the May attack.[15] After meeting light initial resistance Rommel realized that the British forces were retreating – an opportunity he could not resist. Despite his instructions to wait until late May before attacking Agedabia, he pressed into, through, and twelve miles east of Agedabia by the end of the first day. Indications are that Rommel had kept a close eye on the speed and efficiency with which his panzers and vehicles had been refuelled and restocked. This aided in the quick advance.[16] When it became apparent that the British intended to withdraw without decisive action, Rommel decided it was an opportune time to take Cyrenaica with one bold stroke. However, this effort did not progress without difficulty. At the end of the first day the 5th Light Division predicted that it would need four days to replenish its fuel supplies. Rommel intervened in the matter directing that the division unload every available vehicle, return to the resupply point at Arco del Fileni, obtain enough supplies for an advance through Cyrenaica, and return within twenty-four hours.[17]

Rommel was soon confronted by the Italian Commander-in-Chief, General Gariboldi, who was upset that Rommel disregarded orders from Rome. Gariboldi also reminded Rommel that the supply situation was at best tenuous. Rommel persisted in his view that he could not allow an excellent opportunity slip by. "I had made up my mind to stand out from the start for the greatest possible measure of operational and tactical freedom and, what is more, had no intention of allowing good opportunities to slip by unused."[18] Sustainment realities began to impact, however, for several lead elements were stranded for want of supplies and units were strung out twenty-to-thirty miles. For instance, on 7 April Rommel wanted to attack Mechili but could not mass enough combat power due to the scattered units and lack of fuel.[19] Rommel stated that the experience he gained during his advance through Cyrenaica would form the basis for planning his later operations. He felt that the standards he had set, as in any precedent setting operation, were based on something less than average performance and should not be submitted to.[20] If his subordinates thought they had to meet unrealistic demands up to this point they must have thought Rommel ruthless with his later demands – particularly his logisticians.

Although Rommel achieved a great tactical success with his pursuit across Cyrenaica, a large portion of the British forces successfully withdrew to Tobruk, a fortress which was to cause Rommel much grief for the remainder of 1941. By the 8 April, Rommel's forward elements reached Derna while many of his columns were stranded around Tengeder without fuel or water. On the 9 April, Rommel was preoccupied with logistics arrangements and bringing up more troops.[21] Nevertheless, as early as 10 April Rommel announced his intention of attacking the enemy forces in Tobruk.[22] However, by the middle of April, Rommel's first attempt to seize Tobruk was unsuccessful. At this point the Italian *Commando Supremo* urged the German OKW to call a halt before Rommel advanced into Egypt as they were concerned that he would bypass Tobruk and continue the advance. A pause would allow the Afrika Korps to recover its strength through resupply and reorganization. Although Rommel felt that the capture of Tobruk was essential, because it sat astride his lines of communication (LOCs), he also felt it could not be achieved until more German combat units were available – how these additional forces would be sustained was not his concern.[23]

General Halder, Chief of the General Staff, OKH was aware of Rommel's request for additional forces and quickly became concerned that they could not be provided without shifting resources from other critical commitments. Furthermore, he and others became concerned with Rommel's tactical operating style which took him away from overseeing the proper administration of the Afrika Korps. General Halder designated General Paulus to go to Africa, assess the situation, and re-emphasize to Rommel that OKH had only limited resources with which to support him. Upon his arrival in North Africa, Paulus discovered another attack on Tobruk was being planned for 30 April but he refused to approve it until he investigated further. Although he quickly gave his approval, once Tobruk was taken, no further advance was to be made and Cyrenaica would be retained by holding the line Siwa-Sollum. After this second major attack on Tobruk, a stalemate still existed with German forces surrounding the city in depth. Paulus instructed Rommel to pause, reorganize his force, and establish a secure base of supply because his force was too exhausted to continue further operations.[24] On 12 May General Paulus prepared a report on the situation in North Africa. He noted that the logistics posture, including shortages of fuel, ammunition, rations and motorized transport was critical.[25] He was emphatic on the point that no further forces be sent to the theater until enough supply stocks were accumulated. General Halder estimated that Axis forces required 30,000 tons of supplies a month. Indications were that 30,000 tons were for current maintenance of the force and the remainder for the build up of supplies required before a further advance could be undertaken.[26] Furthermore, there was to be no advance beyond Sollum without OKH permission until the 15th Panzer Division arrived.[27]

In early May, Rommel finally realized that his force was not strong enough to mount a successful attack against Tobruk.[28] Although one of Rommel's chief reasons for capturing Tobruk was to improve his sustainment capability, he may have been mistaken for several reasons. First, the port was thought to be capable of handling 1,500 tons per day but could hardly reach 600. Second, the German Navy was concerned about using it for offloading large ships and felt that the ports at Tripoli and Benghazi offered better capabilities (some of this can possibly be attributed to the navy's concern about enemy air). Lastly, there was not even enough coastal shipping capability to employ the port of Benghazi, let alone Tobruk.[29]

The port of Benghazi was underutilized for several reasons beside the shortage of coastal shipping vessels. First, because of a lack of air defence at Benghazi, the port suffered heavy damage. As a result, the only means of getting supplies into the port and discharged was with the use of small coastal vessels. Because coastal snipping capacity was estimated at only about 29,000 tons per month, a large amount of supplies would still have to be moved forward by motorized transport from Tripoli.[30] Additionally, because Benghazi was continually interdicted, coastal shipping only managed to transport 13,000 tons per month and supplies began to stack up at Tripoli.[31] Rommel felt that much more could have been accomplished had the Italians made more of an effort in improving and expanding Benghazi port capacity.[32] Furthermore, there was no suitable logistics headquarters to control the now of supplies forward. This factor, combined with the severe shortage in motorized transport resulted in a clearly insufficient sustainment capability – especially for a situation characterized by long LOCs. Afterward, Rommel admitted that he had not spent enough time to train his forces and make preparations for the advance through Cyrenaica. He attributed the lack of success and resulting stalemate at Tobruk largely to not having an opportunity to make proper preparations.[33]

Once the Afrika Korps assumed a defensive position east of Tobruk during late May, the main supply route was cut by the British fortress. As a result it took an entire day for a resupply column to drive around Tobruk. Although Rommel recognized the need for an improved by-pass road the Italians were unable to complete the project and Rommel did not have the necessary construction assets available. Rommel also realized the extent of the sustainment problem in moving supplies by motorized transport over 1,000 miles. Rommel felt that the solution to reduce the extraordinarily long ground LOG was to have the Italians ship more supplies to Benghazi.[34] He also stated that it was impossible for him to do anything about it as it was an Italian responsibility to get him the supplies he needed. In the meantime,

Rommel had to prepare for the British counter-offensive, *Operation Crusader*, which would be a significant operational success on his part. This analysis will now move to the next major period of the war – the winter of 1941-42 and *Operation Crusader.*

Operation Crusader

In late November 1941 Rommel was making preparations for another assault on Tobruk when the British suddenly attacked to relieve Tobruk. Rommel's logistical staff felt that insufficient fuel and ammunition stocks had been collected with which to sustain another attack. This was because during September and October port installations at Tripoli and Benghazi had been under constant attack and supply convoys across the Mediterranean were interdicted heavily. When the British launched *Operation Crusader* on 18 November, the Afrika Korps and its logisticians were preoccupied with the capture of Tobruk harbor. However, the attack forced Rommel suddenly to turn his attention in the other direction before attacking Tobruk.

After reorienting his forces and conducting several successful battles, Rommel had the British Crusader forces split into fragments and scattered over the desert. Rommel figured that by cutting the British LOCs with a rapid and violent maneuver he could increase their disarray and block British withdraw routes to Egypt. He also informed his Quartermaster that he wanted to capture British supply dumps along the way. Essentially Rommel had taken command of the Afrika Korps at this point because General Cruewell was absent. When Cruewell reappeared he suggested that time should be spent on reorganizing the Afrika Korps, clearing up the litter of the enemy units, and salvaging vast stocks of captured and abandoned materiel before it could be reclaimed by the enemy. Rommel summarized the situation as follows: "The greater part of the (enemy) force aimed at Tobruk has been destroyed; now we will turn east and go for the New Zealanders and Indians before they have been able to join up with the remains of their main force for a combined attack on Tobruk. At the same time we will take Habata and Maddalena and cut off their supplies. Speed is vital; we must make the most of the shock effect of the enemy's defeat and push forward immediately and as fast as we can with our entire force to Sidi Omar."[35] However, both the 15th and 21st Panzer Divisions were short of ammunition and fuel due to the heavy action over the preceding days and were not prepared.

As Rommel pushed forward in his southeasterly drive to the frontier, he bypassed two large British supply depots which remained undiscovered by the Axis forces. If Rommel had been a bit more conservative and mopped up enemy forces as he progressed, he most likely would have found the enemy supply dumps.[36] This would have hindered the British advance and sustained Rommel's forces much longer. However, Rommel's impulsiveness dictated speed over a methodical advance and he suffered the consequences.

Rommel, accompanying the advance elements of 21st Panzer reached the "wire" (border between Egypt and Lybia) at 16.00 directing all efforts once again without the presence the General Cruewell, the Afrika Korps Commander. Travelling at least an hour behind Rommel, Cruewell witnessed enemy formations pushed aside by the spearhead, reorganizing themselves and causing casualties in the trailing elements of his forces. The speed at the head of the column was causing growing attenuation of the body. By the time Cruewell reached the "wire" at Gasr el Abid he found his corps spread from south of Halfaya Pass back in a 50-mile hook to Gabr Saleh with an awesome vehicle casualty rate.

Oberstleutnant Westphal, who in Rommel's absence was the de facto commmander of Panzergruppe Afrika, was attempting to support his commander, now 70 miles away. Without being aware of the dire circumstances his force was in, Rommel was issuing his orders for the following day, the 25th of November, in which he intended to destroy the remnants of the enemy army. Once again he brushed aside Cruewell's concerns over exhaustion and lack of sustainment capability. Rommel then continued to drive eastward far beyond his advance headquarters in the general direction of Habata in search of British supply dumps he had promised his Quartermaster.[37] He was unsuccessful and when returning had his famous incident in attempting to breach the "wire" with his Mammoth command vehicle.[38]

With Rommel and the Afrika Korps scattered about the frontier an attempt was made by the British to link up with the Tobruk garrison. Westphal was watching these developments but was unable to communicate with Rommel or Cruewell. During November 25-26 he tried to contact them and finally contacted General von Ravenstein late on the 26th suggesting that the 21st Panzer Division move towards Tobruk to assure that the front there did not collapse. Although Rommel at first took great exception to Westphal's action, after he examined the situation it was clear he had a threat endangering Tobruk to his rear. The "Dash to the Wire" had reduced the 21st Panzer Division to less than one-half its authorised strength in men and less than one-third in equipment. Nevertheless, Rommel ordered them to attack the New Zealanders and complete the annihilation of the remaining

Tobruk forces. On 1 December the Tobruk corridor had been cut and the port was under siege again. Once the New Zealanders were defeated but before Tobruk was secured, Rommel desired to conduct a second "Dash to the Wire".

On 4 December, Rommel was apprised of the condition of his forces. Although his transport position was eased with the capture of vast numbers of British trucks the advantage was offset by dwindling fuel supplies. Also, losses in terms of personnel and equipment were immense. Of the 250 Panzers with which the Crusader battles started, fewer than forty remained and existing stocks of ammunition were insufficient to fight any battle of consequence. Rommel would be fortunate to acquire enough fuel to retreat, let alone advance any further from his bases.[39] At this point Rommel realized that the main effort should remain south of Tobruk. This was because his formations were too dispersed and were being continually harassed, the cumulative effects of which were beginning to take a toll. As a result, in early December Rommel decided to abandon the Tobruk front and go back to the defensive positions south of Gazala – the same defensive position chosen in May 1941 after the Axis attacks on Tobruk failed.

By late December *Operation Crusader* was over and Rommel was undoubtedly discouraged. "His army had been defeated, and he knew it, not by superior military conception, training, or even prowess-but by logistic inadequacy on the part of his own government and their allies."[40] Rommel felt that after defeating the New Zealanders, on the outskirts of Tobruk, he was robbed of victory by the shortcomings in his sustainment capability. It should be pointed out however that he did not mass his forces in attempting to defeat the Tobruk garrison – his forces were still scattered when he besieged Tobruk the second time. "He would pay more attention himself to that side of affairs in the future, for it was obviously courting disaster to leave such matters in other hands than his own."[41]

Rommel's Second Offensive and the Battle of Gazala

In January 1942 Rommel, by then back at his old start point, was able to launch a counter-offensive to the east from El Agheila. Once again he did not bother to inform his high command nor his allies of his intentions and proceeded in his pursuit of victory. Several factors allowed Rommel to regain the initiative. After conducting an orderly withdrawal to El Agheila, Rommel's army still possessed excellent morale and retained its high efficiency. Second, the Axis supply lines were shortened considerably. This eased significantly the logistical burden. Third, Axis convoys to North Africa were getting through in larger numbers due to more efficient air cover provided by the German Air Force. Finally, Rommel had evidence that the British forces were again in disarray.

British authorities also remained confident because Rommel had incurred heavy losses during *Operation Crusader*, suffered from a lack of reinforcement, and encountered supply difficulties. The significant increase in supply convoys across the Mediterranean had been discounted. During November, the percentage of German cargo that failed to get across the Mediterranean rose to 62% and the amount reaching North Africa was halved from the month before. The British success forced the Axis powers to increase their efforts to protect supply convoys and during late 1941 the Royal Navy lost significant numbers of capital ships. The bulk of the British fleet in the Mediterranean was no longer present and Malta was heavily bombed by the German Air Force which operated from airfields in the bulge of Cyrenaica. When the British were suddenly deprived of the ability to cut off supplies and reinforcements to Rommel, the arrival of Axis supply ships at Benghazi and Tripoli transformed the tactical situation in North Africa and enabled Rommel to resume offensive operations with reorganized forces.

Once again, Rommel had great initial success when he found he had taken the enemy's forward units by surprise. During the first three days of the advance the Axis forces scattered the British forces, inflicted sizeable losses and suffered few themselves. However, the Afrika Korps was unable to stay in close contact with the retreating British forces. This was due to a lack of fuel and the need to pause and acquire enormous quantities of bulk supplies captured in Benghasi. By 2 February Rommel's force was only 35 miles from Tobruk and although triumphant it was exhausted. Rommel was considering another attack because the British forces were extremely weak. However, he decided he did not have enough fuel.[42] General Bastico, the Commander in Chief of Axis forces, reminded Rommel that his mission was to defend Tripolitania and that adequate supplies could not be provided for a further advance. Rommel was satisfied that his position at Gazala would provide a good jumping-off place for future operations.

Although this second offensive had many parallels with the offensive conducted during the previous April it had several key differences. First, there was a sound plan which had been worked out in detail by Rommel's staff. Also, the supply system was better organized – especially for fuel. Finally, with the knowledge that British LOCs were overextended and that large quantities of British supplies, with the exception of fuel, were positioned well forward on the ground, the temptation for Rommel was too great to pass up.[43] Once these supplies were captured a British offensive would be impossible for several months and Rommel could strengthen his own forces.

After a lull of three months, during which Rommel increased his supply stockpiles, he attacked the British positions at Gazala on 26 May 1942 beginning the Battle of Gazala. The British, as Rommel was well aware, were steadily gaining strength faster than the Axis forces.

The British 6th Army could be reinforced more rapidly than Axis forces because the British government was providing all the materiel it could acquire to its forces in North Africa. Large British convoys continued to arrive relatively unimpeded by travelling around the Cape. Furthermore, the British could meet all their fuel needs from refineries located within the theatre.[44] Rommel felt that the British would attack as soon as they felt strong enough, "Our southern flank lay wide open and they had a large choice of possible operations to choose from. A constant threat would hang over our supply lines. Retreat, if we were forced into it by the danger of being outflanked, would be fraught with tremendous difficulties, due to the fact that most of my Italian divisions were non-motorized. But the British were not to have the chance of exploiting their opportunities, for I had decided to strike first."[45]

In less than a day many of the supply dumps of the British XXX Corps at El Adem fell to the 90th Light Division. However, by late afternoon of the second day the 90th Division was separated from the Afrika Korps and the British launched a counterattack. "British motorised groups were streaming through the open gap and hunting down the transport columns which had lost touch with the main body. And on these columns the life of my army depended."[46] Also, British fighters and fighter-bombers had focused their attention on Axis motor transport columns.[47] By the 28th Rommel had reason to be concerned, the Afrika Korps was scattered over a large area, he had already lost 200 tanks, and the 13th Panzer Division was out of fuel and ammunition because it also had become separated from its supply columns.[48] On the morning of the 29th, Rommel led supply columns up to the main body of the Afrika Korps which had taken up defensive positions. Rommel realized that it was too risky to continue the attack before a secure supply route was opened and so directed the efforts of his forces toward sealing off the British in the east and opening a wide gap in the minefields to the west Rommel noticed that the British were not quick to attack his defensive positions so launched another attack on 31 May.

Within two weeks Rommel had won the Battle of Gazala and the British forces were retreating to the Egyptian frontier where a defensive line could be re-established. There would be sufficient time to do so because Tobruk, the key to British sustainment in Cyrenaica, was in Rommel's path. Evidence of the British defeat was present in the form of undamaged motor transport columns left on the roads with abundant supplies. It was less than a week later, on the 21st of June, that Rommel drove into Tobruk. With it came practically everything Rommel's forces needed logistically except water. This included over 2,000 tons of fuel, large quantities of British and German ammunition, 2,000 serviceable vehicles and approximately 5,000 tons of provisions.[49] Characteristically, Rommel decided that it was better to take advantage of the British disorganization subsequent to their defeat at Gazala than to spend time making elaborate plans to besiege Tobruk – he was right!

Tobruk fell easily and his bold triumph led directly to his promotion to Field-Marshal and in Rommel's mind would lead to a quick conquest of Egypt – certainly the high point during his time in North Africa.

Rommel was aware that his forces were worn down, but because he had captured vast quantities of supplies he believed a further offensive possible. Furthermore, Rommel had been promised by *Commando Supremo* that, considering his present location, adequate supplies could only be provided if Tobruk were in his possession. This led him to the idea of exploiting British weakness and precluding their efforts to bring fresh forces westward from Egypt. Rommel realized that his sustainment system would be faced with serious problems once he advanced into Egypt. However, he felt that the supply staffs in Rome were capable of shipping sufficient supplies to ports available in the forward area of operations. "The top Italian authorities could have done this at any time. When I gave orders for the advance into Egypt, I was assuming that the fact of final victory in Egypt being now within reach would spur even the Italian *Commando Supremo* into some sort of effort."[50] Rommel's forces began moving eastward on 22 June.

On 29 June, the last fortress port in the western Egyptian desert, Mersa Matruh, was in Rommel's possession and the British had again suffered heavy losses. As soon as the fortress had fallen, Rommel resumed his eastward movement. There had been a general understanding within the Panzerarmee that after the capture of Tobruk there would be a pause of at least one month. However, when this did not occur the logistics system was not prepared to support a further advance. Captured supplies and materiel certainly played a key role in sustaining the push forward. For example, by this time 85% of the Axis motorized transport consisted of captured enemy vehicles.[51] However, it took time to gather and integrate these assets within the force ones they were captured. Also, ammunition was running short as supplies were not arriving in sufficient quantities when needed. Rommel could visualize his approaching culminating point, "When it is remembered that in modern warfare supplies decide the battle, it is easy to see how the clouds of disaster were gathering for my army."[52] Because Rommel saw the British forces gaining strength with improved equipment and increased shipments of supplies with significantly shortened LOCs he felt it imperative to crush the British forces immediately.

On 1 July, the Afrika Corps began its attack on the El Alamein line. After three days of attempting to crack the British defense, Rommel decided to call off the attack because of his critical supply condition, his severely attritted units, and the strengthened enemy forces. He realized that he had to give his forces a few days' rest and reorganization. His attempts to replenish his supplies were complicated by the extremely long surface LOCs. The ports of Tobruk and Mersa Matruh were still not in use and supplies were being transported from Benghazi and Tripoli 730 and 1,400 miles away.[53] From this point on Rommel could achieve only limited tactical offensive success and the front became static.

Rommel focused all his efforts on preparing for another offensive. It was important that this be done quickly as large quantities of supplies were being shipped from Britain and America and would be arriving in ever increasing numbers by mid-September. Rommel and his staff estimated that by the end of August, the British would have seventy infantry battalions, 900 tanks and armoured vehicles, 550 light and heavy guns and 850 anti-tank guns available for action.[54] They also realized that a superhuman effort would be necessary to sustain Axis forces if they were to be capable of challenging the British build-up. The hurdles in accomplishing this were many.

Beginning the end of July, the Royal Air Force (RAF) had placed priority on interdiction of Axis LOCs from the ports to the front, both the main supply route along the coast and coastal shipping. Ships attempting to disembark in the forward ports at Tobruk, Bardia and Mersa Matruh were constantly harassed. During August, Tobruk, which had become the main Axis port, became the primary target for British air efforts. The German Air Force was over-stretched as only limited assets were available to patrol the coastal road and waters and British air-power grew steadily in strength. As a result, the supplies received in August hardly met the daily requirements of a static combat environment and a build-up of stocks was impossible. Furthermore, the condition of the motor transport fleet was of particular concern. At any one time 35% of the fleet was deadlined and since most of the vehicles were captured, parts could only be obtained through canabalization.

Finally, Rommel felt that the most significant shortcoming with regard to the sustainment of his force was the weakness of the logistics organization supporting him. He felt that because the Italian's were mismanaging the sea LOCs and the Germans could exert little influence over the system, sustainment would remain a restraint Rommel had no influence over the shipping lists, the ports of arrival nor the proportion of German to Italian cargo shipped. Apparently there were enough men, vehicles, and supplies in Italy to meet Axis requirements – the problem was how to get them to the front and to the right forces.[55] Rommel summarized his feelings in the following manner, "It is always a bad thing when political matters are allowed to affect supply or the planning of operations. Where these two questions are concerned, any ill-feelings deriving from other fields must be swept ruthlessly aside and all efforts must be concentrated, regardless of all other considerations, to the one purpose of military victory."[56]

The Battle of Alam El Halfa
Rommel estimated that he had to attack by the end of September even though he understood

German Operations in North Africa: A Case Study of the Link
between Operational Design and Sustainment
....

his predicament in that he was consuming far more than he was receiving. The operation would be the first phase of a major attempt to enter Egypt and capture the Suez. On 22 August, Rommel identified his logistical needs for the operation. He mandated that 6,000 tons of fuel and 2,500 tons of ammunition reach him by the end of August Although the Italians promised to do everything possible and sent 10,000 tons of fuel, including 5,000 tons of aviation fuel, four of the seven ships sent were sunk. By the end of August, only 1,500 tons arrived at Tobruk but Rommel decided he could wait no longer for the reasons already identified.[57] Even if sufficient fuel reached the port it had to be transported to the front – El Alamein is 350 miles by road from Tobruk and it took several days to negotiate the poor coastal road and enemy air attacks. Knowing that the fuel and ammunition shortages would restrict his operation to the vicinity of El Alamein he decided to take the risk of gaining a quick victory at Alam el Haifa.

Once again within a matter of a few hours the attack met stiff resistance, the combat forces encountered fuel shortages and by noon on 1 September, Rommel decided to revert to defensive positions because there was no hope of getting sufficient fuel forward. Although fuel was available in the trains element the roads through the minefields were clogged and supply vehicles were unable to get through to the combat forces. During the morning of 2 September, Rommel ordered a deliberate withdraw, to remove his forces from the British minefields. His reasons were a shortage of fuel, a slow tactical start attributed to the effective minefields, and the continual British air attacks. He had also just been informed that it would not be until 7 September before sufficient fuel supplies could possibly arrive at the port.[58] Rommel's defeat at Alam el Haifa was essentially the beginning of the end for the Axis forces. All the operational sustainment shortcomings Rommel had to overcome at this point were just too much.

Rommel's alternative after taking Tobruk in stride was to pause just east of Tobruk instead of attempting to pursue on to the Suez. By halting east of Tobruk the German Air Force could have been used to support an operation that had already been planned against Malta. The final result was that Malta began to play an ever increasingly important role in interdicting the Axis sea LOCs. By the fall of 1942, the British forces on Malta had regained their strength and succeeded in almost bringing Axis shipping to a standstill. In addition, after pursuing eastward Rommel's forces were even further extended beyond the ports making resupply increasingly difficult.

Rommel was now at the end of a long and frequently interrupted LOC, whereas the British were in directly in front of their well supplied and secured main theater supply base. The flow of supplies to the Germans had almost been shut off while the British received an increasingly steady flow. The Battle of Alam Haifa was the last major Axis offensive operation in Libya and Egypt and was the precursor to the decisive Battle of El Alamein. From this point on Rommel's forces steadily weakened while the British forces grew stronger.

Analysis of the Operational Sustainment Options Available to Rommel

Although Rommel coped with a severely constrained sustainment system by continually improvising to meet his needs, the system could nave been further strengthened in a variety ways. Repeatedly Rommel pointed toward the Italian *Commando Supremo* as the party responsible for his meager materiel resources but certainly other factors contributed to his operational sustainment shortages. As a result, Rommel had several options available to him to improve the sustainment or his force during the course of operations in North Africa and some were carried out with effective results.

On several occasions, Rommel was acutely aware of the presence of British supply storage areas and eased his own sustainment shortfall by capturing and putting them to use. The possibility of capturing enemy supplies certainly affected the conduct of operations in order to shore up his austere logistics posture. Because Rommel's tactics were inherently designed to get into the enemy rear and cut his LOCs there was always a strong possibility Rommel would get a windfall in the form of enemy supplies. Axis forces, particularly in the later stages, lived off of British rations, wore British clothing and used British vehicles and fuel. Although captured supplies were always put to good use and were necessary to maintain the initiative at several critical junctures none of Rommel's offensive operations were initiated solely to gain enemy resources.

When the British railroad was captured at Tobruk, Rommel had great hopes of using it to get supplies up to El Alamein.[59] This would have aided substantially his sustainment capability, especially if the port at Tobruk were employed simultaneously. Because locomotives were not available in theater, nor available for shipment from Italy the railway sat idle. By the fall of 1942 the spoils of British supplies and equipment became a burden. With the front now static British fuel stocks were hard to come by and there were no supplies to keep the captured British equipment operational. For example, because 85% of Rommel's motorized transport was of British and American manufacture, as well as much of his artillery, there were no more British parts and ammunition with which to support them.[60] Reliance on enemy supplies and equipment assisted greatly in getting Axis forces well into Egypt but began to restrain Rommel before he could progress any further.

It is clear Rommel improvised to a great extent particularly with regard to the use of enemy supplies and materiel. However, because he relied on the Italian *Commando Supremo* to keep the sea LOC open and transport sufficient supplies to North Africa, improvisation with regard to operational logistics matters was an area Rommel largely disregarded. There were several instances, however, where the Italians improvised in sustaining the Axis forces. In early 1941, Italian submarines were used to transport fuel to the advance elements of the Afrika Korps.[61] Both the Italians and Germans employed limited coastal shipping in the early stages. Later in 1941 when British interdiction of the shipping lanes became effective air transport was employed for emergency resupply. However, because the Germans had no experience in reinforcing the sand surfaces on the coast and in the desert for landings by amphibious craft and aircraft they relied on the Italians to take care of the matter. Improvisation can be an excellent means of sustaining a force particularly when unforeseen emergencies arise. However, on several occasions, Rommel became dependent on captured enemy supplies, a circumstance which does not bode well for operational planning. When Rommel had to rely upon improvisation to sustain his operations, he found himself at a great disadvantage – especially so when considering that his opponent had little need to improvise logistically.

On several occasions Rommel conducted effective withdrawals. On each occasion he was able to strengthen his force by shortening his ground LOC. However, at no time did Rommel use a withdrawal just to shorten his LOC. During his most dramatic withdrawal, in December 1941, Rommel reduced his LOC by more than 300 miles when he positioned his force at El Agheila. Although he was able to strengthen his force because his ground LOC was reduced by 50%, the primary reason he fell back to El Agheila was because it provided a strong defensive position and was an excellent start point for his next offensive.[62] During the same period of time the sea LOC were open and supplies poured into the ports which assisted greatly in reorganising and sustaining Rommel's forces. All these factors allowed Rommel to rebuild his units and sustain his second major offensive in early 1942 but this was not his primary purpose for conducting the withdrawal.

Speculation on an Improved Linkage between Operational Planning and Sustainment Capability

It is clear in the preceding analysis that Rommel did not pay great attention to sustainment matters while openly admitting that logistics was not his concern. When, during the course of operations, Rommel's forces were slowed because of supply shortages he became personally involved in finding solutions in order to regain the initiative. But this was logistics at the tactical level and reactive in nature. When Rommel addressed operational sustainment shortcomings, he normally accused the Italian *Commando Supremo* of incompetence as they continually fell short of meeting his requirements. However, if a campaign is to be successful, sustainment planning must be an integral component of operational planning and this seems to have been a key deficiency in Rommel's conduct of operations in North Africa.

Rommel's operational planning prior to and upon his arrival in North Africa was negligible. Rommel's perspective on the conduct of operations far exceeded the expectations of the Italian authorities to whom he was supposed to report and from whom he obtained support. There is no evidence that Rommel attempted to build up supplies and organize a sustainment system that would allow him to conduct operation, across North Africa. For this he relied totally on the efforts of the Italians who attempted to restrain him as they seemed to understand the capabilities and limitations of their sustainment system. The British, on the other hand, had a well-planned and organized sustainment system. Seldom did British units run out of fuel and ammunition. Although this could be attributed to the slower tempo of their operations, it was more because of the methodical manner in which their planning and organizing was accomplished. The British employed a forward depot system that provided a base and supply network that eventually covered the entire desert. Although this system was susceptible to enemy raids, because the depots were not mobile, the British forces were well supplied considering the desert environment. Furthermore, the British had access to a prosperous Egyptian base of operations, almost a miniature war economy that remained well secured and supplied throughout operations in North Africa. The British seemed to understand Clausewitz's dictum that the, "army and base must be conceived, as a single whole."[63]

Rommel was forced to deal with significant resource shortfalls as he was conducting operations in a secondary theater and was not receiving priority of support from Germany. This, along with the burden of having to rely on Italian support, placed significant constraints on the number of alternatives Rommel had in conducting his operations. His predicament seemed to drive him in a quest for a decisive battle so that he could finish the war in short order. However, two critical aspects were overlooked in planning his conduct of operations eastward. First, in order to keep his lengthy ground LOC secure, more emphasis could have been placed on securing bases and ports along the coastline as operations progressed. If enough effort had been devoted to protecting the ports with air defense assets and expanding port capacity, surface LOCs certainly would not have been as extended or as vulnerable. Although the necessary resources may have been hard to come by, there is no evidence that any major effort was put into this.

The other factor that should have been confronted was Malta and the British interdiction of the sea LOC. Rommel apparently felt this problem was beyond the scope of his responsibility, but he had to concern himself with this matter if he wanted to conduct major operations. Because he had no operational sustainment system or materiel stockpiles of any significance within North Africa, his operations were dependent upon an easily interdicted sea LOC leading back to Italy. When Rommel influenced the decision to divert sir support from an operation that had been planned to neutralize Malta and instead used it in support of his own ground operations, he put his entire operational sustainment system at risk. Once his sea LOC was interdicted, there were never sufficient resources on the continent to sustain operations for any length of time. Essentially, Rommel's theater support base rested in Italy which had to be regarded as part of his theater of operations.

Having analyzed both Rommel's operational success and failure there seems to be a common thread that runs throughout. When the sea LOC was open, Rommel's forces were well sustained and capable of conducting major operations. When the sea LOC was heavily interdicted, Rommel reached his culminating point within a period of several weeks. Although this is an over simplification, the sea LOC did have a profound impact on Rommel's capability to conduct operations. Because Rommel was forced to rely on one line of support, the British were able to focus their interdiction efforts with tremendous results. Crete was employed as an intermediate supply base but this did not happen until late 1942. If employed earlier, it could have served as an alternate line of support that was closer to Benghazi and Tobruk. Without alternate lines of support there was no redundancy in the sustainment system, so that the interdiction of the single sea LOC had the potential to achieve decisive results.

Another commander who conducted operations in a secondary theater characterized by a undeveloped theater of operations, was extremely successful. Field Marshall The Viscount Slim was methodical in his planning of operations in Burma. He devoted much of his attention in planning operations to the sustainment of his forces. He also took great risks with his sustainment system which was barely sufficient to meet his needs. For example, he introduced an additional division into the theater without an augmentation of sustainment assets at a critical point late in the war.[64] However, when he did so he had a firm grasp of what his sustainment capabilities were and how far they could be stretched.[65]

Several of his operations were designed specifically to strengthen his sustainment system. For example, the capture of Myingyan was designed to gain a river port in order to use the Chindwin River; for transporting supplies and to gain a key road to Meiktila. In order to use the rivers as a means of transporting supplies, Slim directed that a shipbuilding yard be constructed at Kalewa on the Chindwin River. This was accomplished with few outside resources, a classic example of improvisation.[66] Another mode of transportation, employed extensively due to the restricted terrain, was air transport. An entire network of air resupply bases was constructed. This was extremely effective because the British continually maintained air superiority over the theater. Finally, the British were able to get the Alon-Ava and Myingyan-Meiktila railways operating after several bridges were replaced, engines were repaired, and jeeps converted for rail use. Thus another vital mode of transportation was available.

Slim, like Rommel, had to face severe resource constraints and had to face the facts of coalition warfare in dealing with allies and his sister services and meeting their demands. During the An operations, the only method to resupply the force was by air because of the dense jungle. However, the RAF decided the aircraft to support the operation had to be diverted and the operation had to be abandoned. On another occasion, Chiang Kai-shek suddenly demanded an immediate return of all U.S. and Chinese forces under Slim's control. This diverted several U.S. air transport squadrons. In order to overcome resource shortfalls Slim unhesitatingly shifted priorities of support to his forces. This was accomplished, by accepting risk in the assignment of missions thereby assuring that his forces with key roles were not overextended logistically.

Slim's greatest challenge in sustainment came during preparations for crossing the Irrawaddy River. The ground LOG extended over 500 miles from the railhead to the river. There were only five months in which to make the roads and bridges negotiable but it was carried out smoothly. Roads, rivers, rail and air were all used effectively to overcome an extremely long LOG. Slim clearly had a firm grasp of what it would take to sustain a campaign in Surma. The reason he achieved such great success was because his sustainment and operational planning were synchronized.

Implications

The purpose of this monograph was to examine the tension that exists between operational planning and sustainment. From the preceding analysis of Rommel's operations in North Africa, one should conclude that there is a distinct relationship. Commanders cannot permit the shackles of logistics to dictate operational plans. Instead, they must be intertwined if success is to be achieved, particularly in an undeveloped theater of operations. Rommel's experience in North Africa is an excellent example of what can happen if operational design and sustainment are not synchronized.

One key factor that Rommel did not have in his favor was time. Rommel felt that if he were to win in North Africa he would have to do it quickly with a decisive battle. By emphasizing early offensive operations, Rommel consciously decided not to devote his efforts and attention on building a logistics infrastructure on the African continent. Immediately upon his arrival he took the initiative, thus there was no opportunity to stockpile supplies or organize an effective sustainment system. He instead relied on the Italians to look after his sustainment. Slim, by contrast, used time to his advantage and methodically organized an infrastructure that eventually paid enormous dividends. Rominel apparently felt that the sustainment system could be stressed, and still support his forces and, although he came close to making it work, it always fell short when he most needed it – largely because it was so thinly resourced to begin with.

Secure LOCs are a necessity in order to sustain operations. As pointed out earlier, Clausewitz emphasized the importance of insuring that the army and its base of operations are recognized as a "single whole". Because Rommel was dependent upon one tenuous LOC that stretched from Italy, across the Mediterranean, into North Africa, and across the desert there was no alternate means with which to move supplies in large quantities. Emergency resupply by air is not sufficient for large mechanized forces, particularly when the enemy has air superiority. The one suitable road in North Africa for motorized transport ran along the Mediterranean coastline and there were no other adequate roads and no rail lines to employ. Moreover, the Italians were unable to build additional roads and railways or improve what was already available. As a result, there was little redundancy in LOC capability so that the British were able to concentrate their efforts in interdicting an invariable line of support.

Even before his arrival in North Africa, Rommel was informed that extensive operations could not be adequately supported and that his mission was to assist the Italians in holding Libya. There was absolutely no assurance that sufficient quantities of supplies could be provided to Rommel at any time by the Italians. Even after Rommel understood that he was operating in a secondary theater and could not command the resources he needed from Germany, he refused to relent in his efforts to get to Cairo.

Once again as so often seen in other campaigns air superiority was a decisive factor. Although ajr support did not influence Rommel's tactical success it was critical to Ms operational capability. The British use of air strikes against Mediterranean shipping lanes and the ports of debarkation proved decisive. British possession of Malta aided greatly in the Mediterranean effort while forward airfields in Egypt were well within striking distance of Tobruk and the other forward ports. Air resupply was employed, but it was limited and should only be considered as tactical sustainment even though it can have operational significance, as Slim proved.

When operations are not sequenced in accordance with sustainment capabilities, the campaign is in jeopardy as was highlighted by Rommel's experience in North Africa.

Possibly he was doomed from the start based upon his dependence on the Italians and the fact that he could not depend upon his own country to provide the requisite resources. It is obvious that there were differences across the board in the way the Italians and Germans did things militarily. But the key difference from which Rommel may have suffered the most was that the Italian economy was not on a wartime footing. Much more could have been done if the Italian national and military strategies even closely resembled those of its ally. There are serious overtones here for coalition warfare, a subject which is beyond the scope of this paper but vitally important to what occurred in North Africa. Moreover, allies may be the primary means of sustaining operations in undeveloped theaters of operation, the ramifications of which may offer the most important implication of all.

Bibliography

Field Manuals
US Department of the Army. *Field Manual 100-5 – Operations*, Washington, D.C., 1956.

Books
Barnett, Corelli. *The Desert Generals*, New York: Ballantine Books, 1960.
Braddock, D. W. *The Campaigns in Egypt and Libya 1940-1942*, Aldershot: Gale and Polden Ltd, 1964.
Detwiler, Donald S. *World War II German Military Studies, Volume 14: Africa*, New York: Garland Publishing, 1979.
Clausewitz, Carl von. *On War*, Edited and Translated by Michael Howard and Peter Paret, Princeton: Princeton University Press, 1976.

Engles, Donald W. *Alexander the Great and the Logistics of the Macedonian Army*, Berkeley: University of California Press, 1960.
Heckman, Wolf. *Rommel's War in Africa*, Translated by Stephen Seago, New York: Granada Publishing, 1961.
Hinsley, F. H. *British Intelligence in the Second World War*, Volume I, London: Her Majesty's Stationery Office, 1979.
Hinsley, F. H. *British Intelligence in the Second World War*, Volume II, New York: Cambridge University Press, 1981.
Irving, David. *The Trail of the Fox*, New York: Avon Books, 1976.
Jomini, Baron de. *The Art of War*, Translated by Captain G. H. Mendell and Lieutenant W. P. Craighill, Philadelphia: J. B. Lippincott and Company, 1862.

Macksey, Kenneth. *Rommel's Battles and Campaigns*, New York: Mayflower Books, 1979.

Mitcham, Samuel W. *Rommel's War: The Life and Death of the Afrika Korps*, New York: Stein and Day, 1982.

Pitt, Barrie. *The Crucible of War: Western Desert 1941*, London: Jonathan Cape Ltd, 1980.

Pitt, Barrie. *The Crucible of War: Year of Alamein 1942*, London: Jonathan Cape Ltd, 1982.

Playfair, Major General I. S. O. *The Germans Come to the Help of their Ally*, The Mediterranean and Middle East, Volume II, London: Her Majesty's Stationery Office, 1956.

Playfair, Major General I. S. O. *British Fortunes Reach Their Lowest Ebb*, The Mediterranean and Middle East, Volume III, London: Her Majesty's Stationery Office, 1960.

Plairfair, Major General I. S. O. *The Destruction of the Axis Forces in Africa*, The Mediterranean and Middle East, Volume IV, London: Her Majesty's Stationery Office, 1966.

Rommel, Erwin. *The Rommel Papers*, Edited by B. H. Liddell Hart, New York: Harcourt, Brace and Company, 1953.

Slim, William. *Defeat into Victory*, London: Cassell and Company, 1956.

Van Creveld, Martin. *Supplying War*, Cambridge: Cambridge University Press, 1977.

Documents

Toppe, Alfred. *Desert Warfare – German Experience in World War II*, Garmisch, Federal Republic of Germany: Historical Division, European Command, 1954.

Endnotes

[1] US Army, *Field Manual 100-5, Operations* (May 1966), p. 65.

[2] *Ibid.* p. 71.

[3] Donald W. Engels. *Alexander the Great and the Logistics of the Macedonian Army*, Berkley: University of California Press, 1976, p. 122.

[4] *Ibid.* p. 121.

[5] Erwin Rommel. *The Rommel Papers*, edited by B. H. Liddell Hart, New York: Harcourt, Brace and Company, 1953, p. 100.

[6] Martin Van Creveld. *Supplying War*, Cambridge: Cambridge University Press, 1977, p. 164.

[7] *Op Cit.* Rommel, *The Rommel Papers*, p. 103.

[8] *Op Cit.* Van Creveld, *Supplying War*, p. 164.

[9] Major General I. S. O. Playfair. *The Germans Come to the Help of their Ally*, The Mediterranean and Middle East, Volume II, London: Her Majesty's Stationery Office, 1956, p. 15.

[10] Barrie Pitt. *The Crucible of War: Western Desert 1941*, London: Jonathan Cape, 1960, p. 250.

[11] *Ibid.* p. 252.

[12] *Op Cit.* Playfair, The Mediterranean and Middle East Vol. II, p.

[13] *Op Cit.* Van Creveld, *Supplying War*, p. 165.

[14] *Ibid.*

[15] *Op Cit.* Rommel, *The Rommel Papers*, p. 107.

[16] *Op Cit.* Pitt, *Western Desert 1941*, p. 255.

[17] *Op Cit.* Rommel, *The Rommel Papers*, p. 110.

[18] *Ibid.* p. 111.

[19] *Op Cit.* Playfair, The Mediterranean and Middle East. Vol. II, p. 33.

[20] *Op Cit.* Rommel, *The Rommel Papers*, p. 120.

[21] *Ibid.* p. 121.

[22] *Op Cit.* Playfair, The Mediterranean and Middle East Vol. II, p. 35.

[23] *Ibid.* p. 41.

[24] F. H. Kinsley. *British Intelligence in the Second World War*, Volume II, New York: Cambridge University Press, 1960, p. 397.

[25] *Op Cit.* Playfair, The Mediterranean and Middle East. Vol. II, p. 156.

[26] *Ibid.* p. 157.

[27] *Op Cit.* Kinsley, *British Intelligence in the Second World War*, Vol. II, p. 397.

[28] *Op Cit.* Rommel, *The Rommel Papers*, pp. 132-133.

[29] *Op Cit.* Van Creveld, *Supplying War*, p. 167.

[30] *Op Cit.* Playfair, The Mediterranean and Middle East, Vol. II, p. 157.

[31] *Op Cit.* Van Creveld, *Supplying War*, p. 167.

[32] *Op Cit.* Rommel, *The Rommel Papers*, p. 134.

[33] *Ibid.* p. 124.

[34] *Ibid.* p. 136.

[35] *Op Cit.* Pitt, *Western Desert 1941*, p. 416.

[36] *Op Cit.* Rommel, *The Rommel Papers*, p. 166.

[37] *Op Cit.* Pitt, *Western Desert 1941*, p. 420.

[38] *Ibid.* pp. 423-424.

[39] *Ibid.* p. 457.

[40] *Ibid*. p. 461.

[41] *Ibid*. p. 461.

[42] Major General I. S. O. Playfair. *British Fortunes Reach Their Lowest Ebb*, The Mediterranean and Middle East, Volume III, London: Her Majesty's Stationery Office, 1960, p. 151.

[43] Wolf Heckmann. *Rommel's War in Africa*, London: Granada Publishing, 1961, p. 326.

[44] *Op Cit*. Rommel, *The Rommel Papers*, pp. 192-193

[45] *Ibid*. p. 193-194.

[46] *Ibid*. p. 206.

[47] *Op Cit*. Playfair, The Mediterranean and Middle East, Vol. III, p. 227.

[48] *Op Cit*. Rommel, *The Rommel Papers*, p. 209.

[49] *Op Cit*. Playfair, The Mediterranean and Middle East, Vol. III, p. 274.

[50] *Op Cit*. Rommel, *The Rommel Papers*, p. 235.

[51] *Ibid*. p. 245.

[52] *Ibid*. p. 244.

[53] *Ibid*. p. 250.

[54] *Ibid*. p. 265.

[55] *Op Cit*. Playfair, The Mediterranean and Middle East, Vol. III, p. 377.

[56] *Op Cit*. Rommel, *The Rommel Papers*, p. 267.

[57] *Op Cit*. Playfair, The Mediterranean and Middle East, Vol. III, p. 382.

[58] *Ibid*. p. 388.

[59] D. W. Braddock. *The Campaigns in Egypt and Libya 1940-1942*, Aldershot, Hampshire: Gale and Polden Ltd, 1964, p. 116.

[60] *Op Cit*. Rommel, *The Rommel Papers*, p. 245.

[61] Alfred Toppe. *Desert Warfare: German Experience in World War II*, Garmisch, Federal Republic of Germany: Historical Division, European Command, 1954, p. 13.

[62] *Op Cit*. Rommel, *The Rommel Papers*, pp. 173-177.

[63] Carl von Clausewitz. *On War*, translated by Michael Howard and Peter Paret, Princeton: Princeton University Press, 1976, p. 69.

[64] William Slim. *Defeat into Victory*, London: Cassell and Company, 1956, p. 436.

[65] *Ibid*.

[66] *Ibid*. pp. 396-399.

Operating Far from Home: American Logistic Support in the Pacific War

Peter D. Antill

Centre for Defence Acquisition, Cranfield University, Defence Academy of the UK.

Dr Thomas M. Kane

Department of Politics and International Relations, University of Hull

Introduction

All wars are wars of logistics, but this is especially true for World War II, the greatest conflict the world has ever known. It was a war of distance, of projecting combat power, of establishing advanced bases, of using those bases to maintain extended supply lines and where the strategies of the participants were shaped, driven and constrained by logistics. This was particularly so in the Pacific Theatre, both for the United States and its allies on the one hand, as well as for Japan on the other. The role logistics played has been recounted many times, but is probably best summed up by Admiral Ernest J. King:

> "The war has been variously termed a war of production and a war of machines. Whatever else it is, so far as the United States is concerned, it is a war of logistics . . . it is no easy matter in a global war to have the right materials in the right place at the right time in the right quantities."[1]

US forces overcame huge challenges in mounting a campaign across the Pacific Ocean in order to stop the Japanese implementing their strategic goals. The campaign tested US logistics in an extraordinary range of geographical and tactical circumstances over an extended period of time. But just as the war in the Pacific was a war of logistics for the Allies, it was for the Japanese as well. Just because the Pacific War ended in August 1945 with the unconditional surrender of Japan, it should not be forgotten that "the Japanese leaders began the war with a rational, albeit desperate, plan to win."[2] Boiled down to its basics, Japan's military leadership gambled that they could establish a very strong position on the Pacific which would buy them enough time in order to allow diplomacy to work in their favour. The essence of such a plan appeared in the memorandum sent to the Emperor by General Haijime Sugiyama announcing they had attacked Pearl Harbor[3] and in a summary of Japan's military objectives dated 15 November 1941 entitled *Draft Proposal for Hastening the End of the War against the United States, Great Britain, the Netherlands and Chiang* which stated

"Our Empire will engage in a quick war, and will destroy American and British bases in Eastern Asia and in the Southwest Pacific region. At the same time that it secures a powerfully strategic position, it will control those areas producing vital minerals, as well as important transportation routes, and thereby prepare for a protracted period of self-sufficiency."[4]

The Japanese then hoped to make any re-conquest of the Pacific not only daunting in terms of the military power the US would have to deploy but also daunting logistically. Hector Bywater, a British naval writer, writing in *Navies and Nations* in 1929 was aware of the challenge:

" . . . the defense of outlying territories, particularly the Phillipines, Guam and Samoa, opens up the whole question of Pacific strategy . . . Here it suffices to repeat that the American Navy would be powerless to prevent the conquest of the Philippines and Guam in the event of war with Japan. Once lost, they might possibly recovered by an almost superhuman effort. This would involve an amphibious campaign exceeding in magnitude and difficulty anything of the kind that has previously been attempted. It would necessitate the building of an entirely new fleet of warships and auxiliary craft; the conveyance of an army and its impedimenta across the Pacific, the greater part of the route lying within the sphere of enemy naval action; the seizure of intermediate and terminal bases, which would probably be found in a state of defense; the holding of such bases against determined counter-attack; the guarding of communications thousands of miles in length; and finally the development of offensive operations in the advanced war zone on a scale sufficient to force a decision. By no other means of military action could the lost islands be recovered."[5]

It was still a gamble though, as Japan did not possess more than 10 percent of the United States' industrial potential, a fact not lost on Admiral Isoroku Yamamoto, Commander of the Combined Fleet, as he'd seen the USA first-hand, having studied English at Harvard University in the 1920s and travelled extensively through the country.[6]

Admiral Isoroku Yamamoto
(Source: Wikimedia Commons)

The Pre-War Situation

At the start of World War II, the USA was ill-prepared logistically to support a two-ocean war. While the Atlantic Fleet had been gaining some combat experience by engaging Axis submarines, the Pacific and Asiatic fleets had no such opportunity.[7] Added to that, the European and Pacific Theatres were vastly different in terms of geography, strategic situation and size and while a common industrial base and military organisation existed in the USA, the requirements of both theatres were often unique, and where they weren't, there existed a major source of competition for resources, in particular shipping, landing craft and support personnel. Even within the Pacific Theatre itself, the campaign involved several different types of warfare, two or more of which could be underway at any one time: a naval war featuring several large-scale sea battles; an air war, featuring air-to-air, air-to-sea and air-to-ground combat as well as a strategic bombing campaign against the enemy's home islands; an amphibious island hopping campaign featuring both Army and Marine ground forces; and a major ground war in both the Philippines and New Guinea. The Pacific Theatre therefore did not possess the same clear cut distinction of being primarily a land campaign supported by air and naval operations as the European Theatre did. If the Army was dominant in the European Theatre, then in the Pacific Theatre, which service dominated was dependent on exactly where the operation was taking place and when. In the Central Pacific, the Navy and Marine Corps tended to dominate, whereas in the Southwest Pacific, it was the Army and Army Air Force that dominated.[8]

The logistics system that eventually allowed the United States to defeat Imperial Japan had its roots in the 1920s and 1930s as the US Navy absorbed and then implemented the lessons of the First World War. The interwar years do not stand out as a particularly vibrant time for wide-ranging theoretical debates as to the nature of naval strategy, especially with regard to logistics, the one exception being the development of US Marine Corps (USMC) amphibious doctrine. Despite the rate of progress with naval logistic innovation being characterised by some as 'pedestrian'[9], a slow but continuous process was underway that meant planners were gradually making the right decisions in which way to go. If the US Navy had not adopted a different system of supply in the late 1930s / early 1940s then it is entirely possible that the Japanese would have had a much easier time and been more successful.

Following Japan's defeat of Russia during the Russo-Japanese War of 1904-05, her emergence as a world power and her taking control of the former Pacific colonies of Imperial Germany after its defeat at the end of the First World War (Japan had joined the Allies against the Central Powers), scenarios for war with Japan were gamed in American war colleges, including the Naval War College, during the 1920s and 1930s.[10] The USA officially adopted the strategy known as War Plan Orange in 1924, a major assumption being that navy commanders thought that they would be unable to significantly engage the Japanese unless they were within range of their port facilities. In public, US commanders wished to maintain the illusion that they would defend most of their Pacific territories but in reality, recognised that they would not be able to defend the Philippines and Guam in the event of Japanese attack, given the weakness of their forces in peacetime.[11] While the original war plans called for American forces to operate from a base in Manila, a revised version on the plan which came out in 1935 more-or-less admitted that the USA would have to seize the Marshall and Caroline Islands as staging areas before further offensive operations could be contemplated. Despite a number of subsidiary war plans being made, the Army did not think the plan was worth the cost and looked to the 1934 Philippine Independence Act to lessen its commitments in the area. In the event of war, there would be little hope of reinforcing the Philippines quickly and even more time would be required to actually retake the islands.[12]

There was however an alternate way to supply maritime forces, as first demonstrated by the Royal Navy's 'victualling sloops' during the Seven Years War.[13] During the First World War, the US Navy developed the techniques it would need to supply other vital services at sea – this included using a pair of ships as floating work platforms at Queenstown, enabling them to maintain and repair destroyers despite very limited port facilities.[14] This made it possible for naval forces to carry a major portion of their supplies and equipment with them, in a similar fashion to modern ground forces carrying much of what they need in trucks. As it happens, such a concept had been proposed back in 1904 by a civil engineer, A. C. Cunningham[15] and with the US Navy moving the bulk of its fleet to the Pacific after the First World War, local commanders organised the 'Base Force fleet train' to support them[16] and in the Basic Readiness Plan of 1924, announced mobile bases of this sort to support combat forces at sea.[17] However, the Navy eventually returned to the policy of using conventional ports and the concept of fleet logistics, while not dying out, went into hibernation. During the inter-war period, there weren't the funds available to develop new support capabilities and even when the US started gearing up for war in late 1940, the logistics branch had to compete with the rest of the Navy for ships and trained personnel. In October 1939, the USA deployed a force of sixteen destroyers, eight cruisers and an aircraft carrier to Pearl Harbor in Hawaii. While the US Navy had facilities there, it stretched their logistics capabilities to the limit but over time, the Navy learned how to overcome those difficulties[18] to the point where the Base Force and its successor organisations would deliver material to ports and ships in combat zones around the Pacific.

US Marines climbing down into a landing boat during rehearsals for Operation Watchtower, 26 July 1942. The use of scramble nets had been first tested during FLEX 3 (Fleet Landing Exercise No. 3) held at San Clemente, California in early 1937 (Source: US Navy via Wikimedia Commons)

In addition to developing the basis of what would become the naval support services, a number of decisions by different people would eventually prove to be farsighted and vital to the US armed forces as they attempted to regain the initiative from the Japanese. These were:

- **Amphibious Warfare** – it was logical that, if the US Navy would be depending on the capture of ports within the war zone, it needed to field a force capable of doing that. Therefore in January 1920, the US Chief of Naval Operations, Robert E. Coontz asked USMC Commandant George Barnett to develop the concept of an expeditionary force to be used in future campaigns to seize control of island bases.[19] It must be remembered however, that amphibious assault against defended beaches, one of the toughest of operations, was not a USMC speciality at this time, and there was little funding or personnel available to develop such a capability. In addition, amphibious warfare was not well understood, and the debacle at Gallipoli had not endeared such operations to commanders.[20] John A. Lejeune who succeeded Barnett, thought differently however. He saw the importance of amphibious warfare to both the United States and the USMC and directed his staff officer, Earl Ellis, to look at what would be necessary to conduct an amphibious war in the Pacific. He came up with Operations Plan 712 entitled *Advanced Base Operations in Micronesia*[21] which was to serve as a guide to future peace time activity and training. The USMC therefore became a facilitator of naval logistics but in turn, took on some special logistical requirements of its own. The most obvious problem was that beach assault entails special problems of supply, i.e. getting equipment from the ships to the shore without a harbour. In addition, the marines would be conducting the assault under fire, so in many ways, the problems of supply mirror those of assaulting the beach i.e. tactical transport and movement. So in order to overcome these problems, the USMC Equipment Board, under Brigadier General Emile P. Moses procured a number of specialised vehicles, including a landing craft (the 'Higgins' boat) and an armoured, tracked yet amphibious troop carrier, invented by Donald Roebling.[22] Next on the list was a new doctrine – in January 1934, the instructors at the Marine Corps Schools, under the guidance of Colonel Ellis Miller produced a draft report entitled *Tentative Manual for Landing Operations*[23] which divided the problem of conducting a beach assault into six areas, one of which was logistics. It also focused on the importance of the 'combat loading' of ships, so that troops could access important equipment and supplies quickly, and stipulated that goods should packed 'first used, last loaded' so that the most urgent supplies were near the top or the front (depending on the ship), vital supplies should split amongst several ships, so the loss of one ship doesn't cripple the whole operation and that material belonging to the same units should be placed in the same part of the ship, to avoid confusion as to who owns what.[24] While this might seem like common sense, these guidelines ran directly against the principles of normal cargo storage at the time, which emphasised the efficient use of space to load as much material as possible. While there were some lessons the USMC could only learn after entering combat, these tentative steps ensured that they would enter the Second World War with a firm foundation.

- **Submarines** – the Submarine Flotilla Board requested a 1,000 ton vessel with enough speed and range to keep up with the battleship fleet in 1912. Wargames by the US Naval War College thereafter suggested they could act rather like a forward minefield, disrupting the enemy's movements. The First World War proved that they could also be a useful weapon in attacking a country's commercial shipping and although such use was banned under the 1922 Washington Naval Accords, naval planners still considered submarines to be of use in naval actions, as well as useful scout vessels. Therefore, in contrast to their European counterparts, American planners made range and longevity a major engineering consideration, something that would prove useful when President Roosevelt ordered US submarines to counterattack against the Japanese surface fleet and practice unrestricted submarine warfare, only six hours of being told about the raid on Pearl Harbor.[25]

- **Joint Planning** – as already explained, the Pacific Theatre differed from its European counterpart in that land, air and naval combat were all as important as one another and in order to be successful, commanders had to coordinate their actions in all three spheres. Since, in the majority of cases, ground and air forces were reliant on sea lines of communication, the impact of joint operations and therefore logistics cannot be understated. Early operations such as Watchtower (Guadalcanal) brought home the difficulties of joint operations, but at least the US Armed Forces had not only a basic competency, but a basic structure with which to work. The US Army and Navy relied (remembering that at this point, the air force was a part of the army) on a body called the Joint Board to coordinate military activity, until the creation of the Joint Chiefs of Staff in 1942. It could however, only make decisions based on unanimity among its members and was on certain issues therefore, deadlocked. As the possibility of war in the Pacific loomed however, it swung into action, initially by casting aside War Plan Orange in favour of an altogether more pessimistic view of what would be needed. A year later, the Army Chief of Staff (General Malin Craig) commissioned the Board to look at the relationship of strategic air power to warfare in the Pacific. His successor, General George C. Marshall, placed additional emphasis on the support requirements for such air forces.[26]

However, one complicating factor was, at the time of the attack on Pearl Harbor, no overarching theatre command organisation existed in the Pacific. In fact, there were four commands – one Army (Lt General Jonathan M. Wainwright, succeeded by General Douglas MacArthur) and one Navy (Admiral Thomas C. Hart) in the Philippines along with one Army (Lt General Walter Short) and one Navy (Admiral Husband E. Kimmel) in Hawaii. Prior to war, the four commands had operated more-or-less independently and joint planning between them was the exception rather than the rule (unlike the Joint Board above) but with the war starting, it was obvious that unity of command would be a necessity in order to prosecute the war effectively. The Pacific had traditionally been a Navy domain, but a complicating factor was that with the fall of the Philippines, MacArthur had ended up in Australia. Being senior to virtually all the flag officers in the theatre and a national hero to boot, there was strong pressure to make him the overall Pacific theatre commander. The Navy naturally resisted this and after a great deal of wrangling, a compromise was reached whereby Admiral Chester W. Nimitz (who had succeeded Kimmel) became Commander-in-Chief Pacific Ocean Area (CINCPOA) with three subordinate commands – North Pacific, Central Pacific and South Pacific – whereas MacArthur was made Commander-in-Chief Southwest Pacific.[27] While this arrangement managed to traverse the inter-service rivalry and politics of the time, it led to a ". . . duplication of effort and keen competition for the limited supplies of ships, landing craft and airplanes."[28]

War Erupts

Photograph showing (from left to right) the battleships USS West Virginia, USS Tennessee and USS Arizona after the attack on Pearl Harbor, 7 December 1941 (Source: US Navy via Wikimedia Commons)

The Japanese attacked the US Pacific Fleet at their anchorage in Pearl Harbor, Hawaii on 7 December 1941.[29] Shortly after Pearl Harbor, both Germany and Italy declared war on the USA and at the famous Washington Summit between Churchill and Roosevelt, it was decided that the Allies would pursue a 'Europe First' policy, while maintaining something of a holding action in the Pacific. Such a strategy had been embodied in the American Rainbow 5 plan proposed by Admiral Stark in 1940 and agreed to by Marshall, being endorsed by the Joint Board in January 1941 and confirmed with the British. There was however, a certain pressure (from Congress, the public and certain sections of the military) to take some form of offensive action in the Pacific and keep to a very loose definition of 'holding action', if not 'limited offensive'. This meant that there was significant degree of competition between theatres for scarce resources, especially in the latter stages of the war when both theatres saw extensive offensive operations by the Allies.[30]

An early priority after Pearl Harbor was to contain the Japanese advance as far as possible and to protect Australia and New Zealand. To this end, over 75,000 US troops were deployed in the first few months of 1942 (two divisions to Australia, one to New Zealand), a major logistics base was built and advanced bases prepared at such places as New Caledonia and Espiritu Santo on the New Hebrides. While there were plans to build Australia up the same way as the UK was built up to be a major staging area and logistics base for the campaign in Northwest Europe, the vast geography and lack of an adequate road and rail infrastructure prevented that from happening, although Australia did become the lynchpin in the defence of the Southwest Pacific.[31]

While the US Navy was intellectually prepared for the logistic challenges they would face, materially they were less so. The two most critical needs in this area were shipping and advanced bases. The naval strategy of the 1930s had emphasised the need for such bases but no new bases had been built west of Pearl Harbor and the US had forsaken its right to fortify islands in the Western Pacific by signing the Washington Naval Treaty of 1922. In addition, the fleet had not procured nearly enough logistics ships to keep its vessels supplied while at sea. Although the Pacific Fleet's move to Pearl Harbor had highlighted the vital nature of the base force, supply ships only numbered sixty-one in 1941.[32] This shortage is made even more acute when measured against the growth in combat ships when compared to logistics ships. Between 1925 and 1940, the number of destroyers, cruisers and aircraft carriers grew at a rate of more than twice that of logistics ships. In 1940, President Roosevelt authorised the construction of over 125 combat vessels, as compared to twelve support vessels. This was because in peacetime, it was difficult for the Navy to gauge exactly how many support ships were required, so it tended to invest in more tangible assets of naval power. The outbreak of war however, quickly re-balanced the Navy's priorities and by 1945, the base force had expanded to some 315 vessels and the total number involved in naval logistics numbered in the thousands.[33]

Additionally, the joint Army-Navy War Plans of 1941 had assigned the Navy the primary responsibility for sea transportation, with WPI-46 of May 1941 stating the Navy was to "provide sea transportation for the initial movement and continued support of Army and Navy forces overseas. Man and operate the Army Transport Service."[34] Unfortunately, this task was based upon the experience of World War I, mainly a single-theatre war (at least for the United States) with the full availability of the British merchant fleet. The requirements of World War II shipping would be very different, with the tasks facing the US merchant fleet in World War II including:[35]

- Logistic support to forces overseas;
- Lend-Lease shipments to Allies;
- Shipments to sustain Allied populations;

- Imports of raw materials to the United States;
- Normal Western Hemisphere commercial trade.

The upshot of all this was that the Navy simply did not have enough transport and supply ships to handle all these competing requirements, with the majority of its support ships assigned to fleet support, and to cap it all, didn't have enough personnel to man the ships assigned to the Army Transportation Service (which they were reluctant to anyway, given the condition of the ships). To be fair, the Navy had already begun to look at this issue as early as September 1939 when they established Port Directors at the principle US ports to procure (along with the Maritime Commission) merchant vessels to fill emergency Navy requirements. The lack of any centralised control however, led to the formation of the War Shipping Administration in February 1942 which placed the control of all US merchant shipping under one authority.[36] Confronted with this shortage, American strategists revised their requirements and set about massively expanding the numbers of support ships available, but until they started coming online, Nimitz was forced to constrain his actions and so rather than operate in two large fleets as required by pre-war plans, he operated a number of smaller task groups or task forces, which began a series of raids on Japanese bases such as the Gilbert and Marshall Islands, Wake Island, Marcus Island, Rabaul, New Guinea and in April 1942, on Tokyo itself (the famous Doolittle Raid). Without some form of underway replenishment, none of these raids would have been possible, and with each one, the US Navy improved the logistical techniques it would use to support its offensive in the Central Pacific.[37]

The United States had already gained some experiencing in establishing additional bases in the Caribbean, Canada and Atlantic with the 1940 'Destroyers for Bases' deal with the UK. The US was also planning bases in Scotland and Northern Ireland as part of the Lend-Lease Act of 1941, as well as a base on the Galapagos Islands off Ecuador. The site for a refuelling station was selected on the island of Bora Bora (French Society Islands) during December 1941 and an expedition put together which sailed in January 1942. Despite encountering considerable difficulties and revealing many of the planning and administrative problems that still plagued US logistics (inter-service communications broke down, a number of units arrived at the port of embarkation with their equipment uncrated, the equipment that was crated often didn't have labels, proper maps were not available, much of the equipment was unsuitable or packed in such a way as to be almost impossible to unload, and the Navy Construction battalions were not fully trained)[38] there were many important lessons learned, and the United States soon began to construct new bases on Samoa, the New Hebrides and New Caledonia, all of which proved vital to contain the Japanese in the Central Pacific and protect the lines of communication to Australia. As the war progressed however, the use of these bases gradually evolved. Early on, they were of use to the Navy but as the Navy became adept at at-sea resupply techniques, task groups and forces became less dependent on them. As the American counter-offensive rolled across the Pacific, they became useful staging areas for future operations and as American forces approached the Japanese Home Islands, the bases could be used to launch strategic bombing raids against key targets and enabled the Submarine Force to move its logistic support base from Pearl Harbor to Guam which allowed it to strike into Japanese home waters.[39]

The confusion in that early expedition to Bora Bora was due to both the Army and Navy having almost completely separate logistic systems, even down to having separate ports of embarkation, a situation complicated by the fact that the Army had its own shipping, and the Army Air Force and Naval Aviation had their own systems for both procurement and supply. While some progress had been made (the Army had begun to procure small arms ammunition for both services and the Army-Navy Munitions Board had been established to produce plans for industrial mobilisation) there was little effort to coordinate activity and avoid waste and duplication of effort. Furthermore, it would be another three years before any sort of real coordination was attempted.[40] The logistics organisations for both services were very different, and to top that, a significant amount of logistics planning was still carried out by the War Plans Divisions of the individual service staffs. In the Army, the

". . . lack of effective top-level coordination and the dispersion of procurement and supply activities . . . once again threatened to delay the service and supply of the Army as mobilization measures quickened after Pearl Harbor. As had been the case in 1917, the demands of war revealed serious weaknesses in the organizational machinery. There was, in fact no machinery for the close coordination of the whole logistics area anywhere below the Secretary of War himself."[41]

The situation was further complicated by the Army Air Corps who were agitating for increased autonomy. Therefore, in March 1942, the War Department underwent a major reorganisation which included the establishment of the Army Service Forces under General Brehon B. Somervell, based upon the First World War logistics organisation for General Pershing's American Expeditionary Force. Whilst this improved the overall direction, with the supply services taking many of the functions undertaken by the G-4, much of the logistics planning function was subsumed within the War Plans Division of the Army General Staff. In the case of the Navy, much of its logistics planning during the First World

War had been done by the Technical Bureaus under the Secretary of the Navy, while the position of Chief of Naval Operations was not created until 1915. Logistics planning and the setting of requirements were not established under a Deputy Chief of Naval Operations (for Logistics) until the Second World War. The logistics staff however, continued to a great extent, to rely on the Technical Bureaus, in close cooperation with the strategic plans division, for the determination of logistics requirements.[42] Despite this, the Chief of Naval Operations (Admiral Ernest J. King) and the Chief of Staff of the Army (Marshall) saw the need for greater coordination. Marshall redesignated the Army Supply and Services Command as the Army Service Forces and greatly expanded their role (as above) while King tasked his Vice Chief of Naval Operations (Vice Admiral Frederick J. Horne) with the responsibility for the Navy's logistics planning, procurement and distribution services. Horne and Somervell worked closely together for the remainder of the war. The issue of a unified logistics system came up at regular intervals, at the Joint Chiefs level, all the way down to the sub-theatre level.[43] What eventually came to pass, shows how agreements at the higher levels were implemented according to the unique characteristics of each particular theatre:[44]

Admiral Ernest J King
(Source: US Navy via
Wikimedia Commons)

Pacific Theatre – After 1943, the main logistics organisation under Admiral Nimitz was the J4 Section of the Command-in-Chief Pacific's (CINCPAC) Staff and the Service Force Pacific Fleet. The Service Force was responsible for implementing all the US Navy's logistics plans, except for Naval Air and the USMC who had their own logistics organisations. The US Army's plans were put into practise by the component Army Service Forces Command. During 1942 and much of 1943 however, matters of joint logistics and supply were handled pretty much on an ad hoc basis by logistics commands at the CINCPAC level. Initially, it was matters arising out of the establishment and development of advanced supply bases that generated the initial need to look at matters of joint logistics. In essence, the US Navy exercised operational control but each service was still responsible for its own logistics, so problems started to arise at bases that were garrisoned by the US Army. Administration of the army's logistics was shared between the War Department, the Port of San Francisco, the Hawaiian Department and even USAFIA (US Army Forces in Australia) was involved in some way. In the early stages of the war, the only functioning major US Army command was the Hawaiian Department under Lt General Delos C. Emmons, which was given a lot of responsibility for establishing island bases by the War Department. Much of this responsibility was handed out on a ad hoc and piecemeal basis, a situation complicated by the fact that until June 1942, there was no South Pacific Area Commander actually in the post.[45] In July 1942, the US Army established a separate command in the South Pacific under Major General Millard Harmon as Commander, US Army Forces South Pacific Area (USAFSPA), who also happened to be the Chief of the Air Staff under Vice Admiral Robert L. Ghormley, and was responsible to the War Department for the administration and supply of Army forces in that area, but exercised no operational command, assisting Commander, South Pacific (COMSOPAC) with planning. This new command separated these forces from both the Central Pacific and USAFIA.[46] There had however, been some consideration as to a joint logistics system by the Joint Chiefs in early 1942. Joint Purchasing Boards were established in both Australia and New Zealand to take advantage of local resources and to avoid duplication. They also asked the theatre commanders about the desirability of a joint supply system and the possibility of pooling transport resources (in this case, mainly shipping). Nimitz suggested a joint system for the South Pacific (SOPAC) area (under the command of COMSOPAC) linked to the Service Squadron South Pacific and a joint supply base in Auckland, New Zealand, which would include shared access to shipping and storage facilities, while purchasing would be governed by a joint agreement with inter-service coordination. Major General Eammons supported Nimitz's proposal but it was rejected by the US Army due to it having its own shipping, plus it had just established the Army Service Forces and was concerned over the capacity of the Navy's logistics system.[47] The issue was once again examined towards the end of 1942 and an agreement eventually worked out between Somervell and Horne generally followed Nimitz's recommendations and was entitled the 'Joint Logistical Plan for the Support of United States Bases in the South Pacific Area' and included provisions that the:[48]

- Army provided rations to personnel based onshore (except Samoa) which could not otherwise be obtained through the Joint Purchasing Board;

- Navy provided all the fuel;
- Navy provided all locally purchased items through the Joint Purchasing Board, including clothes, construction materials and food;
- Services request items not available from the other sources through their parent services.

Southwest Pacific Theatre – since this theatre was Army dominated, joint logistics did not really become an issue for the first two years. Priorities were generally dictated by General MacArthur and although it was a joint staff, it was treated as an army staff. In addition, the majority if army units coming into the theatre headed for Australia, with MacArthur being charged with the country's defence and the creation of an infrastructure to support future offensive operations. Despite the Army Service Forces establishing a major command for the theatre, in reality it had much less authority than initially envisaged, with much of its supply activity limited to bases in Australia and New Guinea. Because shipping and logistics supply priorities were controlled by General MacArthur, there was some confusion between those commanding the supply services and the CINC's staff regarding exactly who was responsible for what.[49]

Operation Watchtower

The American victory at the Battle for Midway[50] made it possible for US forces to think about taking the offensive in the Pacific War. During early 1942, the Allies had been reluctant to devote resources to such an undertaking as there had been plans to launch an invasion of Europe later in 1942, a plan known as Operation Sledgehammer, and there were shortages in equipment to undertake amphibious operations.[51] When the Allies abandoned Sledgehammer, MacArthur won approval for his offensive. Up until the landing were launched, the services had generally focused their efforts on their own areas of competence, with the US Navy concentrating on a defensive battle to stop further Japanese expansion and the US Army concentrating on establishing Australia as a base of operations and ensuring its survival. After Midway, a limited offensive could be conducted to stop Japan's advance through the Soloman Islands, which included the building of airbases on Tulugi and Guadalcanal, the completion of which would extend Japan's reach throughout the area and allow them to strike at the US ports on New Caledonia and the Fiji Islands.[52] However, no other early operation quite brought into focus the existing logistics problems as Watchtower did. Guadalcanal was to the first American amphibious operation of the war, the first test of amphibious doctrine developed by the USMC and US Navy during the inter-war years, and the initial indoctrination to modern amphibious operations for the US Navy. The naval battles around the Solomon Islands were some of the last clashes between fleets of capital ships with the area of sea off Guadalcanal nicknamed Iron Bottom Sound.[53]

MacArthur had wanted an attack on the Japanese base at Rabaul, but this lay well beyond the range of Allied land-based air power and would have had to rely on carrier air power to support it. The US Navy considered the US Carrier Fleet would have taken unacceptable losses and forced MacArthur into a more cautious strategy, with the initial target Tulagi, being quickly superseded by Guadalcanal after Admiral Kelly Turner had become concerned that the Japanese were building an airbase there. Indeed, when Admiral Nimitz issued the orders for Watchtower, it left only a few weeks for the staff officers to plan the logistics.

This lack of time began to cause problems right from the start. The 1st Marine Division was already on the way to the Southwest Pacific when it received its orders. The Quartermaster had not expected the Marines to go directly into battle and so had not loaded all of the transports ready for combat. This meant that twelve of the ships had to stop at Wellington, New Zealand to have their stores repacked. The quay at Wellington could only hold five ships at a time, so this led to a delay of seven days. As mentioned previously, 'combat loading' takes up far more room on a ship than packing for normal transport and so the division had to leave behind seventy-five percent of its vehicles, fifty percent of its ammunition and thirty-three percent of its rations.[54] Dedicated shipping would not be available to the USMC until late 1943[55] and so up until then, the Marines would have to make do with chartered commercial shipping, which for obvious reasons, could not approach the shore. The Marines therefore had to transport both the combat troops and their supplies from the ships to the beach using the limited number of landing craft available.

Thankfully, the landing on Guadalcanal went unopposed and the 1st Marine Division captured the partially completed airfield with plenty of construction equipment and supplies. The Japanese however started counterattacking by land, sea and air within forty-eight hours of the landing, all while the shore parties were struggling to unload the materiel and get it ashore. The situation was made worse with the fact that the sailors were unloading the supplies and equipment faster than it could be moved off the beach, and so by the end of the first day, around 100 boats were on the shore, all waiting to be processed. This highlighted the necessity of having specialised amphibious transportation assets as the shore parties could have worked more efficiently if the boats had been fitted with ramps, while the few available amphibian tractors proved invaluable.[56] Japanese naval action led to the withdrawal of the US task force and while the Navy tried to get as much equipment and supplies off as possible, the transports still left with the combat transports ten percent full and the remainder around seventy-five percent full. The Marines were stranded with only about half of their food supply and very little heavy or specialised equipment.[57] Without captured food, the Marines would have starved and only had enough ammunition for about four days heavy fighting.[58] Supply shortages would prove to be as big a bane for the Marines as enemy action – almost a week passed before fast moving US destroyers delivered additional supplies and over a month passed before the Marines could return to a normal diet.[59] It wasn't until February 1943 that the Americans could declare a victory in the campaign.[60]

US reinforcements land on Guadalcanal via a Higgins Boat (Source: USMC via Wikimedia Commons)

Operation Watchtower brought the early logistical problems into sharp focus. Many of the logistics problems associated with Guadalcanal resulted from decision taken outside of the South Pacific Area and came from a lack of appreciation as to the logistics situation. The naval elements associated with advanced bases began to request and receive their logistic support directly from agencies in the USA, rather than through CINCPAC while the Army directed its forces were to be supplied directly from their Port of Embarkation at San Francisco. Therefore no-one had joint logistics support at the advanced bases and each service used its own procedures. While the Joint Logistics Plan had been agreed to in July, it was only just starting to be implemented when Watchtower took place. While a supply base had been established at Auckland, New Zealand, it meant there was a very long supply chain leading from San Francisco to Auckland and another one leading from Auckland to Guadalcanal, this one being around fifty percent longer for than the equivalent Japanese supply chain from their nearest advanced base. The situation was made more complex with the base at Noumea, New Caledonia being inadequate for large-scale operations and things didn't start to get better until the base at Espiritu Santo became fully operational in February 1943.[61]

Despite all the things that had gone wrong with the logistic support afforded Operation Watchtower, in the overall scheme of things, they were relatively minor. Ultimately, the Americans had got the 'big things' right, although if the Japanese had taken full advantage of the American's problems then the campaign could have ended in disaster. A telling directive came from President Roosevelt, who, after seeing a series of reports from General 'Hap' Arnold to General Marshall, told the Joint Chiefs to make every effort to support the US forces holding Guadalcanal. If the USA had not planned for long-range logistics during a conflict in the Pacific, if it had not developed a system of amphibious warfare, drawn the Battle of the Coral Sea and won the Battle of Midway and established a string of bases between California and Australia, the counterattack in the Pacific would not have even gotten off the ground.

Learning Lessons

The lessons of the Guadalcanal campaign centred on the importance of planning, coordination and procedure, as well as the duplication and waste caused by separate supply systems. This caused the issue of a joint supply system to be revisited in early 1943, with the Army pushing for a unified logistics system as poor planning, preparation and teamwork had meant that US forces had run unacceptable risks at both Bora Bora and Guadalcanal. Brigadier Leroy Lutes (Somervell's deputy) recommended that

". . . a unified Services of Supply be organized in all theaters for the supply of Army, Navt and Marine forces ashore, and that a unified control of cargo shipping, exclusive of those vessels normally under the fleet commander for supply for vessels afloat be established for the supply of both fleet and shore forces."[62]

Somervell agreed and also proposed that given seventy-five to ninety per cent of forces deployed abroad were US Army, the officer commanding the single supply service also be Army. The Navy objected, preferring merely close coordination. The argument came down to who exactly would control the shipping and shipping priorities. Even while the Marines were fighting on Guadalcanal, the Navy's supply system was evolving during late 1942 / early 1943[63] and was becoming far more decentralised than the Army's with the Navy's system geared towards fleet support and the Army's towards support forces ashore. Essentially the Army's was more structured while the Navy's was more flexible. The end result was that Admiral King and General Marshal issued a directive entitled *Basic Logistical Plan for Command Areas Involving Joint Army and Navy Operations* on 8 March 1943 which instructed that logistics organisations in areas of joint Navy and Army operations be brought under unified command and that theatre commanders organise joint logistics staffs; establish unified supply systems; determine joint personnel and material requirements; prepare consolidated shipping priority lists.[64] Immediately afterwards, Admirals Nimitz and Halsey organised Joint Logistics Boards where Navy and Army officers shared authority over planning.[65] The end result was that CINCPAC's joint logistics procedures in support of amphibious operations in the Central Pacific were the most advanced.

There were still problems however. The Army were pressurising Nimitz to delegate control of the Central Pacific sub-theatre and General Robert C. Richardson Jr, who had succeeded General Delos C. Emmons in taking over the Hawaiian Department and then Commander, Army Forces Central Pacific in August 1943 supported jointness, only so long as it didn't impinge on Army prerogatives. There was therefore no unified logistics system in the Hawaiian area but logistics integration did occur in many forward operating areas and Nimitz's logistics staff was described by one senior officer as the most competent group he had ever worked with[66] and has been described as the only "truly functioning theatre joint staff of the war" serving as a model of later joint staffs.[67] Despite the on-going reorganisations, a number of themes were to recur throughout the war, including:[68]

- A chronic tension between the importance of centralised planning and the requirement of lower-level formations to have flexibility to cope with unforeseen events (as mentioned above);
- The ever-present problems of inter-service rivalry and poor communication (as mentioned above);
- The problem of creating a concrete link between strategic planning and planning the means to carry out that strategy. As Ballantine suggests, logistic plans should be "the link, in short, between the definition of strategic aims and intentions and the execution of plans for the procurement, assembly and delivery of material."[69]

The J4 section of the CINCPAC staff, which replaced the committee system, was directed by Major General Edmond H. Leavey and consisted of:[70]

- J41 – Transportation and Priorities
- J42 – Petrol, Oil, Lubricants (POL)
- J43 – Supply
- J44 – Planning
- J45 – Medical
- J46 – Construction
- J47 – Administration and Statistics

Two branches of the Operations Directorate (J3), Combat Readiness and Communications, were responsible for planning the requirements for ammunition and communications equipment. The direction of logistics planning was now handled by CINCPAC headquarters. Both it and the highly capable Service Force Pacific Fleet (SFPF) evolved due to the necessities of the Pacific campaign – through 1942 the emphasis had been on supporting SOPAC and the battle for Guadalcanal but by early 1943, "a reasonable effective system of logistics coordination existed at the local level in the South Pacific area."[71]

In the Southwest Pacific Theatre, the issue of logistics coordination wasn't as chronic as it was done at the top level via 'centralised planning' rather than at the operational level. As a result, very little of the *Basic Logistics Plan* was reflected in General MacArthur's organisation and few if any changes made to the system of supply at the time. The services each maintained their own system of supply, supported by General MacArthur who determined overall priorities. The Seventh Fleet was supported by Service Force Seventh Fleet (SFSF) while the Army was supported by the Army Service Forces Command for that area. Local sourcing was used as much as possible while the Army provided the USMC with much of its supply, except those items that were unique to the Corps. As in several other areas of the Pacific, the Army provided shore-based personnel with food, while the Navy provided fuel. The Navy also provided support (including spare parts) for the landing craft used by Army amphibious units. One unusual aspect of the area was that it featured a large amount of local shipping of various types, including Dutch, Australian and local vessels – some Army manned, some Navy manned.[72]

In the South Pacific area, the issue of inter-service coordination was more pronounced, as the US Navy and US Army were there in roughly even numbers. Admiral Halsey's preferred answer was for each service to rely on its own sources of supply and undertake local cross-servicing agreements for common items. Admiral Nimitz wanted a more joint approach, so issued a Base Logistics Plan for the area in April 1943 that provided for a Joint Logistics Board with representatives from various component commands. In early 1944, a fully joint logistics staff was established in the SOPAC area with the system of cross-servicing refined, including:

- The Army providing both fresh and dry provisions;
- The Army operating cold storage plants;
- The Navy delivering fresh provisions in refrigerator ships;
- The operation of base repair facilities split between the two;
- The establishment of common stocks of vehicle spares and some types of ammunition;
- The Navy continued to provide fuel;
- The Navy controlled all the shipping within the theatre (although some harbour craft were operated by the Army).

In addition to improving administrative procedures, US forces were faced with a raft of material improvements to the logistics situation. Whereas in 1943-44 the US Army committed one-third of its strength to the Pacific and two-thirds to Europe, the major build up in the Pacific was by the US Navy. Most of the heavy combatant ships went there, as the Atlantic mainly needed destroyers and other anti-submarine vessels, while the older cruisers and battleships could handle the gunfire support needed for amphibious operations. Carrier aviation also played only a small role due to the availability of airfields in both the UK and North Africa.[73] By early 1943, American dockyards had begun to produce ships in staggering quantities and the support services started to receive their share of the new vessels. By the end of the year, the ships available for action had increased almost five-fold, from seventy-seven to 358.[74] This made it possible for the Navy to support major fleet actions and amphibious assaults without the need for either nearby bases or risky improvisations such as at Coral Sea or Guadalcanal. The first major amphibious operation to be supported exclusively by fleet train was Operation Galvanic, the attack by the 2nd Marine Division on the island of Betio, part of the Tarawa Atoll in November 1943.[75] Amphibious transportation improved dramatically after Guadalcanal. By the end of 1942, the production of landing craft and amphibious tractors has increased by a factor of twenty.[76] In addition, British designers had invented several new types of landing craft, due to the British Government's interest in not only landing infantry, but tanks, artillery and other heavy equipment directly onto the beach and the Americans quickly organised a production programme after Pearl Harbor. Among these vessels were:[77]

- LST (Landing Ship, Tank) – this was a 300-foot seagoing vessel that could carry over 2,000 tons of cargo in its huge hold but had a shallow draft that would allow it to land directly on, or very close to, a beach, and disgorge its cargo through bow doors and a ramp. Its slow speed and limited manoeuvrability led sailors to christen it the 'large stationary target' but the Americans were soon adding extra weapons to complement its armament, such as rockets and anti-aircraft guns. It could also carry secondary craft, such as the LCT or LCVP.

- LCI (Landing Craft, Infantry) – smaller, but faster and more manoeuvrable than the LST, this craft could carry almost 200 troops and over thirty tons of cargo, disgorged its cargo down gangways hinged to a platform attach to the bow.

- LCT (Landing Craft, Tank) – this vessel was even smaller than the LCI at 120-feet long, but had a bow ramp that could disgorge either medium tanks or heavy vehicles straight onto the beach.

- LCVP (Landing Craft, Vehicles and Personnel) – had a large bow door, over which thirty-six troops or a single 2.5-ton truck could exit onto the beach.

- LVT (Landing Vehicle, Tracked) – was a tracked amphibious vehicle that could pull itself out of the water and onto the beach using its rubber tracks. Also known as the AMTRAC, early versions could prove unreliable but were to prove invaluable.

All of these vessels were larger than the craft the Marines had had previously, and when the conditions were calm enough and shore conditions suitable, could carry their loads directly to the shore without the time-consuming need to transfer men and material from the transport to the smaller craft.

Coast Guard-manned LSTs during unloading operations on Leyte, 1944 (Source: US Government via Wikimedia Commons)

Taking the Offensive

In March 1943, a military conference was held in Hawaii to determine the objectives for the coming year. Admiral Halsey (South Pacific) was given the task of advancing up the Solomon Islands as far as Bougainville. General MacArthur (Southwest Pacific) was to occupy the northern coast of New Guinea as far as Madang and Cape Gloucester on the island of New Britain. The final objective of these two converging thrusts would be the main Japanese base at Rabaul on New Britain. This operation was given the codename of Cartwheel and would last from June 1943 to March 1944. Key to this were advanced bases and airfields, including both Guadalcanal and Tulagi. Admiral Halsey's forces conducted operations against New Georgia, Vella Lavella, Arundel Island, the Treasury Islands, Erimau Island and Bougainville. MacArthur attacked along the northern coast of New Guinea, as well as Cape Gloucester, New Britain and

Manus Island in the Admiralties. Manus would later become a key base for operations against the Philippines.

In the Central Pacific theatre, Admiral Nimitz had faced a key problem – there were no islands between Pearl Harbor and the objectives (Gilbert, Marshall and Caroline Islands) that could be turned into advanced bases for the operations. For example, Espiritu Santo was over 1,000 miles from Tarawa and Tarawa was 2,100 miles from Pearl Harbor with the challenge being to supply the Gilbert Islands after capture as well as preparing for the following operation against the Marshall Islands.[78] The solution was a mobile logistics base. Under the able direction of Vice-Admiral William L. Calhoun (Commander, Service Force Pacific Fleet) Service Squadron 4 was created and commissioned on 1 November 1943 just before the Marshall Islands operation began. While the atolls of the Central Pacific rarely provided any sort of infrastructure ashore, except space for potential airfields, they often provided excellent protected anchorages for the mobile logistics bases and fleet support units and were valuable as staging areas. This of course, was true for both the USA and Japan, for example, Ulithi Atoll in the Carolines provided a suitable fleet anchorage for the US Navy, as did Truk for the Imperial Navy. The mobile base had enough food to supply 20,000 personnel for thirty days and enough fuel for fifteen days and while the campaign for the Gilberts was underway, fleet oilers could operate unescorted outside the range of Japanese aircraft but for the Marshalls campaign, they had to be escorted.[79]

While the planners for Operation Galvanic attempted to learn the lessons from Guadalcanal, the US would suffer one more near-fiasco before they would perfect the art of getting supplies ashore on a hostile beach. While naval commanders committed themselves to providing more protection for the transport fleet and shore parties were aware of the need to get supplies unloaded quickly, the procedures in place failed to provide the troops with the equipment they needed fast enough.[80] At Tarawa, the US commanders gambled that the morning tide would be high enough to allow the amphibious vessels to pass over the reefs which lay just beneath the waves in front of the beach. This didn't happen and so the landing craft had to disgorge their troops and cargo into chest-high water, a half-mile from the beach. Luckily, Japanese defensive fire remained light during the early part of the day but by the time the third wave of Marines had begun to move ashore, the garrison had decided to defend itself properly and so the landing became a bloodbath. Transport craft had to circle the lagoon waiting for the tide to rise and while some supplies were landed at a pier, they had to be moved solely by hand.[81]

While one cannot blame the logisticians for the tide, and in fact they did an admirable job of getting supplies ashore despite the difficulties, they failed to take into account the Marines' actual needs. The Marines required ammunition, water, medical supplies and heavy weapons on that first day, and very little else. Despite the theory of combat loading being well known and the lessons of Guadalcanal being fresh in the memory, these supplies were not always the initial ones to reach the shoreline. In addition, the Marines, when ashore, had no effective way of communicating their needs with the shore parties. What saved the day were the amphibious tractors (Amtracs), vital for both assaulting the beach and bringing up supplies as they could cross the coral reefs with relative ease. The Marines took 125 Amtracs with them but they needed many more – as combat units became engaged and needed reinforcements and replacements, supplies just had to wait.[82]

After Tarawa, US Navy and USMC commanders subjected their logistics procedures to even more reform, in the run up to the invasion of the Marshall Islands. Admiral R. Kelly Turner insured that sailors and shore parties would train together on the same ship they would use in combat. A palletised system of ammunition supply was developed that made handling quicker plus the USMC doubled the number of Amtracs available to each division to 325 per division. The US Army contributed 100 amphibious vehicles of their own model, the DUKW. The DUKW proved able to carry artillery pieces directly to the shore, solving one of the problems encountered on Tarawa. The Army also introduced something called 'hot cargo', a system of combat loading that included having forty DUKWs already loaded with supplies.[83] It was thanks to these additional measures that the assault on the Marshall Islands proved so successful. The logisticians managed to unload over two divisions worth of supplies without any unexpected delays and while there was a shortage of storage space of the beach, they managed to get around the problem by commandeering an LST and using it as a floating warehouse and storing thousands of barrels of fuel in cargo nets just offshore. In just twelve days, the support ships were completely unloaded and ready for the next operation – the assault on Rabaul.[84]

With offensive operations starting to ramp up in both the European and Pacific Theatres, one problem that would become increasingly acute was the shortage of shipping. Despite the massive increase in US production, it took time for the new ships to become available and there were significant material losses to replace due to action of German U-Boats in the Atlantic, U-Boats and aircraft in the convoy runs to Murmansk, as well as Japanese submarines and aircraft in the Pacific. In addition, it simply took more shipping capacity to move and maintain ground forces in the Pacific than it did Europe. For example, a force of 40,000 troops in Australia required nearly as much shipping capacity as a force of 100,000 troops in the UK. The distances involved and the wide dispersion of forces in the Pacific also mitigated against the creation of central stock reserves and a systematic flow of supplies through depots.[85] In order to continue the Central Pacific campaign, larger amphibious assault shipping was needed, in particular Attack Transport ships (APAs) and Attack Cargo ships (AKAs) for the long distances involved, plus more of the landing ships, such as LSTs and LCVPs, and the Amtracs. The shortage was felt at Bougainville, where Halsey was only able to lift one division as it was being conducted at the same time as the operation against the Gilbert Islands. This competition only intensified in early 1944, as the drive across the Pacific was progressing faster than anticipated at the same time as the Allies were in the final stages of the build-up for Operation Overlord, the invasion of Normandy. In addition, there was competition between MacArthur and Nimitz in the Central and Southwest Pacific Theatres. These simultaneous campaigns in the Pacific was a result of the compromise by the Joint Chiefs of Staff in not assigning a single overall commander in the Pacific (as there was in Europe) and granting equal status to both MacArthur and Nimitz. Indeed, the

". . . central direction of the war was not characterised by hard decisions . . .the committee procedures of the Joint Chiefs of Staff resulted in a strategy of opportunism where it was easier to agree on specific operations as opportunity presented than it was to agree upon a consistent grand design . . . Faced with dilemmas growing out of limitations of resources, when no decision could have satisfied everybody but when a clear-cut decision on priorities . . . might have seemed desirable . . . the Joint Chiefs at times had a tendency to fight the problem, such as accepting over optimistic assumptions about the availability of shipping rather than make a firm choice."[86]

The other great shortage was in Army logistics personnel. Although Europe had an extensive well-developed infrastructure, it would still require large numbers of personnel given that the majority of the Army's combat divisions would be fighting there. The Pacific needed large numbers (despite having virtually the entire US Marine Corps and the Navy's Seabees) as the continued advances were leaving behind islands that needed to be garrisoned and their infrastructure either repaired or developed almost from scratch. Also, in early 1944, seven new divisions were in the process of being transferred to the theatre, bringing the total to twenty divisions, with six in the Central Pacific and fourteen in the Southwest Pacific. These extra divisions all needed transportation and logistic support.

US Navy Seabees unloading cargo onto a landing beach on Iwo Jima, February 1945 (Source: US Navy via Flickr)

The Steamroller Starts Moving

After 1943, US forces in the Pacific Theatre started to launch larger and larger offensives, further and further from their bases. Supplies continually flowed to the frontline and the reforms of the early war years were vindicated. The following points can be made about the logistics of the later campaigns:[87]

- *Large-scale operations conducted at great distances from ports had become routine.* For example, the campaign of the Marshal Islands "took place over 2,500 miles from its base at Hawaii, and many of its ships had come all the way from San Diego. This operation involved twelve carriers, eight battleships and over 355 other vessels, in addition to 1,175 aircraft. The invasion force's amphibious landing ships, which were useful in so many ways, turned out to have enough excess oil capacity to refuel the all of the fleet's minesweepers, minelayers, submarine chasers and other smaller vessels during the voyage."[88]

- *Landing troops, equipment and supplies became quicker and more efficiently done.* For example, during the invasion Biak Island in June 1944, the Americans managed to land 12,000 troops, tanks, artillery and over 3,000 tons of supplies in one day.

- *The US Navy was increasingly able to support entire operations using its mobile service squadrons.* For example, the Cairo Conference in November 1943 decided that the main advance against Japan would be via the Pacific. As a consequence, it was important that the Mariana Islands be taken to provide bases for the new B-29 bombers to begin a strategic bombing campaign against Japan. At the start of the Marianas campaign therefore, the Americans concentrated twenty-five aircraft carriers, fourteen battleships, 496 other vessels, 2,000 aircraft and 127,500 ground troops with the US Navy supplying the entire operation using its mobile service squadrons. Even when both ships and ground force exhausted the available ammunition supplies quicker than expected, the logisticians manage to keep them supplied.

- *The development of major air and naval bases became quicker.* Once Guam had been secured in July 1944, the Americans built air and naval bases there with both Army and Navy personnel completing the work in good time and without any significant interruption.

- *The US Navy had fully implemented the concept of 'mobile basing'.* The fleet of logistics vessels the US Navy built up allowed "the support squadrons to repair warships and stockpile supplies in relatively undeveloped ports. Therefore, when the fighting moved into new areas, the Navy's bases could move with it."[89]

- *The support accorded amphibious operations had become effective, efficient and as just as importantly, flexible.* On 20 October 1944, US forces invaded the Philippines (which had been chosen as MacArthur's next objective, over an assault on Taiwan by Nimitz) with four divisions and a fifth in reserve. This amounted to over 150,000 troops. Upon landing, "some of the beaches proved inaccessible to LSTs. Since the shore parties could not ferry supplies inland without the trucks loaded on those vessels, this disrupted the original logistics plan. Nevertheless, the quartermasters landed as many trucks as they could, constructed pontoon bridges to unload the rest, and did an admirable job despite the unexpected problem. US logisticians had become proficient enough to deal with adversity. Despite the inaccessible beaches, shore parties got 107,450 tons of supplies ashore on 20 October alone."[90]

- These improvements (especially those related to the development of the fleet train and amphibious transport ships) "freed the Navy from logistical requirements which might have otherwise forced the Marines to fight additional battles. Since naval detachments could operate at great distances from their bases, they could bypass enemy-held islands which lay between them and their actual objectives. There were numerous cases in which the US Navy simply isolated Japanese-controlled islands and left the garrison to starve or surrender. This policy saved untold amounts of time, materiel and human life."[91]

The Final Battles

While the battle for the Philippines would carry on for most of the remainder of the war, the US continued to seek additional air and naval bases ever closer to the home islands of Japan with a view to potentially launch an invasion and provide additional facilities to support the strategic bombing campaign. The next two campaigns centred on the capture of Iwo Jima (Operation Detachment) and Okinawa (Operation Iceberg).

Operation Detachment[92] was launched in February 1945 in order to capture Iwo Jima and deny its use as a fighter base with which to intercept raids, to neutralise the radar station there that could give up to two hours warning of an air raid and use it as a base to support the strategic bombing campaign against Japan by providing emergency airstrips where damaged aircraft returning from operations could land (the island was roughly halfway between the Marianas and the Japanese home islands). The battle pitted the 70, 000 marines of Major General Harry Schmidt's V Amphibious Corps against the 21,000-strong garrison under Lt General Tadamichi Kuribayashi. While the marines eventually took the island, they paid a very high price – Iwo Jima was the only Pacific battle where the Japanese inflicted more casualties on the Americans than the Americans inflicted on them. The Americans suffered 23,157 casualties (5,885 killed) while for the Japanese, 216 Navy and 867 Army personnel were captured, meaning that some 19,977 were killed in action.

Operation Iceberg[93] saw the largest amphibious assault launched against the forces of Japan, with eight divisions (five of which made landings on the first day) totalling 190,000 ground troops carried in 430 ships with over 747,000 measurement tons of cargo, staged from Ulithi (in the Carolines), Eniwetok, Saipan and Leyte.[94] As with the operations in the Philippines, there were setbacks but just as with the operations in the Philippines, these were professionally handled by the shore parties so that problems that might have once caused disaster now only caused setbacks instead.[95] The ground forces on Okinawa required a total of 1,256,000 tons of supplies but despite reefs, bad weather, enemy action (including kamikazes) and a poor infrastructure, they unloaded these supplies quickly enough to satisfy the needs of the troops on the ground. The logisticians had come prepared to overcome the problems they encountered and within a day, had cut channels in coral reefs, started to improve the road system leading away from the beaches and built pontoon causeways to facilitate unloading.[96]

Supplies, troops and equipment being unloading onto a beach on Okinawa, 4 April 1945 (Source: US Army via Wikimedia Commons)

The final operation in the Pacific War was to have been the planned invasion of the Japanese home islands, codenamed Operation Downfall. Downfall itself consisted of two subsidiary operations; the first phase was codenamed Operation Olympic, scheduled for 1 November 1945 and targeted at the island of Kyushu. The second phase was codenamed Operation Coronet, scheduled for 1 March 1946 and targeted at the Kanto Plain on Honshu. Olympic would have utilised General Walter Krueger's Sixth Army (582,000 ground troops), Admiral William Halsey's Third Fleet, Admiral Raymond Spruance's Fifth Fleet and the Twentieth Air Force under General Carl Spaatz. Coronet was far less advanced in its planning but would have involved at least two field armies, most probably the First Army under Lt General Courtney Hodges and the Eighth Army under Lt General Robert Eichelberger although earlier planning had cited the use of another army, possibly the Tenth Army, which had been under the command of General Joseph Stilwell from 23 June 1945. Downfall, particularly its second phase, would have seen approximately 1.2 million men transferred to the Pacific from both the USA and Europe, with some 10 million tons of equipment being transferred out of Europe to both the USA and the Pacific Theatre. With these sorts of numbers, it is easy to see that Downfall would have been the largest and most involved logistics operations ever engaged in by the US military. In the end, the invasion didn't need to be carried out due to the Japanese surrender after the US dropped two atomic bombs on Hiroshima and Nagasaki.[97]

Conclusion

To conclude, the development of American logistics capability during the course of the Pacific War made it eventually possible for the US to deploy 600-ship fleets and multi-division assault forces wherever they chose to operate. Those at the highest levels of command saw logistics as the means by which they could bring the massive industrial capacity of the USA to bear against Imperial Japan. For a country that had a less well-developed military organisation, it might have meant having to make difficult choices, but the US was able to pursue multiple options simultaneously. Part of that was being able to resource campaigns in both Europe and the Pacific, so whether the Europe First strategy was a hindrance on the Pacific campaign, or whether the diversion of resources to the Pacific was a strain on the European campaign will forever be debated. It also meant that the US Chiefs of Staff could put off a decision about making one commander or another a 'Supreme Commander' (in the same way Ike was made Supreme Allied Commander in Europe) and resource two (near) simultaneous drives in both the Central Pacific (Nimitz) and Southwest Pacific (MacArthur) theatres. The development of American logistics processes, procedures and systems was one not of radical change, but of gradual reform and correcting mistakes, building upon the work done between the wars about logistic support, mobile base operations and amphibious doctrine. That work allowed the US to take the offensive before the Japanese could inflict even more damage and the operations at such places as Bora Bora, Guadalcanal and Tarawa alerted them to areas that needed additional work while allowing them to continue offensive operations at their own pace.

Ultimately, it wasn't simply a case of having a massive superiority in materiel that decided the outcome of the war in the Pacific, but being able to generate massive amounts of combat power alongside the ability to adequately support it in the field. Logistics is always more than merely providing huge quantities of supplies. Just as vast armadas of aircraft, fleets of ships and armies of soldiers are next to useless without the means by which they can move to where they need to be, engage the enemy, recover their strength and then move again, so vast amounts of supplies lying on the quayside is of no-use to anyone. The two need to be brought together at the correct time, place and in the correct amounts. The US managed to accomplish this with sound planning, strong and flexible support services and effective administration . . . it was the lesson they learned during 1942 and which was applied between 1943 and 1945. While the American logistic system never approached the level of 'jointness' envisaged by General Somervell or agreed to by Admiral King and General Marshall, in some ways this was a good thing. The Army Service Forces were designed for a highly centralised European-style war and while it worked pretty well in the Southwest Pacific theatre, it would not have been suitable for the Navy-run Central Pacific. This required a much more decentralised, flexible system. What came to be was in many ways due to the uniqueness of the two theatres, and jointness in logistics planning was best achieved at the CINCPAC staff level with extensive cross-servicing arrangement in place, both formally and informally. "Could logistics have been made more joint in the Pacific? Certainly. Did logistics work about as well as could be expected owing to the circumstances? Probably."[98]

Bibliography

Antill, P. (2001) *Operation Detachment: The Battle for Iwo Jima*, currently located at http://www.historyofwar.org/articles/battles_iwojima.html as of 5 June 2013.

Antill, P. *Operation Downfall 4: Allied Plans for Olympic and Coronet*, currently located at http://www.historyofwar.org/articles/wars_downfall4.html as of 6 June 2013.

Antill, P. (2002) *Operation Galvanic (1): The Battle for Tarawa November 1943*, currently located at http://www.historyofwar.org/articles/battles_tarawa.html, as of 25 April 2013.

Antill, P. (2003) *Operation Iceberg: The Assault on Okinawa - The Last Battle of World War II (Part 1)* April - June 1945, at http://www.historyofwar.org/articles/battles_okinawa1. html and part two at http://www.historyofwar.org/articles/battles_okinawa2.html as of 5 June 2013.

Antill, P. (2001) *Operation Watchtower: The Battle for Guadalcanal* (August 1942-February 1943), currently located at http://www.historyofwar.org/articles/battles_guadalcanal.html, as of 25 July 2012.

Antill, P. (2001), *Pearl Harbor: The Day of Infamy*, 7 December 1941, currently located at http://www.historyofwar.org/articles/battles_pearl_harbor.html as of 19 July 2012.

Antill, P. (2002) *The Battle of Midway: Turning Point in the Pacific Campaign*, currently located at http://www.historyofwar.org/articles/battles_midwaylong.html as of 19 July 2012.

Ballantine, D. (1998) *US Naval Logistics in the Second World War*, Newport, RI: Naval War College Press.

Barlow, J. (1994) 'Interservice Rivalry in the Pacific' in *Joint Forces Quarterly*, Spring 1994, pp. 76-81.

Budge, K. (2011) 'Logistics' in *The Pacific War Online Encyclopedia*, located at http://pwencycl.kgbudge.com/L/o/Logistics.htm as of 23 May 2012.

Bykovsky, J. and Larson, H. (1957) *The Transportation Corps: Operations Overseas*, Washington D.C.: Office of the Chief of Military History, Department of the Army.

Carter, W. (1998) *Bean, Bullets, and Black Oil: The Story of Fleet Logistics Afloat in the Pacific during World War II*, Newport, RI: Naval War College Press, also located at http://www.ibiblio.org/hyperwar/USN/BBBO/index.html as of 23 May 2012.

Coakley, R. and Leighton, R. (1968) *Global Logistics and Strategy 1943 – 1945*, Washington D.C.: Office of the Chief of Military History, US Army.

Costello, J. (1981) *The Pacific War*, London: William Collins.

Director of the Service, Supply and Procurement Division, War Department General Staff. (1993) *Logistics in World War II: Final Report of the Army Services Forces*, Washington D.C.: Center for Military History.

Donovan, Maj P. (2001) *Oil Logistics in the Pacific War: In and After Pearl Harbor*, Air Command and Staff College, Air University, Maxwell Air Force Base, AL, located at http://www.dtic.mil/cgi-bin/GetTRDoc?AD=ADA407830, as of 23 May 2012.

Dyer, G. (1962) *Naval Logistics*, Annapolis, MD: Naval Institute Press, 2nd Edition.

Ellis, Major E. (1921) *Advanced Base Operations in Micronesia*, Operations Plan 712, later published in 1992 as FMFRP 12-46, located at http://www.ibiblio.org/hyperwar/USMC/ref/AdvBaseOps/index.html as of 26 June 2012.

Furer, Rear Adm. J. (1959) *Administration of the Navy Department in World War II*, Washington D.C.: Office of Naval History, Department of the Navy.

Gray Jr., A. 'Chapter 6: Joint Logistics in the Pacific Theater' in Gropman, A. (1997) *The Big 'L' – American Logistics in World War II*, Washington D.C.: National Defence University Press, also available at http://www.ibiblio.org/hyperwar/USA/BigL/BigL-6.html as of 23 May 2012.

Hastings, M. (2007) *Nemesis – The Battle for Japan 1944-45*, London: Harper Collins Publishers.

Hough, Lt. Col. F., Ludwig, Major V. & Shaw Jr., H. (1958) *Pearl Harbor to Guadalcanal: History of US Marine Corps Operations in World War II – Volume 1*, DC: Historical Branch, HQ USMC. Also available at http://www.ibiblio.org/hyperwar/USMC/I/index.html# as of 27 June 2012.

Huston, J. (1988) *The Sinews of War: Army Logistics 1775-1953*, Washington D.C.: Center for Military History.

Isely, J. and Crowl, P. (1951) *The US Marines and Amphibious War: Its Theory and its Practice in the Pacific*, Princeton, NJ: Princeton University Press.

Kane, T. (2001) *Military Logistics and Strategic Performance*, London: Frank Cass Publishers.

Leighton, R. and Coakley, R. (1955) *Global Logistics and Strategy 1940 – 1943*, Washington D.C.: Office of the Chief of Military History, US Army.

LePore, H. 'Contribution to Victory: The Distribution and Supply of Ammunition and Ordnance in the Pacific Theater of Operations', *Army History*, Issue No. 34 (Spring / Summer 1995), pp. 31 – 35.

Lorelli, J. (1995) *To Foreign Shores: US Amphibious Operations in World War II*, Annapolis, MD: Naval Institute Press.

McGee, W. and McGee, S. (2009) *Pacific Express: The Critical Role of Military Logistics in World War II*, Tiburon, CA: BMC Publications, Amphibious Operations in the South Pacific in WWII – Volume III.

Millett, A. (1991) *Semper Fidelis: The History of the United States Marine Corps*, New York: The Free Press.

Morison, S. (1951) 'Aleutians, Gilberts and Marshalls, June 1942 – April 1944', Volume VII of *History of United States Naval Operations in World War II*, Boston: Little, Brown and Company.

Office of the Chief of Naval Operations. (1946) *US Navy at War 1941-1945 – Official Reports to the Secretary of the Navy by Fleet Admiral Ernest J. King, Commander in Chief U.S. Fleet and Chief of Naval Operations*, Washington D.C.: Department of the Navy, also located at http://www.ibiblio.org/hyperwar/USN/USNatWar/index.html as of 29 May 2012.

Roan, R. (1987) *Roebling's Amphibian – The Origin of the Assault Amphibian*, Command and Staff College Education Center, Marine Corps Development and Education Command (Quantico), currently located at http://www.ibiblio.org/hyperwar/USMC/ref/Roebling/Roebling.html as of 26 June 2012.

Spector, R. (2001) *Eagle Against The Sun*, London: Cassell & Co. (Cassell Military Paperbacks Edition).

Stauffer, A. (1956) *The Quartermaster Corps: Operations in the War Against Japan*, Washington D.C.: Office of the Chief of Military History, Department of the Army.

Thomson, H. and Mayo, L. (1960) *The Ordnance Department: Procurement and Supply*, Washington D.C.: Office of the Chief of Military History, Department of the Army.

Wheeler, R. (1983) *A Special Valor: The US Marines and the Pacific War*, New York: Harper & Row.

Van der Vat, D. (2001) *The Pacific Campaign*, Edinburgh: Berlinn Ltd.

Endnotes

[1] Office of the Chief of Naval Operations. (1946) *US Navy at War 1941-1945 – Official Reports to the Secretary of the Navy by Fleet Admiral Ernest J. King, Commander in Chief U.S. Fleet and Chief of Naval Operations*, Washington D.C.: Department of the Navy, p. 36.

[2] Kane, T. (2001) *Military Logistics and Strategic Performance*, London: Frank Cass Publishers, p. 37.

[3] Costello, J. (1981) *The Pacific War*, London: William Collins, p. 112.

[4] As quoted in *Op Cit.* Kane, p. 37.

[5] Ballantine, D. (1998) *US Naval Logistics in the Second World War*, Newport, RI: Naval War College Press, p. 41.

[6] Spector, R. (2001) *Eagle against the Sun*, London: Cassell & Co., p. 40; Huston, J. (1988) *The Sinews of War: Army Logistics 1775-1953*, Washington D.C.: Center for Military History, p. 425.

[7] *Op Cit.* Office of the Chief of Naval Operations, p. 33.

[8] Gray Jr., A. 'Chapter 6: Joint Logistics in the Pacific Theater' in Gropman, A. (1997) *The Big 'L' – American Logistics in World War II*, Washington D.C.: National Defence University Press, p. 296.

[9] For example: LePore, H. 'Contribution to Victory: The Distribution and Supply of Ammunition and Ordnance in the Pacific Theater of Operations', *Army History*, Issue No. 34 (Spring / Summer 1995), p. 31.

[10] *Op Cit.* Gray, p. 296.

[11] *Op Cit.* Spectre, p. 56.

[12] *Op Cit.* Gray, p. 297; *Op Cit.* Ballantine, p. 34; *Op Cit.* Spectre, p. 57.

[13] *Op Cit.* Kane, p. 39.

[14] Carter, W. (1998) *Bean, Bullets, and Black Oil: The Story of Fleet Logistics Afloat in the Pacific during World War II*, Newport, RI: Naval War College Press, pp. 1-2.

[15] *Op Cit.* Ballantine, p. 33.

[16] *Op Cit.* Carter, p. 2.

[17] *Op Cit.* Ballantine, p. 33.

[18] *Ibid.* p. 36.

[19] Roan, R. (1987) *Roebling's Amphibian – The Origin of the Assault Amphibian*, Command

and Staff College Education Center, Marine Corps Development and Education Command (Quantico), currently located at http://www.ibiblio.org/hyperwar/USMC/ref/Roebling/Roebling.html as of 26 June 2012.

[20] Millett, A. (1991) *Semper Fidelis: The History of the United States Marine Corps*, New York: The Free Press, p. 320; Wheeler, R. (1983) *A Special Valor: The US Marines and the Pacific War*, New York: Harper & Row, p. 1.

[21] Ellis, Major E. (1921) *Advanced Base Operations in Micronesia*, Operations Plan 712, later published in 1992 as FMFRP 12-46, located at http://www.ibiblio.org/hyperwar/USMC/ref/AdvBaseOps/index.html as of 26 June 2012.

[22] *Op Cit.* Roan.

[23] Hough, Lt. Col. F., Ludwig, Major V. & Shaw Jr., H. (1958) *Pearl Harbor to Guadalcanal: History of US Marine Corps Operations in World War II – Volume 1*, D.C.: Historical Branch, HQ USMC, p. 14.

[24] Isely, J. and Crowl, P. (1951) *The US Marines and Amphibious War: Its Theory and its Practice in the Pacific*, Princeton, NJ: Princeton University Press, pp. 43-44.

[25] *Op Cit.* Kane, pp. 41-42.

[26] Watson, M. (1950) *Chief of Staff – Prewar Plans and Preparations*, Washington D.C.: US GPO, pp. 97-101.

[27] *Op Cit.* Grey, pp. 300-301.

[28] Barlow, J. (1994) 'Interservice Rivalry in the Pacific' in *Joint Forces Quarterly*, Spring 1994, p. 80.

[29] For an account of the attack, see Antill, P. (2001), Pearl Harbor: The Day of Infamy, 7 December 1941, currently located at http://www.historyofwar.org/articles/battles_pearl_harbor.html as of 19 July 2012.

[30] *Op Cit.* Grey, pp. 303-304.

[31] *Ibid.* p. 304.

[32] *Op Cit.* Ballantine, p. 96.

[33] *Op Cit.* Carter, pp. 3-9.

[34] Furer, Rear Adm. J. (1959) *Administration of the Navy Department in World War II*, Washington D.C.: Office of Naval History, Department of the Navy, p. 718.

[35] *Ibid.*

[36] *Op Cit.* Grey, p. 306.

[37] *Op Cit.* Kane, p. 47.

[38] *Op Cit.* Furer, pp. 699-705; , R. and Leighton, R. (1968) *Global Logistics and Strategy 1943 – 1945*, D.C.: Office of the Chief of Military History, US Army, pp. 180-185; *Op Cit.* Ballantine, p. 71.

[39] *Op Cit.* Grey, pp. 306-307.

[40] Director of the Service, Supply and Procurement Division, War Department General Staff. (1993) *Logistics in World War II: Final Report of the Army Services Forces*, Washington D.C.: Center for Military History, pp. 198–199.

[41] *Op Cit.* Huston, p. 414.

[42] *Op Cit.* Furer, pp. 695-696.

[43] *Op Cit.* Grey, pp. 308-310.

[44] *Ibid.* pp. 309-310.

[45] *Ibid.* p. 311.

[46] *Op Cit.* Coakley and Leighton, pp. 186-187.

[47] *Ibid.* pp. 187-192.

[48] *Op Cit.* Grey, p. 312.

[49] *Ibid.* pp. 312-313.

[50] For an account of the battle, see Antill, P. (2002) The Battle of Midway: Turning Point in the Pacific Campaign, currently located at http://www.historyofwar.org/articles/battles_midwaylong.html as of 19 July 2012.

[51] *Op Cit.* Coakley and Leighton, p. 388.

[52] *Ibid.*

[53] *Op Cit.* Grey, p. 314.

[54] Lorelli, J. (1995) *To Foreign Shores: US Amphibious Operations in World War II*, Annapolis, MD: Naval Institute Press, pp. 45-46.

[55] *Ibid.* p. 40.

[56] *Op Cit.* Isely and Crowl, p. 127.

[57] *Op Cit.* Costello, p. 326.

[58] *Op Cit.* Spector, p. 195; *Op Cit.* Isely and Crowl, p. 133.

[59] *Op Cit.* Kane, p. 55.

[60] See Antill, P. (2001) Operation Watchtower: The Battle for Guadalcanal (August 1942-February 1943), located at http://www.historyofwar.org/articles/battles_guadalcanal.html, as of 25 July 2012.

[61] *Op Cit.* Grey, pp. 315-316.

[62] Leighton, R. and Coakley, R. (1955) *Global Logistics and Strategy 1940 – 1943*, D.C.: Office of the Chief of Military History, US Army, p. 656.

[63] The US Navy had commissioned a report by the management engineering firm Booz, Allen and Hamilton to study their logistics, with the report appearing in March 1943 recommending a reorganisation of the Navy's administrative services, including the creation of an independent logistics department that had close links with the combat commanders.

[64] Dyer, G. (1962) *Naval Logistics*, Annapolis, MD: Naval Institute Press, 2nd Edition, pp. 166-167.

[65] *Op Cit*. Ballantine, p. 154.

[66] *Op Cit*. Grey, p. 320.

[67] *Op Cit*. Huston, pp. 545-548.

[68] *Op Cit*. Kane, p. 59.

[69] *Op Cit*. Ballantine, p. 108.

[70] *Op Cit*. Grey, p. 320.

[71] *Ibid*. p. 321.

[72] *Ibid*.

[73] *Op Cit*. Coakley and Leighton, pp. 392-394.

[74] *Op Cit*. Ballantine, p. 134.

[75] See , P. (2002) *Operation Galvanic (1): The Battle for Tarawa November 1943*, currently located at http://www.historyofwar.org/articles/battles_tarawa.html, as of 25 April 2013.

[76] *Op Cit*. Leighton and Coakley, 1955, p. 683.

[77] *Op Cit*. Spector, pp. 230-231.

[78] Morison, S. (1951) 'Aleutians, Gilberts and Marshalls, June 1942 – April 1944', Volume VII of *History of United States Naval Operations in World War II*, Boston: Little, Brown and Company, p. 102.

[79] *Ibid*. pp. 105-108.

[80] *Op Cit*. Lorelli, p. 174.

[81] *Op Cit*. Kane, p. 60.

[82] *Ibid*. p. 61.

[83] *Op Cit*. Lorelli, p. 193-202.

[84] *Ibid*. p. 202.

[85] *Op Cit*. Huston, p. 542.

[86] *Ibid*. p. 435.

[87] *Op Cit*. Kane, pp. 62-64; *Op Cit*. Grey, pp. 332-335.

[88] *Op Cit*. Kane, p. 62.

[89] *Ibid*. p. 63.

[90] *Ibid*.

[91] *Ibid*.

[92] For an account of the battle, see Antill, P. (2001) Operation Detachment: The Battle for Iwo Jima, February – March 1945, currently located at http://www.historyofwar.org/articles/battles_iwojima.html as of 5 June 2013.

[93] For an account of the battle, see Antill, P. (2003) Operation Iceberg: The Assault on

Okinawa - The Last Battle of World War II (Part 1) April - June 1945, at http://www. historyofwar.org/articles/battles_okinawa1.html and part two at http://www.historyofwar. org/articles/battles_okinawa2.html as of 5 June 2013.

[94] *Op Cit.* Huston, pp. 556-557.

[95] *Op Cit.* Kane, p. 63.

[96] *Op Cit.* Lorelli, p. 301.

[97] *Op Cit.* Grey, p. 335; See also Antill, P. *Operation Downfall 4: Allied Plans for Olympic and Coronet*, currently located at http://www.historyofwar.org/articles/wars_downfall4. html as of 6 June 2013.

[98] *Op Cit.* Grey, p. 336.

The Largest Amphibious Invasion of All: The Legacy and Lessons of Operation DOWNFALL

Jon T. Hoffman

Deputy Director, Office of the Secretary of Defence, Historical Office.

[Editor's Note: This article originally appeared in the Marine Corps Gazette (August 1995) and as far as possible, has been left 'as written'.]

Introduction

It might seem strange, at first, to look for lessons in an operation that never went beyond the planning stages. But the process of evaluating a historic plan mirrors the challenge that military leaders face in preparing for future operations. In making a decision, we have to form estimates of the likely outcome of each possible course of action for a given scenario. That is a much tougher proposition than making Monday-morning quarterback critiques of actual operations that are already enshrined in the history books. A look at the proposed invasion of Japan thus makes an interesting capstone to a study of amphibious operations in World War II.

The Situation

In June 1945, U.S. leaders had every reason to be optimistic about the Pacific war. Germany's surrender in May had freed the United States, Great Britain and other Allied nations to focus their veteran armed forces against Japan. The Soviet Union was busily transporting units to the far reaches of Siberia in preparation for fulfilling its promise to enter the war against Japan 90 days after the fall of Germany. The long-range bombers of the U.S. Army Air Forces had been pounding the Japanese homeland for several months and were beginning to achieve devastating effects with low-level incendiary raids. The U.S. Navy had sunk the vast majority of Japanese warships and merchantmen. A joint operation had finally secured Okinawa after weeks of bloody fighting and all Services were busily preparing bases there to support air, sea and ground action against the Japanese home islands. Forces of the British Empire were clearing the enemy out of Southeast Asia while the Chinese tied down considerable Japanese strength. Japanese industrial production was plummeting as the island nation ran short of factories, raw materials, and workers. By all rational calculations, Japan was a defeated nation with no logical alternative except surrender to avoid further pointless losses.

Regrettably, many Japanese military leaders did not see things that way. Senior officers, especially those in the Army, believed that anything, to include the complete destruction of their country, was preferable to the dishonour of surrender. Their strategy in the summer of 1945 was simple – they would employ their forces in a suicidal defence against the expected invasion of the home islands. They hoped to make the shores of Japan a much bigger, bloodier version of Peleliu, Iwo Jima and Okinawa. Even if they could not defeat the first landing, they felt that they could inflict sufficient losses on the U.S. to deter subsequent operations and force a negotiated peace more favourable than unconditional surrender. To further this plan, the Japanese refused battle in the air and at sea in the summer of 1945 and husbanded their remaining resources for future kamikaze operations. They also brought home four army divisions from the Asian mainland and created many new ground units with a massive mobilization of nearly two million men.

American leaders agreed with the central thesis of the Japanese strategy. They believed that the public was growing weary of the long war, that they would have to achieve final victory within a year of Germany's surrender. If not, an erosion of popular support for continued fighting would force a negotiated peace. But the Joint Chiefs of Staff were initially divided over how to bring the war to a rapid close. Gen Henry H. Arnold, head of the Army Air Forces, was certain that continued strategic bombing (1,600,000 tons of bombs, to be precise) would bring Japan to its knees. Adms Ernest J. King and William D. Leahy favoured a naval blockade, which would cut off the raw materials necessary to sustain the enemy's war economy. Gen George C. Marshall, Chief of Staff of the Army, thought that only an invasion could force Japanese capitulation within the required timeframe. By June 1945, with no sign of weakening Japanese resolve, the other Joint Chiefs reluctantly agreed to Marshall's point of view. The chiefs were aware of the atomic bomb program, but the first weapon would not be tested until 16 July, so it was not yet an option.

The Invasion Plans

The invasion of Japan, code-named DOWNFALL, had two parts. The first was the seizure of southern Kyushu, which would provide air and naval bases to support further operations. The second assault would capture the Kanto Plain on Honshu, "the industrial and political heart of Japan." These two operations were respectively named OLYMPIC and CORONET. The Joint Chiefs scheduled the main OLYMPIC landings for 1 November 1945 (X Day) and CORONET for 1 March 1946 (Y Day). They also moved away from their earlier reliance on two geographic commands in the Pacific. For DOWNFALL, Adm Chester W. Nimitz would head all Navy forces and run the sea campaign, while Gen Douglas MacArthur would have all Marine and Army ground forces and most of the Army Air Forces in the Pacific under his control and would be responsible for the land war. After MacArthur grumbled about this arrangement, the Joint Chiefs decided that, if "exigencies warranted," he could assume control of the amphibious phase of the operation.

The Sixth Army, composed of 11 Army and 3 Marine divisions, would carry out OLYMPIC. More than 230,000 service and support troops would back up the 252,000 Soldiers and 88,000 Marines in the combat units. Nearly 1,400 transports and amphibious vessels would bring them to the objective. The Fifth Fleet's thirty-six escort carriers, eleven battleships, twenty-six cruisers and 387 destroyers would protect the landing force at sea and provide fire support. The Third Fleet's twenty heavy and light carriers, nine battleships, twenty-six cruisers and seventy-five destroyers would carry out air and surface strikes against targets outside the amphibious objective area. OLYMPIC's ten assault divisions would make it a larger operation than the Normandy landings.

Fifth Fleet would begin its preparation fires on X-8. On X-4 the 40th Division would seize smaller islands off Kyushu, for use as expeditionary naval bases. Beginning on X-2, the IX Corps of two divisions would feint against Shikoku to hold Japanese reinforcements there. On X-Day, three corps of three divisions each would conduct simultaneous amphibious assaults against three separate locations. The V Marine Amphibious Corps (2nd, 3rd and 5th Marine Divisions) would seize a beachhead near Kushikino and then clear the peninsula on the western side of massive Kagoshima Bay. The XI Corps would land in Ariake Bay and take the eastern peninsula. The I Corps would land farther up the eastern coast. The three landing sites corresponded to the only significant coastal plains in otherwise hilly southern Kyushu. Eventually the three corps would move north and establish a defensive line, running from Sendai in the west to Tsuno in the east, which traced the southern exits of passes through the central mountains of Kyushu. If needed, the IX corps and two additional divisions could reinforce the three assault corps.

CORONET's landing of two armies would dwarf OLYMPIC. First Army would land two corps abreast at Kujukuri. The XXIV Corps (three divisions) and III Marine Amphibious Corps (1st, 4th and 6th Marine Divisions) then would seize the peninsula forming the eastern flank of Tokyo Bay. The Eighth Army's X and XIV Corps (three divisions each) would go ashore in Sagami Bay with their initial objectives being Yokosuka and the small peninsula guarding the western flank of the entrance to Tokyo Bay. On Y+10 the XIII Corps' two armoured divisions would land in trace at Sagami and penetrate deep into the enemy rear to a point northwest of Tokyo where they could prevent the movement of reinforcements toward the Japanese capital. In subsequent operations First Army would advance on Tokyo from the east while Eighth Army seized Yokohama and attacked Tokyo from the southwest. In addition to these fourteen assault divisions, MacArthur would have fourteen more divisions (including one each from Britain, Canada and Australia) to feed into the land campaign as needed. Planners never developed a list of naval forces for CORONET but they envisaged that ships and planes would begin preparation fires weeks in advance of the landings.

Japanese Plans

The U.S. had long since broken Japanese codes and thus had a fairly accurate picture of enemy intentions. The Japanese had no similar source of intelligence, but they used their knowledge of previous American operations to deduce the likely U.S. course of action. In particular, they knew that MacArthur preferred to make his amphibious assaults under the cover of land-based air. They also expected an invasion to come after 1 October 1945 at the end of the monsoon season. They were certain the initial objective would be southern Kyushu, because it was within range of American fighters on Okinawa and would provide the air and sea bases needed to complete the strangulation of the home islands and support subsequent operations. They expected twelve divisions in the assault force. They assumed that about ninety days later, US forces would launch an amphibious attack against the Kanto Plain on Honshu. In both cases they even correctly guessed which beaches the Americans planned to use. Based on that estimate, the Japanese concentrated most of their forces in southern Kyushu and the Kanto Plain.

The Japanese defensive scheme for Kyushu had three phases. First, suicide planes and vessels would attack the American fleet as it tried to land the amphibious force. These air and sea kamikazes would include 10,000 aircraft, sixty submarines, nineteen destroyers, 2,000 fast boats , hundreds of midget submarines and manned torpedoes, frogmen with handheld mines and even ground-launched, human-piloted rocket bombs. Second, newly-organized coastal defence divisions, emplaced in fortifications overlooking the beaches would attempt to prevent the landing force from seizing a foothold. Finally, mobile divisions stationed in central locations in the interior would counterattack toward the most threatened locations. In August 1945, the ground forces on Kyushu consisted of 14 divisions and several independent brigades (about 600,000 men), the vast majority of them located in the southern half of the island. The Japanese were also debating whether to send eight more divisions to the island.

In addition to regular military forces, the Japanese organised home defence units. These people, some of them women, had little equipment and meagre training, but they were ordered to attack Allied forces with Molotov cocktails, bamboo spears, kitchen knives and anything else they could lay their hands on. Japanese leaders began indoctrinating the population with slogans such as "One Hundred Million Die Proudly" in order to prepare their people for a fanatical defence of the sacred homeland. Kyushu had 575,000 citizens enrolled in its militia.

The Kanto Plain was defended by twenty infantry and two tank divisions, plus ten infantry and three tank brigades. Tokyo was home to two of the divisions and three of the brigades, to include the Guards division charged with protecting the Emperor and his palace. Another seven divisions were located on Honshu within reach of the Kanto Plain. The only thing easy about CORONET compared to OLYMPIC would have been the absence of sea and air kamikazes, which the Japanese would have used up in Kyushu.

The End of the War

President Harry S. Truman formerly approved the planned invasion of Japan in a mid-June 1945 meeting with the Joint Chiefs of Staff and other senior advisors. He did so based in large measure upon a prediction from MacArthur that casualties would be comparatively low. But those estimated losses were already outmoded by the time the President received them. The OLYMPIC plans had assumed that there would be just 2,000 planes in the home islands and about 260,000 enemy soldiers on Kyushu, with less than half of them located in the south. The casualty predictions also assumed that the U.S would achieve surprise by landing in unexpected locations. By late July, code-breaking had revealed that the Japanese force on Kyushu had mushroomed to half-a-million men (still an underestimation) and most of them concentrating in the south at the precise locations picked for the three main amphibious assaults. There were also indications that the Japanese possessed several thousand more planes than originally suspected.

In early August, Marshall grew sufficiently concerned about the increase in Japanese strength to query MacArthur about developing alternative invasion plans. But MacArthur rejected the intelligence figures as being "grossly exaggerated" and he expressed his strong determination to proceed as planned. Naval analyst Norman Polmar has hinted that MacArthur's stated view that his version of an invasion would be cheaper than any other option was motivated by the general's presidential ambitions, which necessitated his outdoing Gen Dwight D. Eisenhower's Normandy operation.

Neither side put their plans to use. On 16 July 1945, the United States successfully tested the first atomic bomb and made a quantum leap in the scale of firepower. There was considerable debate within the upper echelons of the Government over this new weapon, but President Truman as determined to keep American casualties to a minimum. He soon issued orders to drop the two available bombs on Japanese cities in an effort to convince the enemy that they faced complete ruin if they did not capitulate. The nuclear attacks on Hiroshima (6 August) and Nagasaki (9 August) levelled both cities and instantly killed about 140,000 people altogether. Thousands more died later from radiation poisoning and injuries.

To compound Japanese woes, on 8 August the Soviet Union launched its promised offensive against Japan by invading Manchuria with 1,500,000 troops supported by 5,000 planes. Japan's Kwangtung Army, once the nation's elite force, had been hollowed out during the course of the war as the best divisions were transferred to threatened fronts. Its 440,000 second-class troops, operating without air support, succumbed quickly to the Soviet onslaught. This invasion stunned the Japanese because they had hoped the Soviets would provide them with assistance against the Allies in return for territory, or at least remain neutral in the Pacific war.

Faced with the combined power of many nations and the prospect of further nuclear bombings, the Emperor personally intervened and ordered his government to surrender. That imperial decision was unprecedented in Japan's modern history, since the Emperor traditionally had no direct role in running the country. Even then, the surrender almost did not take place, as some army officers launched a coup with the goal of assassinating the Emperor's advisors and continuing the war. The attempt failed when the War Minister decided at the last minute not to support them (though he did not try to stop them or warn the government either). A number of senior officers (to include the War Minister) committed suicide to avoid surrendering and one admiral even led a flight of kamikaze planes against the U.S. fleet after the Emperor's public announcement of his decision.

The Lessons

Operation DOWNFALL provides three enduring lessons. The first is the danger inherent in choosing what appears to be the best course of action. MacArthur and the joint planners chose southern Kyushu because it was the only part of Japan within range of ground-based fighters, possessed the best sites for air and naval bases, and offered the best springboard for future operations. They selected the Kanto Plain as the follow-on target because Japan's capital and much of her industry were located there, and it provided good country for armoured operations (outside the cities anyway). They chose to go ashore on the widest landing beaches with the best hydrography. The Japanese had no difficulty in using these same factors to determine what the United States would do. As a result, they were every bit as prepared as if they had read our plans. If modern Marines take away one lesson from the history of the Pacific war, it should be that surprise is achieved not so much by secrecy as it is by doing the unexpected. MacArthur masterfully employed that skill in New Guinea but chose to ignore it in 1945. Luckily for thousands of Soldiers, Sailors, Airmen and Marines, Truman's decision to drop the atomic bombs saved them from what might have been MacArthur's greatest folly.

The second striking aspect of the finale of the Pacific war is how heavily it hinged on the decisions of a few personalities. Had the Japanese War Minister supported the coup, it probably would have succeeded and the war would have continued even though we were certain that the Japanese had nothing to gain by doing so. Enemy intransigence would have forced the Allies to invade and destroy that country in much the same way that Adolf Hitler's refusal to surrender resulted in a fight to the finish in Germany. In general, we base our plans on the implicit assumptions that our enemies will make reasonable choices in response to events, but often opponents will not cooperate. We need to keep in mind that knowing our enemy includes knowing whether he is rational, irrational, or perhaps operating with a logic that we do not fully understand.

The final lesson may seem far removed from the daily interests of most Marines, but it might eventually have a profound impact of the future of the Corps and the Nation. During World War II the Joint Chiefs of Staff were equal partners in theory and in fact. Often that resulted in contentious debate, to include the dispute over the best course of action for forcing the surrender of Japan. Sometimes their compromise decisions were not the most effective ones possible, an example being the division of authority for Downfall between MacArthur and Nimitz.

Since the end of the war, the Nation has tried to "fix" its defence system with an ever-increasing emphasis on jointness. In many cases this has resulted in improvements, such as the current system of unified commands that avoids repetition of the MacArthur / Nimitz debate over who should be in charge of an operation. However, the implementation of jointness at the level of the Joint Chiefs of Staffs is effectively stripping the Service Chiefs of responsibility for the overall conduct of national defence and placing it into the hands of the Chairman of the Joint Chiefs. The old system ensured that competing ideas were aired at the highest possible level. The new system increasingly seems to equate effectiveness with the ability of one man and one staff to create and implement a single idea, without serious debate getting in the way. The recommendations of the recent Roles and Missions Commission would only further strengthen this questionable trend. Perhaps it is time to recognise that developing high-level policy is not the same as commanding a combat operation, that putting a single authority is not necessarily the right answer to both situations. The Nation that has always based its political and economic structures on the competition of ideas would do well to put true jointness – the collective wisdom of several services – back into the Joint Chiefs of Staff.

Afterword: The Great Casualty Debate

The recent dispute over the 50th anniversary exhibit of the *Enola Gay* has generated considerable debate over the likely number of casualties U.S. forces would have suffered if President Harry Truman had decided to launch amphibious assaults on the Japanese home islands instead of dropping the atomic bombs. After the war, the common wisdom (supported by memoirs of leaders such as Truman) held that use of the atomic bombs had spared the United States the massive casualties it would have suffered in an invasion of the home islands. Published estimates of American losses in DOWNFALL ran up to one million or more. In the past few years revisionist scholars have argued that those figures were invented after the fact to justify the use of the bomb. The underlying premise is that the United States could have ended the war with a blockade or an easy invasion and so avoided using nuclear weapons.

The most important weapon in the revisionist arsenal is a casualty estimate issued by MacArthur's staff in response to a request from the Joint Chiefs, who needed it for a meeting with Truman that would decide whether the United States would launch OLYMPIC or pursue some other course. The Chiefs made it clear that the President intended "to make his decisions on the campaign with the purpose of economizing to the maximum extent possible in the loss of American lives." MacArthur's staff had one day in which to respond. They answered that they anticipated 50,800 casualties (dead, wounded and missing) in the first thirty days; 27,150 in the next thirty days; and 17,100 in the third thirty days of the operation. In addition they suggested that there might be nearly 13,000 non-battle losses in ninety days. (It was not clear whether these figures included naval losses.) Marshall was not satisfied with this response and hours before the meeting he sent a personal message to MacArthur reiterating the President's concern about casualties and asking for a clarification of the numbers. MacArthur replied that he had not previously seen his staff's estimate and stated that "I do not anticipate such a high rate of loss."

Another estimate, generally ignored by revisionist historians, came from the Joint War Plans Committee. This memorandum, also created in mid-June 1945, noted the difficulty in predicting losses and the wide variance in Japanese resistance in different operations. It then went on to make an "educated guess" that OLYMPIC AND CORONET would result in 193,500 casualties. (Again, it was not clear whether this figure included naval losses.) However, the authors based their calculations on the belief that "the extent of the objective area gives us an opportunity to effect surprise as to the points of landing." A month later the joint planners issued another document that emphasised that MacArthur's forces had inflicted casualties on the Japanese at a 22:1 ratio in comparison to his own losses. They also included a table, however, that showed that the U.S. inflicted losses on Luzon at a 5:1 ratio, and on Iwo Jima at a 1.25:1 ratio. This time the planners stated that "naval casualties will probably be at about the same rate as for Okinawa." Revisionist historians have made frequent use of MacArthur's statements and the 22:1 ration to argue that losses would have been low in an invasion.

There is evidence suggesting that loss rates would not have been as high as in some Central pacific island assaults. For instance, many of the Japanese formations were newly formed and thus poorly equipped and trained. But one example highlights the danger posed by apparently weak Japanese forces. In early 1945 a force composed of 17,000 Japanese sailors and army service troops received last minute orders to defend Manila, which they had previously planned to evacuate without a fight. They were armed primarily with heavy weapons stripped from ships and planes, and the U.S. Army's official history characterised them as "a body of half-trained troops hastily organized into provisional units." But that ragtag outfit inflicted more than 6,500 casualties on the U.S. Army, a 2.5:1 ratio far different from the 22:1 statistic touted by the joint planners and revisionists. Perhaps as significant, a hundred thousand Filipino civilians also died in the battle as the U.S. Army made liberal use of artillery to decrease its own losses. The battle of Manila is relevant because the invasion of Japan would have involved a great deal of the same type of urban combat against just such scratch enemy forces.

There is no way to make an accurate prediction of casualties, but it is certain that an invasion of Japan would not have been cheap. Even if the United States had been wildly successful, the Japanese would have suffered immense losses, both military and civilian, that would have dwarfed those inflicted by the atomic bombings. The Allies and the Japanese alike would have lost tens of thousands more lives in China, Southeast Asia and elsewhere as the war dragged on in those other theatres. And an invasion likely would have triggered the execution of tens of thousands of Allied prisoners in Japanese hands. Assistant Secretary of War John J. McCloy was right in 1945 when he said that "we ought to have our heads examined if we don't explore some other method by which we can terminate this war than just by another conventional attack and landing."

Logistics in Land Warfare: From the Middle Ages to the Gulf War

David Kirkpatrick

Visiting Professor, Cranfield Defence and Security, Defence Academy of the UK.

Introduction

This paper discusses how armies have been supplied at different periods in military history, and the various transport modes which have been used over the last millennium to provide that support (excluding the special problems of amphibious and parachute landings and those of inter-continental expeditionary forces). The discussion is illustrated by some case studies of the logistical problems faced by particular generals, and how these problems constrained their operations. The paper then reviews the desirable and undesirable qualities of armies and of the transport used to support them in the field, comments on the dramatic increase in army requirements during the 20th Century, and advocates that future force planning and budgeting should take a greater account of the logistics requirements of new weapon systems.

Background

Successful military operations have always depended on adequate provision of food, fuel, ammunition and other supplies to military forces in the field. Accordingly, while junior officers study tactics and regimental officers study strategy, generals study logistics. Modern British Defence Doctrine[1] states:

> "The ability to sustain a force, during every stage of a military campaign from force generation, through deployment and operations in theatre, to redeployment and recuperation afterwards, is a critical enabler of fighting power. Sustainability involves the sustenance of personnel, the maintenance and repair of vehicles, equipment and materiel (including associated networks), the provision of combat supplies and service support, and the evacuation, treatment and replacement of casualties. A rigorous assessment of logistic realities is essential to operational planning; indeed, it may be the deciding factor in assessing the feasibility of a particular campaign."

The importance of logistics has been recognised throughout military history:

- "The line between disorder and order lies in logistics" [Sun Tzu]

- "The main and principal point in war is to secure plenty of provisions and to weaken or destroy the enemy by famine." [Vegetius]

- "A general in America must spend twenty hours considering how to feed his army for every one he spends thinking about how to fight it." [Burgoyne]

- "The provisioning of troops is a necessary condition of warfare, and thus has a great influence on operations." [Clausewitz]

- "Fighting the Dervish was primarily a matter of transport. The Khalifa was conquered on the railway" [Churchill]

- "During the last war 80% of our problems were of a logistical nature" [Montgomery]

- "Only a commander who understands logistics can push the military machine to its limits without risking total breakdown" [Thompson]

All these quotations recognise that any army which is short of fuel, ammunition, spares and any of the other supplies which are necessary for effective operations will rapidly become unable to effectively resist a better-supplied enemy. In extreme cases, where an army has insufficient food and water, the bonds of discipline will dissolve as the soldiers' immediate concerns for individual survival override their loyalty to their nation or even to their comrades.

The basic problem of military logistics is that soldiers generally need a daily ration of about 3lbs of food, incorporating sufficient protein, carbohydrate and vitamins, plus several pints of unpolluted water or preferably beer. The adoption of horses as mounts and draught animals increased the logistics problem because they need a daily ration of some 12lbs grain and 14lbs of hay or grass plus ten gallons of water (the scale and composition of the appropriate ration varies with the size of the horse and with its current activity). Early armies which used missile weapons needed replacements for the arrows and sling-stones used in action, and similarly gunpowder-age armies needed to replenish their powder and shot. In the modern age, when armies have acquired an array of complex weapon, communication and transport systems, these systems all need fuel (petrochemical or electric) and spare parts to keep them operational. Furthermore, a modern soldier has every reason to expect a more-attractive diet, better accommodation and medical care, and more scope for recreation than was available to his/her predecessors. It follows that maintaining a modern army in the field involves the procurement, storage and distribution of a multitudinous inventory of items – large and small, perishable and durable, fragile and robust. Managing the flow of such items from 'factory to foxhole' is a daunting challenge for modern logisticians.

Supply by Foraging

In medieval times, when armies were relatively small and their needs were simple, an army on the march could supply itself by foraging, i.e. by plundering the farms, villages and towns unfortunate enough to be on its line of march. However, this procedure broke down when the army either ventured into barren and inhospitable terrain or encountered effective "scorched earth" policies by which the enemy successfully destroyed or hid the food and forage along the army's route. For example, the armies of the First Crusade lost nearly three quarters of their strength to starvation in their march across Asia Minor[2], and the independence of Scotland was maintained not only by occasional Scottish victories over larger and better-armed English armies but by the strategy (known to the Scots as 'good King Robert's testament') of removing any supplies from the path of an invading English army. Problems also arose when a medieval army stopped to besiege a hostile town or castle; it rapidly consumed all the food and fodder in the vicinity, and had to forage throughout an ever-larger area. Concurrently the daily excrement of men and horses (about 1lb and 14lbs respectively) could make the army's camp a sanitary disaster area. Any medieval commander was under enormous pressure to ensure that any siege was brought rapidly to a successful conclusion before his army disintegrated from malnutrition and disease. In 1415, for example, Henry V lost half his army[3] during his five-week siege of Harfleur.

'Morning at the Battle of Agincourt, 25 October 1415' by Sir John Gilbert (Source: Wikimedia Commons)

Even in the Thirty Years War (1618-48), the manoeuvres of armies were largely determined by their need to keep moving, and to operate in areas not previously plundered. Conversely armies regularly ravaged territory from which their enemies might have been supplied, leading often to the unedifying spectacle of opposing forces carefully avoiding each other but plundering and slaughtering in their enemies' homelands. Ultimately this wasteful policy was self defeating, and the resources of the main areas of operation in Germany became so exhausted that even the soldiers starved, despite the most diligent looting and occasional cannibalism.

From the 15th Century onwards, gunpowder weapons played an increasingly important role, first in siege warfare and later on the battle field. It then became important to ensure that an army had adequate supplies of powder and shot, as well as of food and water.

Case Study: Newbury 1643

Re-enactors re-create a battle of the English Civil War (Source: Unknown author, Wikimedia Commons)

In September 1643, King Charles I had almost won the English Civil War. Earlier that year Parliament's western army had been shattered at Roundaway Down, and its northern army (defeated at Adwalton Moor) had been driven to seek refuge in Hull. The sole remaining army under the Earl of Essex (incorporating several regiments of the London Trained Bands, Parliament's ultimate strategic reserve) had marched into the Severn Valley to relieve besieged

Gloucester, and had lost contact with its supply bases in and around London. Essex tried to evade the Royalist army and return to London without a battle, but his army was intercepted in the east-west corridor between the rivers Kennet and Enborne, south of Newbury. Essex dared not risk a river crossing in the presence of an enemy army, and retreat to the west would only have delayed disaster. So all through the 20 September, his army tried to push the blocking Royalists out of the way, but it failed. At the end of the day the Parliamentary army was still cut off from London while the Royalists could be supplied from their main base at Oxford. King Charles was within a whisker of destroying Parliament's most important and last remaining field army. But the prolonged battle of Newbury had used almost all of the Royalists' available gunpowder (four times more than had been needed at Edgehill, the preceding year), and they could not expect more to arrive from Oxford before noon next day. Accordingly the Royalist army withdrew northward during the night, and Essex thankfully marched east to the safety of London.[4] This failure of Royalist logistics allowed the survival of parliamentary democracy in England and prevented England from becoming a despotic monarchy, like other European nations in that period.

Supply by Wagon

By the 18th Century, fighting with smoothbore muskets demanded higher standards of training and ferocious discipline in larger armies recruited by nation states (largely by compulsion and fraud) from the dregs of their respective populations. If such troops were permitted to forage they would seize the opportunity to desert, so the armies in the era of Marlborough and Frederick the Great moved in well-controlled columns with supplies provided in friendly countries by purchasing locally and in hostile countries by wagons carrying supplies from friendly magazines.

The Duke of Marlborough signing the dispatch at Blenheim (Source: Wikimedia Commons)

When in camp, an 18th Century army of 60,000 horses, 30,000 auxiliaries and 40,000 horses would require nearly 100 carts to arrive daily carrying flour and firewood to provide its bread ration, and the timely arrival of animals on the hoof and other provisions. The horses would need some 250 cart loads of grain per day, and many more cart loads of hay or cut grass if they could not find adequate grazing near the camp. In a fertile area, these requirements could be partially met by the orderly purchase of local supplies, provided the army did not stay too long. As and when the army advanced, it would be accompanied by 180 carts carrying bread rations for the next four days, sixty carts carrying bricks to build ovens when the army stopped on the fourth day, and hundreds more carts to carry the officers' baggage. If it planned to besiege an enemy fortress, the army would need a siege train with some 2,000 horses dragging the guns and mortars, and some 3,000 carts carrying gunpowder, shot, and other supplies.[5]

These considerations meant that an 18th Century army relying on wagons could not advance far from its supply bases. If it attempted to do this, its demand for wagons would rise exponentially as the distance from its bases increased and as the wagon drivers, their escorting troops and their draught horses consumed more and more of the provisions they were supposed to deliver. They also meant that it was impractical to campaign in the winter months when the army's horses could not find fresh grazing, and when un-metalled roads become impassable. It followed that 18th Century warfare was indecisive because no army could hope to advance fast and far enough to achieve a knockout blow, even if it succeeded in achieving local superiority in a particular theatre of operations. The superior army could normally advance only a short distance before it needed to halt to allow new forward magazines to be established and/or before it encountered an enemy fortress blocking a node on the road network. In either case, the delay allowed the inferior army to recruit, train and equip fresh troops and thus re-establish equilibrium.

Highland armies fighting for the Stuart Pretenders were a notable exception to these general rules. They could subsist on easily-portable oatmeal, supplemented by plundered livestock, and could therefore advance faster and farther than their Hanoverian opponents.

The French Revolution partially relaxed logistic constraints on the operations of French armies. After the Revolution these armies consisted of well-motivated troops, led by unscrupulous generals, who were often unconstrained by any respect for the laws of property. As these armies conferred the benefits of Liberte-Egalite-Fraternite on the countries they invaded, they thought it only fair that these countries should pay in kind for such benefits and accordingly the armies took what they wanted, especially from the rich. Because these French armies relied more on plunder and less on supply, they moved more rapidly than the wagon-encumbered armies of their enemies (in the Jena campaign, the Prussians had eight times more baggage than the French); because they moved more rapidly they could afford to march dispersed, concentrating for battle as necessary; because they marched dispersed, they could forage more effectively. In this new style of warfare the French armies outmanoeuvred their enemies to win victories in the field, and then poured like a rapid torrent into the heartland of the enemy nation, capturing its capital city and dictating peace. This technique yielded successive victories against France's rivals in Central Europe (although, even there, soldiers were temporarily hungry) but failed when French armies ventured into the less-fertile areas of Spain and Russia.

The problems of supplying an army in this period were vastly eased if it could be supplied by water transport along convenient rivers or canals. A horse pulling a barge can move a load one hundred times greater than when pulling a cart and waterways could be used freely when muddy roads were impassable. Hence, armies fighting in the Netherlands in the 17th and 18th Centuries devoted considerable efforts to capturing the enemy fortresses which commanded the waterways, and thus establishing supply lines to support a further advance. Water transport could play a useful tactical role, but it could not support a rapid strategic advance.

Case Study: American War of Independence

In the 18th Century much of the terrain on the frontiers of the Thirteen Colonies and Canada was undeveloped forest and swamp, where armies could find few provisions, little grazing and where their supply wagons could advance only as fast as passable tracks could be created, often only a few miles per day. Packhorses were able to cross rougher terrain but carried less than the same number of horses pulling wagons. Armies preferred to use water transport on lakes and rivers, but the latter were often interrupted by shoals or rapids which required the bateaux to be unloaded and portaged to the next navigable reach. In 1775 General Arnold used bateaux to transport a small army and its supplies from Augusta to Quebec along the Kennebec and Chaudiere Rivers, but lost many of his supplies when bateaux were wrecked or leaked. His hungry troops became progressively less capable of advance or retreat through steep or swampy portages and only just escaped starvation.[6]

In 1777, General Burgoyne's British army moved south from Montreal, planning to occupy the Hudson Valley and separate New England from the other rebellious colonies. His main army started from St. Johns on the Richelieu River, travelled in bateaux southward along Lake Champlain at about ten miles per day, and disembarked near Fort Ticonderoga at the beginning of July. On 6 July his army occupied the abandoned fort and the following day defeated parts of the retreating American garrison at Hubbardton and Skenesboro. By the 11 July, Burgoyne's army was concentrated at the southern tip of Lake Champlain, only twenty-three miles from Fort Edward on the Hudson. But there his progress slowed dramatically, partly because he has insufficient draught animals and partly because the retreating Americans had felled trees and destroyed bridges to make the terrain even more impassable. The British army did not assemble at Fort Edward till the end of July, having advanced at only one mile per day. Burgoyne's logistic problem was then so severe that he risked sending a small raiding force to seek horses at Bennington, where it was virtually annihilated by superior numbers of American militia. The British army crawled forward from Fort Edward at about half a mile per day until it was able to attack Bemis Heights on 19 September. This logistic-induced delay gave the Americans time to recover their morale, and to assemble large numbers of regulars and militia who defeated the British army and forced its surrender at Saratoga.[7]

Case Study: Russia 1812

When Napoleon planned to invade Russia, he realised that the scale and poverty of the country demanded greater organisation in his approach to logistics. His earlier victories in Italy and Germany had mostly been won campaigning in fertile country within 150 miles of his (French and allied) depots, but Moscow was 600 miles from his current bases in Poland and East Prussia. The French army's supply train was vastly expanded to comprise 9,336 vehicles and 32,500 horses (plus a few thousand more in reserve) and a total capacity of 10,400 tons.[8] But, as the French army moved away from its depots and the supply wagons spent longer en route between these bases and the advancing army, the supply train could deliver progressively smaller quantities, as shown below.

Wagon journey, base to army (days)	2	4	6
Daily delivery to army (tons)	2,400	1,100	670

Even if all of the supply train has been allocated to support the 450,000 men and 150,000 horses in the central group of armies, and even making the heroic assumption that those armies' horses could find sufficient grazing en route, the supply train could not have met the central group's needs for 1,500 tons of food and grain per day after its troops had gone farther than a wagon could travel in three days beyond the Russian frontier (i.e. about half way to Minsk). Once the French armies had gone beyond that point, and had

Napoleon and La Grande Armée on the retreat from Moscow (Source: Wikimedia Commons)

consumed the rations they had carried across the frontier, they had to plunder Russian towns and villages in order to survive. That process was inevitably disorganised and failed to prevent serious shortages; these were exacerbated by indiscipline and rivalry between contingents of different nationalities, shortages of water and the inability of the supply wagons to keep up with the leading troops. By the time the Grande Armee reached Smolensk, about half way to Moscow, half of its soldiers were absent through death, disease or desertion and a similar proportion of its cavalry horses had died through malnutrition and overwork.[9]

Supply by Railway

The business of supplying war was revolutionised by the development of railways, following the initial run by Stephensons's locomotive from Stockton to Darlington in 1825. The British Government soon realised that this new transport system would allow it to move its limited number of troops rapidly about the country to suppress riots by industrial workers. The Russians moved a corps of 14,500 men with all its horses and transport by rail in 1848. The Austrians moved 75,000 men in 1850, and the French astonished military opinion nine years later by deploying (in two months) 600,000 men and 130,000 horses at the start of their war against Austria, of which 230,000 men and 36,000 horses went directly to the theatre of active operations in Italy.[10] A railway train could carry soldiers and supplies ten times faster than they could be moved on foot or in wagons; it could operate when muddy roads were impassable; wood and water were available almost everywhere at all seasons of the year; and a train needed only an engineer, fireman and brakeman rather than the multitude of teamsters needed to move the same load.

The first major war in which railways played a decisive role was the American Civil War of 1861-5 (and discussed more fully in Case Study 1.2). When eleven slave states seceded from the United States to form the Confederacy, it was reasonable for the Southern statesmen to conclude that the sheer size of their new nation made it virtually unconquerable. After all, in the Revolutionary War the vast resources of the British Empire had been unable to conquer the Thirteen Colonies in a coastal strip barely 200 miles deep, and Napoleon, with all of Western Europe at his disposal, had failed disastrously in his campaign 600 miles deep into Russia. The new Confederacy formed a rough rectangle 1,000 by 600 miles (excluding the sparsely-populated plains of Texas and the swamps of Florida which theoretically added another 400 miles to both dimensions) and its leaders expected that it could resist almost indefinitely any invasion by the United States (particularly if additional border states seceded and added on average another 100 miles of depth). This proved to be a disastrous miscalculation. The United States was able to raise large armies, and could use railways (and steamboats where rivers flowed conveniently along the line of operations) to keep these armies supplied as they moved deep into Southern territory. Despite the efforts of Southern cavalry raiders to destroy track and burn railway bridges, Union construction gangs were able to make rapid repairs and keep the supplies flowing.

But away from the railways, the armies had to rely on wagons (like Napoleon) and could not move far from their railheads without suffering the traditional difficulties. The life expectancy of a horse in US army service was about four months so the supply train needed regular reinforcements of fresh horses to keep supplies moving. Most of the American roads were unsuited to heavy traffic, and in bad weather movement was excruciatingly difficult. When the Union Army of the Potomac attempted an outflanking march in January 1863, its many men and wagons churned the unmetalled roads of Virginia into a bottomless mire, and the army came to a helpless halt within a few miles of its starting point (with guns sunk to the axles and mules to their ears).[11] Movement was easier in summer, but the wagon trains accompanying the armies still proved a serious impediment. The Union army of 127,000 men advancing into Virginia in 1864 was accompanied by a train of over 4,000 wagons[12] whose slowness and vulnerability seriously constrained army operations (if the train had been arranged on one road it would have extended over most of the sixty-five miles from the army's starting point on the Rapidan River to its objective in Richmond). The Union advance in 1862-4 across Tennessee and north Georgia (from Nashville through Murfreesboro and Chattanooga, to Atlanta) proceeded in a series of short advances interspersed with pauses during which railways were built or rebuilt to establish a new railhead. Such activities, on this front and elsewhere, involved considerable resources; the United States Military Railroads (USMRR), which operated the railways in recaptured

Southern territory and organised construction and repair of the track, reached a maximum strength of 25,000 men.[13]

Towards the end of the American Civil War, when the defending Confederate forces were negligible, General Sherman abandoned his railway supply line and advanced 300 miles from Atlanta to the sea, foraging in true medieval style and subsisting his Union army on what it could loot in a wide sweep of Georgia farmland.

A British 5-inch howitzer during the Second Boer War circa 1900 (Source: US Library of Congress via Wikimedia Commons)

Many of the logistics problems of the American Civil War recurred in the Second Boer War (1899-1902) in South Africa, where troops needed to be provided with firewood as well as food and water. There were few railways and virtually no roads, so ox wagons found their own routes from point to point across the open veld. The Cape wagon, a design used by the Boers on their earlier Great Trek and by Americans heading across the prairies to California, could theoretically carry four tons but in South Africa its load rarely exceeded one ton. This load could be drawn on level ground by ten oxen, but double teams were needed to go up gradients or across rivers. Oxen travelled no more than ten miles per day and died even more rapidly (of tsetse-borne diseases) than horses in the American Civil War. Initially the British advances to relieve their besieged garrisons in Kimberley, Ladysmith and Mafeking followed the railway lines and were easy to block. Only later in the war, when the British had assembled large forces of cavalry and mounted infantry, they were able to move away from the railways (at least temporarily) to outflank Boer defensive positions.

In the Russo-Japanese war (1904-05) the Russians demonstrated the enormous logistic capabilities of the railway, using the Trans-Siberian line to transport and support an army of 310,000 men in Manchuria. This single-track railway line ran 5,400 miles from Moscow to Harbin Junction and was interrupted by a 100-mile gap demanding a ferry or sledge trip, according to the season, across Lake Baikal. This logistic achievement caused serious apprehensions in India, since it offered the prospect of a similar, but slightly-shorter, line capable of bringing a large Russian army to the North-West frontier.

The supreme masters of railway deployment were the officers of the German General Staff, which quickly realised that a nation surrounded by enemies (as Prussia had been in the 18th Century and as Germany would be again after France and Russia signed the Dual Entente in 1892) could only hope to succeed by moving its forces rapidly from one front to another to meet the most serious threats. The General Staff also realised that a nation which could deploy its forces rapidly at the outbreak of war would thereby gain significant advantages in the subsequent campaign. The effectiveness and problems of railway deployment were demonstrated in the wars of 1866 against the Austrians and of 1870-71 against the French. In both cases, the initial deployment was achieved successfully, but as the invading German armies moved away from their railheads they were forced to operate again in 18th Century style with horses and wagons. Because the railways could deliver supplies faster than they could be distributed, there was monumental chaos and traffic jams at the railheads. In some instances, supplies were left in the railway wagons, effectively taking those wagons out of service and blocking the track; in other cases thousands of tons of supplies were unloaded and left to rot. Fortunately for the Germans the ineptitude of the opposing commanders in both of these wars allowed the Germans to win decisive battles early, and to achieve victory before shortages of food and ammunition became serious.

Even in the railway age, many military campaigns had to be mounted in underdeveloped countries which were unsuitable for wheeled vehicles. In such campaigns, all supplies had to be transported by pack animals (including camels, elephants, horses, mules and yaks) which could carry on their backs only a small fraction of the load they could have drawn in a wagon. When suitable animals were not available, armies had to use hosts of native porters, who had very modest carrying capacity (about one third of a mule load), marched in long vulnerable columns, and had every incentive to abandon their loads at the least excuse.

Very unfavourable terrain could effectively prohibit the operation of large forces. On poor roads through swampy terrain a few wagons can proceed, but each makes the passage more difficult for the wagon following and in a long column the rearmost wagons get bogged down. In South Africa some drifts (fords) support the passage of a few wagons per day but if more try to cross the drift dissolves downstream in a flurry of mud and pebbles and the river is then impassable for several weeks while the drift slowly reforms. The trench warfare of the First World War created a band of virtually-impassable terrain several miles deep where multiple trench lines, shell holes and barbed wire made the re-supply of advancing troops exceptionally difficult.

Case Study: France 1914

In August 1914, the Imperial German Army sought to win the First World War at a stroke, by an overwhelming offensive against France to knock that nation out of the war before the Russian Army could mobilise and attack on the Eastern Front.[14] Since the Franco-German frontier had been heavily fortified, the German Chief of Staff, von Schlieffen, planned an offensive taking the bulk of the German Army through the Netherlands and Belgium to envelop Paris and take the French army in the rear. Schlieffen envisaged that "the last grenadier on the right should brush the Channel with his sleeve" and should march 400 miles to the Seine in twenty-five days.

By 1914, Schlieffen's plan had been modified to omit the invasion of the Netherlands, so that the German armies of the right wing had to funnel through the Liege gap (between the Dutch border and the Ardennes) and then advance west, southwest and south with the outermost troops passing west of Amiens and (ultimately) west of Paris. The railway staff had thoroughly mastered the procedures for deploying large armies, and moved 1,500,000 fully-equipped troops to Germany's western frontiers in ten days. Each corps (about 45,000 men) marching westward was accompanied by 1,164 wagons carrying engineering equipment, field hospitals etc. as well as supplies of food, forage and ammunition, and it was intended that these supply trains should be replenished by Army transport companies shuttling between the advancing troops and the nearest railhead. But with the troops marching almost as fast as the transport wagons, supplies from the rear could be delivered only at increasing intervals.

In practice, the leading troops lost touch with the transport columns almost immediately, and each German army was forced to seek, along the line of march, the 350 tons of food it required per day. Fortunately the country was rich, the season favourable, and captured Belgian and British supplies provided a windfall - otherwise the First Army, at the outer edge of the great German wheel, would have been rapidly reduced to starving immobility. In fact, the men were able to live well, without much recourse to the iron rations they carried, but this did not apply to horses. First Army had 84,000 horses needing nearly 1,000 tons of grain and fodder per day, which could not possibly have been supplied without an astronomical number of wagons - consequently it was expected to search out lush grazing and well-stocked barns. In the event this proved impractical. Some artillery horses died before they crossed the frontier into Belgium. By 11 August, barely a week after the start of operations, one cavalry division had to be withdrawn from action, and by 13 August all cavalry forces on the right wing were ordered to halt and rest for four days. Despite this rest, another cavalry division was withdrawn from action on 19 August, its horses starving and exhausted. The German armies advanced to Mons on 23 August, and later to the battle of the Marne in early September, without adequate cavalry for reconnaissance and increasingly short of artillery.

A steam locomotive taking on water at Burnham Junction in 1947 (Source: Centpacrr via Wikimedia Commons)

The German hopes for success in 1914 relied on railheads being pushed forward about as rapidly as the troops were advancing. But the Belgian and French railways had been thoroughly demolished by their retreating armies, and the railheads lagged, even though the German railwaymen worked themselves to exhaustion. By the battles of the Marne the German Armies of the right wing were being (inadequately) supplied from improvised railheads more than fifty miles away, then regarded as the maximum acceptable distance for supply by horse-drawn wagons, behind the leading troops.

Once the German armies were halted on the Marne and fighting hard against resurgent French and British forces, supply priority was given to the ammunition demanded by quick-firing rifles and artillery (whose consumption had increased thirty-fold since 1870-71). The halted armies were unable to forage each day in new farms and villages, and their situation was untenable, The German armies had to retreat, and could only stabilise the front when they regained close contact with their railheads.

It seems incredible that the grand strategy of the Imperial German Army relied for its success on foraging like a medieval host, and even more incredible that the logistic arrangements were never subjected to the gaming and analysis which were applied to the initial deployment and subsequent operations of combat forces. The failure of the German Army to achieve victory in the opening months of the First World War arose not only from the resilience of the opposing French and British forces but also from an intractable problem of logistics. The war could only be won by a quick advance, but a quick advance could not be supported by the means then available.

Supply by Truck

Although motor transport was used in 1914-18 and played a key role in particular operations (such as the defence of Verdun), its contribution in the First World War was negligible compared to railways in the rear areas and to the backs of men and pack animals near the front. But soldiers of all nations appreciated the potential of wheeled vehicles, which could go wherever there was a reasonable road surface, and of tracked vehicles, which could go almost anywhere. By 1939, the British Army had been motorised, but even that army had to use pack mules to carry supplies in Italy and Burma. Most large armies could afford to motorise only a fraction of their forces, and remained largely reliant on draught horses. The German Army in the Second World War, for example, consisted of two very different elements – the fully-motorised divisions with trucks to supply their rapid advances, and the infantry divisions which marched to battle and were largely supported by horse-drawn wagons. The different performance characteristics of these two elements posed great problems for the German High Command in the invasions of Poland (1939), France (1940) and Soviet Russia (1941), when the motorised divisions raced far ahead of the foot-slogging infantry, and consequently exposed themselves to counterattack (though in practice such opportunities were less evident to the defending commanders, and were rarely exploited). The improved logistic capabilities of the truck enabled the Panzer (armoured) divisions to advance rapidly in a blitzkrieg to achieve decisive victories provided that the campaigns were short and the distances involved were not excessive, for example

- 100 miles – East Prussia to Warsaw

- 200 miles – Belgian border to Channel coast
- 80 miles – River Somme to Paris

In these circumstances the army supply columns (6,600 vehicles carrying 19,500 tons to 103 divisions in 1939) could support the spearheads adequately.

German horses stuck in the Rasputitsa ('quagmire season') on the Eastern Front (Source: Bundesarchiv, Bild 101I-289-1091-26 / Dinstühler / CC-BY-SA via Wikimedia Commons)

The German High Command recognised that the invasion of Soviet Russia[15] would be more challenging since the principal objective, Moscow, was 700 miles from the frontier. Every yard of Russian railway would have to be converted to standard gauge before it could be used by German trains, and Russian demolition of bridges, signals and water towers would have to be urgently repaired. The roads were known to be few and bad. By scouring Europe for every conceivable military and civilian type of truck (2,000 types were used) the German Army preparing to invade Russia in 1941 was given 60,000 tons of transport to support 134 divisions (including thirty-three armoured and motorised divisions). If all this transport had been allocated to these mobile divisions, it could theoretically have supported their operations up to 300 miles into Russia, at which point their further advance would depend on how fast the Russian railways could be converted and repaired. Thus Leningrad, Moscow and Kiev (at 600, 700 and 900 miles respectively from the German bases) were all out of range of a rapid blitzkrieg, and in practice the logistic situation rapidly deteriorated because of breakdowns and partisan activity. By the time the railways had been repaired sufficiently to permit further advance, the Russians had recovered their morale and brought up reinforcements from Siberia, and winter was on the way.

The logistic problems were even worse in North Africa, where German forces had to operate entirely without railways and where the distances were even greater than in Russia.

Case Study: North Africa 1941

In most theatres of operations, opposing armies can expect to find some local food, fuel, shelter, etc. but in the desert they have only the slightest hope of finding anything useful and all their supplies (including water) must be transported from remote bases to the frontline. There are many other special problems, from the sunburn and sores which afflict the soldiers to the higher failure rates and higher fuel consumption of internal combustion engines. Early in 1941, the German High Command sent one light motorised and one armoured division to Sirte, to block the threatened British advance on Tripoli.[16] There was no railway from Tripoli to Sirte (300 miles) so it was planned that the supplies for these two divisions would be transported by 1,170 two-ton trucks – much more than was provided to the divisions then preparing to attack Russia. The total Axis forces requirement of 2,300 tons/day exceeded the unloading capacity of the port of Tripoli (about 1,500 tons/day) so the Vichy French were asked if supplies could be routed via Bizerta. The German High Command realised that any eastward advance would inevitably demand additional vehicles, and explicitly ordered the blocking force to act defensively.

Panzers in North Africa just before the Battle of Sollum, June 1941 (Source: Wikimedia Commons)

However, General Erwin Rommel saw a good opportunity for a quick victory and attacked at the beginning of April, driving the British out of Libya (except for the besieged port of Tobruk) and establishing his leading forces on the Egyptian frontier. This solved the unloading problem, since Benghazi was able to handle up to 750 tons per day, but put his army in an impossible supply position. Most of his supplies still had to come via Tripoli which was now 1,050 miles from the front line[17] and his motor transport was totally inadequate for the task (captured British supplies and transport provided only temporary relief). The Italians succeeded in shipping sufficient supplies across the Mediterranean (averaging 2,700 tons/day in February - May) but these supplies simply piled up at the wharves while shortages exasperated the troops in the front line. Rommel needed to capture Tobruk with its unloading facilities capable of delivering supplies close to the Egyptian frontier. But he admitted that this operation would require another two German armoured divisions whose supplies (at least another 700 tons per day) could neither be landed through clogged Tripoli and Benghazi or transported by his overworked transport columns.

When British ships and aircraft from Malta began to inflict significant losses on Italian shipping in the second half of 1941, the possibility of avoiding this danger by sending supplies via Yugoslavia and Greece to Benghazi was considered. This option was unattractive because it depended on a single-track railway south of Belgrade which had limited capacity and was frequently blown up by partisans. In the summer of 1941, the Luftwaffe tried to establish an air bridge, using transport aircraft and gliders, from Crete to Derna delivering up to 400 tons per day[18]. But the aircraft in transit and the airhead at Derna were vulnerable to the RAF, and even Derna was still quite far (270 miles) from the German front line, so the air route was no substitute for sea transport. Despite the depredations of British air and naval forces based in Malta, the Italians continued to land sufficient supplies (2,400 tons per day) from July to October, but the 2,100 mile round trip from Tripoli to the front was an insuperable problem, absorbing much of the fuel landed before it could reach the Panzer divisions at the front. The situation went from bad to worse when the British attacked in November 1941, and their marauding aircraft and armoured cars forced German transport columns to move only at night.

After his retreat to El Agheila, only a manageable 480 miles from Tripoli, Rommel demanded another 8,000 trucks for his supply columns - this was denied since the thirty-three panzer divisions fighting in Russia could only muster 14,000 trucks between them. But Rommel attacked anyway, advancing first to Gazala (900 miles from Tripoli) in February 1942 and then to El Alamein (1,300 miles from Tripoli) in July 1942. In the course of the second advance he captured Tobruk (with a windfall of 2,000 trucks, 5,000 tons of supplies and 1,400 precious tons of fuel) and thereafter could use its harbour to land supplies. Tobruk was only 400 miles behind the front line, but it could only handle 600 tons per day, and the port was so dangerously exposed to British naval and air forces that it threatened to become the "cemetery of the Italian Navy". Accordingly, the Italians decided to concentrate their convoys on Tripoli and Benghazi, now 1,300 and 650 miles from the front. Sufficient supplies continued to be shipped across the Mediterranean, but only a trickle reached the German-Italian army at the gates of Alexandria.

Since the campaign in North Africa was one of the last major operations undertaken independently by British Empire forces, it has received disproportionate attention from British historians. Many different explanations of the final British victory have been proposed (including a lack of German reinforcements, failures of the Italian Navy and merchant marine, or to the presence of Malta astride Axis supply lines) but the primary cause was an insufficiency of Axis motor transport. This case study demonstrates that a logistics chain is limited by the capacity of its weakest link, and that a long supply chain demands very large resources.

Case Study: France 1944

It was not only the German Army which was constrained by shortages of motor transport. After the Allied victories in Normandy and on the Seine in 1944, the British and American armies were advancing rapidly towards the German frontier when they came to the end of their logistic tether, about 400 miles from Cherbourg and the Normandy beaches. The allied armies had some 1,500 tons of motor transport per division[19], which proved insufficient to support an advance into Germany which could have ended the war nine months earlier, in the autumn of 1944. In such situations soldiers and animals can sometimes struggle on, but machines have an absolute and uncompromising demand for fuel (as well as lubricants, spares, etc.). The immobilised General Patton complained "My men can eat their belts but my tanks have gotta have gas".

Case Study: Russia 1942-45

The Red Army was affected by similar logistic constraints in the later years of the Second World War. Its offensives to liberate its own territory and then to invade Poland and Germany were characterised by a series of limited advances of a few hundred miles[20], interspersed with long pauses while the railways were rebuilt to support a further advance. Russian (and American) trucks were vastly superior as transport systems to the horse-drawn wagons of the American Civil War (see above) and enabled the Red Army to operate farther from their railheads, but supply by truck was, and still remains, limited by the inevitable constraints of tonnage, manpower and fuel consumption.

Supply by Air

During the Second World War, transport aircraft had only limited carrying capacity (the Junkers Ju 52/3M and the Douglas C-47 Dakota each carried about four tons) and were vulnerable to enemy interception in transit and at the point of delivery. German attempts to reinforce their invasions of Holland (1940) and Crete (1941) wrote off hundreds of transport aircraft, and the effort to sustain the Sixth Army trapped at Stalingrad was also very costly and ultimately futile. Transport aircraft could only be used successfully when friendly fighters commanded the air corridor and friendly troops controlled an adequate area around the airfield to which supplies were delivered.

The first Vietnam War[21] (also known as Indochina, 1945-54) was a conflict between a French Expeditionary Force backed by local militia and the Vietminh army which started as a predominately guerrilla army but developed Main Force Units (capable of engaging French units directly) as the war went on. The outcome of the struggle depended on the capacity of the opposing armies to maintain their lines of supply from, respectively, the port of Haiphong and the northern border with China. The French used lorry columns, which were tied to the roads and were repeatedly blocked and harassed by the Vietminh, and some DC3 transport aircraft to drop paratroops and supplies for particular operations. The Vietminh used porters, under strict ideological discipline, to carry their supplies down the Ho Chi Minh and other trails. On long trips, the porters ate 90% of what they carried, but this problem was overcome by using huge numbers - 200,000 porters were used to support the invasion of Laos in 1952. The war was eventually decided by the French attempt to establish a strong base astride Vietminh supply routes at Dien Bien Phu, which was 300 miles from Haiphong and close to the Laos border. The Vietminh used 50,000 engineers and coolies to repair the roads from China after French air attacks; they also used 260,000 porters on jungle trails which the French could not locate or interrupt. The French garrison of Dien Bien Phu had to be supplied by air, using some ninety aircraft, initially to an airstrip inside the perimeter and later (as the Vietminh established AA guns on the surrounding hills and artillery to command the airstrip) by parachute from progressively-higher altitudes. The situation got worse after the Vietminh infiltrated the main French airbases and, ignoring other aircraft types, destroyed many transports on the ground. Soon after, the French garrison had to use ammunition sparingly, and the fortress fell in May 1954.

A US soldier watches a supply drop from a C-130 Hercules during Operation Junction City in early 1967 (US DOD via Wikimedia Commons)

The second Vietnam War[22] (1965-73) can be dated either from the arrival of American Marines to defend the enclave at Da Nang in March 1965 - or from the commitment of American advisers and helicopter units some years earlier. This war presented the US forces with the problem of organising the build up (moving troops, vehicles and equipment to Vietnam in ships which sometimes had to wait twenty days for a berth) and the strategic logistical challenge of supporting 626,000 men[23] at the end of a communications line 11,000 miles long, as well as the tactical logistics problems which had thwarted the French. Airfields were constructed throughout South Vietnam, so that by 1966 nearly everywhere was within twenty-five miles of an airstrip suitable for a C-130 Hercules transport, which could deliver 7,500 gallons of fuel or proportionate quantities (up to fifteen tons) of ordnance, eggs or ice cream. The tactical problems were solved by lavish provision of helicopters and tactical transports operating with total air superiority. Helicopters are a mixed blessing; they can deliver loads almost anywhere, but they gobble fuel and need to be protected during the delivery phase (the US lost 3,000 helicopters destroyed, and many more damaged). A typical US resupply operation to a hill fort would involve twelve CH-46 Sea Knight helicopters delivering some twenty tons supported by twelve A4 Skyhawks and four UH-1E Iroquois gunships. Such lavish logistics plus massive air strikes enabled the US forces to win where the French lost; the US Marines successfully defended Khe Sanh when the Vietcong tried to repeat the earlier victory at Dien Bien Phu. As long as US troops remained in Vietnam and the US taxpayers were prepared to support the immense logistic burden involved (estimates of the financial cost of the war range up to $236bn[24] or $100,000 per soldier year, twenty-five times the French expenditure), the US and South Vietnamese could successfully resist Vietcong pressure.

Case Study: Falklands 1982

In the UK campaign to retake the Falkland Islands[25], "logistics was the principal factor driving planning". The South Atlantic Ocean is even more devoid of useful supplies than the North African desert, and the Falkland Islands themselves are little better. Much of the ground is peat bog, unable to support a wheeled vehicle and interspersed with rivers and boulders. The weather is cold, wet and windy - very unpleasant for camping or bivouacking. Every bean, bullet and drop of fuel for the 25,000 men in the British expeditionary force had to come down a line of communications 8,000 miles long, most of it in twenty-six warships and fifty-four ships taken up from trade (STUFT). The War Maintenance Reserve of the 3rd Commando Brigade, Royal Marines (fuel, ammunition, food and spares) amounted to 9,000 tons to sail with the task force, plus additional supplies for the RN and RAF (total stocks out-loaded from the UK reached 17,000 tons).

The operation suffered because there was no clear definition of the mission when the task force sailed. The expedition could not be sure whether it would have to make an opposed landing on the Falklands, and because it was perceived necessary for the task force to sail from UK as soon as possible, ships were loaded on the basis of an existing plan for the reinforcement of northern Norway. As the diplomatic and military situation clarified, and an opposed landing became virtually certain, stores had to be reshuffled when the task force was at anchor, rolling in the Atlantic swell, at Ascension Island. Fortunately, the airfield at Ascension could be used to receive additional supplies which had not been available when the task force sailed (which provides a good example of the advantages of using complementary transport modes).

Once a landing had been achieved in San Carlos Bay, the shortage of ship-to-shore boats and helicopters (exacerbated by the sinking of the Atlantic Conveyor with three Chinook and five Wessex helicopters aboard) made it impossible simultaneously to move reinforcements ashore from ships, to keep the troops ashore supplied with ninety-five tons per day of food and other stores (including petrol for the generators powering Rapier missile systems) and to move troops and equipment towards Port Stanley. The situation was made worse by the policy that (because of the danger of air attack) ships could only unload in San Carlos Bay for four hours each night, and by many stores being misplaced when ships were forced to withdraw before unloading was complete.

RFA Sir Percivale, which unlike the Sir Galahad and Sir Tristram, came through the Falklands War unscathed (Source: PH1 (AW) Raymond H. Turner II, US Navy via Wikimedia Commons)

Fortunately, the Argentine Air Force concentrated its attacks in San Carlos water on the warships and not a single logistic ship or troop carrier there was hit. Furthermore the Argentinean Army failed to counterattack the beachhead which would have diverted some of the scarce helicopters to ammunition replenishment and casualty evacuation. The action at Goose Green demonstrated that ammunition expenditure of all calibres in a modern firefight was about four times greater than the planned level derived from low level "brush fire" wars. The British invasion force nearly stagnated into a situation where the land force could barely defend its supply ships and the supply ships could barely keep the land force supplied. The deadlock was broken by the marching (a.k.a. yomping) capacity of Royal Marine Commandos, helped by their few tracked vehicles, which allowed them to advance (largely on foot) from San Carlos to attack the mountains around Port Stanley. But the shortage of logistic support continued to constrain operations, and also encouraged the British gamble of landing 5th Infantry Brigade troops at Fitzroy which cost the British forces forty-three dead and many more wounded or deprived of their equipment when the landing ships "Sir Galahad" and "Sir Tristram" were bombed.

The Falklands campaign showed again that logistics are of paramount importance, and MoD's report to Parliament drew attention to the need for enhanced logistics support for operations outside the NATO area.

Case Study: Gulf War 1991

The logistics problems in the Gulf War[26] replicated in many ways, the earlier desert war in North Africa in 1940-3, but with the advantage that fuel was provided free and on site by Saudi Arabia. Other logistics problems, such as the mechanical unreliability of British tanks and the enormous need for daily supplies of fresh water (4.5 litres/head/day), proved very familiar. The 45,000 UK Service personnel deployed to the Gulf were accompanied by 15,000 vehicles and 400,000 tons of freight, of which about 10% was carried by air and the rest by sea. The 1st (UK) Armoured Division had 25,800 men of which almost half were logistics personnel delivering the 2,000 tons per day which the Division required to maintain itself (this requirement rose to 6,000 tons per day during active operations). Even allowing for the inclusion of logistics personnel in the division, this represents a substantial increase in logistics requirements over the 650 tons/day needed by an Allied armoured division in World War II. Modern armoured divisions have much more equipment (vehicles, radio sets, etc) than their predecessors of half a century ago, and their expenditure of ammunition is also substantially greater.

It is notable that the British Army chose to use trucks and support helicopters to move these prodigious quantities of supplies inland from the port at Jubail, 250 miles to its forward depots, when a light railway would have been considerably more efficient. It is also notable that £291m of the £1073m cost of that Division's contribution to the war was expended moving it to and returning it from the area of operations.[27]

Supply Lines and Transport Modes

It is possible, from this review of logistics achievements and difficulties in various periods of history, to draw some conclusions from a logistics perspective of the desirable and undesirable qualities of armies, of their equipment, and of their supply arrangements.

In an ideal army, the soldiers themselves would be frugal and hardy, able to subsist on a handful of rice or oatmeal and resistant to the diseases in their area of operations. The ideal army would not have soldiers who demanded civilian standards of living at all times, or officers who similarly brought a lavish lifestyle into the field. The ideal army's front-line equipment (weapons, etc) should ideally be light, so that much of it is portable by the soldiers themselves (so it helps if the soldiers are physically strong). All front-line systems should be simple to operate, should have low consumption of fuel and ordnance (precisely-aimed shots and shells are preferable to random bombardments), and should be robust and reliable to minimise the need for replacement or repair. These qualities yield low requirements for manpower to operate and support the systems, and low demands on the army's supply lines. The transport systems which provide the army's mobility should (for the same reasons) be robust and reliable, and have low fuel consumption.

But, however ideal the soldiers and equipment of an army may be, they will always require a supply line. The capacity of the supply line is determined by the size of the army and the intensity of its operations, and the length of the supply line is determined by the practicable routes (by land, sea and air) from the army's permanent base to its area of operations. Supplies, fuel, reinforcements, etc. can be carried in a variety of transport modes from factory, depot or warehouse to the front line along one or more supply lines in parallel. Each supply line may involve several successive modes of transport (generally at least two, since rear-area transport is unsuitable for the forward area and vice versa), which have at different times included:

- Railroads
- Trucks (wheeled or tracked)
- Horses / mules
- Porters

- Ships / barges
- Fixed-wing aircraft
- Helicopters

A UN fuel damp at Pusan, South Korea in March 1952 (Source G. Dimitri Boria, US Army via Wikimedia Commons)

The capacity of each supply line is inevitably limited by its worst bottleneck, which might be a shortage of transport vehicles or escorts, or constraints on loading/unloading capacity at one of the interfaces between transport modes. The supply line's capacity may also be affected by weather or by enemy operations.

There are several desirable qualities associated with logistic supply lines, which should ideally be:

1. Fast, and therefore responsive to unforeseen demands for particular supplies or for personnel reinforcement or evacuation; fast re-supply also minimises the stocks required in the theatre of operations;
2. Economical of manpower and fuel resources for operation and support of the transport vehicles and their escorts:
3. Flexible in the chosen route and point of delivery, and hence responsive to

changes in the location of the force to be supplied and/or able to avoid or surmount enemy interdiction operations.

4. Little affected by adverse weather

Railways are very economical but rely on a fixed (and hence vulnerable) infrastructure of track, signals, sidings, water towers, etc. Fixed-wing aircraft are fast but can only land at pre-prepared airstrips. Helicopters are supremely flexible and need virtually no infrastructure, but are extravagant of fuel and require large amounts of skilled manpower and spares for maintenance and repair. Trucks are comparatively slow and require many drivers, but they can go wherever there is an adequate roadway (and tracked versions can go across country) unless the weather is particularly unfavourable. Ships are relatively slow and require suitable ports for loading and unloading, but have large cargo capacity and can vary their transit route if necessary to avoid contact with enemy forces. All these vehicles can be allocated sufficient crews to permit continuous operations, pausing only for loading and unloading.

Human and animal transport has been used throughout history and was still used in the 21st Century, when there is a shortage of vehicles and/or when the terrain in unsuitable for them. Their capacity is limited - a pack horse can carry about 220lbs and a soldier can carry around half that (65lbs on the Some in 1916 and 120lbs across the Falkland Islands in 1982) - and their endurance is limited by physiological needs for food and sleep at acceptable intervals. Accordingly, their speed is limited to about a dozen miles per day, less in unfavourable terrain and more under operational pressure. They are prone to diseases which do not affect mechanical vehicles, but their ingenuity and determination often allows them to surmount obstacles and shortages and to deliver vital supplies to where they are required.

In principle, it is possible to deliver any desired quantity of supplies over any distance, using whatever transport mode is available, by assigning sufficient resources to the task. In practice, the volume of resources required rapidly becomes unaffordable and unmanageable, as the desired quantity and distance increase. In real operations, an army commander has a given level of logistic resources, which circumscribes those operations which he can undertake successfully. The limitations set by the army's logistic resources can sometimes be stretched by the ingenuity of a commander and the determination of his troops, but this is more difficult in a modern army where complex equipments resent improvisation. The available level of logistic resources has always determined (in medieval, Napoleonic and modern times) how fast and far an army can advance and how far from its base it can be sustained.

Historical Trends

In the course of history, some developments have facilitated the task of supplying armies in the field. The increasing European cultivation of the potato in the 17th and 18th Centuries provided a crop which could substitute for bread, and which soldiers could gather and prepare more easily than grain. The invention of tinned food in the 19th Century allowed soldiers a more-varied diet, and eased the problems of food transportation and storage. In parallel, developments in horse harnesses and road surfacing made supply by wagon progressively more efficient, and in the last 150 years the introduction of railways, trucks, aircraft and helicopters have provided a range of transport modes of much greater capability and payload/fuel ratios than those available to earlier commanders from Caesar to Napoleon.

However, these increases in capability have been offset by concurrent increases in an army's requirements for equipment and supplies. Medieval swords and spears could be used for years, needing only occasional repair, but a modern army needs weapon systems and vehicles to confer firepower and mobility. These weapon systems and vehicles must be accompanied by appropriate ready-to-use stocks of ammunition, fuel and spares (as well as the test equipment and tools needed for maintenance and repair) and a logistic supply chain to ensure replenishment of these stocks as required. Modern weapon systems have a prodigious appetite for ammunition because they need more shots to achieve a hit (Napoleonic soldiers made one hit per 400 shots but US soldiers in Vietnam made one in 600,000). The soldiers in a modern army need (and deserve) better standards of food, hygiene, accommodation and medical care than were available in earlier times; these requirements increase the support services which must accompany a modern army and the logistics needed to transport and to resupply those services. The combined demands of the soldiers and their equipment have inflated and continue to inflate the resources needed to transport an army and to support it in the field. This trend is manifest in the increasing daily requirement of a division in the field; indicative values in tons per day are shown below, with the higher value characteristic of active combat operations:

Napoleonic	20-35	Ex fodder
First World War	80-250	Ex fodder
Second World War	350 - 650	
Gulf War 1991	2,000 – 6,000	

The size and equipment of an army division has varied through 19th and 20th Centuries, and supply requirements vary between different nations and different types of division, but the historical trend is unmistakeable.

It follows that while modern armies have considerable tactical mobility conferred by their many trucks and support helicopters, they require very large logistic resources to deploy a task force and support it in the field. If those logistic resources are not available in sufficient quantity, the capability of the task force is strictly limited.

Decisions on the procurement of new defence equipment should therefore take explicit account not only of its life cycle cost (which includes the personnel and supplies required for direct support of the equipment, as arranged under its Integrated Logistic Support[28] plan) and of its military operational effectiveness, but also of the cost of the logistic resources required to deploy the equipment (plus associated personnel, fuel, spares and support equipment) to the envisaged area(s) of operation, to maintain it there for as long as necessary, and afterwards to repatriate it to the home base.

USNS San Jose, a US Navy combat stores ship of the Mars-class, which served in both the Vietnam and Gulf Wars, as well as providing support to the Australian-led INTERFET peacekeeping mission to East Timor (1993) and supported the hospital ship USNS Mercy after the December 2004 tsunami (Source: J L Guerrero, US Navy via Wikimedia Commons)

Conclusions

The preceding accounts of historical operations have demonstrated that logistics is important, and that the capacity of a logistics system is set by the capacity of its most restrictive link or interface. The system must operate coherently to provide the frontline troops with the right volume and mix of supplies to maintain those troops and their equipment in optimum condition for efficient use, and the required mix depends on the troops' speed of advance and their intensity of operations. Modern logistics vehicles are much more efficient than earlier types, but that is counterbalanced by the high expectations of modern troops for creature comforts and rapid casualty evacuation, by the greater rate of ammunition usage by modern weapon systems and by the greater number of vehicles, radios and other equipment associated with a modern army division. Thus, in contrast to a medieval army which found it easier to supply itself when moving than when stationary, a modern army finds it easier to sit still than to move because movement demands ever-increasing logistic resources.

In the 18th Century, the amount of equipment, transport and supplies required by a European army had increased to such an extent, relative to the capacity of the transport modes then available, that the movement of such armies became extremely ponderous. Warfare became accordingly indecisive, because the superior force could not drive home its advantages. Today, modern transport systems provide much greater capacity and flexibility, but a modern army has an exceedingly large requirement for the regular delivery of fuel, ammunition and other supplies. Small contingents can be deployed rapidly to fight ill-armed guerrillas, but the deployment and support of a large force, equipped for a major high-intensity conflict, demands careful planning and enormous resources.

Accordingly, the assessment of any new weapon system should take explicit account of its associated logistic requirements. Future force planning and equipment procurement policies must seek to reconcile the conflicting goals of force, mobility and economy.

Endnotes

[1] MoD. (2011) *Joint Warfare Publication 0-01 - British Defence Doctrine*, 4th Edition, Shrivenham: DCDC, November 2011, pp. 2-8.

[2] Dupuy, R & T. (1993) *Collins Encyclopaedia of Military History*, London: BCA, p. 339.

[3] *Ibid.* p. 445.

[4] Day, J. (2007) *Gloucester and Newbury 1643*, Barnsley: Pen & Sword, pp. 189 and 194.

[5] Chandler, D. (1990) *The Art of Warfare in the Age of Marlborough*, Staplehurst: Spellmount Ltd.

[6] Huston, J. (1991) *Logistics of Liberty*, Newark, DA: University of Delaware Press.

[7] Seymour, W. (1982) *Yours to Reason Why*, London: BCA.

[8] van Creveld, M. (1977) *Supplying War*, Cambridge: Cambridge University Press, p. 63.

[9] Smith, D. (2002) *Armies of 1812*, Staplehurst: Spellmont Ltd.

[10] *Op Cit*. van Creveld, p. 82.

[11] McPherson, J. (1989) *Battle Cry of Freedom*, New York: Ballantyne Books, p. 584.

[12] Fuller, J. (1958) *The Generalship of Ulysses S. Grant*, New York: Da Capo Press Inc., p. 227.

[13] Katcher, P. (1992) *The American Civil War Source Book*, London: Weidenfield Military, p. 169.

[14] *Op Cit*. van Creveld, Chapter 4.

[15] *Ibid*. Chapter 5.

[16] *Ibid*. Chapter 6.

[17] Kershaw A. and Close, I. (1968) *The Desert War*, London: Phoebus, p. 37.

[18] Buckingham, W. (2009) *Tobruk*, Stroud: The History Press Ltd, p. 304.

[19] *Op Cit*. van Creveld, p. 144.

[20] Macksey, K. (1976) *Tank Warfare*, London: Panther Books, p. 222 says 250 miles is ambitious.

[21] Thompson, J. (1991) *The Lifeblood of War*, London: Brasseys, pp. 133-186.

[22] *Ibid*. pp. 193-219.

[23] *Op Cit*. Dupuy, p. 1333.

[24] Maclear, M. (1981) *The Ten Thousand Day War*, New York: Avon Books, p. 355.

[25] *Op Cit*. Thompson, pp. 249-288.

[26] See for example White, M. (1995) *Gulf Logistics - Blackadder's War*, London: Brassey's (UK); Pagonis, W. (1992) Moving Mountains: Lessons in Leadership and Logistics from the Gulf War, Boston, MA: Harvard Business School Press.

[27] Atkinson, R. *The Prediction of the Costs of Military Operations*, unpublished paper.

[28] Kirkpatrick, D et al. (2004) *Integrated Logistics Support and All That – The Wiley Guide to Managing Projects*, New Jersey: John Wiley & Sons Inc., pp. 597-620.

Part Two // Defence Acquisition

Single Service Procurement: The Royal Navy's New Hunter Killers

Steve Robinson

Centre for Defence Acquisition, Cranfield University, Defence Academy of the UK.

"The Astute Class will become a cornerstone of UK Defence capability and the benefit they will bring to our Royal Navy cannot be overstated." – Lord Drayson, Former Minister for Science and Innovation

HMS Astute on the shiplift outside the Devonshire Dock Hall after launch (Source: PoorTom via Wikimedia Commons)

Introduction

In January 2001, one hundred years to the day after construction began on Holland 1, the Royal Navy's first submarine, the first steel that was to become HMS Astute was laid down at Barrow-In-Furness, Cumbria. This new Astute Class of nuclear powered hunter-killer submarine (SSN) is the most technologically advanced of her type ever produced for the Royal Navy[1] and the programme for its design, build and in-service operation, has become a rich source of political, economic, technical and programme management experiences and lessons.

Nuclear-powered attack submarines are at the heart of the Royal Navy force structure. They have a wide variety of roles and are capable of deployment either as an integrated layer of defence within a Task Force or independently in advance of such a force.[2] The Astute Class will provide the Royal Navy with the means to support this policy well into the 21st Century. They are planned to have improved communications facilities to support joint operations and an enhanced capability to operate in the littoral (close to the shore) compared with previous classes.

HMS Tireless (a Trafalgar-class submarine) near the North Pole in 2004 (Source: Chief Journalist Kevin Elliott, US Navy via Wikimedia Commons)

To ensure that sufficient forces are available for operations, the MoD has had a requirement since at least 2004, for a defined number of submarines to be ready to deploy at short notice. To meet this requirement eleven Swiftsure and Trafalgar Class submarines were in service in 2004 – the oldest of which had entered service in 1974. To replace these submarines, the MoD had originally planned to purchase eight Astute Class submarines, but in 2007 this was revised to seven.[3] The Astute Class will progressively replace both the Swiftsure and Trafalgar Classes[4], which are planned to be decommissioned in 2010 and 2022 respectively.

The Astute Class submarines are required to undertake a range of tasks including:[5]

- Support the Vanguard Class submarine & the Successor Deterrent
- Anti-Submarine Warfare
- Anti-Surface Ship Warfare
- Surveillance and Intelligence gathering
- Land attack using Tomahawk Land Attack Missiles (TLAM)

The contract requirement for both the Astute Class submarines and their support is specified in function and performance terms, giving the prime contractor, BAE Systems, the responsibility to achieve the specified performance which will build on that of the Trafalgar Class, updated with a new submarine combat system and a much greater weapon load. It includes the Rolls Royce PWR2 pressurised water reactor plant used in the more recent Vanguard Class submarine, and a range of specific improvements to achieve the required through life capability.[6]

This case study offers a broad examination of the Astute Programme in order to identify and examine the implications of key decisions that have been made and to consider how these implications may have relevance to the direction and management of similar defence acquisition programmes.

HMS Spartan (a Swiftsure-class submarine)
(Source: defenceimagery.mod.uk)

Background – The Chronology

In June 1991 (equivalent of the current MoD Initial Gate) approval was given to proceed with a programme of studies to define the Batch 2 Trafalgar Class Boat (now known as the Astute Class). This programme of studies led to the issue of an Invitation to Tender for the design and build of an initial batch of three boats.[7]

In July 1994, as a result of concerns over the overall affordability of the programme, the Minister (Defence Procurement) and Treasury approved that further risk reduction studies be undertaken in parallel with the formal bidding phase of the programme. To maintain an effective competitive environment, contracts for risk reduction were awarded to both bidders, GEC Marconi (now BAE Systems Maritime-Submarines) and Vickers Shipbuilding and Engineering Ltd. GEC-Marconi was subsequently identified as MoD's preferred bidder in December 1995. Using the commercial policy of No Acceptable Price No Contract (NAPNOC), a Prime Contract was placed with BAE Systems in March 1997 for the design, build and initial in service support of the first three of the class.[8]

During 2002, the MoD and BAE Systems recognised the full impact on the Astute programme of the long production gap between the Vanguard & Astute Classes, and the significant difficulties that had been encountered following the introduction of Computer Aided Design (CAD). These problems were reported in National Audit Office's (NAO) *Major Projects Report 2003*. They arose in part because the Astute Class was the first UK submarine programme to use CAD techniques, and the complexities of these were underestimated. The problems contributed to a cost increase of £886m and a time delay of forty-three months to the programme.[9]

BAE Systems is responsible for the design and build of the vessels and provision of all equipment, including the combat system and for demonstrating functional performance. Under the MoD Smart Procurement Initiative, a fully Integrated Project Team (IPT) was formed in early 2000 for the Astute Class and other elements of new capability required for the existing Swiftsure and Trafalgar Classes. The submarines are assembled in the Devonshire Dock Hall at Barrow-in-Furness which is the largest submarine building construction complex of its kind in Europe. This hall was designed to hold four vessel hulls simultaneously and two in build.[10]

In February 2003, MoD and BAE Systems concluded an agreement to provide greater certainty about the delivery of the submarines by restructuring the programme.[11] The contract was amended in December 2003 to reflect this agreement. Although still under a single prime contract, the price for the design, development and production of the First of Class was separated from the pricing of the second and third submarines. The First of Class element of the contract was incentivised through a 'Shareline' arrangement which allowed the company and the MoD to share cost under/over-runs.

Operator and maintainer training specific to the new Astute submarines was arranged to be provided through the Astute Class Training Service (ACTS) PFI contract.[12] This contract was let with FAST-Training Services Ltd in September 2001 and a contract amendment required to realign ACTS with the delayed submarine build programme was signed in July 2004. Training delivery was planned at this time to be initiated in December 2012. The contract covered training for the first three boats only because, at the time of contract award, there was no approval for the build of later Astute Class Submarines. Further approval was received in 2007, to include provision the fourth boat within the ACTS.

ACTS comprises of Command Team Training, Ship Control Training and Manoeuvring Room Training simulators, Weapon Handling & Loading Rig along with various classrooms and office space. The training facilities are housed in a purpose built Astute Training Facility (ATF) located at Faslane in Scotland, which was completed in 2004. ACTS is undergoing progressive acceptance of the eight training elements.

In July 2006, an Astute Class Support Review Note was approved to implement an Initial Astute Support Solution for four years and five months elapsed time, up to the end of December 2012.

A further order for boat four was placed on 21 May 2007[13], which covered initial build work prior to agreement of a whole boat contract and price.

In 2009, £139m was removed from the Astute Programme budget for the period 2009 – 2013, as part of the MoD 2008 Equipment Examination to reduce short-term budget pressures. This was done by slowing down production of the second, third and fourth boats and deferring boats five, six and seven. This increased the total programme costs in the longer term by a net £400m.[14]

In March 2010, approval for the Initial build activities of boat five was given and long lead items were ordered for boat six.[15]

In October 2010, there was a significant development for defence acquisition with the Strategic Defence and Security Review[16], which was the first full defence review since 1998. The Review was undertaken during a major on-going military commitment in Afghanistan and with a shortfall reported by the Department of up to £42bn (which included funding for the Successor nuclear deterrent programme) between the anticipated defence budget and forecast spending over the coming decade. As the Review noted, such a shortfall made "painful, short-term measures unavoidable", such as reducing or cutting military capability. Two of the most significant measures taken by the Review were extending the build programme of the Astute Class submarine and cancelling the Nimrod maritime patrol aircraft. The Review also changed the Joint Strike Fighter (JSF) variant to be carried on the Queen Elizabeth class aircraft carrier.

As a consequence of the SDSR, an option was taken in 2010 to defer the introduction of the Successor Programme and to consequently delay the Astute Programme to maintain steady production. This added another £330m to the Astute Programme cost and delayed the In-Service date for boat four by sixteen months. The SDSR also announced plans with the main industrial partners to reduce the cost of the entire submarine business by £900m over the next decade.

During MoD Planning Round 2011, boats two to seven were further delayed to align with the deferred Successor Programme and avoid a production gap in the submarine construction industry. This added a further £266m to the Astute Programme cost, bringing the total increase in costs to over £1bn. The cost increase rises to over £1.9bn when the technical difficulties and capability changes made since the original approval for boats one to three was taken in 1997.[17] In procurement terms, this equates to substantially more than the cost of acquiring a further boat.

The SDSR did however endorse the political, military and industrial requirement for a seven-boat Astute Programme. As part of the Astute class programme's objectives including the sustainment of submarine building capability for the Successor Programme, the build schedule for Astute boats was extended by an average of fourteen months per boat. The build schedule for the whole class was extended by a further ninety-six months and the average deferral in the previous three years of twenty-eight months per boat.[18] As a result of extending the Astute Class build programme, the MoD recognised the need to operate older boats beyond their out of service dates, work a smaller fleet of Astute submarines harder, or reduce scheduled activity for the submarine fleet. Therefore the MoD was also reporting that the Astute submarines would not meet the Royal Navy requirement for sufficient numbers of submarines to be available for operations over part of the next decade.[19]

In recognition of the requirement to sustain key skills and the submarine building capability, BAE Systems launched a new recruitment initiative in October 2012 to recruit around 150 professional engineers, specialising in mechanical, electrical, design, power and propulsion, quality and nuclear.[20] Although available to the Astute Programme, the majority of the new staff will be assigned to the Successor Programme.

A ten-year contract with Thales was agreed during May 2013 to maintain Royal Navy sensor systems which includes worldwide support and repairs on the Astute Class sonars, periscope system and electronic surveillance systems.[21]

Background – The Capability

The Astute Class submarine is a 7,400 tonne nuclear-powered hunter-killer (SSN) designed to be the most technologically advanced of her type ever produced for the Royal Navy.[22] The performance requirement is an extension of the performance of the Trafalgar class Batch 1 fleet planned to be decommissioned by 2022, which has begun with HMS Trafalgar being decommissioned in December 2009.

The seven Astute Class submarines are designed to be the stealthiest and most capable submarine of her type and have the capacity to circumnavigate the globe without surfacing, limited only by their food storage capacity. Able to deploy rapidly, they are powered by the PWR2 reactor that can run for their twenty-five year lifespan without refuelling. As this reactor was designed for use on Vanguard Class SSBNs, the Astute class submarines are about thirty per cent larger than previous Royal Navy SSNs, which were powered by smaller diameter reactors.

The bridge fin of the Astute Class is, as with other Royal Navy submarines, specially reinforced to allow surfacing through ice caps. The class can also be fitted with a dry deck shelter which allows for the Special Forces (Special Boat Service) Swimmers Delivery System to deploy whilst the submarine is submerged.[23] This reinstates a capability available on the Swiftsure class.

A maximum speed of twenty-nine knots was originally specified for the class, but it has been reported that this speed has not yet been demonstrated due to a propulsion design problem. It is as yet unclear if this problem can be overcome, and at the launch of HMS Ambush, the Royal Navy only stated she was "capable of speeds in excess of twenty knots".[24] This and other Guardian media articles provoked the consternation of HMS Astute's Commanding Officer, Commander Steven Walker, who replied in the same media – "I have seen the boat outperform anything I have served on in the past and I have yet to operate her in all the submarine war fighting arenas. There are still challenges to overcome but these are not safety related or I would not be at sea with her right now".[25]

Engineered to be the stealthiest submarine of her type, construction involves more than 39,000 acoustic tiles to mask the vessel's sonar signature, giving the class a better stealth quality than any other submarine previously operated by the Royal Navy.[26] The design includes the following significant improvements over current fleet submarines:[27]

- The latest, fully integrated submarine combat system which receives data from the boat's sensors and displays real time imagery on all command consoles;
- Increased weapons load including Spearfish and Tomahawk Land Attack Missile

(TLAM). The TLAM are capable of hitting a target to within a few meters within a range of over 2,000km. The class will also be able to fire the new "tactical Tomahawk" currently under development;

- An 'optronics' periscope in place of hull penetrating masts;
- External actuation for all control surfaces to reduce hull penetrations and simplify aft end construction;
- A digital control and information system for the submarine, to minimise costly cabling;
- Several detailed improvements to avoid outdated equipment, improve operability and save cost.

The propulsion system for the Astute Class has been made even quieter through the use of revolutionary design and manufacturing techniques and materials. With rafted sections throughout the boat, machinery noise is not passed into the environment around the vessel and crew noise is isolated from the outer hull. New designs of coatings, tiles and paints have been deployed to stop the submarine reflecting enemy sonar. Although deployable for extended periods, Astute is fitted with the very latest systems to convert waste products into substances that cannot be detected in her wake. Combined, all of these attributes mean that an enemy will find it very difficult to detect the presence of an Astute class submarine, even when operating in close proximity to their sensors. It therefore allows the crew to operate undetected and remain at the front line of naval operations for longer periods of time.

Fitted with the latest version of the Thales S2076 integrated sonar suite, Astute possesses one of the most sensitive acoustic sensors ever to put to sea. Able to detect noise across the full range of frequencies, this sonar is able to track and classify multiple targets at vast ranges. Whilst still reliant on a human ear, S2076 relieves many of the pressures associated with this demanding task. Contributing to the submarine's exploitation of the acoustic environment is the very latest in environmental suites, able to accurately monitor changes and shifts in the marine environment, enabling the crew to exploit the slightest variation to the full. Astute is not fitted with traditional optical periscopes[28]; instead she has a high definition optical system passing images through fibre optic cable into the control room for the operator to review on a large screen. This, coupled with huge advances in night vision equipment and thermal imaging, means that when operating just below the surface, the crew's collection of visual information is excellent. Astute's remaining above water sensors allows the crew to fully exploit the electromagnetic spectrum in order to determine enemies' intentions and movements. The crew can use these for its own benefit, or relay the intelligence back up the chain of command, so that the information can inform the wider force. The sensors also enable the crew to detect hostile aircraft before they enter its battle space.

This all combines to give Astute a significant 'edge' over any adversary and enables the crew to control where and when it operates, whilst remaining hidden from the enemy. A continuous and accurate assessment of this advantage is paramount to all submarine operations.

Following the prominent first wave role of TLAM in all recent land campaigns, the Submarine Service has remained the sole custodian of the United Kingdom's TLAM capability. Astute can be deployed carrying over fifty percent more missiles than previous classes. This includes the latest variant of the TLAM, which has an extended range, improved accuracy and greater in-flight interaction, making it a more modern and versatile weapon. Using this system, Astute is able to patrol a coastline and deliver a surgical strike in support of land forces several hundred miles away.

HMS Ambush alongside RFA Diligence
(Source: defenceimagery.mod.uk)

Astute retains the most traditional ability of the Submarine Service – to search for, track and destroy enemy ships and submarines. This capability has been enhanced by the boat's sonar fit and can safeguard the transit of surface vessels – be it a deployed carrier battle group or the merchant vessels essential to the UK's economy. The Spearfish heavyweight torpedo provides an effective anti-ship capability.

Some concern has been raised over the possible overstretch of Astute capability given her lack of a sub-launched Anti-Ship Missile (ASM). The optimal load for Astute should be twenty-four Spearfish torpedoes and fourteen TLAM missiles, but no more than nine missiles for anti-ship operations might normally be available in the best conditions. Any increase in TLAM will limit Astute's anti-ship capability given her reliance on Spearfish for anti-ship operations.

One possible operational tactic, experimented with previously by the Royal Navy, of having SSNs effectively locked inside so-called "Launch Boxes", a sector of ocean where the submarine is required to lurk continuously, ready to fire its TLAMs in support of land operations is of concern. With only seven SSNs available in the future fleet, committing submarines to this style of operation would mean having few submarines available for other tasks, from shipping-interdiction to fleet protection to Special Forces insertion.[29] Astute recently proved her ability to launch TLAM during a deployment to the USA completed in 2012. She successfully fired two missiles from the Gulf of Mexico accurately hitting targets in Northern Florida.[30]

Astute has a Ship's Company of 150, comprising eighteen Officers, sixty-two Senior Rates and seventy Junior Rates. Of this total, only ninety-eight would normally be taken to sea, with the remainder staying alongside employed in the Essential Shore Support Group (BAE).[31] Astute is the first Royal Navy submarine class to have a bunk for each member of the ship's company, ending the practice of 'hot bunking ', whereby two sailors on opposite watches shared the same bunk.

An estimated 5,000 BAE Systems personnel are employed directly as a result of the programme together with other staff within agencies and the supply chain.[32]

Background – Equipment Delivery

The following review of progress across the design, build and operation of the Astute Class makes reference to all seven boats within the class:

- Boat 1-HMS Astute
- Boat 2-HMS Ambush

- Boat 3-HMS Artful
- Boat 4-HMS Audacious
- Boat 5-HMS Anson
- Boat 6-HMS Agamemnon
- Boat 7-HMS Ajax

The First of Class, HMS Astute, was launched on 8th June 2007. HMS Ambush was launched in January 2011. HMS Artful is under construction, the final weld has been made thus completing the hull.

HMS Astute successfully completed her first dive, deep dive and full power trials during early 2010. A back dated In-Service Date based was declared and agreed by the Investment Appraisal Board in July 2010. HMS Astute continued with the Contractor Sea Trials and was subsequently commissioned in August 2010.[33]

In October 2010, HMS Astute was involved in a grounding and collision incident whilst on sea trials off the west coast of Scotland. She was floated off after twelve hours and following evaluation returned to the Clyde Naval Base under her own power. Repairs were completed in November 2010. The inquiry into the incident reported that in addition to human error, "a number of additional causal factors were present including some deficiencies with equipment", however the report went on to conclude from the inquiry panel findings that the failures were specific to HMS Astute.[34]

HMS Ambush completed a five month deployment to the USA, and commenced sea trials in September 2012 and was commissioned in March 2013. HMS Astute continues trials in the Bahamas and the Eastern Seaboard as she prepares for her first operational patrol towards the end of 2013.[35]

A number of quality assurance problems have been reported in the national media concerning the first Boats built. Due to the failure of a pipe cap, made of incorrect material although construction records indicated the correct metal had been used, HMS Astute was forced to surface following a leak that was flooding a compartment. A number of other problems have been identified, including the wrong type of lead being used in a reactor instrument, and other quality issues leading to early corrosion of components.[36]

This and other Guardian reports critical of the performance and potential safety of HMS Astute resulted in Rear Admiral Simon Lister, Director Submarines, MoD Defence Equipment & Support (DE&S) replying:[37]

"I would never allow an unsafe platform to proceed to sea and the purpose of the extensive sea trials HMS Astute is undertaking is to test the submarine in a progressive manner, proving that the design is safe, that it has been manufactured correctly and that she is able to operate safely and effectively. This process reflects the nature of HMS Astute as both a prototype and an operational vessel. We have always known that it would be necessary to identify and rectify problems during sea trials and this is what we have done. All the issues noted in the story have either already been addressed or are being addressed. In particular, while we do not comment on nuclear propulsion issues, or the speed of our submarines, I can assure you that, once HMS Astute deploys operationally, we do not expect there to be any constraints on her ability to carry out her full combat role for the Royal Navy."

Boats three to seven were delayed due to the retention of resources on HMS Astute to resolve technical issues and MoD direction that the programme be slowed to realise early year savings.

HMS Audacious is in the build stage which will include the incorporation of an uprated chilled water plant and other mechanical modifications identified as a result of the earlier builds. In March 2010, approval for initial build activities for HMS Anson was given, and Long Lead Items were ordered for HMS Agamemnon

In June 2012, the order was placed for the manufacture of the nuclear reactor for HMS Ajax alongside the refurbishment of Rolls-Royce's manufacturing facility in Raynesway, Derby and the development and production of the first reactor for the Successor class SSBN.

HMS Astute has not yet demonstrated its 'top speed' key performance measure as trials had not completed by the in-service date as originally planned. Further trials are planned before the submarine is ready for military operations.

Issues, Observations & Questions

A number of key case study issues, observations and questions arise from the Astute Programme that provides fundamentally important references for review and critical assessment. These include:

How to build resilience into a complex programme such as Astute to ensure continued viability in the face of substantial schedule and production volume changes?

Irrespective of the UK's defence needs, no complex programme can live in a political or economic vacuum, particularly when the timescale from the concept phase of the programme to decommissioning of the Astute Class is around sixty years. Difficult choices are inevitable when balancing defence capability with affordability across the lengthy timescales associated with major defence programmes. The Astute Programme has already encountered changes in Government and defence policy, industrial capability, a downturn in national economic performance, and the threats facing the UK, which have required programme rebalancing. The longer the programme timescale, the more likely that changes will be necessary to the performance requirement, schedule and cost. In almost all circumstances, except for a significantly reduced capability requirement, these changes are likely to result in programme cost growth and the increase in risk.

The key to retaining programme resilience is to recognise the potential for these changes, difficult as they may be to predict, and to ensure that they are identified as risks that can be quantified and managed. The implications of production volume options can be modelled and assessed in the concept stage, however it is much more difficult to quantify externally enforced changes to a build programme, as the cost of this is, in most instances, optimised to ensure the most productive use of labour and facilities, and management of the supply chain. Programme resilience is driven at a strategic level by a steadfast coalition at the Programme Board level, particular with the sponsor, and a demonstration at the programme team level of excellent programme, risk and benefits management capability. It is unlikely in the case of the Astute programme for even these levels of strategic resilience to have mitigated against the external effect of an overheated defence programme.

It's important to consider the extent to which technical difficulties encountered early in the programme, particularly with the use of CAD techniques, had detrimentally impacted confidence in the programme and its vulnerability to externally enforced change.

In all cases, and at all stages, programme viability remains fundamentally important: the strategic alignment of stakeholders cannot exist in its absence. Significant deferral in the Astute build schedule introduced significant additional programme cost, however the programme has remained viable when considered in the context of Defence capability and industrial capability needs.

How best to manage the relationship between the Trafalgar decommissioning schedule and the Astute and Successor Programme build schedules, to ensure affordable sustainment of the UK maritime defence capability?

An obvious observation here is to ensure the effective alignment of all associated programmes through common governance and programme / portfolio management arrangements. However, this alignment is complicated when external financial pressures impose significant changes to the individual programme schedules, as has been the case on the Astute Programme.

The problem of programme alignment across an enterprise to achieve strategic goals is not just restricted to complex defence programmes. It was recognised as such a significant issue that it gave rise to the Office for Government Commerce (OGC), then subsequently the Cabinet Office, Management of Portfolios (MoP) Initiative.[38] Within this initiative, the portfolio is defined as:

"The totality of an organizations' investment (or segment thereof) in the changes required to achieve its strategic objectives"

MoP helps organisations answer the fundamental question 'Are we sure this investment is right for us and how will it contribute to our strategic objectives?'

Investment is the keyword here, because portfolio management is about investing in the right change initiatives and implementing them in a way that maintains the primacy of achieving the strategic objectives. MoP seeks to achieve this by ensuring that:

- The programmes and projects undertaken are prioritised in terms of their contribution to the organisation's strategic objectives and overall level of risk

- Programmes and projects are managed consistently to ensure efficient and effective delivery

- Benefits realisation is maximized to provide the greatest return (in terms of strategic contribution and efficiency savings) from the investment made.

Although generic in nature, the application of the MoP approach may have a stronger part to play in complex, long duration programmes such as the Astute Programme. The strategic objective of the UK maritime portfolio is the sustainment of Deployed and High Readiness Force submarine operational capability. Clearly, strategic decisions made in the context of the broad portfolio of Swiftsure, Trafalgar, Astute and Successor Programmes have a significant impact on submarine operational capability.

Delays in approval of the Successor Programme required rescheduling of the Astute Programme, which may have an impact on the In-Service life of the Trafalgar Class and will impact achievement of the strategic objective. In addition, the need to sustain a viable on-shore submarine building capability adds a further dimension to the portfolio, which has a direct impact on the affordability of achieving the strategic objective.

The SDSR direction to extend the Astute build programme on the Future Force 2020 requirement thus causing a deficiency in this capability was noted by the Defence Select Committee. Chair of the Committee, Rt Hon James Arbuthnot MP, said:

> "This is a clear example of the need for savings overriding the strategic security of the UK and the capability requirements of the Armed Forces. The Government needs to outline its plans to manage the gap left by the loss of these capabilities and lay out detailed plans for their regeneration."

A question to consider here is whether the more extensive use of Portfolio Management techniques, properly applied, would have would have made it possible to sustain the Deployed and High Readiness Force Submarine Operational capability without the need for loss and subsequent regeneration.

How best to ensure alignment of the Astute Build and Successor Programme schedules in order to sustain the UK submarine building capability?

The Defence Industrial Strategy of 2005 was clear in the explicit need to sustain the UK's Key Industrial Capabilities including submarine design and build. It was seen as confirming BAE Systems as the UK's 'national champion' in this area. Prior to this, the Defence Industries Council had warned that "the continuation of a totally open market approach would see the UK lose almost completely, the strong industrial base that has supplied our armed forces and UK sovereignty could be threatened."[39]

The subsequent publication of the National Security Through Technology Paper[40] in 2012 was less explicit, stressing that open competition would be used by the MoD to fulfil defence requirements unless other procurement strategies were essential for UK national security by protecting UK Operational Advantage and Freedom of Action. This paper was highlighted as the industrial policy until the next SDSR expected to be held in 2015 and that it superseded the earlier Defence Industrial Strategy.

Nuclear technologies are specifically referred to in this procurement strategy, however equipment platforms such as ships and submarines are not. This is an example of where the political environment within which a programme such as Astute exists can change significantly during the life of the programme.

Notwithstanding this evolution of the UK's Defence Industrial Policy, the sustainment of industrial capability relies in practice on a long-term agreed schedule of defined workload to plan and optimise the use of labour and facilities. Ideally this scheduled workload should avoid significant and unscheduled peaks and troughs as this will inevitably results in the sub optimal use of resources, reduction in productivity and consequently an increase the overall cost of the programmes being delivered.

Unavoidable and substantial gaps in workload are likely to require the implementation of a Human Resource Strategy to best manage the availability of industrial capability. This can be based either on sustaining the workforce and facilities through a workload gap or running down the capability then regenerating it when needed. The later approach however may result in an increase in long term costs as productivity will almost certainly be detrimentally impacted by the utilisation of unskilled labour.

There are many parallels here to a similar problem being encountered in the surface shipbuilding industry. There is a significant workload gap between work completing on the Queen Elizabeth Carrier Programme and the ramping up of work on the Type 26 Global Combat Ship Programme. In this case, a Terms of Business Agreement (ToBA)[41] exists between the MoD and BAE Systems which includes a requirement arising from the Defence Industrial Strategy of 2005 to maintain Key Industrial Capability through such a gap. However implementing this requirement is costly and can have the perverse effect of paying staff when there is no work available to be undertaken. Irrespective of the benefits or disadvantages of sustaining industrial capability in this manner on surface ships, no such commercial arrangement is in place to sustain submarine building capability.

Given that BAE Systems has only the one facility for submarine production in Barrow-in-Furness, it is essential that an enterprise level perspective is taken in the scheduling and use of all available resources. It is also important that gaps in the use of resources are quantified early in order that to increase the likelihood of the successful implementation of the Human Resource Strategy.

One question to consider is how might the MoD best optimise the alignment and minimise potential cost increases on the Astute & Successor Programmes, given the likelihood of future workload gaps?

How could the Astute Programme be made more flexible in responding to changes in build quantity and rate?

An issue requiring consideration here is the practicality of using shadow procurement strategy options and any investment that could be made in the development of decision support tools. The implications of the class size being reduced in quality is certainly an option that would be detailed within the Business Cases at both the Initial and Main Gate approval stages and it is clearly the case that early decision making to reduce the production requirement is made less detrimental if made early and before the procurement of long lead items. However flexibility comes at a cost, the later the decision is made to procure long lead items the higher the likely production costs.

Similarly designing flexibility into a programme to change production build rate comes at a cost. If there is a strong likelihood that this will occur then early consideration should be given to investment in the development of an agreed decision support model that enables both the supplier and customer to assess the impact that will result from such changes.

A point to consider is the balance of investment that may need to be made in ensuring that all key senior stakeholders including particular the sponsor and politicians remaining robust and aligned in support the existing programme. The use of a decision support model may not prevent inevitable changes in build quantity and rate, but it may ensure that agreed evidence of the implications are available, better understood and communicated.

How best to manage the achievement of future efficiencies on the Astute Programme to achieve enterprise level savings targets without detrimentally impacting programme performance and quality?

The benefit of the sustained use of best programme management approaches and tools feature strongly here, however broader portfolio level issues need to be considered.

It is likely that future savings arising from efficiencies in the way that both the MoD and BAE Systems operate will be required and assumed in the MoD Programming Round before the means by which these savings will be achieved have been identified.

The Submarine Enterprise Performance Programme (SEPP) the partners of which include the MoD, BAE Systems, Babcock Marine and Rolls Royce aims to improve long term affordability of the submarine enterprise in build and support. This programme is managed by DE&S and will be seeking to ensure an achievable level of future savings across the submarine enterprise but how should this be implemented to ensure that this it done without a detrimental impact on the Astute Programme. Should an enterprise level agreement along the lines of that in place with BAE Systems though the Surface Ships ToBA be put in place or should the enterprise savings requirements be embedded within the programme contracts for Astute and Successor? Although partnering clearly has a part to play in achieving future savings, what is likely to be the preferred commercial approach that best meets the UK Defence capabilities need and affordability criteria?

Conclusions

This case study includes of number of essential observations for the critical review of a major defence acquisition programme, particularly in respect to programme changes that have been required as a result of external strategic factors. Although currently less than half way into this programme many of these observations are significant. Undoubtedly more will result from operational deployment and in-service experience.

Astute programme success should be viewed, as with any programme, in the context of time, cost and performance. Each of these aspects will have a weight of importance, as determined by stakeholders that will vary throughout the programme's life cycle. Cost and affordability have undoubtedly been the predominant factors underlying changes to the programme since the concept phase. The programme has been significantly impacted by external changes in Government and defence policy, global and economic performance, and the need the balance defence expenditure. These factors have resulted in extended programme timescales which have consequently resulted in programme cost growth which underlines the inevitable law that programme cost is proportional to programme timescale. This cost increase crudely equates to substantially more than the cost of acquiring a further boat. An important point to consider is how the required programme savings may have been achieved more efficiently.

Astute is a complex programme that includes a significant number of performance improvements over current submarines. Inevitably this results in significant technical risk. It was the first UK submarine programme to use CAD techniques, the complexities of which were underestimated. This contributed to a substantial increase in programme cost and delay from which lessons must be learned on the Successor Programme. Other technical problems have been evident, although there is no reason, given the success of recent sea trials to suppose that these will prevent Astute being accepted into service. Despite the difficulties that have been encountered the submarine is widely recognised as the stealthiest and most capable submarine of her type in the world.

The Astute programme has been complicated by two maritime portfolio issues: maintaining an efficient submarine building capability to enable an affordable Successor Programme, and providing the Future Force 2020 capability to protect the UK nuclear deterrent, and naval task groups, through the availability of a Deployed and High Readiness Force of submarines. In the case of the first issue, the Astute and Successor Programmes are inextricably associated via the facilities and finite availability of skills required to ensure achievable and affordable build programmes. The retention of a UK industrial submarine building capability, to ensure Freedom of Action and Operational Advantage in BAE

Systems, comes at a cost. Secondly and as a result of the extended Astute build programme it has been recognised that it will be necessary to operate older boats beyond their out of service dates, work a smaller fleet of Astute submarines harder, or reduce scheduled submarine activity. It has been consequently reported that the Astute submarines may not meet the Royal Navy requirement for sufficient numbers of submarines to be available for operations over part of the next decade. It is worth considering how these maritime portfolio issues may have been managed differently.

Looking to the future, more challenges still lie in wait for the Astute Programme, particularly related to an on-going financial challenge. The MoD Planning Rounds include a requirement to deliver further savings across the whole submarine business over the next decade through SEPP to enable affordability of the Successor Programme. This will inevitably introduce further risk back into the Astute Programme.

The Astute Programme provides a wealth of learning from experience that will not only be invaluable to the successful management of the future maritime programme but also more broadly across defence acquisition.

Endnotes

[1] Royal Navy. (2013) 'Submarines' webpage, http://www.royalnavy.mod.uk/The-fleet/submarines as of 11 July 2013.

[2] Naval Shipbuilding. (2013) 'North West England's Shipbuilding – Astute Submarines' webpage at http://www.navalshipbuilding.co.uk/navalship_warships.asp?ID=WAR1&catID=5 as of 11 July 2013.

[3] National Audit Office. (2011) *Ministry of Defence – Major Projects Report 2011*, HC1520-I, dated 16 November 2011, at http://www.nao.org.uk/report/ministry-of-defence-the-major-projects-report-2011/ as of 11 July 2013.

[4] National Audit Office. (2013) *Ministry of Defence - Major Projects Report 2012*, HC684-I, dated 10 January 2013, at http://www.nao.org.uk/report/ministry-of-defence-the-major-projects-report-2012/ as of 11 July 2013.

[5] Willett, L. (2005) ' Astute, Trident and SSGN: Land Attack for the Royal Navy Submarine Service', *RUSI Defence Systems*, Summer 2005, at http://rusi.org/downloads/assets/30willett.pdf as of 11 July 2013; *Op Cit*. Naval Shipbuilding, 2013.

[6] Armedforces.co.uk. 'Submarines – Astute Class', located at http://www.armedforces.co.uk/Europeandefence/edequipment/edsea/edsea1a1.htm as of 11 July 2013.

[7] National Audit Office. (2008) *Ministry of Defence – Major Projects Report 2008*, HC64-I, dated 18 December 2008, at http://www.nao.org.uk/report/ministry-of-defence-major-projects-report-2008/ as of 11 July 2013.

[8] Global Security. (2011) 'Astute SSN Program History' webpage, currently located at http://www.globalsecurity.org/military/world/europe/hms-astute-history.htm as of 11 July 2013.

[9] National Audit Office. (2004) Ministry of Defence – Major Projects Report 2003, HC195, dated 23 January 2004, at http://www.nao.org.uk/report/ministry-of-defence-major-projects-report-2003/ as of 11 July 2013.

[10] BAE Systems. (2013) 'Maritime: Submarines' webpage at http://www.baesystems.com/our-company-rzz/our-businesses/maritime---submarines as of 11 July 2013.

[11] *Op Cit* . National Audit Office, 2008.

[12] Navy Matters. (2013) website currently located at http://navy-matters.beedall.com/ as of 11 July 2013.

[13] Naval Technology. (2012) 'SSN Astute Class Nuclear Submarine, United Kingdom' webpage, located at http://www.naval-technology.com/projects/astute as of 11 July 2013.

[14] *Op Cit* . National Audit Office, 2011.

[15] *Op Cit* . Naval Technology, 2012.

[16] HM Government. (2010) *Securing Britain in an Age of Uncertainty – The Strategic Defence and Security Review*, Cm7948, October 2010, at http://www.direct.gov.uk/prod_consum_dg/groups/dg_digitalassets/@dg/@en/documents/digitalasset/dg_191634.pdf as of 11 July 2013.

[17] *Op Cit* . National Audit Office, 2011.

[18] *Ibid* . p. 29.

[19] *Ibid* .

[20] *Op Cit* . BAE Systems, 2013.

[21] Monaghan, A. (2013) 'Thales wins MoD contract for servicing electronics of Royal Navy fleet' in *The Guardian*, 28 May 2013, at http://www.guardian.co.uk/uk/2013/may/28/thales-contract-royal-navy-electronics?INTCMP=SRCH as of 11 July 2013.

[22] *Op Cit* . BAE Systems, 2013.

[23] Willett, L. (2004) 'The Astute Class Submarine – Capabilities and Challenges' in RUSI Defence Systems, Summer 2004, located at http://www.rusi.org/downloads/assets/Willet.pdf as of 11 July 2013.

[24] Hopkins, N. (2012) 'Britain's nuclear hunter-killer submarines were doomed from the start ' in *The Guardian*, 15 November 2012 at http://www.guardian.co.uk/uk/2012/nov/15/astute-hunter-killer-submarines-doomed?INTCMP=SRCH as of 11 July 2013.

[25] Hopkins, N. (2012) 'HMS Astute: quality control the key to restoring hunter-killer sub's reputation' in *The Guardian*, 16 Nov 2012, located at http://www.guardian.co.uk/uk/2012/nov/16/hms-astute-sub?INTCMP=SRCH as of 11 July 2013.

[26] Shipping Times. (2007) 'Countdown to launch first Astute submarine at Barrow shipyard', located at http://www.shippingtimes.co.uk/item577_astute.htm as of 11 July 2013.

[27] *Op Cit* . Naval Technology, 2012.

[28] BAE Systems (2013a) 'The Astute Launch – Fascinating Facts' at http://production. investis.com/astute/about/facts/ as of 11 July 2013.

[29] See http://ukarmedforcescommentary.blogspot.co.uk/p/future-force-2020-royal-navy. html.

[30] *Op Cit* . Royal Navy, 2013.

[31] *Op Cit* . BAE Systems, 2013a.

[32] Wikipedia. (2013) 'Astute-Class Submarine', located at http://en.wikipedia.org/wiki/ Astute-class_submarine as of 11 July 2013.

[33] *Op Cit* . Royal Navy, 2013.

[34] Ministry of Defence. (2012) *Report of the Service Enquiry into the Grounding of HMS Astute on 22 October 2010*, 22 April 2012, located at https://www.gov.uk/government/ uploads/system/uploads/attachment_data/file/27118/astute_grounding_si_report.pdf as of 11 July 2013.

[35] *Op Cit* . Royal Navy, 2013.

[36] *Op Cit* . Hopkins, 16 November 2012.

[37] Ministry of Defence. (2012) 'Allegations of cost-cutting on Astute submarines' on the *Defence Talk* website, at http://www.defencetalk.com/allegations-of-cost-cutting-on-astute-submarines-45576/ as of 12 July 2013.

[38] Management of Portfolios (MOP), 1st edition, June 2010, see http://www.mop-officialsite.com/.

[39] Wikipedia. (2012) 'Defence Industrial Strategy' webpage, currently located at http:// en.wikipedia.org/wiki/Defence_Industrial_Strategy as of 12 July 2013.

[40] Ministry of Defence. (2012) National Security Through Technology – Technology, Equipment & Support for UK Defence and Security, Cm8278, February 2012, currently available at https://www.gov.uk/government/uploads/system/uploads/attachment_data/ file/27390/cm8278.pdf as of 12 July 2013.

[41] House of Commons Public Accounts Committee. (2011) 'Supplementary written evidence from the Ministry of Defence' in *Ministry of Defence – The Major Projects Report 2010*, HC1696, January 2011, at http://www.publications.parliament.uk/ pa/cm201011/cmselect/cmpubacc/687/687we05.htm as of 12 July 2013; Ministry of Defence. (2009) *Terms of Business Agreement Relating to BVT Surface Fleet Limited and its Business*, Contract No. MCP/001, July 2009, located at https:// www.gov.uk/government/uploads/system/uploads/attachment_data/file/16847/

BAESystemsSurfaceShipsTermsofBusinessAgreementREDACTED.pdf as of 12 July 2013.

Single Service Procurement and the British Army's Main Battle Tank

Dr. Peter Tatham and Prof. Trevor Taylor

Centre for Defence Acquisition, Cranfield University, DCMT Shrivenham.

Introduction

In November 1986, shortly after Vickers Defence Systems (VDS) had acquired the former Royal Ordnance Factory (ROF) in Leeds (for £11m), the company began work on the design and development of a new tank which, they proposed, would replace the ageing fleet of Centurions (dating from the 1960s) and also the newer Challenger 1s (first ordered in 1978) which were both unreliable and had poor gunnery accuracy. The first nine turrets were built (seven at Leeds and two at VDS' original factory in Newcastle) on a private venture basis prior to the issue of the Staff Requirement.

The perceived requirement for a new Main Battle Tank (MBT) took place against the backdrop of the "Levene" reforms to UK defence procurement which placed a premium on achievement of value for money through competition and taut contract conditions. Although in the pre-contract discussions VDS argued that there was a need to provide the new fleet of tanks quickly (to fill a capability gap), and that a single tender contract would safeguard employment (some 2000 jobs) at both Leeds and Newcastle, the company's reputation was poor having delivered unreliable tanks over budget and late in previous contracts. As a result, a full competition was unavoidable and this took place at the end of the decade, with the final tank being delivered in 2002.

A Challenger 2 pictured during live firing exercises in Grafenwöhr, Germany.
(Source: Cpl Wes Calder, RLC from defenceimages.mod.uk via Flickr)

CR2 - Doctrine

Whilst the decision to procure a new MBT coincided with the fall of the Berlin Wall in 1989 and then the Conventional Forces in Europe Treaty of 1990, there was perceived to be a continuing (but reduced) requirement for such a system. This will be discussed in greater detail later in this Case Study. The procurement decision also coincided with the doctrinal developments that saw the introduction of the manoeuvrist concept. Thus, whilst the Chieftain and, to a lesser extent, the Challenger 1 MBTs had a movement capability, unlike Challenger 2 (CR2), they could not be seen as a key component of the implementation of manoeuvrist doctrine.

CR2 - Organisation

The introduction of CR2 took place at the same time as the major revision in the role and *modus operandi* of the Armed Forces and, as part of this, the MOD's Planning Assumption was that a large scale conflict would entail a "warning time" of ten years. As a result, the number of armoured regiments in the Army was under severe pressure and, as part of the conditions tied by the MoD to the introduction of the CR2, the tank fleet was reduced from some 900 Chieftain/Challenger I to 386 CR2. This was formally achieved as part of the 1990 "Options for Change" reductions in the size of the Armed Forces which, in effect, saw the loss of five Armoured Regiments.

CR2 - Equipment

The provision of the CR2 MBT proved to be a complex undertaking that reflected, to a large extent, a number of external influences such as the emergence of a number of larger entities within the Defence Industrial Sector, and the influence of the Levene reforms mentioned above. As a result, this section of the Case Study will be broken down into the phases of today's CADMID Cycle (although the Downey Cycle was formally in place then).

The Concept Phase

As indicated above, VDS anticipated the requirement for a new MBT and, furthermore, concluded that it was a "must win" competition. To achieve this, they built a new factory at Leeds (at a cost of some £14m), and planned for production to be split equally between this and the existing Newcastle facility. Recognising the implications of the Levene reforms, they also began to identify their own core competencies, and to review what should be sub-contracted. As a result of this work, VDS approached the competition by selecting the high value subcontractors based on value for money and confidence in their reliability.

This represented a major change of strategy for the company which had previously relied on UK companies with whom they had operated for many years but, having changed their procurement approach, VDS did little in the way of upskilling their Purchasing Department to deal with the new challenges. The result was a list of over 500 sub-contractors and, although some were mandated by the MOD e.g. the 120mm rifled gun from Royal Ordnance (part of BAE Systems) and the engines from Rolls Royce (part of Caterpillar Inc), other major parts were brought from Canada and France. This exemplified the growing internationalisation of the arms sector, but also placed VDS at a disadvantage in some instances – for example, the 386 fire control systems for the CR2s bought from CDC of Canada (now part of General Dynamics) were dwarfed by a parallel order of 8,000 systems by the US for the Abrams tanks.

As a result, VDS moved from a previous position in which only 50% of their production was "bought in" to 80% - in effect changing the nature of their work from "production" to 'assembly'. Furthermore, many of the "sub" contractors were actually significantly larger companies than VDS and as a result, VDS was unable to flow down the MOD's Terms & Conditions as the large suppliers would not accept them and VDS could not enforce compliance.

The Assessment Phase

The formal competition for the new MBT was held between:

- VDS (UK): Challenger 2
- General Dynamics (USA): M1A2 Abrams
- Krauss Maffei (Germany): Leopard 2
- GIAT (France): Leclerc

It is interesting to note that, given the perceived wisdom that National Governments would always prefer their National arms companies, it proved necessary for the MOD to subsidise the bids from USA, France & Germany in order to achieve the desired competition.

As a result of the Invitation to Tender (ITT), the MOD (unusually) made a qualified recommendation to buy either the Leopard 2 (elderly, but proven and reliable) or the Abrams (modern, but with a novel and expensive gas turbine engine). The MOD did not shortlist the CR2 as they did not believe that VDS had the capacity to deliver to time and cost. When this decision was taken to cabinet in 1991, the views of the key players are summarised below:

Prime Minister (Margaret Thatcher)	• Why do we need a new tank at all? • If one is necessary, would VDS be able to deliver to cost/ time?
Defence Secretary (Tom King)	• No strong defence differentiators between the two short listed bidders
Foreign Secretary (Douglas Hurd)	• Some potential export benefit from CR2. • Neutral over short listed bidders.
Trade Secretary (Peter Lilley)	• Indigenous MBT production capability gave huge political kudos. • Embodied spirit of national engineering excellence. • Major political benefit in an election year (Leeds constituencies were marginals).

It is interesting to note that none of these four decision makers appeared to be particularly concerned with price and, much to the surprise and consternation of the MoD Project Team, the Trade Secretary's view eventually prevailed with VDS emerging as the declared competition winner.

The final MoD contract presented VDS with three key issues:

• First, the main contract set new standards and conditions for a prime contractor in terms of the scope of what had to be delivered and how. The contract penalties for failure were severe.

• Secondly, the package of contracts that made up the CR2 programme amounted to almost £2bn (at the peak over ninety percent of the VDS order book) making it the largest Armoured Fighting Vehicle (AFV) programme in Europe. But the financial size of VDS and even Vickers plc (the parent company) were quite small compared to a contract of this magnitude.

• Third, the complex technical and programme risks were new to VDS, the AFV supply chain and the MoD. Unlike virtually all previous major defence contracts the risks were to be managed entirely by the prime contractor who was also held to be totally responsible and accountable. Furthermore, in line with the Levene model, very demanding conditions were placed on VDS and, given that the advice of the MOD CR2 team on the winning bid had been overturned, it is unsurprising that these conditions were robustly enforced in the subsequent contract.

A Challenger 2 coming ashore during an amphibious landing exercise in Gosport, Hampshire. (Source: Cpl Kellie Williams, RLC from defenceimages.mod.uk)

CR2 – Development & Manufacture

Previous MBTs built by VDS followed a recognisable technical design, namely a mechanically simple layout with a diesel engine, 105mm or 120mm rifled gun, fixed sights (all pointing in the same direction as the gun) with rudimentary night observation functions, a simple fire control computer to calculate gun pointing and the capability to hit a moving target whilst the tank itself was static. However, the requirements for CR2 were an order of magnitude more complex and well outside the traditional capabilities of VDS. For example, the design of the CR2 included a computer-controlled diesel engine management system, a high performance 120mm gun, a panoramic stabilised commander's sight linked to a gunner's sight including a high performance night sight, two laser rangefinders and a sophisticated NBC system. Furthermore, VDS had never designed an MBT for contracted levels of reliability which were to be incorporated in the first-off production tank through to the last tank produced, with no variations in quality across the production run.

The six year development phase started in earnest immediately after contract signature for an initial 140 tanks in June 1991 and, in order to achieve success, VDS conducted a completely new type of development programme for the prototype vehicles. The most notable feature was the use of reliability growth trials (RGT) which required vehicles to undertake a set trials regime of mobility and firing based on a typical war profile called a battlefield day. The RGT was the single most expensive part of the development programme requiring three MBTs full time over three years conducting hundreds of battlefield days.

The development phase ostensibly went well with MoD concluding a follow-on contract for around 260 tanks, and with the NAO reporting no time or cost overruns in 1994 or 1995. Indeed, VDS managed to develop initial vehicles that met the specified tests, however the first completed production-standard CR2 MBTs delivered to the British Army were discovered in October 1995 to be well below the reliability requirement. This led, under the contract terms, to the stopping of payment and the imposition of Liquidated Damages. These included the cost of keeping existing Challenger 1s in-service until the CR2 problems were fixed - however long that took the company. In turn, the lack of payments meant that the vehicles already under construction either had to stop until the reliability problems had been solved, or would continue being built but would be known to be unreliable and fixed an undefined later date - all at the company's expense. Potentially, the financial penalties were sufficient to cause the parent company, Vickers plc, to be at risk of declaring bankruptcy.

The operational impact of this failure was considerable, for example the first Regiment that was planned to migrate to CR2 had already disposed of their Challenger 1 tanks but had to have them re-issued. More broadly, the image of VDS, British tank engineering and defence industry in general were at an all time low particularly with the MoD, Army and NAO. That said, there was no doubt that the MoD used the CR2 programme as a very public example of their strict adherence to the new competitive environment wherein the prime contractor, rather than the customer (ie the MOD), took the technical and financial risks.

In the face of the severe financial difficulties faced by the company, it undertook a major re-structuring programme. This included the freezing of all salaries (from Board level downwards) until the performance improved. In addition, the shopfloor workers had their long-standing arrangement for 'piece-rate' pay stopped and replaced with a flat hourly rate. Nevertheless, despite the dire financial position of the company, the Trades Unions held a ballot for strike action which received overwhelming support. The strike arrangement consisted of a one day a week stoppage for one month. In response, the MoD Project Team were furious and blamed the VDS management team for this situation, and there were even rumours in the MoD and NAO of cancelling the entire contract and buying the American M1A2 Abrams.

The crisis developed further when the VDS Board announced the closure of the entire Leeds factory (that had only been built some five years earlier) with the loss of some 900 staff, and the movement of the outstanding CR2 production from Leeds to Newcastle. This was aimed at reducing the company's overheads that were judged to be excessive due to the 'unnecessary' duplication of manufacturing between the Leeds and Newcastle sites. The financial situation was, indeed, difficult as the MoD had, by this stage, stopped paying VDS for CR2 and the tanks themselves were being stored as they were finished in a purpose built shed on the Leeds site all at VDS expense.

Fortunately, the changes to the business produced quick results. Within a few months the MoD agreed to a new accelerated development programme, and VDS agreed to take responsibility for the reliability failures as the prime contractor. As an example, although the company had planned to select their contractors on the basis of proven reliability, in practice they had to cast the net rather wider and this resulted in much of the estimated eighty two percent by value of each CR2 being bought-in from relatively unknown or inexperienced sub-contractors. As part of this process, VDS developed a number of improved supplier management teams which, working closely with their quality control colleagues (itself an innovation), resulted in greater supplier control and communication as well as quality improvement groups both in VDS and with the suppliers. Joint VDS/supplier closed loop action systems were introduced involving an electronic system to jointly track and identify problems at source thereby implementing corrective and preventative action.

With a two year programme of business change, CR2 re-testing and re-building, progress was good and reliability improvements were recorded from July 1996. The MoD was sufficiently satisfied to allow the formal handover of CR2 to the Army in 1998, with the final tank being delivered in 2002. However, the financial impact on the business was considerable and it is estimated that the original £2bn CR2 contract finishing with an overall profit margin of 1.5 percent compared with the planned 9 percent.

A Challenger 2 patrolling outside Basra during Operation Telic 4. (Source: MoD via defenceimages.mod.uk)

CR2 – In Service

The original CR2 fleet was purchased in two tranches:

- June 1991: 127 MBTs and thirteen Driver Training Tanks (DTTs)
- July 1994: 259 MBTs and nine DTTs

As part of the latter decision, it was decided to mandate the use of 230 120mm rifled barrels that had already been ordered from the then Royal Ordnance factory so that they could be retro-fitted to the Chieftain tanks. It was argued that these barrels were available "at no cost" when it was decided to replace the whole Chieftain fleet with CR2. However, in doing so, the UK was out of step with most other European armies that had adopted a 120mm smooth bore barrel as standard.

A Challenger 2 on a night exercise.
(Source: army-technology.com)

It is understood that the Challenger 2 Capability Sustainment Programme (CSP) (that is designed to maintain the system's capability until 2035) will incorporate the Challenger Lethality Improvement Programme (CLIP) which includes the replacement of the rifled barrel with a smooth bore version. This would have the benefit of allowing the use of ammunition available from a wider range of sources as well as, potentially, allowing the same smooth bore barrel to be used as part of the direct fire unit of Group 2 of FRES.

CR2 – Training

As noted above, previous generations of MBTs built by VDS followed a recognisable technical design with fixed gun sights pointing in the same direction as the gun and rudimentary night observation functions. They incorporated a simple fire control computer to calculate gun pointing, and the capability to hit a moving target whilst the tank itself was static (but with relatively low probability of success). Whilst this form of design led to comparatively high training requirements and crew skill, the requirements for CR2 were an order of magnitude more complex. The intention was that tank crews, with little training background, should be able to engage a moving target whilst on the move themselves with a high probability of a hit, rapid target switching and high speed of subsequent engagement. A key element was that the commander should have the means to identify and prioritise the next target while the gunner was busy engaging the last one. This clearly generated technical requirements (a sight giving the commander broad field of vision), training needs and considerable trust of the gunner's performance by the commander.

However, within the Land Environment, the support for CR2 is seen as the first successful application of the "systems approach to training". The result was a suite of training aids that provide the necessary understanding and experience to allow the various crew roles to be filled successfully. One of the more recent developments is the use of a live firing solution called the Enhanced Capability for Armoured Training System (ECATS) which allows a sub-calibre round to be fired within a certain range bracket in which the trajectory is a close approximation to that of the full effect charge. The key reason for this approach (apart from reduced barrel wear) is that the ECATS round costs some £7 – versus some £1,200 for the standard Armour Piercing Fin Discarding Sabot (APFDS) round.

CR2 – Logistics

Although originally supported by a traditional MOD-managed arrangement, the Challenger Innovative Spares Provision (CRISP) contract was signed in 2000 with BAE Systems as the Prime Contractor and Lex Multipart Defence (LMD) as the key sub-contractor. Through this contract, LMD was appointed the "custodian" of the legacy consumable spares inventory; whilst future stock is procured by LMD based on their assessment of the MOD's demand forecasts and their own inventory management routines that have been developed in a variety of non-military contexts. In 2007, it was estimated that CRISP has delivered:

- 89% reduction in the MOD inventory under LMD custodianship.
- 27% increase in spares availability
- 95% on time in full delivery direct to units in barracks or on exercise
- 90% reduction in lead time.
- 33% reduction in costs.

Moving forward from this success, the future support to CR2 arrangements are being developed by the IPT as part of the broader proposed contract between the MOD and BAE Systems called the Armoured Support Vehicle Initiative (AVSI).

A Challenger 2 from the Queen's Royal Hussars, attached to the 1st Royal Regiment of Fusiliers (1 RRF) Battlegroup at Camp Coyote, Kuwait in 2003. (Source: Cpl Paul Jarvis, RLC from defenceimages.mod.uk)

Although there were undoubtedly a number of changes associated with the remaining lines of development, not least those relating to the introduction of the Bowman communications system (see Case Study 2.5), the main acquisition lessons can be gleaned from the LODs were discussed above.

Summary

In summary, the chequered story of the acquisition of Challenger 2 took place in parallel with a sea change in a number of significant areas. Firstly, the platform was procured against the background of the development of the manoeuvrist doctrine and the end of the Cold War. Whilst it might be argued that the latter did not have a direct effect on the acquisition process *per se*, in practice it might have meant that Challenger was seen as a less pressing capability and, therefore, one that could be used as means of demonstrating the government's resolve to get to grips with defence procurement. It should not be overlooked that even the much criticised Challenger 1 was operated with considerable success in the 1991 war against Iraq, albeit after extensive preparations.

This determination to improve defence procurement reflected the Thatcherite free market vision, and was exemplified by the Levene reforms which emphasised the need to deliver Value for Money for taxpayers through arms' length competition. This, in turn, led to a determination on the part of the MOD that the prime contractor should shoulder a greater burden of the risk in delivery of the system within the agreed price.

Unfortunately, VDS was ill-prepared to take on this role. The company itself reflected the down-sizing the Defence Industrial Base and the sale by the government of some its former nationalised assets (ie the Royal Ordnance Factories). At the same time, it was attempting to transform itself from a relatively low technology "metal bashing" company to one which created value through the integration of the best in breed equipment from around the world. However, it is clear that the early stages of the CR 2 procurement reflected the lack of preparedness for the challenges of the new roles in many areas of the company and these were reflected in the poor quality of the initial production tanks.

Nevertheless, after considerable readjustment, including the reduction of some 50% of the workforce and the closure of the Leeds factory, the company was able to improve its performance across the board, and CR2 proved its worth as a key element of the Army's orbat in March 2003.

Single Service Procurement and UORs: Buying the British Army's New Capability

Peter D. Antill and Jeremy C. D. Smith

Centre for Defence Acquisition, Cranfield University, Defence Academy of the UK.

Introduction

During the recent conflicts in both Iraq and Afghanistan, the problems of providing protected mobility to troops on the ground, especially in view of the limited availability of support helicopters, has received attention from the media, from coroners and in Parliament. The vehicles in service at the time were either: fast and agile but lacking protection against mines and Improvised Explosive Devices (IEDs); or much better protected, but slow with relatively high operating costs. In addition, it was considered that tracked vehicles were viewed as more aggressive, while wheeled vehicles were less intimidating, had a greater range, a higher top speed, and a lower maintenance burden. The pressure was on to have something done, from the Prime Minister, through Lord Drayson (at the time the Minister for Defence Procurement), all the way down to the heads of both the Defence Procurement Agency (DPA – Sir Peter Spencer)[1] and the Defence Logistics Organisation (DLO – General Sir Kevin O'Donoghue).[2]

The MoD had three options available to it to fill what it perceived to be a capability gap: go through the standard acquisition cycle; upgrade any existing capability; or acquire capability using the Urgent Operational Requirement (UOR) process. Using the standard acquisition cycle was not really practical as time was of the essence and the MoD had been criticised for the delays (and cost overruns) caused to projects as they moved through the CADMID cycle.[3] As will be described below, the second option has been implemented in so far as the 'Snatch' Land Rover, Warrior IFV and FV432 have been concerned, while option three was used to acquire new vehicles, such as the Mastiff and Foxhound.

Vehicles Then In-Service

These included:

'Snatch' Land Rovers

Following a competition in early 1991, the MoD placed a contract worth £50m with what is now NP Aerospace to supply 1,000 lightly armoured 4x4 vehicles, a contract which also covered design and development. The vehicle was a version of the Land Rover Defender 110, with NP Aerospace fitting a special ballistic protection system which was integral to the vehicle and made from advanced fibre-reinforced composite materials. They were widely used in Northern Ireland and on peacekeeping missions where the threat environment was considered low, in roles such as internal security, ambulance, explosive ordnance disposal, logistics and communications. Other users included the United Nations High Commissioner for Refugees (UNHCR), the BBC, the French Ministère des Affaires and the Canadian Department of National Defence.[4] There is also Snatch 2 and its variants:[5]

- The baseline vehicle has 12v electrics, left-hand drive (LHD) and an air-conditioning unit (ACU) but is only used for training;
- The 2A variant has 24v electrics, right-hand drive (RHD) and an ACU;
- The 2B variant has 24v electrics, no ACU and is for use in Northern Ireland only.

Their use in Iraq and Afghanistan was criticised because, despite being armoured against small arms fire, the vehicles had proven susceptible to IEDs and over thirty-seven casualties were attributed to the vehicle's lack of protection.[6] Such was the disillusionment, that armed forces personnel started calling it the 'mobile coffin'.[7]

A Snatch 2 12v Land Rover (Source: I Wish I Was Flying via Flickr)

Warrior

A comparatively well-armed and armoured (having a 30mm Rarden cannon and 7.62mm chain gun) infantry fighting vehicle (IFV) which grew out of the 1970s MCV-80 project. The initial 1967 proposals to consider a replacement armoured personnel carrier (APC) were followed by in-house Ministry of Defence (MoD) feasibility studies running between 1968 and 1971. There followed several years (1972 – 1976) of initial industrial work and MoD option studies (known as Project Definition 1) with Full Project Definition (Project Definition 2) lasting for a further two years (1977 – 1978). This was carried out by GKN Sankey after they had been chosen as prime contractor for the MCV-80. In 1978, a parallel evaluation started of the American XM2 (now in service as the M2 Bradley Infantry Fighting Vehicle) with full development of the MCV-80 starting in 1979. By 1980 there were three prototypes of the MCV-80 in use, and by January 1984 negotiations regarding an initial production order were well advanced, with the MoD contracting GKN Defence for the full development of variants and additional vehicles based on the design. MCV-80 was accepted for service in November 1984 under the name 'Warrior' with a reliability rating well in excess of target. Production began in Telford, Shropshire in January 1986 with the first production batch numbering 290 vehicles, 170 of which were infantry section vehicles, while 120 were specialised variants. The Warrior entered service in May 1987 with the 1st Battalion, Grenadier Guards. Although the original requirement was for 1,053 vehicles (enough to equip thirteen battalions), the reductions in the size of the British Army as a result of Options for Change meant that only eight mechanised infantry battalions would be equipped with Warrior. A total of 789 vehicles were produced by GKN Defence, the final deliveries being made in early 1995. In addition, after extensive trials, Kuwait selected an export variant, the Desert Warrior in late 1992, with an order for 254 being placed in August 1993. Final deliveries were made in late 1997. As a side note, the earliest vehicles are nearly twenty-six years old and present an increasing maintenance burden and require upgrading.[8]

A Warrior IFV (Source: Davric via Wikimedia Commons)

FV432

In June 1956, the GKN Fighting Vehicle Development Division (FVDD) was awarded the contract to develop and construct four prototype and ten trials vehicles of the FV420, a light, unarmoured, tracked vehicle to be delivered by March 1958. In addition, they were given the contract to design and develop the FV430 family of armoured personnel carriers (APCs) with an initial requirement for four prototypes and thirteen test vehicles to undertake troop trials. Alongside this, Royal Ordnance (now part of BAE Systems, Global Combat Systems) were contracted to build another seven vehicles for troop trials under GKN's design parentage, with all these vehicles being delivered by late 1961. In 1962, GKN Sankey were given the production contract to build the FV432 APC along with design and development contracts for a number of variants, including the FV431 Light Tracked Load Carrier (which didn't enter service) and the FV434 Armoured Fitters' Vehicle. The first production vehicles were built at the GKN facility in Wellington, Shropshire with the vehicle entering service in late 1963. By the time production finished in 1971, around 3,018 vehicles had been built in three distinct models – the Mark 1, Mark 2 and Mark 2/1. The FV432 replaced the Saracen (6x6) APC in British Army service but was itself replaced by the Warrior IFV. It had a welded steel hull that provided protection against small arms fire and shell splinters. Despite being in service for almost fifty years, it is still in British Army service in a number of variants, including troop carrier, ambulance and command vehicle.[9]

An FV432 APC (Source: Plushy via Wikimedia Commons)

Option Two: Upgrading Existing Capability

Snatch Vixen

Deployment started in late 2008 with Snatch vehicles being upgraded by Ricardo Specialist Vehicles and NP Aerospace as the original design authority, the programme being run by the Specialist & Utility Vehicles Integrated Project Team (IPT). Between 150 and 200 vehicles were eventually fielded. The main improvements centre on an improved armour package (elements of which had already been tested as part of the upgraded Land Rover Weapons Mount Installation Kit – WMIK) with underbody and wheel arch blast deflectors, as well as an enhanced engine and drive-train package, essential given that the vehicle now weighs in at 4.1 tonnes. In addition, the British Army is working on a Snatch Vixen Plus variant which would raise the overall weight to 4.7 tonnes with additional armour protection.[10]

Warrior

Warrior had already received upgrades such as the Battle Group Thermal Imaging (BGTI) programme in 2005 which replaced the image intensification sights then being used on Warrior, equipping the gunner with a sight that features a day / thermal imager and eye-safe laser range finder and the commander with a monitor and flat screen display and access to both the Bowman and battle management systems being procured under separate contracts. More recently, both the Theatre Entry Standard (Herrick) (TES(H)) and Warrior Capability Sustainment Programme (WCSP) upgrade programmes have begun, covering both the short and long-term development of the vehicle. The WCSP contract was awarded to Lockheed Martin UK on 2 November 2011 and is estimated to have a value of £1bn, which includes not only demonstration and production costs, but also MoD programme costs and Government Furnished Equipment (GFE). The WCSP actually includes a number of separate elements including the Warrior Fightability & Lethality Improvement Programme (WFLIP), the Warrior Enhanced Electronic Architecture (WEEA) and the Warrior Modular Protection System (WMPS).

The WEEA was developed by Lockheed Martin UK to allow the vehicle to be upgraded in the future when new electronic systems become available, while the WMPS is essentially a modular system for mounting different armour packages on the vehicle, allowing armour to be changed as the situation dictates or for damaged sections to be replaced easily. The turret is being modified to accept the fully stabilised CTAI International 40mm Case Telescoped Cannon and Ammunition (CTCA) system while retaining the 7.62mm chain gun to the left of the main armament as well as applique armour. The Bowman digital communications system will be installed, with the three crew members getting digital displays and day / night cameras providing 360 degree situational awareness. The WCSP also includes an Auxiliary Power Unit (APU) and an environmental control unit (which includes air conditioning) that will integrate into the NBC[11] system. This upgrade work will be done alongside the existing Warrior Base Overhaul Programme (WBOC). The eleven WCSP demonstrator vehicles will undergo extensive testing through 2013 and 2014 with the demonstration phase ending in 2016. Around 380 vehicles will then be upgraded between 2018 and 2020. Meanwhile, the TES(H) programme was a continuation of the upgrade work done on vehicles serving in Iraq with around seventy vehicles having been modified by the end of 2011 at the Defence Support Group (DSG) facility at Donnington. The upgrade includes over thirty modifications which have enhanced the vehicle's protection and survivability. A new suspension system and lower ratio final drive has restored its speed and manoeuvrability (especially at low speeds) as the modified vehicle weighs in at around forty tonnes, compared to the original vehicle's twenty-five. It includes two counter-IED systems and a Modular Protection System (MPS) that can be tailored to a specific deployment, typically applique passive armour and bar armour to the chassis, bar armour to the turret and an underbelly armour plate, although it can accept Explosive Reactive Armour (ERA).[12]

FV432 Mk. 3 Bulldog

In early 2002, BAE Systems (by then the designated design authority for the FV432 vehicle) completed a Systems Demonstrator that was first displayed in July that year. The demonstrator had a Cummins Engine Company (CEC) B-Series six-cylinder turbocharged diesel engine (250hp) which met EURO II regulations, coupled to a new Allison X200-4C fully automatic, electronically controlled transmission, already installed in the latest BAE Systems M113A3 APC, along with a new cooling system. The vehicle was found to be 500kg lighter, allowing for the placement of additional armour without affecting driving performance. By mid-2003, this and three additional prototypes (with a new damper suspension system from Horstman Defence Systems) were undergoing trials at the British Army's Infantry Trials and Development Unit (ITDU) at Warminster, Wiltshire. In November 2005, the DLO awarded BAE Systems an £80m contract (with an additional £15m for support in early 2006) to supply subsystems so that ABRO[13] could upgrade 500 FV432 APCs to a standard that included the new engine and drive train, an ERA package, air conditioning, thermal blanket, protected commander's position (in

some cases this will be the Selex Galileo Enforcer Remote Controlled Weapon Station)
and an IED detection system. A follow-on contract worth £70m for an additional 400
vehicles was signed in May 2007, with final deliveries taking place in early 2011.[14]
All 908 vehicles currently in-service have been upgraded to the FV432 Bulldog Mk.
3 standard, with another 117 in storage having additional passive armour added to the
upper part of the suspension.

Option Three: In The Market

However, given both the operational and political urgency (for example, a Ministerial target
was set to get Mastiff into Iraq by 31 December 2006)[15], upgrading vehicles currently in
service would, while being quicker than the normal acquisition cycle, still take time and
so it was decided that the requirement would have to be met by a Military-Off-The-Shelf
(MOTS) purchase utilising the third option, the UOR process. After a review by a number
of subject-matter experts and capability managers of what was available, a list of ten Key
User Requirements (KURs) was produced. While these have been applied to the Mastiff
acquisition, the MoD has in fact bought a wide range of vehicles in significant numbers to
fill the capability gap.

The first Mine Resistant Ambush Protected (MRAP) vehicles appeared in Iraq as
Explosive Ordnance Disposal (EOD) and combat engineer vehicles. The original designs
were based on experience of both the South African and Rhodesian bush wars and
generally featured a V-shaped or curved lower hull that deflected the blast from a land
mine or IED around and away from the vehicle. They also tend to be fully enclosed, a
hint as to their origin as EOD vehicles, with heavy ballistic glass fitted to windscreens
and viewing ports. As the IED threat increased in both Iraq and Afghanistan, MRAP
vehicles were seen to be the safest method by which armed forces personnel could move
around in hostile terrain, given that IED strikes were killing hundreds of personnel each
year. The early MRAP vehicles, although far better protected than Humvees or 'Snatch'
Land Rovers, were not designed as troop transports and so were seen as being a bit too
heavy, too tall, and too bulky for either the urban environment of Iraq or the mountainous
regions of Afghanistan. New designs appeared, which took into account the tactical
needs of the users and the operating conditions in-theatre. However, some criticism was
voiced as to their effect on the counter-insurgency effort, encouraging troops to ride in
these vehicles rather than patrolling outside and interacting with the local population.[16]
To cater for the needs of the British Army with regard to protected mobility, the MoD
has bought:

Mastiff, Wolfhound and Ridgback

A Mastiff Protected Patrol Vehicle (PPV) – a variant of the US Cougar MRAP vehicle (Source: I Wish I Was Flying via Flickr)

The MoD initially ordered 108 Force Protection Industries Incorporated (FPII) Cougar MRAP vehicles (known in British service as the Mastiff).[17] The MoD was given a deadline of twenty-three weeks to have Mastiff in-theatre and so the basic vehicles[18] were upgraded to UK specifications by Coventry-based NP Aerospace at the UK base in Akrotiri, Cyprus, where some REME and RLC[19] personnel were given training as well. The initial batch of ten vehicles was then flown to Iraq to meet the Ministerial deadline, a classic UOR procurement where urgency generally outweighed cost or an extended assurance process.

This initially rushed procurement was followed by the purchase of additional 'upgraded' versions of Mastiff 1, Mastiff 2 and a small but growing number of Mastiff 3[20] as well as thirty ex-USMC vehicles (which entered service in 2009) to be used for training.[21] The total number of Mastiff vehicles has reached about 300. On top of that, 177 Ridgback (4x4) and 101 Wolfhound (6x6) have been received, meaning that the entire Cougar-based fleet will have risen to about 600 vehicles during 2012, making a vital contribution to protected mobility and overall force protection.[22]

There were doubts as to whether something quite so large and lumbering could fulfil the UOR and concerns about its potentially adverse effect on the equipment programme and, in particular, the Future Rapid Effects System Utility Vehicle (FRES (UV)) project. However, Mastiff has proven to be an operational success, although there have been other factors which have complicated things, and these have included:

- The Commercial Environment – NPA took on the task at a significant commercial risk pending the award of an MoD contract. At that time, the Specialist & Utility Vehicles Integrated Project Team (SUV IPT) was the Design Authority but with Mastiff 2, the role passed to NPA and has since moved again to Integrated Survivability Technologies Limited (a joint venture between FPII and NPA).

- Procurement Strategy – Given the timescale, the strategy was to look for a MOTS solution, with the key issues being the choice of the base vehicle, developing enhanced protection, and systems integration. The urgency of the requirement was underlined by a number of people, including the SUV IPT Leader and Lord Drayson.[23] The Defence Vehicle Dynamics (DVD) Trade Show was a useful showcase for viewing a number of different contenders, with information also coming from the Defence Science and Technology Laboratory (DSTL).

- Innovative Support – Given the speed at which this procurement was undertaken, there was little time to consider innovative support arrangements, such as Contracting for Availability or Contracting for Capability. Some $4m of spares were ordered with the vehicles, based on the only usage data then available, provided by the USMC. This initial spares batch reflected the understanding that UORs have a one-year life (later amended to three).

- International Context – the procurement was also influenced by the international nature of the operations in both Iraq and Afghanistan with a number of Coalition partners having deployed Cougar-based vehicles.[24] While this might have led to opportunities for shared support and learning lessons regarding interoperability, it actually led to some unhelpful competition over priorities and resources. At the time, NP Aerospace were not allowed to source alternative suppliers of spare parts and had to use US manufacturers, who themselves were required by US law to satisfy the demands of the USMC first, the MoD finding that significant quantities of spare parts originally intended for the UK were diverted.[25] While Mastiff and Ridgback were conducted as Foreign Military Sales (FMS), Wolfhound was a Direct Commercial Sale (DCS) allowing the UK to have a little more control.

In UK service, the Mastiff family of vehicles includes[26]:

- Mastiff 1 / 1.5: Contract Awarded – August 2006; Deployed – December 2006; First Operational Use – March 2007. Variants – troop carrier, battlefield ambulance.

- Mastiff 2: Entered Service – late 2008; Deployed Operationally – March 2009. Enhancements – improved lights and upgraded brakes; Variants – troop carrier, battlefield ambulance and enhanced communications vehicle.

- Mastiff 3: Entered Service – early 2011; Enhancements – increase in internal room and integrated communications equipment.

- Ridgback (4x4): Ordered – February 2008; Arrived in UK – August 2008; Deployed – May 2009; Variants – troop carrier, battlefield ambulance, command post vehicle.[27] In October 2008, NP Aerospace was awarded an £81m contract by DE&S to convert Cougar (4x4) MRAP vehicles to the enhanced Ridgback PPV specification. A total of 171 vehicles were converted, with modifications that included additional passive armour, enhanced situational awareness, bar armour, weapons, wire cutters, new seats to enhance crew survivability, Bowman and counter-IED electronics. Some seventy-two of the troop carriers are armed with the Salex Galileo Enforcer Remote Controlled Weapon Station which can be fitted with a 7.62mm machinegun, a .50 cal M2 heavy-barrelled machinegun or a Heckler & Koch 40mm Grenade Machine Gun.[28]

- Wolfhound (6x6): Ordered – April 2009; Entered Service – late-2010; Variants – Utility (eighty-one), Explosive Ordnance Disposal (thirty-nine) and Military Working Dog (five). This vehicle is a 6x6 version of Mastiff that was developed by Integrated Survivability Technologies Ltd. Equipment includes Bowman, counter-IED electronics and a protected weapon station.[29]

There was some initial resistance to Mastiff, which led to criticism of some of its capability shortcomings. One area of concern was safety, an issue which is being looked at by the Protected Mobility Team (PMT) and Army Headquarters, Andover. It is considered a priority, with current issues including the vehicle's ability to deal with water hazards (canals are common in Helmand) and crew egress in an emergency. But if allowances are made, the vehicle actually fulfils the capability requirements very well. Indeed, Mastiff has, overall, received a good press, for example – "The procurement of Mastiff has largely been a real success story for the MoD and, in particular, for Minister of Defence Equipment and

Support, Lord Drayson"[30] warranted by good performance in-theatre.[31]

Vector

The MoD ordered 180 UK-built Pinzgauer Vector alongside the Mastiffs.[32] The Vector, originally designed by Steyr-Daimler-Puch of Austria, was developed and placed in quantity production in less than nine months, being based on the Pinzgauer (6x6) chassis, with a new armoured body designed by BAE Systems. It also incorporated power-assisted steering, an anti-skid braking system, electronic traction control, run-flat tyres, an air conditioning system, the Bowman communications system and electronic counter-measures (ECM) devices. While better than the Snatch Land Rover, it has been found that the Vector does not provide the sort of protection against mines and IEDs that other vehicles do and so has been relegated to use in lower threat areas. All 180 vehicles had been delivered by the end of 2007 but by 2013 had been withdrawn from active service in Afghanistan and returned to the UK.[33]

Foxhound

A Foxhound PPV in Afghanistan (Source: defenceimagery.mod.uk)

The Ocelot PPV had been in development by Force Protection Europe (FPE – formerly a subsidiary of FPII) since early 2009 with FPE working alongside Ricardo Specialist Vehicles to meet the requirements of the British Army for a light PPV with a high-degree of protection and good mobility. After the production of five trials vehicles and following extensive ballistic and blast testing in 2009, the Ocelot was selected as the preferred solution in September 2010, over that of the Supacat SPV 400. In November 2010, FPE was awarded a £180m contract covering the supply of 200 Ocelot LPPV (known as Foxhound in British Army service) plus an initial purchase of spare parts with deliveries to run from 2011 through to mid-2012. FPE was taken over by General Dynamics Land Systems in 2011. The first thirty-five vehicles were handed over in late 2011 and deployment to Afghanistan started in mid-2012. Additional contracts were placed in mid-to-late 2012 for 100, twenty-five and fifty-one vehicles, bringing the total ordered to 376. Foxhound Theatre Entry Standard includes an air conditioning system, Bowman, electronic jamming equipment, Barracuda thermal reduction covers, a GPS navigation system and a pair of roof-mounted 7.62mm machineguns.[34]

Panther

The BAE Systems Panther, based on the Iveco Defence Vehicles LMV (4x4), was chosen to fulfil the British Army's Future Command and Liaison Vehicle requirement, with some 401 vehicles being ordered, although due to issues arising during trials, it wasn't accepted for service until mid-2008. The vehicle has been designed with a compact profile, enabling one vehicle to be carried in a Chinook helicopter or two in a C-130 Hercules. Of the 401, 326 are of the Group 2 standard and come with the Selex Enforcer 7.62mm Self-Defence Weapon (SDW) and Surveillance Target Acquisition (STA) with the remaining seventy-five fitted for, but not with, the SDW/STA. All Panther vehicles have an integrated floor protection system and a modular armour package, but BAE Systems also fitted the SDW/STA, rear pod, roof, two banks of four smoke dischargers, Health and Usage Monitoring System (HUMS), a fire detection and suppression system and a driver vision enhancer. In addition, a number have been upgraded to Theatre Entry Standard (TES) with additional ECM equipment, larger roof hatches, a rear view camera, a protected engine compartment, a new rear cargo pod, Bowman (which reduces the crew complement), additional armour and a redesigned engine air intake.[35]

*A Panther command vehicle at the UOR Equipment Demonstration in Salisbury, Wiltshire
(Source: defenceimagery.mod.uk)*

Warthog

A further development of the STK Bronco, this vehicle was ordered in late 2008 to replace its
direct predecessor, the Viking. The Warthog comes in four variants (ambulance, command,
repair and recovery, as well as troop carrier) and includes spall liners, appliqué armour, a
mine protection kit, Bowman communications equipment, counter-IED electronics, wire
cutters, grenade launchers and a Platt roof-mounted weapon system. All 115 vehicles had
been delivered by mid-2011.[36]

Jackal and Coyote

The Jackal (originally known as the Supacat High Mobility Transporter) is designed to
transport loads of between three and six tonnes across difficult terrain and comes in 4 ×
4 configuration, while the 6 × 6 variant is known as the Coyote in British Army service.
The Jackal is powerful enough to tow loads up to four tonnes in weight, in addition to
carrying its payload of just over three tonnes. It comes with variable height suspension,
enabling ground clearance and load height to be adjusted, giving the vehicle a smooth
ride in difficult terrain. Each tyre has both a large diameter and wide cross section, which
gives the vehicle a high off-road mobility and reduces ground damage. The design of

the vehicle allows the customer to specify the configuration such as personnel capacity and body type.[37] Approximately 455 Jackals and seventy-six Coyotes have been bought since 2006.[38]

A Jackal PPV at the Defence Vehicle Dynamics (DVD) show in 2008
(Source: defenceimagery.mod.uk)

Husky

Between 2008 and 2009, the MoD ran a Tactical Support Vehicle (TSV) programme to find suitable light and medium weight vehicles, the contract for which was worth around £700m. In April 2009, the MoD placed an order for 262 Husky Tactical Support Vehicles (TSV) with Navistar, these vehicles being based on a much-modified International MXT chassis, itself based on a DuraStar / 4000 Series medium duty truck platform. Navistar subsequently announced in September 2010 that it had received a second delivery order valued at $56m from the MoD for additional Husky TSV utility variants. Deliveries commenced in October 2010 and finished in mid-2011.[39] Around 333 Husky TSVs have been bought meaning that both Supacat and Navistar products account for 864 of the 1,916 vehicles (45%) bought by the MoD since 2006.[40] This has led Supacat and Navistar to form a partnership (a Memorandum of Understanding was announced on 19 June 2013) so as to cover the likely support requirements for their respective vehicles as they are taken into the British Army's core capability.[41]

A Husky PPV (Source: defenceimages.mod.uk)

Conclusion

With an urgent need to counter the growing threat of IEDs in both Iraq and Afghanistan, and political pressure building due to adverse press coverage and Coroner's reports, the MoD has successfully filled a specific operational requirement in a relatively short period of time, by upgrading current capability and by acquiring new capability, utilising the UOR process. This is important, as the MoD has recently stated that there will be an increasing emphasis on buying MOTS solutions where appropriate.[42] Success in the short term has not come without cost in the longer term however: the Mastiff, for example, was acquired without any real examination of the issues surrounding the generation of a Through Life Capability Management (TLCM) plan, effectively leaving that to after the signing of the Post-Design Services contract; and maintenance and repair has been complicated by the lack of visibility of, and difficulties in, the management of spares. All this, and the lack of an overall fleet management system, means that there will be a shortage of operating and support data and information available to the MoD as it transfers these vehicles into its inventory as core capability, a decision that was taken only in May 2013. In an age of austerity, the project is likely to cost several hundred million pounds over the next decade, with money having to be re-allocated from the Army's £5.5bn AFV 'funding pipeline'. Over £100m alone is expected to be spent in the refurbishment of the 300-or-so Mastiff vehicles that are now in-service but will be withdrawn from Afghanistan by the end of 2014. DE&S has been preparing business cases (thirteen in total) for Army Headquarters in Andover to allow the Defence Support Group (DSG) to begin regenerating the vehicles. Around fifty-three Jackal 4x4 and twenty-one Ridgback 4x4 vehicles have been brought back to the UK.[43]

Endnotes

[1] The Iraq Inquiry. (2010) 'Sir Peter Spencer – Transcript', dated 26 July 2010, currently located at http://www.iraqinquiry.org.uk/media/48689/20100726pm-spencer.pdf . Accessed: 6 August 2013.

[2] DLO Microsite, located at http://webarchive.nationalarchives.gov.uk/+/http:/www.mod.uk/DefenceInternet/MicroSite/DLO . Accessed: 6 August 2013.

[3] Concept Assessment Development Manufacturing In-service Disposal. For example, see National Audit Office. (2007) *Ministry of Defence – Major Projects Report 2007*, HC98-I, London: TSO, 26 November 2007, p. 5.

[4] BBC News Website. (2009) 'Q&A: Snatch Land Rovers', currently located at http://news.bbc.co.uk/1/hi/uk/7703703.stm. Accessed: 6 August 2013; Wikipedia. (2012) 'Snatch Land Rover', currently located at http://en.wikipedia.org/wiki/Snatch_Land_Rover. Accessed: 6 August 2013; Jane's Information Group. (2013) 'NP Aerospace CAV100 Armoured Personnel Carrier', posted on 5 March 2013 in *Land Warfare Platforms – Armoured Fighting Vehicles* at ihs.janes.com, Accessed: 16 July 2013.

[5] *Op Cit*. Jane's Information Group, 'NP Aerospace CAV 100 armoured personnel carrier'.

[6] BBC News Website. 'Inquest into only female UK soldier's death resumes', currently located at http://news.bbc.co.uk/1/hi/uk/8542288.stm. Accessed: 6 August 2013.

[7] Sturke, J. (2008) 'Snatch Land Rovers: the mobile coffins of the British army', dated 1 November 2008, currently located at http://www.guardian.co.uk/uk/2008/nov/01/snatch-land-rovers-army. Accessed: 6 August 2013.

[8] Jane's Information Group. (2013) 'BAE Systems Warrior Infantry Fighting Vehicle', posted 14 January 2013 in *Land Warfare Platforms – Armoured Fighting Vehicles*, located on ihs.janes.com. Accessed: 16 July 2013; Foss, C. (1994) *Warrior Mechanised Combat Vehicle 1987 – 94*, Oxford: Osprey Publishing, July 1994, New Vanguard Series No. 10.

[9] Jane's Information Group. 'BAE Systems, Global Combat Systems FV432 armoured

personnel carrier', posted 29 November 2011 in *Land Warfare Platforms – Armoured Fighting Vehicles* at ihs.janes.com. Accessed: 16 July 2013; Crusader 80. (2013) 'Royal Engineers FV432 Armoured Personnel Carrier' webpage at http://www.crusader80.co.uk/432.html as of 16 July 2013.

[10] *Op Cit.* Jane's Information Group, 'NP Aerospace CAV 100 armoured personnel carrier'.

[11] Nuclear Biological Chemical.

[12] Defense Industry Daily. (2011) 'WCSP: Britain's Warriors to Undergo Midlife Upgrade', currently located at http://www.defenseindustrydaily.com/WCSP-Britains-Warriors-to-Undergo-Mid-Life-Upgrade-05967/. Accessed: 6 August 2013; *Op Cit.* Jane's Information Group, 'BAE Systems Warrior Infantry Fighting Vehicle'.

[13] Formerly the Army Base Repair Organisation – it became a trading fund (and hence known as ABRO) on 1 April 2002 and was subsequently merged with the Defence Aviation Repair Agency (DARA) on 1 April 2008 to become the Defence Support Group (DSG). See Wikipedia. (2013) 'Army Base Repair Organisation' webpage at http://en.wikipedia.org/wiki/Army_Base_Repair_Organisation as of 17 July 2013.

[14] *Op Cit.* Jane's Information Group, 'FV432 armoured personnel carrier'.

[15] Author's conversations with members of the MoD's Protected Mobility Team, dated 26 January and 24 February 2010. See also 'Defence Secretary orders new vehicles for troops in Iraq and Afghanistan', located at http://webarchive.nationalarchives.gov.uk/+/http://www.mod.uk:80/DefenceInternet/DefenceNews/MilitaryOperations/DefenceSecretaryOrdersNewVehiclesForTroopsInIraqAndAfghanistan.htm . Accessed: 6 August 2013. Ministerial interest has continued throughout the vehicle's entry into service and deployment, for example, PM Gordon Brown made a statement to the House of Commons on 8 October 2007, confirming that additional Mastiff vehicles had been ordered as a priority for the forces serving in Iraq and Afghanistan. See Hansard, Commons Debates, 8 October 2007, Column 24, located at http://www.publications.parliament.uk/pa/cm200607/cmhansrd/cm071008/debtext/71008-0004.htm#column_21 . Accessed: 6 August 2013.

[16] Neville, L. (2011) *Special Operations Patrol Vehicles – Afghanistan and Iraq*, Oxford: Osprey Publishing, September 2011, New Vanguard series No. 179, p. 41.

[17] Foss, C. (2006) 'UK unveils Mastiff and Vector protected vehicles', posted 20 September 2006, in *Jane's Defence Weekly*, at ihs.janes.com. Accessed: 6 August 2013.

[18] See http://www.gdls.com/index.php/products/mrap-family/cougar6x6 for specs. Accessed: 6 August 2013.

[19] Royal Electrical and Mechanical Engineers, Royal Logistics Corps.

[20] See http://www.army.mod.uk/equipment/23248.aspx for overview. Accessed: 6 August 2013.

[21] Email dated 12 January 2012, from Tim Foreman, DE&S Public Relations Office.

[22] Ripley, T. (2013) 'British Army UOR fleet moves into core' posted 24 June 2013 in *Jane's Defence Weekly* at ihs.janes.com. Accessed: 6 August 2013.

[23] Drayson, Lord. (2006) 'Speech to the Future Carrier Conclave', Royal United Services Institute, 18 September 2006, located at http://webarchive.nationalarchives. gov.uk/+/http://www.mod.uk/DefenceInternet/AboutDefence/People/Speeches/MinDP/ SpeechToTheFutureCarrierconclave18September2006.htm . Accessed: 6 August 2013.

[24] Such as Iraq, Canada, Croatia, Georgia, Hungary, Italy and Poland. See Wikipedia. (2013) 'Cougar (vehicle)' webpage, located at http://en.wikipedia.org/wiki/Cougar_(vehicle) . Accessed: 6 August 2013.

[25] National Audit Office. (2009) *Support to High Intensity Operations*, HC508, 14 May 2009, London: TSO, p. 13.

[26] See Conners, S. (2009) 'Mastiff 2 and Ridgeback reach Afghanistan' posted 12 June 2009 in *Jane's Defence Weekly* at ihs.janes.com . Accessed: 6 August 2013; Foss, C. 'Change of the Guards: European Land Systems Part 2 – the UK' posted 22 June 2009 in *Jane's Defence Weekly* at ihs.janes.com . Accessed: 6 August 2013.

[27] Army Technology Website. (2011) ' Cougar Ridgback 4x4 MRAP Armoured Vehicle, United Kingdom' Webpage, located at http://www.army-technology.com/projects/cougar_ ridgback/ . Accessed: 6 August 2013.

[28] Jane's Information Group. (2013) 'General Dynamics Land Systems – Force Protection Cougar Mine Resistant Ambush Protected Vehicle', posted 28 February 2013, in *Land Warfare Platforms – Armoured Fighting Vehicles* at ihs.janes.com. Accessed: 6 August 2013.

[29] *Ibid*.

[30] D'Arcy, M. (2008) 'Mastiff the Protector' in *Defence Management Journal*, Issue [40] (February), at http://www.defencemanagement.com/article.asp?id=329&content_ name=Land%20Vehicles&article=9186 . Accessed: 6 August 2013.

[31] See for example http://www.gdls.com/index.php/products/mrap-family/cougar4x4 ; Feickert, A. (2011) *Mine-Resistant Ambush-Protected Vehicles: Background and Issues for Congress*, dated 18 January 2011, Report No. RS22707, available at http://www.fas. org/sgp/crs/weapons/RS22707.pdf , p. 2. Accessed: 6 August 2013.

[32] *Op Cit*. 'UK unveils Mastiff and Vector protected vehicles', posted 20 September 2006.

[33] Jane's Information Group. (2013) 'BAE Systems Vector Protected Patrol Vehicle', posted 5 March 2013, in *Land Warfare Platforms – Armoured Fighting Vehicles*, available at ihs.janes.com. Accessed: 6 August 2013.

[34] Jane's Information Group. (2013) 'General Dynamics Land Systems – Force Protection

Europe Ocelot Light Protected (Foxhound) Patrol Vehicle', dated 5 March 2013, in *Land Warfare Platforms – Armoured Fighting Vehicles* at ihs.janes.com . Accessed: 6 August 2013.

[35] Jane's Information Group. (2013) 'IVECO Defence Vehicles Light Multirole Vehicle (LMV)', posted 2 April 2013 in *Land Warfare Platforms – Armoured Fighting Vehicles*, at ihs.janes.com . Accessed: 6 August 2013; Jane's Information Group. (2013) 'British Army Armour Upgrades for Iraq and Afghanistan' in *Land Warfare Platforms – System Upgrades*, posted 3 October 2012. Accessed: 7 August 2013.

[36] *Op Cit*. 'British Army Armour Upgrades for Iraq and Afghanistan', posted 3 October 2012.

[37] Jane's Information Group. () 'Supacat HMT (High Mobility Transporter)' in *Jane's Police and Homeland Security Equipment*, posted 1 July 2013 at ihs.janes.com. Accessed: 7 August 2013.

[38] *Op Cit*. 'British Army UOR fleet moves into core', posted 24 June 2013.

[39] Jane's Information Group. (2013) 'Navistar Defence (International) range of military vehicles' in *Land Warfare Platforms – Logistics, Support and Unmanned*, posted 13 March 2013 at ihs.janes.com. Accessed: 7 August 2013; Anderson, G. (2013) 'Supacat and Navistar form UK vehicle support partnership' in *Jane's Defence Weekly*, posted 19 June 2013 at ihs.janes.com. Accessed: 7 August 2013.

[40] *Op Cit*. 'British Army UOR fleet moves into core', posted 24 June 2013.

[41] *Op Cit*. 'Supacat and Navistar form UK vehicle support partnership', posted 19 June 2013.

[42] Ministry of Defence. (2012) *National Security Through Technology: Technology, Equipment and Support for UK Defence and Security*, CM8278, February 2012, London: TSO, pp. 20 – 21.

[43] *Op Cit*. 'British Army UOR fleet moves into core', posted 24 June 2013.

Patience is a Virtue: The Case of the British Army's Assault Rifle

Peter D. Antill

Centre for Defence Acquisition, Cranfield University, Defence Academy of the UK.

Introduction

Few items that have come into service with the British Army have caused more controversy over their operating lives than that of the SA80 (Small Arms for the 1980s) series of weapons. This family of small arms, chambered for NATO's 5.56x45mm ammunition, consists primarily of the L85 Individual Weapon and the L86 Light Support Weapon, but also includes the L22 Carbine and L98 Cadet Rifle. The L85 and L86 replaced the L1A1 Self-Loading Rifle, L4A9 Bren Light Machine Gun, L7A2 General Purpose Machine Gun and L2A3 Sterling Sub-Machine Gun. Officially handed over on 2 October 1985, production had reached over 323,920 when it finished in 1994.[1]

From top to bottom: SA80A1, SA80A3 and SA80 Carbine Mk. I
(Source: Author's Collection)

This case study looks at the background, development history, problems and controversies surrounding this assault rifle, concentrating on the political interference with the project (both national and international), the questions over the supposed testing and the continual reliance on 'quick fix' solutions. Such problems and controversies have always generated interest in specialist publications, the general media and the political sphere, with the result that there was a lot of material available on the weapon and its history, in this case, much of it critical – "a weapon or weapon system is usually written about because of its innovative design, its impact on the field of battle, or even on world events. This book is probably unique among all others on small arms because its subject, the SA80, is none of the above, and will be remembered for all the wrong reasons."[2]

Background

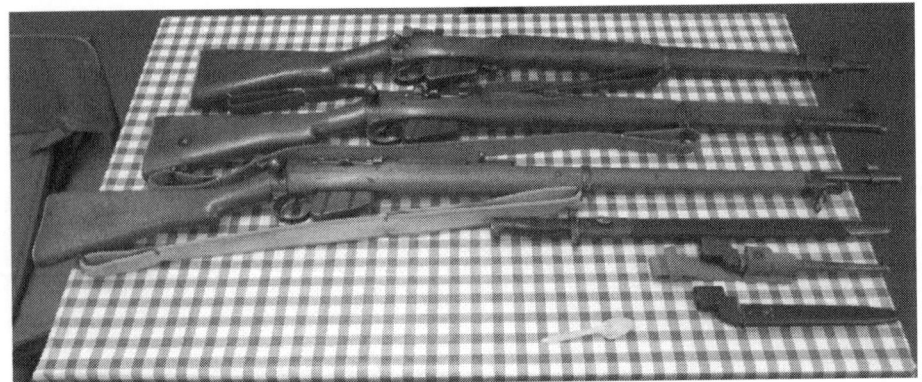

From bottom to top: Mk. I Magazine, Lee Enfield (MLE); No. 1 Mk. III Short, Magazine, Lee Enfield (SMLE); No. 4 Mk. I Lee Enfield (Source: Author's Collection)

Soon after the end of World War II, the British Army looked to replace its No. 4 Lee Enfield rifles, which while being accurate and reliable, were based on technology dating back to the late 1880s.[3] Experience during both world wars, and even the Korean War, questioned the need for infantry to have weapons chambered for full-power cartridges that are accurate out to as much as 2,000 yards.[4] "In fact, despite the evidence that most shooting during WW1 was at short range, armies continued to show an interest in full-power rifle/MG rounds."[5] World War II showed the need for infantry to be armed with light, selective fire weapons that required an "effective range of fire much longer than of submachine gun, but shorter than of conventional semi-automatic or bolt-action rifles."[6] After several years of research, development and testing, the UK had developed the .280/30 cartridge (in metric terms, 7x43mm) and the EM-2 rifle to fire it, officially adopting them in August 1951 as the 'Cartridge, SA, Ball, 7mm Mk1Z' ('Z' denoted the use of nitrocellulose propellant) and the 'Rifle No. 9 Mk 1', after they had been entered into the NATO Standardisation Trials of 1952.[7] Due to both national and international politics however, this decision was reversed as NATO (under pressure from the USA) decided to go for a different calibre[8] and so the UK adopted the 7.62x51mm chambered L1A1 Self-Loading Rifle (SLR) on 1 March 1957.[9]

From top to bottom: EM-2, EM-2 without the optical sight / carrying handle and an FN FAL (Source: Author's collection)

The immediate background to the SA80 lies in the decision in the late 1960s, to start looking for a replacement for the L1A1 SLR. The 7.62x51mm NATO cartridge that it fired had always been considered overpowered by the British[10], even though it was designed as a compromise between the American .30-06 cartridge and the British .280 round. The nature of the compromise meant it was little more than a .30-06 cartridge with a shorter case and the round therefore fell between the two camps, that is, it was not quite as powerful as the rounds it replaced but too powerful to be a practical assault rifle cartridge.[11] NATO adopted it in 1954 and the British, having been forced to adopt it and keep the cartridge and the rifle that fired it in service for what would turn out to be three decades, decided that next time, the decision would be based on firm technical and tactical requirements. Or so they thought. Once again, the British looked at data from both world wars and Korea but by this time could include data from the war in Vietnam.

They decided that any future ammunition requirement would be based on the theoretical maximum engagement range that came out of an analysis of this data, which turned out to be around 400m.

The foundations for what would eventually become the Enfield Weapon System (EWS) were laid in the early 1970s. In 1970, the Director General Weapons (Army) asked Royal Small Arms Factory, Enfield to conduct a study, to be finished by the end of 1971, with the following objectives:[12]

- To define what sort of target a future weapon should be able to hit and what criteria should be set out that would constitute defeating said target;
- To assess a range of ammunition calibres, ranging from 4mm to 7.62mm with regard to an effective range of between 400 and 600m;
- To look at a variety of weapon configurations with regard to a requirement that it be lighter than the current standard weapon and easier to handle;
- To investigate the possibility of incorporating an area-effect capability (for example, a rifle grenade);
- To investigate what was happening world-wide, with regard to the design and procurement of small arms.

RSAF Enfield reported back in December 1971 with the following findings:[13]

- The size of the target was determined as being 450mm x 900 mm (approximately 18in x 35in) and the criteria as being an energy of 466j, that being necessary to defeat the best steel helmet then in use (West Germany);
- An optimum calibre of around 5mm for both an Individual Weapon (IW) and a Light Support Weapon (LSW);
- It was unlikely that unconventional systems (such as caseless ammunition or flechette projectiles) would be able to be developed adequately in the timeframe stipulated so a conventional cartridge was recommended;
- There were no definite conclusions as to how best to incorporate an area-effect capability, although a grenade launched from the weapon's muzzle was considered preferable;
- Most small arms manufacturers were utilising advances in materials and technology to improve weapon handling, reduce weight and even offer unconventional solutions.

RSAF Enfield then looked at the system configuration, and came to the conclusion that:[14]

- Both the IW and LSW should be of an unorthodox configuration with a straight butt, which would give a shorter overall weapon, save weight and improve handling;
- The weapons have a calibre of around 5mm;
- Both weapons being able to fire accurately out to about 600m;
- The commonality of components be as high as possible;
- Have a capability to fire on both semi-automatic and fully-automatic;
- Both weapons be gas operated;
- Both have a multi-lug breech-operating system;
- The two weapons should be fitted with an optical sight similar to the SUIT on the L1A1;
- If possible, the weapon would have a three-round burst limiter included;
- For both weapons to have a cyclic rate of between 300 and 1,000 rounds per minute;
- The prototype LSW use a combined open / closed bolt operation – this would improve reliability and lower the chances of a 'cook-off' after fully automatic fire but mean a more complicated mechanism and lower commonality of components.

The result of this preliminary work was General Staff Target (GST) 3815, published in 1972.[15] This document concentrated the project's future direction and laid down guidelines to be followed during the next two years of feasibility work. These guidelines were:[16]

- The weapons would be in 4.85mm calibre, keeping the LSW as light as possible at the expense of having the IW fire a round that was slightly more powerful than optimum;
- The weapons are as light as possible, in a bullpup configuration and be adaptable to either left or right-handed use by a unit's Armourer;
- The weapons would have an optical sight that was as good as or better than the SUIT;
- They would be capable of accepting a night sight;
- Further research into the possibility of having an area-effect capability would be undertaken;
- Definite designs would be produced.

Early Development

RSAF Enfield began their feasibility work by looking at the ammunition. They eventually produced a 4.85x49mm cartridge that gave better performance and lower recoil energy than the 5.56x45mm M193 round. RSAF Enfield produced twelve weapons (eight IWs and four LSWs) to test various concepts and design features (for example, one was chambered for 5.56mm and another had a 40mm under-slung grenade launcher fitted) which resulted in a Feasibility Study report being submitted in March 1974.[17] Its conclusions were:[18]

- The 4.85x49mm cartridge meets the requirements set;
- More work needs to be done on producing an area-effect capability;
- The SUSAT (Sight Unit Small Arms Trilux) performance was satisfactory and improved weapon accuracy;
- The LSW had a limited sustained fire capability due to the heat produced during automatic fire, which could also impact barrel wear, affecting accuracy – a way around this would be to have a 'quick-change' barrel facility, similar to the Bren gun but this would increase cost and weight, as well as reduce the commonality of parts between the IW and LSW. An increase in its rate of fire would require the weapon to be belt-fed and contravene the GST which required a common magazine feed;
- Firing single shot produced more hits per rounds fired than the other modes of operation so the burst limiter and rate of fire control were judged to be unnecessary. It is a shame that the three-round burst option was eventually dropped as it should prove a more accurate option than full automatic and potentially conserve ammunition, a useful factor during the heat of battle when re-supply might be problematical. As a counterpoint, the M16A1 when it was upgraded to the M16A2, had a three-round burst capability included;
- Any requirement for left-handed operation should be handled by Armourers at the unit level;
- An assessment regarding the need for night sights did not reach any conclusions.

From top to bottom: An L1A1 SLR, two Enfield Individual Weapons and an Enfield Light Support Weapon (Source: Author's collection)

Following this, the first REME Ease of Maintenance (E of M) assessments took place in May 1974 followed by the issue of the formal General Staff Requirement (GSR) 3518 that defined the characteristics of the weapons system that would enter service.[19] Following additional user trials and another REME E of M assessment, RSAF Enfield incorporated a number of design changes to the weapons including changes to the trigger mechanism, removing the three round burst capability and strengthening the body and trigger housing mechanisms. The official unveiling of the new system took place on 14 June 1976 a year before the NATO Ammunition Trials were to begin. By allowing the Press and Public to view these weapons, which were in fact hand-built prototypes, it confirmed the MoD's faith in these weapons and that the "weapon would enter service without a hiccup, and the US Army and the rest of NATO would switch to 4.85mm when they saw what a great round it was."[20] Unfortunately, this optimistic attitude was to be undone, as alluded to above, by the actions once again, of the lead player within NATO – the USA. Backtracking slightly, continuing trials in the USA suggested that the new AR-15 assault rifle developed by Eugene Stoner and chambered for 5.56x45mm (.223) ammunition was superior to the M-14, the rifle chosen to chamber the 7.62x51mm cartridge. The Ordnance Department recommended that development should be pursued with a view to replacing the 7.62mm rifle, which had only been formally adopted for service two years before.[21] With the US Air

Force ordering the rifle in 1960 to replace the M2 Carbine and adopting it in 1964, while the US Army finally followed suit in February 1967. The British .280 cartridge, which, it must be remembered, had been shelved for over a decade by that point, had proved to be far ahead of its time with the USA replacing the M14 with the M16A1 in most combat units by the end of the decade.[22] The M16A1 was designed to use the M193 cartridge but this has been the subject of considerable controversy over its reported lack of stopping power, reported by troops in Vietnam and since.[23]

The USA's use of the 5.56x45mm cartridge in the M16 and its gradual introduction into service by several other countries within the Alliance led to an unusual situation of the Alliance having one official round and one unofficial round – "standardisation was thrown out the window."[24] This situation led to NATO agreeing to hold another set of Standardisation Trials with a Memorandum of Understanding (MoU) being signed in 1976, and the trials scheduled to take place for approximately two years from April 1977 with a report expected in early 1980. Where these trials differed from the ones in the 1950s, was that "no common arm was expected to emerge."[25] These would be overseen by the NATO Small Arms Test Control Commission (NSMATCC), at Cold Meece in the UK, Hammelburg and Meppen in West Germany.[26] The decision to choose a cartridge to supplement, rather than replace, the 7.62x51mm cartridge meant that it was highly unlikely that a true intermediate general-purpose cartridge would be considered and only a cartridge substantially smaller than 7.62mm would prevail.[27] The majority of entries into the competition (with the exception of the British and the West Germans) were 5.56x45mm with various combinations of bullet heads and charge weights, meaning that it was hardly a surprise when the 5.56x45mm won out. Although the British 4.85x49mm round performed well, it was not sufficiently better than the 5.56x45mm cartridge to prevail, given that several members were already using the calibre, the most important of whom was the USA who was unlikely to consider anything different in any case. Once again politics, rather than technical performance, scuppered the British cartridge. The only sweetener for the Europeans was that NATO decided to use the Belgian SS109 round instead of the American M193, which proved to have better accuracy, long-range performance and penetration. This was designed to be fired from a barrel with a fast 1:7 twist as opposed to the M193 that was designed to be fired from a barrel with a slow 1:12 twist – "it was seen by some as payback time after the defeats in the trials of the 1950s, as the USA had to re-barrel their M16s to accommodate the new NATO round."[28]

The British XL64 and XL65 (as they had been designated) weapons had performed poorly during the test, with almost 700 incidents being logged by the REME Armourers (a number that was probably under the genuine total), mainly due to the weapon system still being in the early stages of development. This included such faults as a failure of spot welds on the body assembly, failure to extract the empty case from the chamber, failure to eject an empty case, double-feeding and failure of the trigger / sear mechanism – many of which were associated with the ingress of sand and dirt into the weapon. The results from the NATO Trials were accepted after which the shape of the weapon started to change dramatically. These new models incorporated many design changes intended to simplify production and reduce manufacturing costs, as well as incorporating the lessons learned at the NATO Trials to improve the function of the trigger mechanism, the ammunition feed and the bolt, rod and carrier assemblies. It was obvious that sorting out these problems and converting the weapon from 4.85x49mm to 5.56x45mm would take time and push back the In-Service Date (ISD), therefore increasing development costs. At the same time this was happening, the Conservative Government under Margaret Thatcher, intent on selling off almost anything that was government-owned, set up a study group in 1980 to look at how Royal Ordnance worked, including its facility at Enfield – this did not bode well for the long-term future of the RSAF.

Three Production Rifles were built, in order to test the new design features and alterations that had come about due to the NATO Trials, but results were disappointing. Further tests and modifications would be needed – the LSW suffered from the same problems as well as a low first-shot accuracy when fired on single shot and automatic. This led to a postponement of the user-trials until late 1981 while the Ordnance Board Trials began in February of that year. Trials by the Ordnance Board are intended to examine aspects such as the safety of weapons and ammunition under development as well as their suitability for service. The Ordnance Board initially used 'controlled condition' tests, simulating both general environments and extreme ones, to provide data on the weapon and the ammunition. In theory, these should have highlighted areas of weakness that would need to be addressed before the weapon and its ammunition went into full production and were meant to continue right through to the weapon's early service life. Unfortunately, they failed to uncover a whole host of problems that only came to light when the weapon had been subject to the rigours of actual usage.[29] One such example being a cold test, where weapons were soaked and then placed in a freezer. One weapon split its barrel (which led to new specifications for metal and stress relief being issued) but this test failed to account for real conditions in the arctic, where high winds can drive snow into various parts of the rifle, causing ice to clog up the weapon. There were four phases, those being Phase A (February 1981 – December 1982), Phase B (April 1983 – April 1984), Phase C (April 1985 – July 1987) and Phase D (April 1988 – December 1988 and environmental trials between 1988 and 1990).

These ran alongside the Infantry Trials and Development Unit (ITDU) trials between 1981 and 1984. The ITDU, based at Warminster, are supposed to assess weapons and their ammunition before they go into production, putting them through a series of tests that would represent a mixture of both training and tactical environments, to determine whether the weapon system had met the criteria as laid down in the User Requirements Document (URD). It is supposed to give an independent, accurate and reasoned assessment of any weapon system that has been sent to them for trial and give considered reasons for why any part of it should be modified or why it did not come up to scratch. The weapons they tested should have been very similar to the weapons that went forward to the Troop Trials and so the faults found there, should have been found during the User Trials by the ITDU. Criticisms have been raised and questions still need to be answered over the quality of the ITDU User Trials, the first being that according to one source, everything was done by the book – weapons were stripped, cleaned, fired and carried according to a strict adherence to rules and regulations, not necessarily how the actual user would do things.[30] Second, if the tests on the weapon represented the most severe environmental and handling conditions, how could they have missed so many of the problems that were shown up later? Third, did the soldiers, who had actually performed the tests, write the actual reports? Fourth, as many different people came and went from the project, perhaps it became more and more difficult for the Army to form a definitive opinion as to what its 'ideal' rifle would look like – soldiers are posted on a regular basis and therefore move onto different jobs. Fifth, how easy would it have been to raise objections, point out problems and cause dissent, especially given the impact on one's promotion prospects? "If the ITDU had undertaken what was asked of them and conducted serious trials when necessary . . . perhaps future problems would have been reduced."[31] This was on the back of the statement by the then Defence Secretary, John Nott, in May 1982, that Royal Ordnance would be sold off to the Private Sector, floatation being scheduled for 1986. Following this was the RSAF Final Comparison Report produced in 1983, where the 'new build standard' of weapon was put forward as the definitive design for mass production and compared to the GSR 3518, this comparison surprisingly being done by RSAF Enfield, rather than the MoD. Given that the order book at RSAF Enfield needed to be full in order for the Government to be able to sell it off at a good price to the Private Sector, is it any wonder that they found that they had met the majority of the requirements set out in the GSR, with barely a footnote to say that any areas of concern would be sorted out in the near future? Next, the ITDU completed their Trial No. 35/83 titled 'The Final Evaluation of Small Arms for the 80s to meet GSR 3518 (1983)' where they concluded that during "all activities the IW proved itself to be a robust, reliable weapon that suffered from few stoppages."[32]

Acceptance into Service

On 17 January 1984, a Provisional Acceptance Meeting was held in Room 254 of the Old War Office Building, Whitehall, under the chairmanship of Brigadier C W Beckett to examine the suitability of the SA80 weapon system for service with the UK Armed Forces. A member of the ITDU gave a short introduction to the weapon system and explained the components of and differences between, the IW and the LSW, an unusual occurrence as one would have thought that the people there would have been those with a high degree of knowledge of the project, given it was a meeting to accept the items in question into service. This meeting followed on from a pre-acceptance meeting held on 5 January. The meeting recognised that a large number of modifications had been incorporated into the latest model (but not necessarily all the modifications that might be needed) as a result of the Ordnance Board and ITDU Trials and that as far as they were concerned, the IW and LSW were safe and suitable for service, with some provisos. One of those being the work still needed to be done on the LSW, which was still not acceptable for service due to its inability to group shots to an acceptable standard and continued reliability issues (especially in terms of the failure of the breech to close properly). Another was that further modifications were in the pipeline and that no-one had tested or approved the methods that were going be used once the weapons moved over to full-production. In effect, they were accepting a weapon for limited production whose design characteristics were still subject to change with future modifications being untested and untried, which had never been produced in large quantities or using mass production methods. "Given the number of problems already encountered on basically hand-built weapons, it would seem a profound leap of faith to think that "gearing up" for full production would be "relatively trouble-free"."[33] In addition, the Radway Green magazine was still under development, forcing the IW to continue using the M16 magazine.

As well as accepting the IW for limited production, another acceptance meeting was scheduled for September, focusing on the LSW, to give RSAF time to investigate the continued accuracy and reliability problems with the hope that these could be sorted out to a satisfactory degree. In the meantime, an accuracy meeting was held on 9 April 1984 under the chairmanship of Colonel J C Langlands in order to 'clarify' aspects of the operational requirements for the LSW. As it stood, the LSW was supposed to deliver effective suppressive fire out to a range of 600m but no-one had defined 'effective' suppressive fire. The problem the LSW had was that it was accurate enough when firing single shots, but produced two distinct groups when firing fully automatic bursts (the first round would hit in one place, the subsequent shots hitting in another). It was therefore decided to amend the accuracy statement in the GSR so that it was vague enough to encompass what was hoped the LSW would be able to achieve after eight months of further work. This included having a trained soldier, at 100m: being able to put a five-round group on a target within a diameter of 100mm; being able to produce an average burst size of 300mm in diameter with five, two-to-five-round bursts while firing at five different aiming marks; being able to produce a 400mm diameter group while firing twenty rounds in bursts of between two and five rounds fired at a single aiming mark. In addition, the Mean Point of Impact (MPI) for both the single shot and automatic fire groups should not deviate significantly (however that might be defined, which it wasn't) and be capable of producing comparative grouping qualities at 600m.[34]

A Steyr AUG (StG 77) assault rifle (Source: MoserB via Wikimedia Commons)

The ITDU then undertook comparative trials, between the LSW, the FN Minimi, the HK13 and Steyr AUG, alongside the Bren LMG and GPMG.[35] The trials staff seemingly preferred the Steyr for its ease of stripping, ease of handling, user control of the weapon, low recoil, lack of cook-off and overheating problems, light weight, reliability and accuracy when shooting on automatic, although it did not quite meet the GSR criteria for single shot accuracy. It was this, and the fact that it used a different magazine to the one on the IW that meant it was not acceptable to the Ordnance Board (in addition, what impact would it have had on Royal Ordnance's impending sell off?). It was agreed at the Acceptance Meeting on 13 September 1984, that given the improvement in accuracy due to additional modifications of the weapon in the intervening months (a different design of bipod, a strut incorporated under the barrel supporting the bipod, an additional pistol grip under the butt and a fold-over shoulder support brace) and the improvement in reliability expected by replacing the firing pin and extractor as well as the SUSAT sight azimuth screws, the weapon was accepted for limited production.[36]

Early Problems

RSAF Enfield was awarded the contract to produce the first 175,000 weapons in June 1985 with the first weapons being handed over to the 1st Battalion, Worcestershire and Sherwood Foresters in a public ceremony on 2 October 1985.[37] The ceremony was dampened slightly by firstly one of the LSWs having black electrical tape around the bipod (to stop the legs springing open and accidently injuring the holder)[38] and secondly Lord Trefgarne revealed that the weapon system had cost £500 million over the last fourteen years to develop. However, the general optimism and praise for the weapon system is evident in early publications, although a number of problems were quickly highlighted, by interested parties examining the new IW and LSW:[39]

- The cocking handle was on the right-hand side, along with its ejection to the right means that the weapon has to be fired from right shoulder, problematical for left-handed shooters, as well as causing problems while firing from left of cover.
- Weight – an SA80, fully loaded with SUSAT is just 80g lighter than the L1A1.
- Balance problems – the bullpup design along with the position of the SUSAT sight, the use of stamped sheet steel for the main body and nylon for the pistol grip and fore-grip, makes the weapon butt-heavy, a factor that exacerbates the high recoil when firing on automatic.
- High-sighting plane – the firer has to expose more of him or herself to fire over cover.
- Hard trigger pull – has an impact on accuracy.
- The position of selector switch and magazine release catch on the left-side of the weapon but away from the pistol grip means the firer could lose target acquisition if he needs to change magazine or the rate of fire. Also, the magazine release catch could be accidentally pressed when carried against the chest.
- The sling cannot be used as an aid to shooting.
- The shoulder-butt strap was configured to sit too high when the LSW was in the shoulder and served no useful purpose.
- The lack of a changeable barrel and belt-feed option on the LSW might limit its sustained fire capability.

Additional early problems included[40]:

- The discovery that the weapon could fire if dropped muzzle first onto a hard surface with the safety off from more than three metres.
- The rate of fire was between 50 and 100 rounds per minute less than expected.
- The LSW occasionally ejected a case into the firer's face and magazines were difficult to fit when the bolt was closed.41
- Concern that use of the SUSAT would lead to the infantryman loosing track of the 'bigger picture' and ignoring dangers on the edge of their peripheral vision.[42]

Also, projected costs had risen from the 1978 figure of £320 to the 1983/4 figure of £523 or £799 if the SUSAT and its bracket are added.[43]

Testing of the weapon system continued with both Ordnance Board and Troop Trials into the early 1990s. Both sets of tests, which included an interim report made in July 1986 and a final report in January 1987, indicated that while the weapons remained very accurate (and therefore excelled on the range) problems remained despite attempted 'quick-fix' solutions, primarily centred on the reliability of the weapons especially during environmental trials and the build quality of individual components. Anonymous letters being sent to the press and MPs showed that unease and disillusionment were spreading through the Armed Forces especially in the light of the fact that, after fifteen years of development, things were still not sorted out. The Ordnance Board trials still showed a poor Mean Time Before Failure (MTBF) rate, even though the figures were generally massaged to include only critical failures rather than critical, serious and minor failures – "**NB** In the original trials any number of stoppages that could be cleared by the firer were not counted as failures. In the trials of the modified weapon more than one stoppage, including those that can be cleared by the firer, counts as a failure."[44] Inclusion of the latter two categories meant that IW would fire on average two magazines before an incident occurred, while the LSW fired only one. The Troop Trials, some of which were in Norway, some of which were in the jungle, found these faults:[45]

- Bayonet – tip breaks, fails to stay on, the retaining clips on the frog fracture, wire cutter distorts if used to actually cut wire, sharpening stone falls off.
- Blank Firing Attachment (BFA) – carbon build-up after firing causes problems in removal, leading to the screw being damaged when this is tried;
- Bipod – does not stay in when in the up position, the retaining screw sometimes falls out;

- Body Locking Pins – either seize up or fall out;
- Bolt – erosion from gases around the firing pin hole, fails to close or function properly if dirt, dust or sand get into the locking lugs;
- Butt – pulls out the retaining screws if pressure is applied via the sling to the rear sling loop;
- Butt Strap – stop lugs break, making the item unusable.
- Cleaning Kit – oil bottle leaks or cap splits, pull-through snaps or cannot be pulled through barrel, combination tool breaks or falls apart, brushes break or unwind or just inadequate to do the job, the rod 'T' piece fails to lock.
- Common Weapon Sight (CWS – a modern night sight) – difficult to attain the proper eye relief when wearing a helmet.
- Ejection Opening Cover (EOC) – breaks or freezes shut in arctic conditions.
- Ejector – fails to work, works erratically, still occasionally ejects case into firer's face, and in arctic conditions it freezes and fails to work.
- Extractor – sharp edges can cut brass from the case with the debris causing it to jam.
- Firing Pin – springs can lose strength and allow weak strikes, the tip fractures after long bursts on automatic.
- Functioning – ammunition fails to feed properly, rounds fail to eject, insufficient gas to cycle the weapon (especially in arctic conditions when locking lugs are fouled up), weapon fails to function unless spotlessly clean and well-oiled.
- Gas Plug – carbon deposits make removal difficult and doing so sometimes causes damage preventing re-assembly and gas-system operation.
- Guide Rod Assembly – spring weak, guide rods can distort or become loose.
- Hand Guards – brittle (especially in arctic conditions) with no means of repair once cracked due to heat shield inserts.
- Hold Open Device – fails to function and the button breaks off.
- Iron Sights – fracture if struck at the right angle, while the retaining screw breaks.
- Magazine Catch – fails to lock magazine when a full magazine is loaded, sometimes releases the magazine when the weapon is carried across the chest, in arctic conditions the magazine can freeze in place.
- Muzzle Cover – no way of keeping it secured on the weapon, use in arctic conditions causes it to freeze to the flash eliminator and shrapnel effects if fired through.
- Rear Sling Loop – distorts or pulls off the butt if any pressure is applied.

- Sight Rail – inconsistent welding leads to failure, rusting occurs under the rail itself.
- SUSAT – loss of adjusting screw lock nuts, loose sight clamp, range drum prone to jamming, eye lens prone to misting up and the rubber cap and front hood fill with snow in arctic conditions).
- Top Cover – catch fails leading to the cover opening.
- Trigger Mechanism – trigger fails to reassert when weapon set on 'R', the hammer stops distort and break, interceptor sear jams on hammer stud, safety sear does not always engage on the hammer fully or occasionally at all.
- Sight Cover – too rigid with no method of retention.
- Sling – plastic parts break.

In addition, the body extension was too weak to fully take the stress of the LSW's weight away from the barrel leading to it becoming bent, periods of automatic fire would lead to overheating and a residue build-up that would impede the full forward movement of the gas assembly and bolt carrier.[46] And none of this was apparent to those who carried out the User and Troop Trials earlier in the decade? Royal Ordnance was eventually sold off to British Aerospace on 2 April 1987 for £190 million with the contract for the second tranche of weapons still to be signed, being held back as a 'sweetener' for whoever bought Royal Ordnance:

"The new revelations will increase suspicions that the system was ordered simply as a device to make Royal Ordnance an attractive proposition for privatisation. The cost of the development and production of the gun is understood to exceed £300 million."[47]

"One expert has suggested that the gun was chosen to help give Royal Ordnance a full order book ready for privatisation."[48]

After the sale, British Aerospace discovered that the viability of producing the second tranche was in question, unless production costs could be brought down or the price increased due to the delays in delivery of the first tranche. Given that the price they had contracted for was fixed, and found to be £100 less than the weapon's true cost, it was decided to move production to a new facility at Nottingham, at a cost of £15 million, the excuse being that the site at Enfield was outdated, too large and the buildings the wrong position, shape and size for diversification or improved production. The fact that the

RSAF was located on a site that was highly desirable to redevelopers for commercial and residential property was not, apparently, part of the equation. Neither was explaining why the new facility could not be built on a site the size of RSAF Enfield or the money spent on upgrading the facilities already there. Finally, and despite all the problems listed above, whether due to political pressure or a misguided belief that these faults would be fixed soon, the Full Acceptance Meeting was held in October 1987, the recommendation being that the weapon was suitable to be accepted for full service, "in the face of clear, tabulated evidence to the contrary".[49]

Operation Granby, LANDSET and the HCDC

A British Infantryman (1st Battalion, The Staffordshire Regiment) during training exercises as part of Operation, Desert Shield (Source: PFC John F. Freund, US Army via Wikimedia Commons)

The SA80 would see serious combat for the first time, not on the North German Plain facing a Warsaw Pact invasion of West Germany, but in the deserts of the Middle East where approximately 43,000 British troops were deployed between 1990-1991 during Operation GRANBY. This operation was conducted firstly, to protect Saudi Arabia and then secondly, to liberate Kuwait from Iraqi occupation, fulfilling UN Resolution 678. The experience they had with the weapons blew the contention that the majority of problems associated with the IW and LSW were due to arctic conditions out of the water. Moreover, problems were being encountered in all climatic conditions and only exacerbated in arctic or desert environments, for example, even

"after the most careful preparation, of those whom I observed, not one managed to complete the CQB [Close Quarter Battle] course without at least one stoppage and some had repeated stoppages. Some 50% of these appeared to be magazine related and a further 30% may have been caused by the ingress of dirt. What happens in the Gulf, happens in Wales, too; and there is not too much sand flying about in Sennebridge. None, in point of fact."[50]

Indeed, the problems encountered with the use of these weapons in desert or sandy conditions, far from being new ones, had been apparent at the beginning of 1987, with a internal Army document outlining a 'sand ingress problem'[51], as well as the various User and Troop Trials from 1981 onwards.

"It came as no surprise to me that the soldiers in the Gulf should have had these problems, since it was reported to me, by a person involved in the recording of the 1985 trials, that the SA80 had been submitted to the standard sand test *three times* and each time it failed, miserably. To that person's knowledge, it was never re-submitted after the last failure and, quite clearly, no work had been done since to solve that particular and most significant shortcoming."[52]

A report, entitled 'Equipment Performance (SA80) During Operation Granby (the Gulf War)', undertaken by the Land Systems Evaluation Team (LANDSET) after the conflict had finished, was scathing in its criticism of the weapon system. To quote:

"SA80 did not perform reliably in the sandy conditions of combat and training. Stoppages were frequent despite the considerable and diligent efforts to prevent them . . . It is extremely difficult to isolate the prime cause of the stoppages. It is, however, quite clear that infantrymen did not have CONFIDENCE in their personal weapon. Most expected a stoppage in the first magazine fired. Some platoon commanders considered that casualties would have occurred due to weapon stoppages if the enemy had put up any resistance in the trench and bunker clearing operations. Even discounting the familiarisation period of desert conditions, when some may have still been using the incorrect lubrication drill, stoppages continued to occur."[53]

A copy of the report was leaked to the press in August 1992, causing a furore. The MoD initially denied any knowledge of it (via *The Daily Telegraph* who was then sent a copy by a reader), then dismissed it as a 'fake', then claimed it was 'unofficial' and then grudgingly 'semi-official'. But it refused to go away, especially as it was clearly an official report listed under 'User Trials (Infantry Trial and Development Unit No. 20/91, 10 – 20 March 1991)'.[54] Many of the major papers and shooting magazines carried articles about the SA80 and the issues highlighted in the LANDSET report, with many quoting directly from the report itself.[55] This included units procuring as many SLRs, Bren guns and GPMGs as they could. Why? "The fact is that the older generation of weapons: Bren, GPMG, SLR and Sterling, were designed for reliability and for functioning in adverse conditions."[56] It was also found that the problems with both the IW and LSW effectively turned British tactical doctrine on its head, with the LSW being fired using rapid single shots as full automatic fire caused overheating and affected accuracy with a split group risking friendly fire incidents, while the SA80 was often used on full automatic as the troops felt there was a reduced tendency to jam.[57] Pressure quickly built on the Government from MPs around the House of Commons, including the Liberal Democrat defence spokesman Menzies Campbell, who wrote to Sir Nicholas Bonsar, Chairman of the Commons Defence Select Committee for a Parliamentary enquiry to be held. Thus, the first real independent investigation into the SA80 saga surrounded the issues arising from the Gulf War and was taken up by the House of Commons Defence Committee who investigated the matter in early 1993.[58]

The Committee looked at several areas concerning the SA80 including its characteristics, accuracy, problems associated with firing from the left shoulder, performance with regard to other weapons, sales, the view of the user, faults, their causes and modifications to overcome them, the in-service date, reasons why faults were not corrected before acceptance and volume production, the length of time taken to introduce modifications, its reliability in sandy conditions and therefore its performance during Operation Granby, and the trials conducted. The evidence collected included a large amount of written evidence from the MoD and an interview (conducted on 22 April 1993) with several witnesses involved with the procurement of Army equipment, including Major General Anthony C P Stone (Director General, Land Fighting Systems), Colonel Donald R Wilson (Land Systems Operational Requirements), Colonel Martin E Romilly OBE (Project Manager, Infantry Weapons) and Lt Colonel Keith M Cook (Ordnance Board of the MoD). Of course, conspicuous by their absence was anyone actually involved in using the weapon on operations, particularly in the Gulf, or Government ministers, firing range staff or unit armourers. While the Committee were to some extent, dazzled by their trip to Warminster to fire the weapon under ideal conditions and out-manoeuvred by the MoD which was "achieved by giving the impression of full-cooperation and by bowing their heads to criticism that would be forgotten within months, if not weeks"[59], they still managed to level these criticisms at the MoD for their handling of the £384 million project[60]:

- Thirty-two faults were corrected at a cost of £24 million AFTER the first weapons had entered service;
- The ISD slipped (due to various factors) from 1983 to 1986 and the Committee expected "the Ministry to be able to show real and quantifiable improvements in procurement performance as a result of the present risk management initiative";
- That the weapon was accepted into service at a premature stage in its development and that the faults that became evident soon after it entered service should have been detected and corrected during the Ordnance Board, Main User and Troop Trials. The Committee summarised that the "lesson the Ministry have learned is that the general usage of the weapon should be tested in the hands of soldiers during the design and development phase. We have to express some surprise that it has taken over three hundred years of personal weapon usage by the British Army to discover this fact";
- The Committee was "astonished that the Ministry should accept into service, and pay for, equipment such as the cleaning kit that appears to us to verge on the shoddy. We do not believe that a commercial organisation would have been prepared to accept and pay for goods which subsequently turned out to need so many modifications";
- The length of time required to fix faults had been far too long (up to four years in some cases) and urged the MoD to examine "its arrangements for making modifications to in-service equipment to determine where time savings can be made";
- The weapon that was accepted into service could only be fired from the right shoulder, causing problems to left-handed shooters, especially those with strong left-eyes and causing problems in urban patrolling situations, such as firing around the left of cover;
- That better export sales have not been achieved;
- The Committee accepted the MoD line that the LANDSET report represented a grassroots view of the performance of the weapon but should not be considered as the full picture and that the modifications that had been introduced and were being retrofitted solved many of the problems alongside the use of the correct cleaning regime. Nevertheless, they were concerned that it was only on the eve

of a major conflict that the correct cleaning regime for sandy conditions began to be disseminated and that this "delay could have had disastrous consequences and we look to the Ministry to ensure that it does not happen again". The fact that the incorrect cleaning drills were still being used by some troops was a cause for concern and that "the Ministry investigate why this was so and what lessons can be learned."

- That overall, the "SA80 is a highly accurate weapon which is now sound when properly maintained. Its accuracy puts it into a different generation of weapon from earlier rifles. It needs to be treated with respect for its higher technology. However, it was delivered late and had many defects that, in our view, should have been detected and put right before it entered service. We trust that the MoD have learned from this costly story and we will be seeking evidence of this when examining future procurement cycles."

One thing the HCDC didn't pick up on was the inconsistencies in the results of the accuracy trials between the SA80 and L1A1. The L1A1 was fired over open sights while the SA80 was fired using the SUSAT optical sight, which has a set four-power magnification. Naturally, the better results were used to highlight the improvement in accuracy that the new system would give the troops but the bias in the trials was never picked up. Surely a more 'level-playing field' and truer indication of the difference in accuracy would have been to hold trials that compared the L1A1 firing both over its iron sights and using the SUIT optical sight with the SA80 firing both over the optional iron sights and using the SUSAT optical sight. While there is little chance that this would have altered the outcome, it would have given a more accurate picture as to the rifles' relative accuracy but also proved that the L1A1, fitted with the SUIT optical sight, was a more accurate rifle than it was ultimately given credit for.[61]

Continuing Problems

By the second-half of the 1990s, with all the 'quick-fix' remedies applied to the SA80, it finally seemed as if things were beginning to improve – "this is the first chance I've had to shoot one extensively. One criticism of the rifle has been the lack of reliability, but my shooting companion and I put over a thousand rounds through our test rifle with only two malfunctions, neither attributable to the rifle."[62] However, events continued to point towards issues that still remained unresolved and user confidence in the weapon remained low – "unlike the case of the M16, complaints about the qualities about the SA80 have continued to simmer underneath the surface."[63] As a result, the IW and LSW were suspended from the NATO Nominated Weapons List, a list of those weapons used within the Alliance for testing ammunition that is seeking NATO qualification, in early 1997[64] - a move that was embarrassing for the MoD and Government Ministers.

But by then, even the MoD had been driven to the point of despair, with the Defence Procurement Agency (DPA) ordering a full appraisal of the weapon, in work that was carried out by Heckler & Koch GmbH (then a subsidiary of British Aerospace) between 1995 and 1997.[65] The team from Heckler & Koch, led by Ernst Mauch, reported in 1998 with a list of modifications that they felt would improve the weapons' performance.[66] At the same time, if confirmation were ever needed as to the astonishingly uncritical evaluation undertaken by the ITDU on the SA80 weapon system (and in particular the LSW) during the User Trials, the Commandant of the ITDU ordered an investigation to be carried out in 1998 into exactly this point. The report, entitled 'LSW Trials Investigation 1981 – 1996', was to assess the outcomes of the trials, not to prove how critical or uncritical they had been of the weapon but to highlight any areas that might leave the organisation open to criticism should any awkward questions be raised in the future. No particular priority was given to this, as only a single Warrant Officer was asked to carry out the investigation, but he approached his work diligently and with an open mind. The report, dated 8 July 1998, concluded that:[67]

- The reports stated facts that were not even mentioned in the recommendations;
- The guidelines set out in the GSR and GST pointed the ITDU in a particular direction as regards the suitability of the LSW but which were ultimately irrelevant as the MoD were going to accept the LSW whatever happened;
- Personnel reading the reports may not have interpreted them correctly;
- Not enough trials were done on the LSW;
- It was not until faults really became obvious that they started to trial the weapons properly;
- Decisions taken during the early part of the LSW's development were politically orientated and that someone further up the chain of command wanted the LSW accepted, whatever its performance, for some unspecified reason.

The MoD Look to Heckler & Koch

Meanwhile, following their recommendations, Heckler & Koch were awarded a contract in mid-1998 to modify 200 L85A1 and L86A1 weapons to the new 'A2' standard so that comprehensive climatic trials could be undertaken. This batch of weapons was delivered in January 1999, with the MoD conducting trials at: the US Army's Cold Regions Test

Centre in Fort Greely, Alaska (cold / dry); Small Arms School, Warminster, Wiltshire, UK (temperate); Seria, Brunei (hot / wet); and Kazma, Kuwait (hot / dry) with a range of different NATO ammunition types. The majority of these trials were completed in July 1999 and the final report delivered to the Minister of State for Defence, Geoff Hoon, in December. The report concluded that Heckler & Koch had indeed solved the problems encountered during the previous twenty years by intensive and in-depth testing of both materials and their designs.[68] As a result, the Government decided to award Heckler & Koch the contract to modify around 200,000 SA80 rifles to the new 'A2' standard.[69] This however was only part of the story, as the MoD, in its review, had also looked at more drastic options:

> "Industry experts also confirm that the UK MoD had considered replacing its entire armoury of 300,000 5.56 mm SA80 rifles with Colt M16 systems, prior to Heckler & Koch's (H&K) GBP92 million (USD179 million) revamp of the weapon in 2000."[70]

> "After various attempts at denial, and years of applying minor fixes that eased some problems but failed to solve the big ones, the Ministry of Defence bowed to the inevitable in 1997. They considered buying the M16 and M4 "off the shelf", but in the end commissioned HK to undertake a thorough revamp of the SA80 (HK was by this time owned by Royal Ordnance, so was in effect a British company - it has since been returned to German control)."[71]

M16 variants (Source: Offspring 18 87 via Wikimedia Commons)

The planned upgrades were given urgency when it was revealed that the troops had continued to have problems with the weapons system during the operations in Kosovo (Operations Allied Force and Joint Guardian)[72] and Sierra Leone (Operation Palliser)[73]. This extra work however, would mainly be undertaken by Heckler & Koch at their factory in Oberndorf, near Stuttgart with a small amount being undertaken by the small contingent located on the RO Nottingham site. The closure of RSAF Enfield and the movement of production to Nottingham had been greeted locally as an indication of long-term job security but restructuring within BAe would see the manufacture of large ordnance move to Barrow-in-Furness and with the contract to refurbish the SA80 going to Heckler & Koch, the site finally closed in late 2001 due to a lack of orders and sold for redevelopment, another pool of skills and experience being dissipated forever.[74] "The politicians had finally won, and the British Armed Forces of the future would perforce need to buy a foreign weapon system manufactured by foreign workers, but paid for by British taxpayers."[75]

The new 'A2' version was officially unveiled by the Rt. Hon Adam Ingram, Minister of State for the Armed Forces, on 18 October 2001, the coincidence being that it was sixteen years, almost to the day, from when the SA80 was first handed over and about the same time as the RO Nottingham site was being closed. While a lot of rhetoric was being banded about, especially in terms of the weapon being "probably the most reliable rifle in the world"[76], nothing was said about "the fact that Britain lay bereft of any domestic small arms manufacturing capability whatsoever."[77] On top of that, the cost of the programme had risen, from £80m to modify 300,000 weapons, to £92m to modify 200,000 weapons, with the remaining 100,000 being cannibalised and used for spares or being made available for export sale.[78] The SA80 weapon system was finally admitted back onto the NATO Nominated Weapons List after the 'A2' variants began to be issued, in March 2002, with the Parliamentary Under-Secretary of State for Defence, Dr Lewis Mooney, confirming that the MoD would not seek to obtain the re-admission of the A1 variant as that was the weapon being replaced.[79] The changes to the weapon include:[80]

- A new cocking handle, made of shaped nylon polyamide, which doubles as a cartridge case deflector;
- A new magazine, which is slightly longer, more curved and comes with a smoother spring feed action;
- The LSW has a heavier barrel;
- A new gas plug and cylinder made from superior materials;

- The catch spring has been widened to prevent jamming in the gas feed during re-assembly;
- The gas blowback cycle has been improved;
- One-and-a-half locking nuts removed from the barrel extension / chamber to accommodate a different extractor shape, which should also guide empty cases away from the ejection port;
- An all-new bolt head that has a larger, more robust extractor;
- The cartridge ejector has a new rim and a stronger multi-wire spring;
- The carrier has been polished to reduce the friction between it and the top-most cartridge in the magazine;
- A new sturdier firing pin has been installed, made from high-strength, quenched and tempered steel, with the stop moved from the rear to the front;
- The ejection port has been enlarged to improve the round ejection pattern;
- The magazine housing has been reinforced with additional welding to prevent it breaking;
- The weight of the hammer has been increased by 9g to prevent misfires caused by 'bouncing';
- The bolt release catch has been strengthened;
- A new recoil spring with a higher compression has been installed to even out the rate of fire.

FN Herstal Minimi – para version (Source: Davric via Wikimedia Commons)

Problems in Afghanistan?

With Heckler & Koch converting some 3,000 weapons per month, the new A2 variant was due to be supplied to the 3rd Commando Brigade in March 2002. However, the UK's commitment to operations in Afghanistan (Operation Herrick) accelerated that process and the SA80A2 was first fired in anger by troops from the 2nd Battalion, The Parachute Regiment (2 Para) during fighting around Kabul in February.[81] The fighting in Afghanistan, where British forces have been involved in operations against the Taliban as part of the International Security Assistance Force (ISAF)[82], as well as the invasion of Iraq (Operation Telic) in 2003 and the subsequent conflict there, have all proven major testing grounds for the new weapons. At the same time as the 'A2' variants were being issued, the MoD also purchased 149 FN Herstal Minimi LMGs for use by the troops in Afghanistan, a number that would quickly rise to over 300, which were bought under an Urgent Operational Requirement (UOR) and designated either the MG L108A1 (the standard version) or the MG L110A1 (the para version). This presents an interesting turnaround, as the standard FN Minimi was trialled and rejected in 1984 as it did not meet the GSR accuracy requirement but it seems that "the GSR was conveniently ignored rather than put lives at risk."[83]

While 2 Para did not have any major issues with the weapons, at least three major stoppages were reported by the Marines of 45 Commando during operations in June and July. This sent the alarm bells ringing all the way back to the MoD and the Defence Secretary, Geoff Hoon, ordered an immediate investigation with a team from the ITDU, DLO and Heckler & Koch under the command of Colonel Fraser Haddow, going out to Afghanistan to investigate the failures.[84] The team interviewed the members of the patrol who had experienced the problems, inspected the weapons and the Marines then prepared their weapons for firing and conducted an exercise on the firing range. Of the twelve weapons used, only two performed to standard. The team looked at this outcome and concluded that[85]:

- The Marines could not clean their rifles properly due to worn out, missing or incorrect brushes (not neglect);
- They were not oiling the weapons according to instructions in the cleaning pamphlet;
- Magazines became damaged easily;
- Safety catches were difficult to operate;
- Muzzle covers expanded in the heat and fell off, exposing the bore to dust and sand.

The Marines were then instructed in cleaning their weapons using the correct procedures and in a re-run of the test, this time using twenty-four Marines, only one rifle failed.

The team concluded that the problems had been caused by not using the proper cleaning regime. To prove the point, they set up a trial using two Chinook helicopters, with a group of twenty-four and another group of twelve Marines (the control group) who disembarked seven times, in conditions approximating what would be found on operations, followed by firing their weapons on the range. The group of twenty-four Marines who had followed the new regime had a reliability rate of 87 percent while the control group had a reliability average of only 17 percent. It seemed that the team had proved their point and that the problems were the fault of the User. What the report also mentioned were recommendations that a replacement muzzle cover was required, a weapon cover was needed to prevent dirt and dust getting into the mechanism, the safety catch should be made of stronger material and the instruction leaflet needed to be clearer.[86] With the blame being placed squarely on their shoulders, the Royal Marines reacted angrily, arguing that the weapon was inherently difficult to clean under operational conditions, the quality of the cleaning and maintenance kit was poor and the instructions, running to thirty pages, was difficult to follow. The CO of 45 Commando, Lt Col Tim Chicken, defended his troops against the accusations.[87] A stand-up row even occurred back in the MoD between the Army and the Royal Marines[88] with senior Army officers suggesting that the Royal Marines had caused the problems deliberately as they viewed themselves on a par with the Special Forces and wanted to be issued with the Heckler & Koch G36 assault rifle.[89] However, in an unusual show of solidarity, the Parachute Regiment agreed with the Royal Marines, with a former officer in the Parachute Regiment dismissing the claims that the Marines were to blame and calling the weapon an "unmitigated disaster" and that the "first time I had concerns was when the magazine fell out onto my boots on exercise."[90] Royal Marine officers branded the report a "whitewash"[91] and stated that if "you're jumping out of a Chinook into that kind of heat and dust, it wouldn't matter how clean the rifle was beforehand. The minute you got off, it would be covered in shit."[92]

G36 assault rifle (Source: Domok via Wikimedia Commons)

Arguments continued through 2002 with the MoD seeming to waver between first, replacing the rifle altogether[93] and then deciding to keep the weapon and start a confidence building exercise[94]. The trials were however, exposed as being conducted under controlled conditions, with hessian matting being laid on the firing points at the ranges being used during the trails, ammunition being drawn from factory-sealed boxes, the use of brand new magazines and SA80A2 weapons being transported to the trials in sealed bags.[95] Despite this, the MoD maintained that the weapon would be in service until at least 2015 and has in fact seen service in Afghanistan until the present day as well as Iraq during the invasion of 2003 and the conflict that followed, until British forces were withdrawn in 2009. Although criticism of the IW seemed to die down as time went on, the same cannot be said for the LSW. With continued complaints coming from deployed units over its lack of firepower in the suppressive role, something highlighted when it was first introduced and related to the use of a 30-round magazine and non-changeable barrel, an alternative had to be found, and quickly. In another 'quick fix' move, the DPA then began trials at the US Army's Yuma Proving Ground in Arizona, of four weapons, which included the Minimi, the Heckler & Koch MG43, the Israeli Military Industries Negev and the South African Vektor Mini SS. The DPA then selected the Minimi and MG43 for further testing in cold and hot-wet environment trials.[96] Both FN Herstal and Heckler & Koch were then asked to submit tenders by the middle of February 2003 to supply 2,472 LMGs, with an initial batch of 200 being delivered by the end of the year and the remainder being delivered within three years.[97]

The MoD subsequently selected the Minimi[98] but questions must be asked as to the objectivity of the selection decision. How could both the Viktor and Negev have failed the initial tests when their country's armed forces operate in arid, dusty conditions and surely would have been tested in such environments? With no small arms manufacturing capability left in the UK, both the Negev and the Viktor would have to be made under license and imported, the problem being that the main contenders for such a contract would have been FN and Heckler & Koch who were fielding their own weapons. The clear favourite was probably the MG43 as Heckler & Koch were the company that had just been awarded the contract to revamp the IW and LSW but given that the British Army were already using the Minimi in substantial numbers, the decision had effectively been made.[99] The MoD extended its purchase of the FN Minimi LMG to 4,000 units, as well as additional firepower upgrades including 9,000 night sights and 2,000 under-slung grenade launchers at a cost of around £30m, with another £35m of additional funding available if necessary. By the end of 2005, every infantry battalion was re-equipped, giving an eight-man section, four-times the capability of its World War II equivalent. Each section is split into two four-man fire teams, each with 1 x SA80A2, 1 x SA80A2 with grenade launcher, 1 x SA80A2 LSW and 1 x FN Minimi.[100]

In Retrospect . . .

While the procurement of this weapon system can be criticised on many levels and for many reasons, the main ones are:

- Firstly, the SA80 was built around the major components of the Armalite AR-18 system, which the designers at RSAF Enfield used virtually unchanged, with the initial prototypes being put together through the purchase of several AR-18s by the MoD for use in trials. This was followed by a visit from Stan Carroll, then the Director of Small Arms at RSAF Enfield, to see what manufacturing processes Sterling were using to produce the AR-18 (built under license), being shown around the factory by David Howroyd, the General Manager, as Sterling were interested in obtaining any work that might be sub-contracted out. None however would be forthcoming, as RSAF Enfield obtained a similar capability through the acquisition of similar machines from the same manufacturer (probably the real reason for the visit).[101] Indeed, the use of the AR-18 mechanism was confirmed by James Edmiston, the former owner and managing director of the Sterling Armament Co. Ltd at Dagenham and until the late 1980s, a successful British private arms company:

"In 1976 Edmiston and his designer, Frank Waters, saw the prototype SA80 at the British Army Equipment Exhibition in Aldershot. It was a bullpup design, a squat rifle with a minimal butt, and its operation looked curiously familiar.
'Frank was allowed to take it apart,' Edmiston told *The Observer*. 'He found our bolt carrier, our magazine, and parts out of our gun. These weren't even copies. They had bought some of our guns and were using the parts to make the SA80 prototype.'
A former weapons designer with Royal Ordnance confirmed that claim. He added that the original prototypes, basically an amalgam of the Armalite AR18 and the bullpup design of the old RO EM2 were good, promising guns . . . 'but the design was fiddled with by committees in the MoD and Royal Ordnance.' The gun, he says, has never been the same since."[102]

"Not once did Enfield ever ask Sterling for information on the AR18 . . . I know of at least one component that they 'copied' incorrectly which could well have made a difference to reliability."[103]

In their enthusiasm to embrace the AR-18 design (produced by Arthur Miller after Eugene Stoner had left the company), the design team overlooked the original thinking behind the weapon. The multi-lugged rotating bolt had its roots in the .30 calibre automatic rifle designed before World War II by Melvin M Johnson and the short-stroke gas piston was based on that used in the German Gewehr 43 rifle, itself based on the Soviet Tokarev SVT40. The AR-18 was designed to meet the requirements of less-developed countries, lacking the fine engineering facilities required by the AR-15 / M-16 and so made extensive use of sheet-metal stampings and spot welds which would only require basic metal tooling, common in most countries. The multi-lugged, front locking, rotating bolt was seen by both Armalite and Enfield as a solution to the problem of body weight with the AR-18 utilising a single metal pressing to form the body, while plastics, alloys and case-hardening of metal components provided the remainder. Thus the AR-18 was seen as an inexpensive export weapon to supply in military aid packages to allies around the world and was never seen as a serious alternative to the AR-15 / M-16. Low production costs have a trade-off however, in terms of the quality of components and materials used as well as the weapon's reliability under adverse conditions. Equipping Third World militias with such a weapon was one thing, using it as a basis to equip the British Army was a different story.[104]

There was also a misunderstanding over the impact that moving away from the traditional means of manufacturing small arms components would have. The precision components that made up the bolt-action Lee Enfield and the L1A1 SLR were machined by hand from solid blocks of metal while the EM-2 was made from the same sort of machined components as well as wood. The SA80 however was made from pressed steel and plastic – such materials would not go together with the same tolerances that properly machined components would, in this case, one or two microns. "Critically, Hance and his successors failed to come to terms with the realities of a new way of mass-producing guns, pioneered by the Germans during the second world war and taken up by the Americans."[105]

• Secondly, two aspects of the design were always going to cause problems, both of which were inter-dependant. First, the method by which the breech was locked involved a multi-splined bolt which was always going to be highly vulnerable to any foreign matter which managed to get into the weapon. Second, the reciprocating cocking handle meant that, even with an ejection cover fitted, it necessitated a slot running two-thirds the length of the body through which dust, sand and dirt could enter and an open or broken ejection cover just made the situation worse.[106]

- Thirdly, the LSW, a light-weight magazine-fed 5.56x45mm support weapon, firing with a closed bolt and a fixed non-changeable barrel was always going to have problems related to its rate of fire and overheating and the MoD has now purchased the FN Minimi to replace it in section support – "of the Gulf conflict one can say that the case for replacing the present LSW with the Minimi, Ameli or a similar seriously configured light machine gun was never more amply demonstrated."[107]

- Fourthly, there has been a major question over the propellants used in the ammunition manufactured by the UK. Prior to the NATO Standardisation Trials in the late 1970s, 5.56mm / .223 ammunition had been manufactured for several years here in this country but not specifically for military use. With the NATO decision to adopt 5.56mm as a second round (more specifically the Belgian SS109 cartridge), the UK started producing 5.56mm ammunition (the M193 cartridge) initially for its M16A1 weapons but also in anticipation of the adoption of its own 5.56mm small arm. It was decided that the ammunition would be boxer primed for ease of manufacture, while propellant would be bought in until a home-developed alternative was available. In 1980, the first bulk order for propellant for use in the RG ammunition was for ball powder from Pouderie Belge (PRB) as used in the M193 ammunition being used at the time. In 1982, an NNN type of propellant was developed by Nobels Explosive Co. Ltd, which at the time was a subsidiary of ICI Ltd, who in turn ran the Government-owned factory at Powfoot on a management basis. Given that cut tubular propellant is generally cheaper than ball powder, it was natural that ICI would produce that type of propellant in order to minimise costs, a right they had under the terms of the contract and even had the Government recognised the disadvantages inherent in the use of cut tubular propellant as opposed to ball powder, there was nothing they could do about it.

Thus the 5.56mm ball round that was approved in 1984 was loaded with 23.46gn of NNN cut tubular propellant. Cut tubular propellant has a slower and more progressive burn rate as compared to ball powder, which results in lower chamber and gas port pressures, which have a direct impact on cyclic rate and functional reliability. In addition, ball powder is smaller and compacts better than cut tubular propellant and so more propellant can be used in a cartridge case. Given that just about everyone else who uses 5.56mm ammunition uses ball power propellant, that fact should be seen as an indication as to its impact on how a weapon functions. Added to this, is the multi-lugged Stoner type of bolt used in the SA80, a direct derivative of the bolt used in the AR-15 / M16 and AR-18. In all these weapons, the locking lugs require a movement of 22.5° to lock / unlock the bolt, but differences exist in the 'dwell time' (the time its takes the carrier to move in order for the bolt to lock / unlock) with the AR-18 having a much shorter 'dwell time' than the SA80. This, combined with the greater chamber and gas port pressures associated with ball powder which is used in the USA and most other countries that have 5.56mm weapons, means that greater energy is given to the parts of the weapon that need it, resulting in a faster and more positive action as well as the extraction and ejection of the spent case, the picking up of a fresh round out of the magazine and its placement in the chamber with the weapon's action ready to fire again. Therefore the action of the AR-15 / M-16 and AR-18 is able to overcome a greater degree of fouling than that of the SA80 due to it being inhibited by its slower, more sluggish action. It is unclear as to why something as basic as the propellant used and its impact on the cycling of the SA80 has not been investigated – even the £92m Heckler & Koch upgrade was mainly focused upon reducing friction within the system (indirectly easing the problem).[108] Such an impact was admitted to in the questions posed by the HCDC:[109]

"Mr Trotter.
1640. Could I, before doing that, follow up on the ballistic matter? Would the range be different?
(Lieutenant Colonel Cook) The propellant will alter slightly the rate of fire of the weapon and that can have consequences on the functional reliability and indeed mechanical reliability.
1641. So there may be more jamming?
(Lieutenant Colonel Cook) It is possible but not necessarily so.
(Major General Stone) Different manufacturers of different ammunition produce a different energy in their round. Depending on the propellant you can have either a higher or lower energy. Clearly if you fire a low energy round the recoil, the movement of the working parts, is less precise perhaps than a higher energy round. Conversely, if you have a very energetic round it might force the working parts to the rear too severely. That is the sort of difficulty we are talking about."

- Fifth, one of the most telling criticisms has been the almost complete lack of export orders. Bar a small number of weapons that have been supplied to Nepal, as well as Jamaica, Zimbabwe and Mozambique as foreign aid, there have been no other significant enquiries. The exception to this is Venezuela, whose Special Forces trialled the weapon in the mid-1990s with an eye to replacing their FN FAL rifles, but was so discontented with the weapon that they didn't proceed with the project any further.[110] "Lucrative overseas sales are usually the result of a successful weapons system and exports of SA80 speak for themselves."[111] The Falkland Islands Defence Force (FIDF) chose the Steyr AUG, as did Ireland, Australia and New Zealand. "FIDF conducted comparative trials and found that the AUG outperformed the SA80 in every respect and vastly outclassed it in terms of functional reliability."[112] On top of the lack of export orders, the rifle was dropped from the NATO Nominated Weapons List in 1997[113], only being readmitted in March 2002. Finally, the SA80 has always been rejected by British Special Forces units, who have tended to go for the Colt 5.56mm M16 rifle or M4 carbine (or the examples made under license by Diemaco, a Canadian company, known as the C7 rifle or C8 carbine) or more recently the Heckler & Koch G36 assault rifle. In addition, the Pathfinders (from the Parachute Regiment) and Brigade Patrol Troop (from 3rd Commando Brigade) have also used these weapons whenever they can, although the improved reliability of the SA80A2 has caused this to be a less common event.[114]

- Sixth, there is a massive question mark over the roles of the Ordnance Board and the ITDU, as well as the trials they conducted. As mentioned above, the range, suitability and rigorousness with which these trials were conducted are all in question, given that most of the initial faults that were found were done so after the IW had been accepted for service and had to be corrected at a cost of £24m.[115] In addition, Heckler & Koch, who had been subcontracted to do some work on the training ammunition, rang one of the officers on the project in 1985 and reported that the weapon went off if you dropped it. The officer immediately went to the armoury to source a weapon and dropped it – it went off. A dangerous safety flaw had been discovered after supposedly exhaustive testing by the Ordnance Board and ITDU, whose trials were later revealed to be far too biased towards tests in the laboratory, rather than conducting those in conjunction with tests conducted in the field by combat troops. "The second area of concern, or where we have learned a major lesson, is the need to have sufficiently comprehensive user-trials during design and development and to test the general usage of weapons in the hands of soldiers and not necessarily rely solely on clinical tests which we might assume have covered all sorts of angles".[116] The MoD and Army realised, too late, that there was a huge difference between the weapons used in the pre-acceptance trials which were hand-built using traditional techniques and those rolling off the mass production lines. There was also little in the way of proper project management – the soldiers would demand a change, the engineers would introduce the change but due to time pressure, the change would not be properly tested. The change would fail and another quick-fix solution sought. Plus it would take time for the changes to be fitted to all the weapons in service, totalling over 300,000 by the time production ceased.[117] Instead of starting production slowly, and introducing properly tested modifications as faults were found, the Government and the MoD moved heaven-and-earth to get the weapon into service, ignoring any criticisms that came in:

"We were under a lot of pressure in those days to get something in as quickly as possible. The self-loading rifle was becoming increasingly expensive to maintain and the user had set us the demands of an in-service date of 1983."118

"Initially it was the plan that we would have a low rate of production such that as soon as difficulties became apparent with the small number in the field, we could take action quickly to put that right. Now, as you will be aware, we had the problem of the in-service date, we were slipping like mad, and there was increasing pressure from the user to get this weapon into service to replace the aging self-loading rifle and so we made the error, if you like, of increasing the rate of production to satisfy the pressures and demands which were upon us."119

- Seventh, there was a missed opportunity to extensively trial an after-market modification in the form of the Datestyle Muzzle Stabilizer, designed in 1980 by Richard Cave. This was originally designed as a recoil reducer on a 7.62mm long-range pistol. Further trials on a FN FAL rifle and M16 rifle proved promising, with the company coming to the conclusion that if fitted to the IW and LSW, it may well improve the firing groups of both weapons. Apart from a muzzle brake being fitted to two '0' series LSWs, one of which was the only model to have a changeable barrel, the issue of using the muzzle blast to help control the weapon and for improving performance, seems to have been completely neglected. The ITDU conducted a two-day trial that included an AR-15, an L1A1, an IW and an LSW, all of which were fired in the keeling and standing positions. All the weapons involved showed a marked improvement in group size of between thirteen and sixty-one percent for the AR-15, of between twenty-six and fifty-five percent for the L1A1, of between eighteen and seventy-seven percent for the IW and between forty-one and sixty-eight percent for the LSW. An interesting side-effect seemed to be that the stoppages caused by poor ejection seemed to have diminished. As a result of the trial, a letter was sent by Andrew Watt of Datestyle to Royal Ordnance on 9 March 1992, asking for 10,000 rounds to continue trials at Warminster which gained a positive response from Royal Ordnance via a letter from Mike Kennedy over the signature of Ken Malia on 23 March 1992 indicating they would be prepared to proceed with the trials. Three days previous to that, Datestyle had sent a letter to LSOR2 outlining their proposals. On 14 April 1992, a letter arrived from Major P H Williamson MBE at LSOR2 indicating the MoD had 'no requirements' for any such muzzle stabiliser. This was confirmed by a letter from Colonel R H Forsyth, Project Manager Infantry Weapons, Procurement Executive, MoD dated 28 September 1992 (in response to Datestyle's letter to the Secretary of State for Defence dated 2 September 1992) merely repeating the official line that despite some initial teething problems, the Armed Forces were very happy with the weapon that met all their operational requirements and so further evaluation of the muzzle stabiliser was pointless.[120]

- Eighth, and perhaps most tragically of all, is the loss of a national UK firearms design and manufacturing capability, as a result of the closure of the RSAF Enfield site in October 1988 while "most of the skilled gun makers, designers and ballistics staff at Enfield accepted redundancy. A fair number have since set up independent companies and consultancies".[121] RO Nottingham closed in 2001, as a result of restructuring in BAe and the lack of firm orders for small arms. In the dogmatic rush to sell off as much Government-owned industry or utilities as possible, the commercialisation, privatisation and then sell-off of RSAF Enfield left the UK's small arms manufacturing in the hands of a privately-owned corporation who were not accountable to the government and once production of the SA80 had ceased, there was nothing to stop them selling the site off for commercial development and profit. Even Heckler & Koch, once a subsidiary of BAe, has been bought out by a consortium of employees in December 2002 and is now an independently-owned company again, which begs the question, once the MoD contemplates the replacement of the SA80, who will it turn to? Whichever business is chosen, will mean reliance on a foreign company, for not only the acquisition of the weapons themselves, but for spares and logistic support too.

Conclusion

The history of the SA80 weapon system is one that almost beggars belief. Given that the system was first unveiled in mid-1976, a year before the NATO Standardisation Trials, it has taken almost thirty years for the British Army (and by extension the Royal Marines and RAF Regiment) to finally be equipped with an assault rifle that combines phenomenal accuracy with a decent level of reliability, particularly in adverse environmental conditions. This however, is only one half of the overall SA80 weapon system. The LSW too has had problems in reliability, in accuracy while firing on fully automatic (the split group syndrome) and in overheating (with the lack of a changeable barrel), which produced an inability to conduct sustained fire in order to fully suppress a target. It has therefore been relegated to the position of being a long-range rifle, its place being taken by the FN Herstal Minimi. It is almost inconceivable that after that length of time and the expenditure of over £500m on its development and almost continuous modifications and upgrades, only one half of the weapon system is functioning correctly. Indeed, it is in the process of being upgraded to an 'A3' standard due to lessons coming out of operations in Afghanistan – such upgrades involving lighter, improved sights[122], new handgrips that contain a quadruple Picatinny rail adaptor system[123], polymer 30-round magazines and a Vortex flash eliminator that allows a suppressor to be fitted, useful for command and control during fighting in built-up areas.[124] The other half has finally been recognised as being incapable of performing the job it was designed and produced for, to be replaced by a weapon that was first trialled nineteen years before and only rejected because it didn't quite meet the GSR accuracy requirement.

It has thus taken almost twenty years since it was first issued, but SA80A2 seems to be the gun the Army should have had in the late 1980s, not perfect but a lot better. As highlighted above, a number of criticisms can be levelled at the MoD in relation to the procurement of this weapon system but in retrospect, these are the factors that really stand out:

- The role of politics, in the first case, national – "It was accepted for service because of commercial and political pressures, not for sound military reasons"[125], which has left the UK without a domestic capability to design and produce small arms, the most basic of our Armed Forces weapons.
- Again, the role of politics, but in the second case, international – for it is "a story of the decline of British engineering, the sacrifice of skills for political and financial gain, a complacent cold war military bureaucracy, and Britain's role as America's subservient ally in Europe."[126] Let's not forget that twice in the space of less than

thirty years, was a British-designed small arm, firing a British designed and tested intermediate calibre cartridge, sacrificed on the altar of NATO standardisation, under pressure from the USA who were adamant that their calibre would be the one chosen as the new 'standard'.

- The role of the Ordnance Board and ITDU and the suitability of the trials they (supposedly) conducted.
- The concentration and reliance on 'quick-fix' solutions, denying or ignoring anything was wrong until concrete evidence was leaked into the public domain and ignoring the reports that were coming back from the actual users themselves – the soldiers.

Postscript

On a separate but related note, while criticism of the SA80A2 and LSW have died down (the latter due to its relegation to a longer-range rifle and being replaced by the FN Herstal Minimi) in recent times, the same cannot be said for the ammunition used by all three weapons, and indeed by the majority of the small arms used by NATO countries – the 5.56x45mm cartridge. As mentioned above, the NATO Standardisation Trials in the early 1950s saw the adoption by NATO of the 7.62x51mm cartridge, the USA's preferred choice. Frustratingly, for the proponents of the smaller calibre, trials by the US in the latter part of the decade suggested that the new AR-15 assault rifle, chambered for the new 5.56x45mm (.223) cartridge, was superior to the M14, which was chambered for the 7.62x51mm cartridge. The Ordnance Department recommended that development of the AR15 should continue, in order to replace the M14, which had only been adopted for service two years earlier. *Endnote 127* The US Air Force ordered the AR15 (designated the M16 in military service) in 1960 to replace the M2 carbine, and formerly adopted it in 1964. The US Army did the same in February 1967. The British .280 cartridge had proved itself to be far ahead of its time with the USA replacing the M14 with the M16A1 in most combat units by the end of the decade. *Endnote 128* The M16A1 was designed to use the American M193 cartridge but this has been the subject of considerable controversy over it's lack of stopping power, reported even then by troops in Vietnam.[129]

A selection of cartridges, from left to right: 6mm SAW, 6.5 Grendel, 6.8 Remington SPC, 7mm Bench Rest, .280/30 British, 7mm-08, 7mm Second Optimum (Liviano), .276 Pedersen, .308x1.75", 7.62x51mm NATO (Source: JamesL85 via Wikimedia Commons)

In fact, these problems of lethality have never really disappeared, for if "the 7.62mm was overpowered, the 5.56 was distinctly underpowered for military use, being essentially a small game ("varmint") cartridge. In fact, the 5.56x45mm is illegal for deer hunting in many areas of the US".[130] This lack of lethality has been evidenced in the conflicts in Iraq and Afghanistan, especially for those troops using the M4 and M4A1 carbines, which in this case primarily equates to US Special Forces. The problem seems to relate to the difference in velocity that the SS109 round leaves the M4 (792m/s) as compared to the standard M16 (884m/s). The SS109 is most lethal when it strikes a target at a velocity of 731m/s or greater, after which the bullet starts to tumble and fragments along the cannelure causing a miniature explosion, enhancing the size of the wound cavity. For a standard M16, the range at which the SS109 round drops below 731m/s is around 200m, as opposed to the M4, where this occurs at a range of less than 100m.[131] This has led the USA to procure a new 5.56x45mm cartridge, the Mk 262, which fires a 77gn (5g) bullet at 832m/s from a 16in barrel, while fragmenting at velocities as low as 610m/s, meaning it will have enhanced lethality at about 300m for a 16in barrel and 250m for the 14.5in (M4) barrel. The problem with the lack of lethality of 5.56x45mm ammunition at ranges over 300m has also plagued the British Army, which has seen combat operations in both Iraq and Afghanistan (where some 50% of engagements occur over 300m).[132] The problem has been partly tackled at least, by firstly the re-introduction of large numbers of 7.62mm L7A2 GPMGs which are deemed to be "essential" for operations and have provided a "battle-winning capability" at platoon, even section-level.[133] Secondly, has been the procurement under an Urgent Operational Requirement (UOR) of 440 7.62x51mm LM7 semi-automatic rifles from Law Enforcement International (LEI) who beat competition from Heckler & Koch, FN Herstal and Sabre Defence Industries. The rifles will be brought into service under the designation L129A1 and will be issued to 'sharpshooters', who are service personnel who complete a designated course of instruction and are regarded as being a grade below that of 'sniper'. 'Snipers' will continue to be issued with the Accuracy International L115A3 rifle (in .338 Lapua Magnum) but the new L129A1 will enable soldiers to effectively engage targets between 300m and 800m alongside the GMPG, finally filling a capability gap.[134]

The L115A3 from Accuracy International (Source: Luhai Wong via Wikimedia Commons)

Endnotes

[1] Jane's Infantry Weapons. (2009) 'L85A1/L85A2 5.56mm Individual Weapon' webpage, located on the Jane's Website (http://www.janes.com) as of 16 July 2009.

[2] Raw, Steve. (2003) *The Last Enfield: SA80 – The Reluctant Rifle*, Cobourg, Ontario: Collector Grade Publications, p. xxxi.

[3] The lineage can be seen starting with the Mk. I Lee Metford rifle which was approved for service on 22 December 1888, the Mk. I Lee Enfield rifle which was approved for service on 11 November 1895, the No. 1 Mk. III SMLE which was approved for service on 26 January 1907 and finally the No. 4 Mk. I Lee Enfield which was approved for service on 15 November 1939. See Skennerton, Ian. (2007) *The Lee Enfield – A Century of Lee Metford & Lee Enfield Rifles & Carbines*, Labrador, Queensland: Arms & Militaria Press.

[4] Hitchman, Norman et al. (1952) *Operational Requirements for an Infantry Hand Weapon*, Operations Research Office, Johns Hopkins University, Chevy Chase, MD, June 1952.

[5] Williams, Anthony G. (2009) 'Assault Rifles and their Ammunition: History and Prospects' webpage, dated 11 June 2009, currently located at http://www.quarry.nildram. co.uk/Assault.htm, as of 16 July 2009.

[6] Popenker, Max R. (2009) 'Enfield EM-2 / Rifle, Automatic, caliber .280, Number 9 Mark 1 (Great Britain)' webpage, located at http://world.guns.ru/assault/as59-e.htm as of 17 July 2009.

[7] Popenker, Maxim and Willliams, Anthony G. (2004) *Assault Rifle: The Development of the Modern Military Rifle and its Ammunition*, Ramsbury: Crowood Press, p. 54; Raw, Steve. (2003) *The Last Enfield: SA80 – The Reluctant Rifle*, Cobourg, Ontario: Collector Grade Publications, p. 224.

[8] *Op Cit*. Popenker and Williams, 2004, p. 55. See also Cary, Lucian. (1951) 'That New British Rifle' in *True* Magazine, MacFadden Womens Group, December 1951. Reproduced in Dugelby, Thomas B. (1980) *EM-2 Concept and Design: A Rifle Ahead of its Time*, Toronto: Collector Grade Publications, pp. 141 – 148; Ezell, Edward C. (1974) 'Cracks in the Post-War Anglo-American Alliance: The Great Rifle Controversy, 1947-1957' in *Military Affairs*, Vol. 38, No. 4 (December 1974), pp. 138 – 149.

[9] For a much more in depth look at the EM-2 story, see Antill, P. 'EM-2 – A Rifle Ahead of its Time: The EM-2 (Rifle No. 9, Mk. I)' in Moore, David. (Ed) (2011) *Case Studies in Defence Procurement and Logistics – Volume I: From World War II to the Post Cold-War World*, Cambridge: Cambridge Academic Press, pp. 109 – 125.

[10] See for example Jane's Ammunition Handbook. '7.62 x 51 mm cartridge' webpage, currently located on the Jane's Website (http://www.janes.com) as of 17 July 2009; Houghton, Cpt J M. 'UK Small Arms for the Eighties (SA80)' in *REME Journal*, April 1983, p. 31.

[11] *Op Cit*. Jane's Ammunition Handbook. '7.62 x 51 mm cartridge' webpage, 25 January 2005.

[12] *Op Cit*. Raw, 2003, p. 15.

[13] Hooton, E R. (1986) 'The Enfield Weapon System: New small arms for the British Army' in *Military Technology*, March 1986 (3/86), p. 120.

[14] *Op Cit*. Raw, 2003, pp. 16 – 19.

[15] *Op Cit*. Houghton, 1983, p. 34.

[16] *Op Cit*. Raw, 2003, p. 26.

[17] *Op Cit*. Houghton, 1983, p. 34.

[18] *Op Cit*. Raw, 2003, p. 31.

[19] *Op Cit*. Houghton, 1983, p. 34.

[20] *Op Cit*. Raw, 2003, p. 35.

[21] *Op Cit*. Popenker and Williams, 2004, p. 60.

[22] Wikipedia. (2009) '.280 British' webpage', located at http://en.wikipedia.org/wiki/.280_British as of 16 July 2009.

[23] Williams, Anthony G. (2009) 'Assault Rifles and their Ammunition: History and Prospects' webpage, dated 11 June 2009, currently located at http://www.quarry.nildram.co.uk/Assault.htm, as of 16 July 2009; Cutshaw, Charles. (2004) 'Barrett's M468 special-purpose carbine', Jane's International Defence Review (May 2004), posted on http://www.janes.com on 02 April 2004; Kirby, Charles. (1985) 'Bullpup – Getting to Grips with the New Service Rifle' in *Handgunner*, Nov / Dec 1985, p. 36.

[24] Upchurch, Lee. (1985) 'Enfield Weapons System' in *S.W.A.T.*, December 1985, p. 56.

[25] Dugelby, Thomas B. (1984) *Modern Military Bullpup Rifles*, London: Arms and Armour Press, p. 55.

[26] *Op Cit*. Raw, 2003, pp. 49 – 53.

[27] *Op Cit*. Popenker and Williams, 2004, p. 62.

[28] *Op Cit*. Raw, 2003, p. 55; See also *Op Cit*. Popenker and Williams, 2004, p. 62.

[29] *Op Cit*. Raw, 2003, p. 68.

[30] *Ibid*. p. 75.

[31] *Ibid*. p. 76.

[32] Quoted in *Ibid*. p. 85.

[33] *Ibid*. pp. 86 – 87. Also see Ministry of Defence. *Record of an Acceptance Meeting to Consider the Suitability of the Enfield Weapon System Light Support Weapon (SA 80 LSW) for Introduction into Service Held in Room 254 Old War Office Building on 13 September 1984*, D/OR12/2/8/36, dated 19 September 1984 (Restricted), p. 2 for a brief description of the 17 January 1984 meeting.

[34] *Op Cit*. Ministry of Defence, 19 September 1984, Annex A.

[35] *Ibid*. Annex B.

[36] *Ibid*. p. 10.

[37] Steadman, Nick. (1986) 'The Enfield Weapon System' in *Armed Forces*, Volume 5, Number 2 (February 1986), p. 71.

[38] Stevenson, Jan A. (1985) 'Britain Adopts New Enfield' in *Handgunner*, Nov / Dec 1985, p. 65; *Op Cit*. Steadman, February 1986, p. 72; *Op Cit*, Raw, 2003, p. 102.

[39] Fleming, Burton. (1985) 'Britain's New Bulldog' in *Combat Weapons*, Summer 1985, pp. 66 – 69; Hooton, E R. (1986) 'The Enfield Weapon System: New small arms for the British Army' in *Military Technology*, March 1986 (3/86), pp. 120 – 128; Karwan, Chuck. (1989) 'The Last Enfield' in Lewis, Jack. (Ed) *The Gun Digest Book of Assault Weapons*, 2nd Edition, Iola, WI: DBI Books, pp. 116 – 125; Kirby, Charles. (1985) 'Bullpup – Getting to Grips with the New Service Rifle' in *Handgunner*, Nov / Dec 1985 (No. 31), pp. 25 – 36; Kirby, Charles. (1986) 'Service Rifle SNAFU' in *Handgunner*, May / June 1986 (No. 34), pp. 19 – 23; Steadman, Nick. (1986) 'The Enfield Weapon System' in *Armed Forces*, Volume 5, Number 2 (February 1986), pp. 71 – 75; Steadman, Nick. (1986) 'Update on UK SA80 Programme' in *Armed Forces*, Volume 5, Number 9 (September 1986), p. 401; Stevenson, Jan A. (1985) 'Britain Adopts New Enfield' in *Handgunner*, Nov / Dec 1985, pp. 59 – 66; Upchurch, Lee. (1985) 'Enfield Weapons System' in *S.W.A.T.*, December 1985, pp. 38 – 39, 56 – 57.

[40] *Op Cit*. Steadman, September 1986, p. 401.

[41] Willis, Guy. (1989) 'The long and the short of it – the SA80 family' in *International Defence Review*, January 1989, p. 68.

[42] Gelbart, Marsh. (1997) 'The SA80 Assault Rifle: A Costly Disaster' in *Machine Gun News*, April 1997, p. 25.

[43] *Op Cit*. Raw, 2003, p. 103.

[44] Williams, Anthony G. (2007) 'SA80 – Mistake or Maligned – and What Next?' webpage, dated 04 October 2007, currently located at http://www.quarry.nildram.co.uk/SA80.htm as of 16 July 2009; Also see *Op Cit*. Raw, 2003, p. 135.

[45] Kirby, Charles. (1989) 'SA80 – A Rival for Reising?' in *Handgunner*, September / October 1989, pp. 55 – 58; *Op Cit*. Raw, 2003, pp. 149 - 151.

[46] Kirby, Charles. (1989) 'SA80 in Section Support' in *Handgunner*, November / December 1989, pp. 55 – 60.

[47] Macrae, Callum. (1992) 'Revealed: MoD told in 1985 new rifle was a dud' in *The Observer*, 23 August 1992, p. 7.

[48] Macrae, Callum. (1992) 'Secret report damns Army's assault rifle' in *The Observer*, 16 August 1992, p. 1.

[49] *Op Cit*. Raw, 2003, p. 153.

[50] Kirby, Charles. (1993) 'Cassandra and the Rifle' in *Handgunner*, February / March 1993, p. 39.

[51] Wright, Col A P. (1987) *SA80 Full Acceptance*, Loose Minute – dated 24 February 1987, D/DGW (A) 18/41/6.

[52] *Op Cit*. Kirby, February / March 1993, p. 45.

[53] The Army Rumour Service. (2009) 'SA-80' webpage located at http://www.arrse. co.uk/wiki/SA-80 as of 7 August 2009.

[54] See Waters, Daniel. http://www.thegunzone.com/556dw-10.html. Also, *Op Cit*. Raw, 2003, p. 176.

[55] *Op Cit*. Macrae, 23 August 1992, p. 7; *Op Cit*. Macrae, 16 August 1992, p. 1 and p. 20; McIlroy, A J. (1992) 'Gulf troops 'feared rifle would not fire'' in *The Daily Telegraph*, 22 August 1992, p. 2; Stevenson, Jan A. (1992) 'Service Rifle Scandal' in *Handgunner*, October / November 1992, pp. 22 – 29.

[56] Stevenson, Jan A. (1993) 'Service Rifle Scandal – part 2' in *Handgunner*, February / March 1993, p. 13.

[57] *Op Cit*. Gelbart, April 1997, p. 26.

[58] House of Commons Defence Committee. (1993) *The SA80 Rifle and Light Support Weapon*, Session 1992-93, Third Report, HC728, London: HMSO, 9th June 1993.

[59] *Op Cit*. Raw, 2003, p. 180.

[60] *Op Cit*. HCDC, 9th June 1993, pp. viii – xv; Kemp, Ian. (1993) 'MoD handling of SA80 buy berated' in *Jane's Defence Weekly*, 31 July 1993, p. 26; Stevenson, Jan A. (1993) 'Service Rifle Scandal – Part IV' in *Handgunner*, December 1993, pp. 34 – 38.

[61] *Op Cit*. Raw, 2003, p. 106.

[62] Thompson, Leroy. (1996) 'The SA80 (L85A1) Individual Weapon: Britain's Assault Rifle' in *S.W.A.T.*, February 1996, p. 68.

[63] *Op Cit*. Gelbart, April 1997, p. 27.

[64] House of Commons. (2000) 'SA80 Rifle' in Hansard Written Answers for 10 July 2000 (pt 6), 10 July 2000, Column 377W (also available online at http://www. publications.parliament.uk/pa/cm199900/cmhansrd/vo000710/text/00710w06.htm); House of Commons Defence Committee. (1999) 'Letter from the Minister of State for Defence Procurement on the SA80 Weapon System' in *Annual Report of the Committee for Session 1997 – 98: Report and Annexes with Proceedings of the Committee and Appendices*, First Special Report, HC273, 10 March 1999 (also available on http://www. publications.parliament.uk/pa/cm199899/cmselect/cmdfence/273/273r04.htm).

[65] *Op Cit*. HCDC, HC273, 10 March 1999; BBC News. (1999) 'Desert 'too tough' for Army's rifle', posted 11 March 1999 and located at http://news.bbc.co.uk/1/hi/uk/294758.

stm as of 13 August 2009; Butcher, Tim. (1999) 'Army's rifle doesn't work in the desert, MoD admits', posted 11 March 1999 and located on www.portal.telegraph.co.uk/ htmlContent.jhtml?html=/archive/1999/03/11/ngun11.html as of 21 December 2001 (posted 11 March 1999).

[66] Bruce, Robert. (2003) 'Afghanistan Report: Has Britain Really Fixed the Disastrous SA80?' in *S.W.A.T.*, May 2003, p. 50.

[67] *Op Cit*. Raw, 2003, pp. 97 – 98.

[68] House of Commons. (2000) 'SA80 Weapon System' in *Hansard Written Answers for 24 Jan 2000 (pt 19)*, 24 January 2000, Column 70W (also available online at http://www. publications.parliament.uk/pa/cm199900/cmhansrd/vo000124/text/00124w19.htm); See also *Op Cit*. Raw, 2003, pp. 277 – 278.

[69] House of Commons. (2000) 'SA80' in *Hansard Written Answers for 23 June 2000 (pt 4)*, 23 June 2000, Column 318W (also available online at http://www.publications. parliament.uk/pa/cm199900/cmhansrd/vo000623/text/00623w04.htm#00623w04.html_ sbhd6 as of 14 August 2009.

[70] White, Andrew. (2007) 'In the line of fire: close quarter combat fighters call for improved small arms", located on the http://www.janes.com website as of 11August 2009, posted 12 March 2007 (in *International Defence Review*, April 2007).

[71] *Op Cit*. Williams, 04 October 2007.

[72] Ministry of Defence. (2000) *Kosovo: Lessons from the Crisis*, Cm4724, London: TSO, paragraphs 8.35 – 8.37; Gander, Terry. (2000) 'UK fires up SA-80 programme', posted 11 September 2000, located on Jane's Website (http://www.janes.com) as of 10 June 2009; Tweedie, Neil. (2000) 'Infantry chief says gun must go', posted on 24 July 2000, http://www.telegraph.co.uk/news/uknews/1350127/Infantry-chief-says-gun-must-go.html as of 18 August 2009.

[73] BBC News. (2000) 'Minister confirms UK rifle 'jammed'', posted 31 July 2000 and located at http://news.bbc.co.uk/1/hi/uk/859812.stm as of 17 August 2009; Butcher, Tim. (2000) 'Soldier's rifle failed in battle, says secret report', posted 31 July 2000 at http:// www.telegraph.co.uk/news/uknews/1351052/Soldiers-rifle-failed-in-battle-says-secret-report.html, as of 17 August 2009; Evans, Michael. (2001) 'Troubled Army rifle gets thumbs down from SAS', posted 7 August 2000, at http://www.times-archive.co.uk/ news/pages/time/2000/08/07/timnwsnws01009.html, as of 3 August 2009; McKillop, James. (2000) 'Senior generals ignored by MoD', posted on 11 August 2000, located at http://www.theherald.co.uk/news/archive/11-8-19100-2-26-12.html as of 12 July 2009.

[74] Evans, Michael. (2000) 'Parting shot for weapons firm', posted on 9 August 2000 and located at http://www.times-archive.co.uk/news/pages/tim/2000/08/09/timnwsnws01010.

html as of 30 August 2009; Foss, Christopher F. (2000) 'BAE Systems RO Defence to close Nottingham facility in 2001', posted 25 August 2000, located on Jane's Website (http://www.janes.com) as of 18 August 2009.

[75] *Op Cit*. Raw, 2003, p. 280.

[76] Sengupta, Kim and Bruce, James. (2001) 'This 'reliable' gun's 82nd revamp has cost the taxpayer £80m, but still the SAS refuse to use it', posted on 23 January 2001 and located on *The Independent* website (http://www.indepedent.co.uk) as of 12 August 2009.

[77] *Op Cit*. Raw, 2003, p. 281.

[78] National Audit Office. (2002) *Ministry of Defence: Progress in Reducing Stocks*, HC898, Session 2001-2002, TSO, London, 20 June 2002, p. 16.

[79] House of Commons. (2002) 'SA80A1 / SA80A2' in *Hansard Written Answers for 22 Jul 2002 (pt 18)*, 22 July 2002, Column 758W (also available online at http://www.publications.parliament.uk/pa/cm200102/cmhansrd/vo020722/text/20722w18.htm).

[80] Sen, Philip. (2001) 'Revamped SA-80 "among the very best"', posted 30 October 2001, located on the Jane's Website (http://www.janes.com) as of 10 June 2009.

[81] Sen, Philip. (2002) 'Upgraded SA-80 goes to war', posted 16 April 2002, located on the Jane's Website (http://www.janes.com) as of 10 June 2009.

[82] ISAF in fact came under the auspices of NATO and amounted to over 35,000 military personnel from twenty-eight NATO and fourteen non-NATO countries.

[83] *Op Cit*. Raw, 2003, p. 294.

[84] Gander, Terry. (2002) 'As the SA-80's woes continue, it looks like time to start again', posted 11 July 2002, located on Jane's Website (http://www.janes.com) as of 10 June 2009; Tweedie, Neil and Savill, Richard. (2002) 'Army's £93m revamped rifle 'still misfiring'', posted 6 July 2002, at http://www.telegraph.co.uk/news/uknews/1400531/Armys-93m-revamped-rifle-still-misfiring.html as of 19 August 2009; Rayment, Sean. (2002) 'Scrap British rifle and buy Heckler, say the generals', posted on 7 July 2002, located at http://www.telegraph.co.uk/news/uknews/1400622/Scrap-British-rifle-and-buy-Heckler-say-the-generals.html as of 19 August 2009.

[85] *Op Cit*. Raw, 2003, p. 295.

[86] Jane's Information Group. (2002) 'British forces do battle with rifle maintenance mythology', posted 17 October 2002 and located on the Jane's Website (http://www.janes.com) as of 10 June 2009; Navy News. (2002) 'Testing Times for New Weapon', posted 13 November 2002 at http://www.navynews.co.uk/articles/2002/0211/1002111301.asp as of 12 May 2009.

[87] *Op Cit*. Bruce, May 2003, p. 51.

[88] Rayment, Sean. (2002) 'Marines blamed for rifle failure', posted on 21 July 2002

and located at http://www.telegraph.co.uk/news/uknews/1402063/Marines-blamed-for-rifle-failure.html as of 19 August 2009; Smith Michael. (2002) 'MoD under pressure to abandon SA-80 rifle', posted on 22 July 2002 and located at http://www.telegraph.co.uk/news/uknews/1402138/MoD-under-pressure-to-abandon-SA-80-rifle.html as of 19 August 2009.

[89] Norton-Taylor, Richard. (2002) 'MoD may have to abandon main rifle', posted 18 July 2002 at http://www.guardian.co.uk/uk/2002/jul/18/military.richardnortontaylor as of 19 August 2009; Smith, Michael. (2002) 'Army trials of new SA-80 rifle 'were fudged'', posted on 26 July 2002 at http://www.telegraph.co.uk/news/uknews/1402602/Army-trials-of-new-SA-80-rifle-were-fudged.html as of 19 August 2009; *Op Cit.* Raw, 2003, p. 295.

[90] *Op Cit.* Smith, 26 July 2002.

[91] *Op Cit.* Rayment, 21 July 2002.

[92] *Op Cit.* Smith, 22 July 2002.

[93] Rayment, Sean. (2002) 'Army to scrap 'unreliable' SA-80 rifle', posted on 10 August 2002 and located at http://www.telegraph.co.uk/news/uknews/1404117/Army-to-scrap-unreliable-SA-80-rifle.html as of 19 August 2009.

[94] BBC News. (2002) 'Faulty Army rifles to be retained', posted on 17 September 2002 and currently located at http://news.bbc.co.uk/1/hi/uk/2262685.stm as of 19 August 2009.

[95] Smith, Michael. (2002) 'Army chief 'wanted rifle scrapped'', posted on 26 September 2002, at http://www.telegraph.co.uk/news/uknews/1408410/Army-chief-wanted-rifle-scrapped.html as of 19 August 2009. *Op Cit.* Smith, 26 July 2002. *Op Cit.* Raw, 2003, p. 299.

[96] Kemp, Ian. (2002) 'UK begins testing new light machinegun', posted 01 August 2002, located on the Jane's Website (http://www.janes.com) as of 20 August 2009.

[97] Kemp, Ian. (2003) 'Light gun selection progresses', posted 24 January 2003, located on the Jane's Website (http://www.janes.com) as of 20 August 2009.

[98] Kemp, Ian. (2003) 'UK selects FN Herstal machine gun', posted 30 May 2003, located on the Jane's Website (http://www.janes.com) as of 20 August 2009.

[99] *Op Cit.* Raw, 2003, p. 302.

100 Smith, Michael. (2003) 'Army admits defeat over SA80 light machinegun' posted on 29 May 2003 at http://www.telegraph.co.uk/news/uknews/1431349/Army-admits-defeat-over-SA80-light-machinegun.html, as of 20 August 2009; Jane's Information Group. (2003) 'United Kingdom' from Jane's Defence Industry, posted 20 June 2003 and located at Jane's Website (http://www.janes.com) as of 10 June 2009; Harding, Thomas. (2005) 'Army gets £30m new firepower to take on al Qa-eda and the Taliban' posted 19

October 2005 at http://www.telegraph.co.uk/news/uknews/1500917/Army-gets-30m-new-firepower-to-take-on-al-Qaeda-and-the-Taliban.html, as of 20 August 2009.

[101] *Op Cit.* Raw, 2003, pp. 21 – 22.

[102] Macrae, Callum. (1992) 'How the Army got second best' in *The Observer*, 23 August 1992, p. 7.

[103] Meek, James. (2002) 'Off target', posted on 10 October 2002 and located at http://www.guardian.co.uk/uk/2002/oct/10/military.jamesmeek, as of 19 August 2009 (quoting James Edmiston).

[104] *Op Cit. Raw*, 2003, pp. 23 – 24.

[105] *Op Cit.* Meek, 10 October 2002.

[106] *Op Cit.* Raw, 2003, p. 154.

[107] *Op Cit.* Kirby, February / March 1993, p. 47.

[108] *Op Cit.* Raw, 2003, pp. 309 – 310.

[109] *Op Cit.* HCDC, 9th June 1993, p. 4.

[110] TripAtlas.com. (2009) 'SA80' webpage, currently located at http://tripatlas.com/SA80 as of 10 August 2009.

[111] Bloom, Pete. (2000) 'SA80 – The Rifle That Dared to Call Itself "The Last Enfield"' in *Target Sports*, February 2000, p. 59.

[112] *Op Cit.* Stevenson, October / November 1992, p. 29.

[113] http://www.parliament.the-stationery-office.co.uk/pa/cm199900/cmhansrd/vo000710/text/00710w06.htm - Question put to Dr Moonie from Mr Quentin Davis MP, 20 July 2000, Column 377W.

[114] Elite UK Forces Website. See http://www.eliteukforces.info for the articles entitled 'Diemaco C7 Assault Rifle', 'SA80A2 Assault Rifle' and 'SAS Weapons - C8 SFW Carbine (L119A1)'. Retrieved 10 August 2009.

[115] *Op Cit.* HCDC, 9th June 1993, p. x.

[116] *Ibid.* p. 18.

[117] *Op Cit.* Meek, 10 October 2002.

[118] *Op Cit.* HCDC, 9th June 1993, p. 13.

[119] *Ibid.* p. 18; *Op Cit.* Meek, 10 October 2002.

[120] *Op Cit.* Raw, 2003, pp. 199 – 203; *Op Cit.* Kirby, February / March 1993, pp. 47 – 51.

[121] Steadman, Nick. (1996) 'Britain Builds the Bullpup: Genesis of the SA80' in *Fighting Firearms*, Spring 1996, p. 15.

[122] White, Andrew. (2006) 'UK assault rifle to receive lighter, improved sight', posted 28 April 2006 and located on the Jane's Website (http://www.janes.com) as of 21 August 2009.

[123] White, Andrew. (2007) 'UK MoD seeks further upgrades for SA80 rifle', posted 23 August 2007 and located on the Jane's Website (http://www.janes.com) as of 21 August 2009.

[124] White, Andrew. (2009) 'UK forces take on small-arms lessons from Afghanistan', posted on 02 September 2009 and located on the Jane's Website (http://www.janes.com) as of 23 February 2010.

[125] *Op Cit*. Gelbart, April 1997, p. 27.

[126] *Op Cit*. Meek, 10 October 2002.

[127] *Op Cit*. Popenker and Williams, 2004, p. 60.

[128] *Op Cit*. Wikipedia. '.280 British' webpage'.

[129] *Op Cit*. Williams, 11 June 2009.

[130] *Op Cit*. Cutshaw, http://www.janes.com, 02 April 2004.

[131] *Ibid*.

[132] Drummond, Nicholas & Williams, Anthony G. (2009) *Biting the Bullet*, October 2009, located at http://www.quarry.nildram.co.uk/btb.pdf as of 23 February 2010.

[133] *Op Cit*. White, 02 September 2009.

[134] White, Andrew. (2009) 'UK selects 7.62mm Sharpshooter weapon for Afghan ops'', posted on 24 December 2009 and located on the Jane's Website (http://www.janes.com) as of 22 January 2010; Mail on Sunday. (2010) 'British troops to get U.S. rifles to tackle Taliban' posted on 17 January 2010, located at http://www.dailymail.co.uk/news/article-1243851/British-troops-U-S-rifles-tackle-Taliban.html as of 23 January 2010; Drury, Ian. (2010) 'British troops get new Sharpshooter weapon to blast Taliban . . . because their weapons have a longer range than ours' posted on 18 January 2010, located at http://www.dailymail.co.uk/news/article-1244085/British-troops-new-Sharpshooter-rifle-blast-Taliban-half-mile-away.html as of 23 January 2010.

Tri-Service United Kingdom Project Management

Dr Jeffrey Bradford
Defence and National Security Consultant

Introduction

The publication of the United Kingdom government's landmark 1997 Strategic Defence Review has illustrated the latitude which a newly elected government has in being able to redefine the nation's defence posture. After the previous administrations efforts to draw down the defence establishment following the end of the Cold War it could be suggested that the Strategic Defence Review provided a new intellectual framework for warfighting structures as well as the machinery of government overhaul for peacetime management of the British armed forces and defence procurement.[1]

This case study wishes to consider one facet of the latter aspect, that of the Smart Procurement Initiative and the nature of its departure from previous practise. Whilst future procurement programmes will immediately benefit from such approaches what of those 'guinea pigs' which were underway at the time of transition? One of the most fundamental projects of the time was the Bowman communications programme, which affected each of the three armed services down to its operational foundations. In order to perceive the benefits of Smart Procurement practises the case-study will consider the Bowman programme in order to understand previous efforts in order to contextualise both the nature of developments and their significance.

Project Bowman involved the procurement of a modern communications system for the British armed forces. Its aim was to supersede the existing Clansman system, providing simultaneously backwards compatibility with current systems and an architecture, which will be compatible with systems developed in the future by Britain or her NATO allies.[2]

The existing Clansman system was derived from attempts to rationalise the various systems developed to meet British needs during the Second World War. The Larkspur programme of the 1940s and 1950s introduced for the armed services a reduced variety of equipment and greater commonality. Its successor, Clansman, sought to build on these efforts with an initial plan to operate five basic radios.

The Clansman project was regarded as a success, which set several important markers for its successor. First the procurement of a family of equipment led to more logical decisions being taken as to the number of suppliers and manufacturers of the hardware. This was in contrast to earlier efforts of a 'bottom-up' nature where radios were sourced from several suppliers and then combined to form a communications system. Commonality meant that man portable radios were designed to be integrated with vehicles when necessary in a simple manner. Third, for industry Clansman had a large and lucrative export value.[3] The successor Bowman program was clearly under pressure to match these features in addition to the mere technical requirements of the programme.

A Clansman PRC-320 radio, which was issued down to company level
(Source: Wikimedia Commons)

During the 1980s the military requirements for the successor to Clansman began to emerge. The need to replace the existing system was summarised by the Commandant of the Signals School, "Clansman is mahogany and brass whereas modern radio is silicone and plastic".[4] The new system needed to be able to transmit digital data as well as voice in order to facilitate the exchange of data between surveillance and target acquisition systems such as JTIDS, BATES and ADCIS.[5] An important point to note when considering the evolution of the programme is that Bowman was originally envisaged as Clansman plus a limited data transfer capability.[6]

A further characteristic of the new equipment was the central importance of software. The software involved in the new generation system facilitates ease of use by the operator, improved diagnostic capability, as well as the ability to emulate different wavelengths, with the appropriate sensors attached. The software engenders flexibility to the system and facilitates the transfer of data from different mediums.

Among the challenges for the definers of the military requirement were to communicate the potential for the future to the entire defence organisation. After all, the Royal Signals possessed only a small fraction of the communications equipment required by the three armed services. Educating the customer base and obtaining a consensus as to the future potential of Bowman was critical. As described by one source, "We [the Military requirements team] were thinking about digitisation in 1985."[7]

The Bowman performance requirements were generated by a system of working groups, a scientific working group based at DERA[8], a programme group responsible for the production issues, and a requirements group of tri-service military officers and executive assistants. The project manager was served by a reporting structure built both from formal and informal sources.

The problem identified by one official with this structure was that it was somewhat of a hostage to fortune insofar as the personality at key nodes within the structure could cause considerable damage to its efficiency if they did not gel well together. A further complication was that of conflicting organisational cultures. Civil servant project managers found risks with military officers whose reporting chain and future career prospects were not directly affected by their views. On occasion this could lead to problems for the project managers of individual members informal communications channels outside of the project team structure.[9]

The early military requirement was generated during the Cold War before the Ministry's adoption of the COEIA framework.[10] The documentation generated by this effort exceeded 120 pages. In generating the initial costings there were three factors aside from defence inflation which would influence the cost of the project. Firstly, the requirement was not to replace radio equipment on a unit for unit basis. The need for communications equipment for vehicles as well as the change in organisation and the use of communications would increase the volume of units required. Second, was the issue of installing the equipment into various platforms. Lastly, there was a need to purchase a communications 'backbone' to construct the system.

Formal Start of the Programme

In September 1988, following ministerial approval, the Bowman project started in earnest. The programme was divided into two stages. The first stage aimed to procure advanced battlefield radios which can interface with a range of command information systems. Stage two envisaged Bowman evolving into a high capacity data transmission network with an improved management information system.[11] Each of these two stages would consist of a feasibility study and production demonstration and actual production phase. These phases were planned to overlap so that feasibility study stage 2 would run concurrently with production demonstration phase 1.

The Ministry of Defence procurement strategy had several distinct facets. Firstly Bowman was to be procured with no formal development phase, the objective being to minimise technological risk and delivery time. The plan was to move from a demonstration phase straight to production [12]

A second facet of the Ministry of Defence procurement strategy was the use of a cardinal point specification for Bowman. By specifying the minimum critical characteristics for the equipment the Ministry could then stand back and allow industry the freedom to develop solutions. However, the list of these characteristics numbered over 1,000. Furthermore by awarding two demonstration contracts the Ministry hoped to emphasise competition throughout the process of procurement.

An important element in translating the cardinal point specification was the creation of a tri-service Bowman Military Team. This organisation was situated between the Procurement Executive and industry as a body which could translate the requirements into practical terms. An extreme example was that the specification required that the radios be coated in a paint with particular characteristics. Industry could choose to paint them shocking pink. However, consulting the Military team would enable them to realise that the customer would much prefer green. The Military Team could not however advise industry directly to make changes that would incur costs above those budgeted for. If green paint cost a larger amount contractual issues would then need to be considered.[13]

The third strand to the project involved placing the financial burden on the defence industry to carry out the conceptual studies. The Ministry of Defence further realised that few companies could bid for Bowman alone it therefore encouraged the formation of project teams from industry to bid for the project, which was estimated in 1992 as being worth some £2 billion, if it could reproduce Clansman's export success it could ultimately be worth double that figure. The Ministry strategy reflected evidence given by the Chief of Defence Procurement to the House of Commons Committee of Public Accounts. The conclusions of the Committee suggested that;

"we note that he [Chief of Defence Procurement] will place particular emphasis on achieving value for money from sole source supplies, on risk management, on reducing through life support costs and on the provision of information to industry."[14]

Emergence of Industry Bidding Consortia

In the autumn of 1991 three consortia declared their intention to tender for the Bowman programme. The groups known as Arrowhead, Crossbow, and Yeoman comprised companies from across the defence electronics industry in the UK and overseas. By April 1992 formal tenders had to be submitted to the Ministry of Defence. By this point a fourth bidder from the United States had submitted a tender.

The Arrowhead bid arose from Anglo-French collaboration between GEC-Marconi and Thomson-CSF. Given the desire to minimise risk by procuring off the shelf technology, the Arrowhead group were able to offer a recently developed product due to enter service with the French army. GEC's communications director noted, "Thomson already has a state-of-the-art system with the RP4G. There is no point on spending money on developing duplicate technology".[15] Defence industry critics suggested that the Anglo-French bid offered the Ministry of Defence, "short term off the shelf benefits derived from a policy that has the purpose of creating long term employment for Frenchman".[16]

Yeoman represented the efforts of Siemens Plessey and Racal Radio. The division of labour between the companies was planned so that Siemens were responsible as the prime contractor and project management whilst Racal would design, develop, and manufacture the radios. Both companies in the Yeoman consortium had had recent export successes with the Raven system to the Australian Army and Jaguar to the Canadian Army.

The Raven system was a vehicle based VHF radio designed by Siemens-Plessey. This contract provided an entry to supply the raven Advanced VHF radio manpack for the Australian Army against nine other competitors in May 1997.[17] Racal's Jaguar system had by 1993 been adopted by over 40 countries with sales worth over £300m. Racal's involvement as a subcontractor providing 10,000 Jaguar 2000 units to a Canadian company, as the hardware element of its IRIS C3 system. The contract was valued at some £70m.[18]

Yeoman intended to use these products as a base for designing the Bowman family of radios. The striking difference between Arrowhead and Yeoman was the latter indication that it would field new products should it be successful.

The Crossbow bid represented a transatlantic bid to supply the future Bowman system. ITT Defence teamed with British Aerospace (BAE Systems) and others, emphasising the value of procuring a system compatible with that of the United States for use in future coalition operations. A second facet to the Crossbow bid was the implication that technology transfer of the American SINCGARS system would be made available to the UK and likewise the Bowman technologies could be transferred to the United States.[19] Figure 1 summarizes the composition of the teams involved, their proposed solutions for the Bowman requirement:

Team Name	Companies	Equipment	Strengths
Arrowhead.	GEC-Marconi (UK). Thomson-CSF (Fr).	PR4G VHF, Scimitar HF, HaveQuick II UHF.	Proven technology. Cryptography. Involvement in BATES and ADCIS programmes.
Crossbow.	ITT Defence (US). British Aerospace (UK). Northern Telecom. Hunting. Harris. Cossor.	SINCGARS VHF, Falcon RF5021 HF, HaveQuick II UHF.	United States involvement gives access to R&D and Compatibility with US armed forces.
Yeoman.	Siemens Plessey (Ger). Racal.	VHF based on improved Jaguar system.	Experience as Prime contractor for Ptarmigan and successes with Australian Raven system and VICDS demonstrator.
Hughes.	Sensors and Communications Systems division (US).	Equipment in service with the United States armed services.	Reputation. Low risk. Possible economies of scale.

Figure 1: Details of Bowman project groups.[20]

In the competition for the initial contract, defence observers noted that lobbying efforts had focused upon securing UK jobs.[21] GEC argued that its failure to secure Bowman would lead to closure of one of its facilities. Yeoman argued that should Crossbow be awarded the contract it would mean the end of radio manufacture in the UK. Crossbow on the other hand sought to stress that much of its manufacturing would occur in Canada.

There were further industrial developments relevant to the programme during the tendering period. The export success of Thomson CSF's PR4G to Spain, the Netherlands as well as France in 1992 meant that most of the European business for VHF radio was becoming dominated by the French firm.

In August 1993 the contracts for the stage one project definition (PD1) were awarded. Yeoman and Crossbow were the successful bidders and each received a £25 million ($37.5 million) contract to supply samples of production equipment for evaluation by the army.[22]

The Defence Procurement Agency (what was the Procurement Executive and is now Defence Equipment & Support) (Source: Adrian Pingstone via Wikimedia Commons)

Official Scrutiny

Parliamentary scrutiny of the Bowman continued through the mechanism of the Committee of Public Accounts annual review of major projects. The Chief of Defence Procurement, during questioning about the nature of delays or 'project slippage',was keen to emphasise the uniqueness of the Bowman procurement strategy;

"Through the feasibility process we have deliberately kept two people in play with two quite different technical solutions to the problem. Firstly, we have a lot of fascinating competitive pressure on the two to perform well but, equally, we have alternative technical solutions should one prove to be more difficult and expensive than the other." [23]

In terms of progress this evidence related to the feasibility stages of Bowman. A more complete report on the successes and problems of the programme was not completed until the publication of the National Audit Office annual report into Ministry of Defence projects during the summer of 1996.

During this period prior to the National Audit Office report the defence industry had not stood idle. ITT Defence appointed a new director during 1995 who had worked for Plessey's for a decade and had been involved in the development of Bowman's predecessor Clansman.[24] This was an appointment which seemingly placed the right industrial expertise at the head of one of the competitors for the production of Bowman. Furthermore in the political manoeuvring for the contract it provided the Crossbow team with another arrow in their quiver.

In December 1995 the Committee of Public Accounts criticised the Ministry of Defence handling of the programme noting that Bowman, "is now four years late, and which has forced the British Army to continue to use the 1960s technology Clansman system, at an extra cost of £200 million ($312 million)".[25]

The burden of sharing the Research and Development costs of Bowman as the project became increasingly delayed began to become apparent for Racal, part of the Yeoman team. In June 1996 profits fell by over a third in the radio communications business. The company blamed this partially upon increased expenditure on the Bowman programme.[26] The National Audit Office noted that the companies had to spend more than envisaged before the contracts were agreed with the MoD's blessing because the programme has proven "more technically complex than was envisaged".[27]

The National Audit Office annual review of projects in 1995 published a detailed examination of the progress of Bowman.[28] The report outlined the rationale behind the two stage procurement programme which aimed to maximise the ability to deliver the near-term requirements of stage 1 whilst allowing a longer period of time for the more complex C3I studies comprising stage 2 to be developed.[29]

The six month trial of the Yeoman and Crossbow equipment was due to be undertaken starting in March 1996. However the report noted that this was not possible due to the fact that, "the companies could not meet this deadline and this, together with the requirement to provide troops for Bosnia, caused a delay".[30]

In terms of achieving the planned in-service date of December 1995 the report noted that this figure had slipped already to April 2000 or a change of 52 months. The reason cited was that, "two years of the slippage are attributed to unforeseen technical difficulties and the rest is deferment due to budgetary constraints".[31]

An examination of these two factors in greater detail yields an interesting insight into the management of the programme. One of the key features of Bowman was its reliance on current technology to minimise risk and delays. The National Audit Office noted that neither hardware nor software difficulties were the cause of the two-year delay but rather the framework for conducting the technical studies.

The plan was for the feasibility study stage 1 to be of a collaborative nature linking the Ministry of Defence (in a leading role) with the companies, the scientific community and the end user.[32] In practise the use of two competitive teams meant that both were reluctant to release data of a commercially sensitive nature which their competitors might use in order to win the production contracts. This meant that the Ministry of Defence became responsible for more of the work than was initially envisaged.

As to the budgetary constraints that caused the remainder of the delay, the National Audit Office highlighted the broader issues of procurement and the Bowman project's place within them. The Procurement Executive budget co-ordinates the individual project budgets into an aggregated figure. Should this figure exceed the available budget then options have to be applied to bring this into line with the funds available. These options included,

> "The deferral, descoping or cancellation of projects. The projects selected for such action are not necessarily those which have themselves experienced slippage or budget overruns: rather the Department aims to choose those projects where the operational or financial penalties are least."[33]

In terms of these criteria Bowman had been delayed no less than four times in the four years prior to 1995. These delays subsequently led to rising operational costs for the legacy system. Maintaining Clansman beyond its life span had rendered it vulnerable to changing standards across NATO which have led to expenditure in order to keep Clansman effective until Bowman's eventual introduction. Conservative estimates in 1994 placed the financial cost of this as being £50 million per year.[34] This estimate said nothing of the operational hazards of using an out-dated communication system.

The final problems identified by the National Audit Office referred to the issues of Government furnished equipment and information. In order for the contractors to design and manufacture an appropriate product, the government has to supply information about the platforms where such a device needs to be mounted. In the Project Definition Stage 1 (PD1) the Ministry of Defence has to obtain platform information (for ships, vehicles etc.) from the relevant design authority, which was often a commercial company, and pass it onto the contractors. The report described the problems, "many design authorities are unwilling to release proprietary information... Secondly the Department usually have to bear the costs of the design authority assembling the information".[35]

Regarding Government furnished equipment in the context of Bowman, this tended to refer to the vehicle platforms submitted for installation of Bowman or its accessories. Problems in this field refer to some platforms such as ships being difficult to schedule being available for refit. Further some high volume platforms such as the Army's Land Rover fleet exist in a variety of slightly different specifications.[36] The consequence is that if the vehicles differ from the specification submitted to industry the Department becomes liable financially for any special costs incurred in modification. The administration of this activity led to the creation of a database known as the Bowman Installation Requirements Database which enables each platform in service to be checked easily.

An issue related to the installation of Bowman arises when considering projects in their early stages or later. The future scout vehicle TRACER for example was sufficiently in the future for only the vaguest of data to be supplied to them. However the MRAV future armoured vehicle was more advanced and urgently required details as to volume, power requirements and so forth.[37] Although the in-service date for Bowman had moved to March 2002 that would not have been the end of the project. Installation and retro-fitting of Bowman was expected to take a further six years, therefore a full brigade was expected to be operational with Bowman by the end of 2002 and the whole armed forces to be converted by the end of 2008 to the new architecture.

By the end of 1996, Racal Radio, one of the Yeoman companies was experiencing increased financial difficulties. After issuing a profits warning to the financial markets the Chairman of Racal noted that the global market in defence communications was predicted to drop from $2.4 billion in 1996 to $1.9 billion in 2001.[38] This prediction highlighted just how important the Bowman contract with its in service support contract and export potential would be to UK players in the defence electronics sector.

Industry Reaction to Programme Delays

Following this announcement Racal declared its intention to combine with ITT Defence of Crossbow in its bid for Bowman. Having spent £4 million on development and predicted a need to spend a further £50 million before the production contract was granted, clearly the board of Racal felt that it had to be involved with the winning bid at all costs.

1997 brought about further corporate developments. Siemens Plessey declared early in the year that it was seeking a partner or an outright buyer for its defence electronics business. The company's rationale was that, "increasing competition and pressure for strategic alliances meant the business was too small to stand alone".[39]

By March 1997 the Ministry of Defence was forced to acknowledge these developments and formally accepted the merger of the two consortia bidding for the Bowman programme.[40] Crossbow and Yeoman would become Archer because neither group was prepared to invest £50 million in further development costs without the guarantee of receiving the production contract. The Ministry of Defence decided to accept the proposal because it believed that asking new companies to compete for the programme would only add further delays. As noted by one official;

> "The requirement for the competitors to provide private venture funding was tantamount to inviting them to play roulette and put £25m on black! Is it surprising that they decided not to wait for the ball to drop?"[41]

In April 1997 an agreement was signed between Archer, the companies holding shares in Archer and the Ministry of Defence which sought to define the new relationship for the duration of the project. Crossbow and Yeoman had previously spoken to the Ministry about combining to form Archer in 1995, but when the talks fell dormant so did the planned Ministry response, leading to a surprise for the organisation when Archer was formed. Meanwhile, domestic political developments were leading to a change of political administration, which had been involved with Bowman since the start. The incoming Labour government was committed to conducting a defence review.

Within months of the 1997 UK general election and the Labour victory, GEC was cleared to be able to make a bid for Siemen's defence electronics business.[42] By late summer the ownership of the new Archer consortium became clear. The stakes in the new company were 30% each to Racal and Siemen's of the original Yeoman team and 40% to ITT Defence - the United States key player within the Crossbow team. In naming the contractors selected to develop the VHF system within Bowman, the Ministry of Defence, "chose not to have an open competition".[43] The reasons cited for this by Archer Communications were that;

> "The only companies capable of fulfilling these requirements were the ones in the two original consortia ... competition is at the heart of Archer. It is not something that has been thrown away".[44]

During the summer of 1997 military evaluations of communications systems by the United States and British armed forces had led to a re-evaluation of technical requirements.

The VHF transceiver planned for Bowman had a data transfer rate twice that of the US SINCGARS system. However in US Force XXI related exercises, the forces employed found it necessary to use systems with a data transfer rate six times greater.[45] Meanwhile US contractor ITT Defence is working with the US Army to develop a capability twice that used in the Force XXI exercises. A US Army official described the process of digitisation as being akin to, "giving birth to a bale of barbed wire".[46]

By late autumn 1997 the sale of Siemens defence business had been confirmed. Both GEC and Thomson-CSF were unsuccessful in their efforts and instead the company was split with DASA acquiring the German interests and British Aerospace the UK and Australian facilities. The £320m purchase of Siemen's defence interests at this juncture meant that British Aerospace had acquired a 30% stake in the Bowman programme which should be guaranteed to go into production with Siemens as part of the Archer Communications team.[47]

In February 1998 Archer issued tender requests for the HF radio requirement and Local Area Sub-systems worth $300 million.[48] The Managing Director of Archer noted that Bowman was far more complex than Trident and that Bowman would be the largest conversion programme since the Second World War involving 25,000 vehicles from 1,000 types and 130 families.[49]

Furthermore Archer's Chief Executive gave a practitioners definition of the ministry's improved procurement process or 'smart procurement' as it would influence Bowman;

"Smart procurement says don't place it all in one contract because it will take you forever to negotiate. So bite off sensible chunks of work and place contracts for that and then negotiate the rest".[50]

A further proposal within the smart procurement framework was the idea of single integrated project teams or IPT's, an amalgam of personnel from all the relevant areas such as contracting, military requirements and so forth for the duration of the project. In terms of this concept the Bowman programme appeared to have measured up well. The contracts staff had been closely tied in, if not co-located geographically, with the project team since the early stages of the project.

Some staff located in London had access through specialised computer terminals to the Bowman project office and could contribute rapidly. Furthermore, Archer Communications were to supply the Procurement Executive with a terminal linking the Bowman team to their computer network as well as having limited access to those operated by the Bowman project office.[51]

In April 1998, the competitors for the Local Area Sub-systems contract, which aimed to facilitate multimedia communications between command vehicles, was announced. The two consortia pitted Racal and Thomson-CSF against a group known as 'The Command Team' comprising Hunting, Bae (BAE Systems) and CDC of Canada. Archer expected to announce the winning bid later in 1998 [52] The solutions are compared in Figure 2 below:

Companies	Equipment	Strengths
Racal Radio & Thomson-CSF	ATM solution. Internal data rate (in principle) of 155 Mbps. Upgrade capacity to 622 Mbps +.	* Scalability to handle future communication systems integrated into Bowman. * expansion capability.
Hunting Engineering, Siemens Plessey, CDC Canada, and BAe SEMA (BAE Systems).	MOSAIC VEDS solution. 155 Mbps bandwidth (can be upgraded to 622 Mbps +). ATM protocol for MOSAIC VEDS whilst the VIDS, vehicle based system will have IP protocol (26 Mbps expandable to 52 Mbps).	* Command Team believe ATM protocol outdated. More 'future-proof' by mixing protocols. * IP offers superior communications to ATM (According to Command Team).

Figure 2: Composition of Bowman LAS project teams.[53]

The announcement of the invitation to tender for the Local Area Sub-systems contract led to intensified political lobbying efforts by the companies involved. One industry source suggested that the contract's main significance was in terms of positioning for future communication projects;

"Whoever wins the LAS is in pole position for replacement of the [British Army's] Ptarmigan and other future communications systems up to strategic level... These could be worth a total approaching 1.6 billion pounds to the winner."[54]

The political lobbying had elements similar to those observed in earlier stages of the Bowman programme. The Hunting team indicated that production of their LAS proposal would be conducted in Britain at the same site as Bowman's radio elements. Furthermore the Hunting team intimated that the involvement of Thomson-CSF (the alternative to their own proposal) would see intellectual property rights being held outside Britain. Racal subsequently stated that they would produce 100% of the LAS in the UK and that intellectual property rights in their bud would reside with the Ministry of Defence.[55]

The publication of the annual National Audit Office report concerning major Ministry of Defence projects sought to consider the changes in the structure of the procurement of Bowman.[56]

The NAO felt that the reason for the creation of Archer and the collapse of its continuous competition strategy lay in the original requirement;

"The original requirement had been expressed in terms of a performance specification, rather than a detailed technical specification and design".[57]

However, in considering the generation of the military requirement it is important to note that by specifying performance criteria, the customer could revise it in order to benefit from the rapid improvements in technology. It could be suggested that this technique was not incompatible with the proposed Smart Procurement Initiative whereby prior to production future equipment will be assessed to ensure that it has not been rendered less effective than envisaged due to environmental change.

The technical problems for the contractors led to their requesting further time thus pushing back the in-service date. Further the technical problems required the companies to spend more on their development increasing their risk, given that the team that lost would receive no compensation.

The Ministry's response to having had its competitors merge was to accept the merger but proceed on a single source (NAPNOC) basis.[58] In value terms the Ministry of Defence believed that Bowman would use NAPNOC for 10% of the project costs with the remainder being on a competitive basis.[59]

The NAO in their findings saw strengths and weaknesses in this revised strategy. In positive terms the Ministry of Defence would have full visibility of the contractor's pricing. On the negative side the Department has no precedents to refer to. The Ministry had no experience of procuring a communications system of this type by this method before. The Clansman system was produced in a different industrial, administrative and legal environment, which limited its teaching value for those wrestling with the Bowman programme.

After the intense period of the 1990s, Bowman finally worked its way towards being fielded though felt pressure from the emergence of battlefield digitization (the early UK effort being known as Network Enabled Capability or NEC). In 2001, against a backdrop of intense defence industry change, the Ministry of Defence awarded CDC Systems (General

Dynamics) the £1.7 billion contract.

The Bowman system entered service in Iraq (2004) and subsequently Afghanistan in a limited manner with a major software upgrade paving the way for more full functionality in 2008.[60]

A soldier of the Royal Signals with a Bowman 325 man pack radio in Lashkar Gar province, Afghanistan (Source: defenceimagery.mod.uk)

Conclusion

This case study has sought to show the project management aspects of Bowman as well as the progress of the project and the changing industrial and political conditions throughout the 1990s. Attached to this case study are selected data about the progress of Bowman from National Audit Office reports concerning costs incurred until the late 1990s, as well as the changing predictions of the volumes required.

What was conceived in the late 1980s as a gentlemanly incremental upgrade in capability became hostage to technological fortune as the information revolution and fast innovation of the 1990s and early 2000s threatened to change the program shape. Among the many lessons of Bowman it could be suggested there are three key outcomes.

Firstly, no matter the procurement plan, the defence industry will as a matter of necessity incurred by the length of the program change shape to survive in order to secure the business.

Second, the ability to reach a decision on requirements relatively rapidly and move the program forward was essential.

Third, as the Royal Navy often remark, "no plan survives contact with salt water" building on Prussian military wisdom. The late 1980s definers of Bowman could only vaguely perceive digitisation, NEC, and C4ISTAR. The length of procurement exposed Bowman to all these developments and left the project team in a quandary of moving to production or trying to capture the developments in the programme, akin, as stock traders remark on when to buy a share whose value is continually falling, hoping it will bottom and turn around as "catching a falling knife".

A member of the King's Royal Hussars with a Personal Role Radio in Afghanistan (Source: Cpl Paul Morrison via Flickr / defenceimagery.mod.uk)

APPENDICE ONE: SELECTED DATA

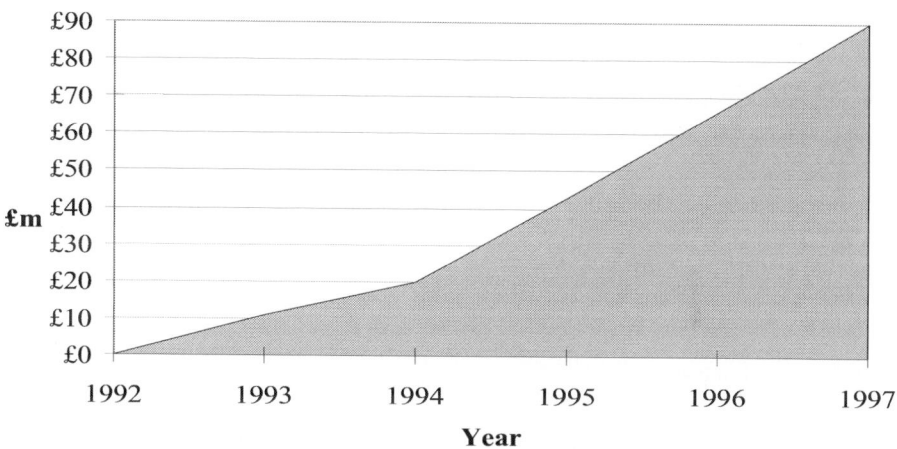

Figure 3: Costs incurred during Bowman programme during the 1990s.

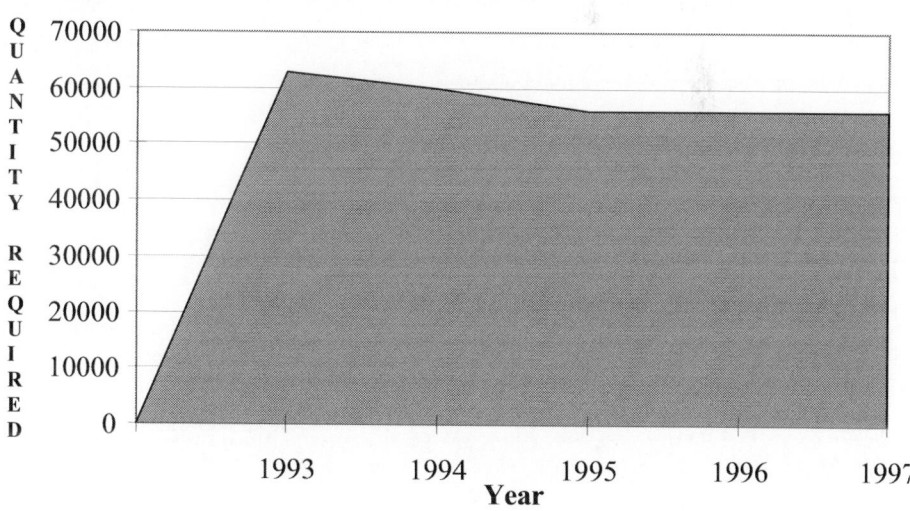

Figure 4: Unit volume of Bowman systems required during the 1990s.

Endnotes

[1] For details of the Strategic Defence Review see Her Majesty's Stationery Office. *Strategic Defence Review: Modern forces for the modern* world (London: HMSO 1998). For earlier efforts see Options for Change and Front Line First. For commentary see Codner, M. *Policy topped but Treasury tailed ? The Strategic Defence Review.* The Officer 10 (4), 1998, pp. 30 - 33. Also Codner, M. *The Strategic Defence Review - A good job.* RUSI Newsbrief, 18 (8), 1998. pp. 57 - 59.

[2] Witt, M. 'Bowman's many strings' in *Military Technology* (Nov. 1992). p. 64.

[3] *Ibid.* pp. 62 - 64.

[4] McLean, D J. 'Future radio' in *Journal of the Royal Signals institute* 19 (4) (Summer 1990). p. 253.

[5] *Defence Industry Digest* 8 (8) (Dec. 1991). 'Bowman'. The acronyms refer to JTIDS - Joint Tactical Information Distribution System. BATES - Battlefield Artillery Target Engagement System. ADCIS - Air Defence Command Information System.

[6] Discussions with Ministry of Defence, Abbey Wood. June 1998.

[7] Discussion with serving officer May 1998.

[8] The Defence Evaluation and Research Agency (DERA) was the fore-runner organization to the Defence Science & Technical Laboratory (DSTL) and QinetiQ.

[9] Discussion with Ministry of Defence, Abbey Wood. June 1998.

[10] Combined Operational Effectiveness and Investment Appraisal process or COEIA.

[11] Jane's International Defence Review 5/1992. 'Battle begins for Bowman'. p. 434.

[12] *Jane's Defence Weekly* (08/02/92). 'Costing out the options'. p. 205.

[13] Discussions with Ministry of Defence, Abbey Wood. June 1998.

[14] House of Commons. *HC143 Committee of Public Accounts 10th report: The 1990 statement on major defence projects and the 1989 summary of post costing activity.* (London: Her Majesty's Stationery Office 13/07/92). p. viii. para. 9.

[15] *Jane's Defence Weekly* (02/11/91). 'Arrowhead to bid for Bowman'. p. 846.

[16] *Defence Industry Digest* 8 (8) (Dec. 1991). 'Bowman'. p. 2.

[17] *International Defence Review* 28 (5) (May 1995). 'Australia seeks combat net radio'. p. 21. Also *Ibid.* 30 (5) (May 1997). 'Australia advanced VHF manpack'. p. 21.

[18] *Jane's Defence Weekly* (14/08/93). 'Battlefield electronics: Update'. p. 22.

[19] *Jane's Defence Weekly* (22/08/92). 'Bowman battle begins'. pp. 27 - 30.

[20] *Jane's International Defence Review* 5/1992. 'Battle begins for Bowman'. pp. 434 - 435. See also *Jane's Defence Weekly* (22/08/92). 'Bowman battle begins'. pp. 27 - 30.

[21] *Defence Industry Digest* 9 (12) (April 1993). 'Bowman and beyond'. p. 3.

[22] *Jane's Defence Weekly* (28/08/93). 'Contract award takes Bowman forward'. p. 11. Note monetary figures are 1993 values.

[23] House of Commons. *HC42 Committee of Public Accounts 1st Report: Ministry of Defence: The major projects report (1993).* (London: Her Majesty's Stationery Office 23/11/94). p. 17. para. 28.

[24] *Financial Times* (31/05/95). 'Craen comes back to communications at ITT'.

[25] *Financial Times* (01/12/95). 'Defence ministry criticised over weapons projects'. All monetary figures in 1995 values.

[26] *Financial Times* (06/06/96). 'Racal to reorganise data products side'.

[27] National Audit Office. *HC677 Ministry of Defence: Major projects report 1995.* (London: Her Majesty's Stationery Office 09/08/96). Part 3. p. 24. para. 3.9.

[28] *Ibid.* Part 3. pp. 21 - 29.

[29] *Ibid.* Part 3. p. 22. para. 3.5.

[30] *Ibid.* Part 3. p. 23 - 24. para. 3.8

[31] *Ibid.* Part 3. p. 24. para. 3.12.

[32] *Ibid.* Part 3. p 25. para. 3.15.

[33] *Ibid.* Part 3. para. 3.19. pp. 25 - 26.

[34] *Ibid.* Part 3. para. 3.23. p. 26.

[35] *Ibid.* p. 27. para. 3.28.

[36] *Ibid.* p. 28. para. 3.30.

[37] Discussions with Ministry of Defence, Abbey Wood. June 1998. MRAV and TRACER morphed into the FRES program.

[38] *Financial Times* (04/12/96). 'Hold-ups force Racal on to the defensive'.

[39] *Financial Times* (28/02/97). 'Siemens seeks defence partner'.

[40] *Financial Times* (21/03/97). 'MoD accepts radio bid by merged rivals'.

[41] Discussions with Ministry of Defence, Abbey Wood. June 1998.

[42] *Financial Times* (12/07/97). 'GEC bid for Siemens' defence business cleared'.

[43] *Financial Times* (29/08/97). 'Battlefield systems deal to secure 7,000 jobs'.

[44] *Ibid.*

[45] *International Defence review* 30 (9) (Sept. 1997). 'Bandwidth boost sought for Bowman'. p. 13.

[46] *International Defence Review* 30 (9) (Sept. 1997). 'International digitisers wrestle with reality'. p. 38.

[47] *Racal Business Bulletin* (05/11/97). 'Acquisition of Siemens Plessey by BAe and impact on Archer'.

[48] *Jane's Defence Weekly* (04/02/98). 'Smart procurement will keep Bowman on track'. p. 20.

[49] *Ibid.* See also Archer Communications Systems Ltd. *UK Armed Forces conversion to Bowman.* (1997). This publication indicates the scale of the conversion effort: 260 Ships & boats, 450 Aircraft, 23,000 Land vehicles, 180 Buildings, and 120,000 people from the services and the reserves.

[50] *Ibid.* p. 21.

[51] Discussion with Ministry of Defence, Abbey Wood. June 1998. The Procurement Executive became part of the Defence Procurement Agency or DPA which in turn is currently known as DE&S following the DPA / DLO merger.

[52] *Racal Business Bulletin* (01/04/98). 'Racal Radio and Thomson-CSF team collaborate for Bowman LAS bid'. See also *Ibid.* (20/05/98). 'Racal Radio submits Bowman LAS bid'.

[53] *Jane's Defence Weekly* (08.04.98). 'Bowman advance gathers speed'. p. 12. See also *Electronic Times* (05/05/98). 'Military might of Bowman'. p. 20. ATM is described as, 'Asynchronous transfer mode (ATM) was developed to take advantage of the massive bandwidths available on modern fibre optic cables, and is now a global open standard'. Scalability is described further, 'ATM is able to cope with multiple speeds on one network. This means that no protocol conversion is incurred when crossing narrow transmission paths, typically wan links or copper turret junction boxes in armoured vehicles'.

[54] *Defense News* (18-24/05/98). 'U.K. Bowman network bidding turns political'. p. 4 & 44.

[55] *Ibid.* p. 44.

[56] National Audit Office. *HC695 Ministry of Defence major projects report 1997* (London: Her Majesty's Stationery Office 13/05/98). pp. 34 - 40.

[57] *Ibid.* p. 35. para. 3.19.

[58] *Ibid.* p. 144. NAPNOC is defined in the report as, 'The Department's policy for non-competitive pricing which seeks to replicate the pressures of competitive procurement in which a price is secured at the outset through the tendering process. Under the NAPNOC policy, non-competitive contracts are only placed when a price has been agreed which reflects what it should cost an efficient contractor to carry out the work. NAPNOC contracts must, therefore, be priced before a contract is placed'.

[59] *Ibid.* p. 36. para. 3.22.

[60] See H Kenyon, *U.K. Communications on Target* (Signal online: 2001), A Baddeley, *Bowman hits the mark* (Signal Magazine: 2004), Defense Update, *Bowman General Dynamics UK* (2005: Issue 3), H Kenyon, *Bowman Achieves Full Operational Capability* (Signal online: 2008) for more recent developments.

European Collaborative Procurement – The Multi-Role Armoured Vehicle Programme

....

Peter D. Antill

Centre for Defence Acquisition, Cranfield University, Defence Academy of the UK.

Introduction

This is a case study of British, German and French acquisition and how plans for the process evolved. It highlights not only the overall timeline of events, but the overlapping requirements and the politics of forming a collaborative venture and procurement strategy. Not only that, but it also looks at how a single project can be linked to wider political purposes, including industrial restructuring and the creation of a European armaments agency.

A New Requirement

Most armies in the world operate a mix of wheeled and tracked armoured personnel carriers and infantry fighting vehicles to carry their infantry around and undertake essential support roles. Tracked vehicles tend to have better mobility across rough terrain than their wheeled counterparts, but the overall trend since the end of the Cold War has been the steady increase in the use of wheeled vehicles leading to a more balanced fleet in many armies.

Tracked Infantry Fighting Vehicles (IFVs) normally have greater armour protection, mobility and firepower than Armoured Personnel Carriers (APCs), but their most significant drawback is the very high acquisition and total life cycle costs. While early wheeled APCs were often based on 4 x 4 truck chassis, the latest ones are 6 x 6 or even 8 x 8. With advances in technology (better engines, drive trains, suspension and tyres), they can often have a cross-country mobility that matches the tracked IFVs. They are also easier to maintain and have lower life cycle costs, and have very good road speed, and hence better strategic mobility.

In the early 1990s, both the French and German Armies had a requirement for a new family of wheeled armoured vehicles, called the VBM (Vehicules Blindes Modulaires or Modular Armoured Vehicle) in France and GTK (Gepanzerte Transport – Kraftfahrzeuge) in Germany. The French required them to have high cross-country mobility, so that they would be able to keep up with the LeClerc MBT that was just coming into service (from

Giat Industries), have modular protection, a good load carrying capability and be simple to maintain. It was intended to replace the fully tracked AMX-10P and wheeled VAB (4 x 4) vehicles, with up to 3,000 vehicles being needed.

Examples of contemporary IFVs: BAE Systems Warrior (Source: davric via Wikimedia Commons) and an SPZ Marder (Source: Kombat via Wikimedia Commons)

The German requirement was very similar, in that the vehicle should replace the Transportpanzer 1 (6 x 6) and the M113 series of tracked APCs. As a result, a new consortium was formed to bid for the new vehicles. It consisted of Giat Industries, Panhard, Krauss-Maffei and Mercedes-Benz. It was formed in order to develop an entire family of 4 x 4, 6 x 6 and 8 x 8 wheeled APCs that had excellent cross-country mobility and had common automotive systems. Just before the formation of this consortium, Giat Industries, as a private venture, built the prototype of a new 8 x 8 high mobility demonstrator, which they called the Vextra. This could have been an effort to seize *de facto* project leadership.

It was initially expected that the consortium would eventually become a joint venture company, which would design, bid for and hopefully produce the family of vehicles. For a number of reasons, this failed to materialise, and Germany went ahead on its own with the GTK project.

The UK MoD had been looking at a requirement for a Multi-Role Armoured Vehicle, and Roger Freeman, the then Minister of State for Procurement, met with both his French and German counterparts in February 1995. The UK requirement was initially for both a tracked APC (known as the M1P1 and to be procured on a national basis) and a lighter wheeled vehicle (known as the M2P2). Both would replace the current tracked FV432, the wheeled Saxon (4 x 4) APC and the particular members of the Alvis Scorpion family of tracked reconnaissance vehicles that would not be replaced by TRACER (Tactical Reconnaissance Armoured Combat Equipment Requirement).

At the time (mid-1990s) the British Army's armoured infantry battalions were equipped with the Warrior IFV, and the armoured regiments had started to receive the Challenger 2 (the final delivery being on 17 April 2002). However, many older vehicles still served in support roles, and their shortcomings were highlighted in the Gulf War. The UK Minister made it clear that he preferred to have two consortia competing for the UK needs. The UK subsequently decided to join the German GTK project, as our requirements were very similar to Germany's, and the project was seen as a way of entering the proposed European Armaments Procurement Agency.

Rationalisation

The end of the Cold War brought political, geographical and strategic changes to Europe, and a challenge to the Defence Industry. For with the disappearance of the 'threat' from the Soviet Union and its military alliance, the Warsaw Pact, the states of Western Europe and North America sought a peace dividend, to release funds for reinvestment in other pressing domestic needs. As a consequence, defence budgets shrank considerably, meaning fewer orders being made for new equipment and upgrades. This had an impact on the defence industrial base, with a number of mergers and acquisitions meaning fewer companies (in the USA at any rate) chasing fewer contracts, both at home and abroad.

The aerospace sector in the United States led the way in regard to rationalisation. A number of key mergers and buy-outs resulted in the contraction in the number of American companies to just four: Boeing, Lockheed Martin, Hughes-Raytheon and Northrop Grumman. A similar process started with regard to land systems. BMY Combat Systems (which was owned by the Harsco Corporation) and the Defence Systems Group of the FMC Corporation joined together to become United Defense, L.P. in 1994 (which makes the Bradley Mechanised Infantry Combat Vehicle), with a gradual shift of its production facilities from California to Pennsylvania.

General Dynamics Land Systems bought some of the business units from Lockheed Martin (who had acquired them from General Electric), as well as Teledyne Vehicle Systems who build the AVDS 1790 diesel engine, as well as armoured vehicle upgrades and suspension. General Dynamics are the prime contractor for the M1 Abrams MBT and Wolverine Heavy Assault Bridge, but has enlarged its overall product line to include a number of other weapon and transmission systems.

Europe, however, was slow to respond to the new challenges, the exception being ammunition manufacturers, who have been reduced to one major supplier in both France (Giat) and the UK (originally Royal Ordnance, now part of BAE Systems), and two in Germany (Diehl and Rheinmetall). With regard to armoured vehicles, in Europe as a whole there were twenty-three companies (compared to two in the US) that were facing increased competition for fewer contracts. Many experts believed that rationalization was becoming inevitable, but was complicated by the fact that land system collaboration did not have an enviable record (the MBT-70 and SP-70 artillery systems were just two examples), let alone European collaboration as a whole (for example Trimilsat and Horizon).

The OCCAR

The Eurocopter Tiger (Source: Dmitrij Rodionov via Wikimedia Commons)

In 1994, Germany and France promoted the notion of a European armaments agency which would improve the management of joint projects. In particular, 'juste retour' – where the proportion of contracts under a particular programme awarded to firms from a given country is in proportion to the funding that country has contributed to the programme – would cease to operate as a basis for allocating contracts. Both Britain and Italy expressed an interest in joining the emerging organisation. British membership was *de facto* justified on the grounds of the UK involvement in the MRAV / GTK / VBM project. The Franco-German agency emerged in 1996 and was called the Joint Organisation for Arms Cooperation by the European Parliament, but has been more commonly known as *Organisation Conjointe de Coopération en matière d'ARmement* (OCCAR).

The new multinational procurement organisation was originally envisaged as eventually becoming part of the Western European Union (WEU), but instead has linked itself to the European Union (EU) and European Defence Agency (EDA). It has concentrated on steadily formalising its cooperative approach to research and development. It originally incorporated four joint programmes for its original members – UK, Germany, France and Italy – which were the Eurocopter Tiger, Euromissile's Roland surface-to-air missile, as well as the Milan and HOT anti-tank missiles. OCCAR members now number six (Belgium and Spain having since joined) with another six associated countries also taking part in various programmes. These are Finland, Sweden, Poland, Luxembourg, the Netherlands and Turkey.

At the time, it seemed likely that the MRAV programme would come under OCCAR's umbrella. Other candidates included the Cobra counter-battery radar, the Brevel target drone, the Trimilsatcom military communications satellite, the TRIGAT anti-tank missile, the Helios / Horus reconnaissance satellite, a future surface-to-air missile (FSAM) and the PzH2000 155mm howitzer. The aim of OCCAR was to promote cost effectiveness, the rationalisation of programmes and contracting procedures, the appointment of some transnational design authorities, greater competition, and replacement of 'juste retour' by a multinational multi-programme balance (that is, removing the politically sensitive work share agreement for each project, and assigning it over a number of programmes).

However, the OCCAR nations had differing attitudes to both the development of a common defence policy (which is different to arms cooperation) and to the integration of the WEU into the EU. The UK traditionally had a distrust of both concepts. But the call by Prime Minister Tony Blair during the informal EU summit in Portschach, in late October 1998 for 'fresh thinking' on European collaboration and cooperation meant a change of direction, confirmed by the 'Joint Declaration on European Defence' published at a Franco-British summit at St Malo in December. Some UK sources (such as Saferworld, a foreign affairs 'think-tank') pointed out that Article 223 of the Treaty of Rome exempts the production of, and trade in, arms and materials of a defence nature from the usual necessity to conduct a competition for public contracts. The European Commission subsequently indicated that Article 223 does not give member states any general exclusive powers, or that there are areas of national security, which are not covered by subsequent treaties (a reference to the 1992 Maastricht and 1997 Amsterdam Treaties). Besides, new cross-border industrial linkages and mergers make the application of national arms export policies very difficult, and show the need for a common approach, if not policy.

Continued splits over a common defence policy, as well as European defence and security issues (such as the cost of NATO expansion, the future role of the WEU and Organisation for Security and Co-operation in Europe (OSCE), Bosnia, Albania and Kosovo) and differing national industrial philosophies meant that this issue rumbled on for years. A small step in the right direction was achieved in late 1998 when the UK, Italy, France and Germany gave OCCAR the legal power to place and manage contracts, as well as employ its own staff.

Countries that want to join OCCAR have to meet certain criteria, such as agreeing with the principles of cooperative development and purchase, and joining one of the programmes being handled. At the time, one strong contender to join was the Netherlands, which was looking to join the MRAV project, to replace its YPR-765 APCs (a modified and upgraded M113) and M577 command vehicles. This came after the Dutch ruled out the Italian Centauro (due to the lack of opportunity for industrial collaboration in the development phase of the programme) and the American M2 / M3 Bradley replacement (which still hasn't become available).

A Dutch YPR-765A1 APC (Source: Rasbak via Wikimedia Commons)

The Start of Procurement

In January 1996, the German MoD (the lead organisation which defined the baseline vehicle) issued an invitation to tender (ITT) to a number of German companies, who gradually teamed up with a number of companies from the United Kingdom. Finally, in March 1997, the two consortia submitted their individual proposals to the German Bundesamt für Wehrtechnik und Beschaffung (the Federal Office of Defence Technology and Procurement – BWB) to develop a wheeled family of vehicles. The first consortium (the Eurokonsortium, later known as ARTEC – ARmoured vehicle TECnology) consisted of GKN Defence (UK), Krauss-Maffei, Rheinmetall / MaK, Wegmann (Germany) and Giat (Italy) with the second one (TEAM International) having Vickers Defence Systems and Alvis Vehicles (UK), Henschel Wehrtechnik / KUKA (Germany) and Panhard (France) coming back to the project. The British requirement was for around 1,100 vehicles, with an initial batch of 200 (with 200 for both France and Germany as well), with seven possible versions:

- Armoured Personnel Carrier (180).
- Command Vehicle (470).
- Communications Vehicle (110).
- Armoured Treatment and Evacuation Vehicle (185).
- Armoured Repair and Recovery Vehicle (quantity undecided).
- Armoured Mortar Vehicle (quantity undecided).
- Mortar Fire Control Vehicle (quantity undecided).

Although the M2P2 was required to operate behind the Forward Edge of the Battle Area (FEBA) it was to have good armour protection and mobility, with a low signature, and have a reasonable upgrade potential. This was especially important with regard to the armour, so it could be upgraded to the same level as the M1P1 if necessary. The M1P1 was required to operate in the FEBA, and have the mobility to keep up with the Challenger 2 and Warrior Mechanised Infantry Combat Vehicle (MICV).

Battle is Joined

As the date for the announcement drew closer, so the war of words became stronger, and started to take on the shape of the opening rounds in the battle to dominate Europe's armoured vehicle industry. Both sides vigorously lobbied their respective Ministries of Defence, and the German procurement agency, theBWB. GKN's Managing Director claimed that whoever would win this contract would lead the consolidation of the industry. While rumours began to mount that the Eurokonsortium had won, Vickers led a last minute attempt to persuade both the UK Ministry of Defence, and German BWB of the virtues of their consortium's bid. The company claimed that the Germans had rushed the decision in order to get it through the Bundestag (Parliament) before the general election, due to be held later that year.

Vickers argued that Britain was in danger of being railroaded into a decision due to German political ambitions that may not be in the best interest of the British taxpayer, and that if their consortium won, more work would come to the UK due to the involvement of both Vickers and Alvis. This was disputed by GKN, who insisted that all the design work for their bid was done equally, and work on the first batch of 600 vehicles would be shared evenly between the UK and Germany. There was also concern from Vickers about the move late in the competition towards favouring an 8 x 8 configuration, even though a 6 x 6 configuration was favoured originally, and it only had a short period of time to enter an 8 x 8 design.

Vickers also wanted a delay in the announcement so that both sides could build a prototype, instead of purely relying on the scrutiny of designs, a move that had attracted some criticism. Additionally, German sources indicated that some in the Bundesheer (German Army) were concerned about the anticipated decision to go forward with the Eurokonsortium proposal. The Bundesheer favoured a 6 x 6 vehicle for the troop carrying role, with a small number of 8 x 8 vehicles for a number of specialised roles, such as command posts, or 120mm mortar carriers. An 8 x 8 would have greater internal volume and cross-country mobility, but it would also be more expensive to procure, operate and maintain (up to fifteen per cent).

Both GKN and Vickers were looking to add to their order book as GKN (who made the Piranha wheeled vehicle and Warrior MICVs) only had orders until the end of 1999 and needed a new order to secure 500 jobs in Telford as production of the Desert Warrior (for Kuwait) was coming to an end. Vickers needed orders (despite the probable orders for tanks to South Africa and Qatar), as the order for the British Army's Challenger 2 tanks was now running down, and it had a workforce of 1,500 split between Leeds and Newcastle. The loss of the contract would be a major blow to the company, and possibly to the northeast, which had seen a number of large-scale job losses in recent years.

Eurokonsortium Wins

On 22 April 1998, it was announced that the Eurokonsortium of GKN, Krauss-Maffei, Wegmann, Rheinmetall / MaK and Giat had won the competition, estimated to be worth up to £3bn. This was to provide vehicles for the UK, France, Germany and the Netherlands as well, with Italy, Spain and Poland expressing an interest. The programme was to be managed by the new Organisation for Joint Armament Co-Operation (OCCAR). While details about the share of the work remained sketchy, it was believed that Germany would provide the engine, transmission and the complete running gear, the UK would provide the baseline armoured hulls (drive modules) and France the mission module.

There was a question over the continuation of the project as the losing consortium (TEAM International – Vickers / Alvis / KUKA / Henschel and Panhard) applied to the Federal Court of Comptrollers (BRH) in Germany arguing that the rules of the competition had been unfairly changed during the process. The Court overruled this, but at the same time, questioned the validity of the GTK calculation by the German MoD suggesting that instead of the DM6 billion ($3.3 billion) the Ministry of Defence had quoted, the project may cost closer to DM8 billion for the procurement of the 3,000 vehicles.

There were still however, some questions as to the continued French involvement with the project. Some industrialists in France (as well as some in the UK) saw the selection of Eurokonsortium as another step in the German strategy to become the predominant player in the European land warfare systems industry, with the tacit approval of both the UK and French Governments.

The issue was further complicated by the fact that Vickers had started talks with Giat Industries, with a prospect of closer ties between the two companies and the possibility of a joint venture to manufacture an armoured IFV to meet French requirements. This, incidentally, was started about the same time Vickers was talking to GKN about a possible merger, which didn't come to anything in the end, due to a disagreement on price. Vickers declared that it had not given up on the order, as there was a review scheduled after the initial stage. Vickers was also seeking support from a number of German MPs who had backed the company and its partners.

There were claims that the order was pushed through by the 'Bavarian Mafia', as the key German companies in the GKN consortium were based in Bavaria. Vickers stated that although it was disappointed at not winning the contract, its order book was healthy (£1.5bn) and had strong hopes of increasing its export orders for the Challenger 2.

The win however was welcomed by GKN, which stated that it would safeguard the 500 jobs at its site in Telford, and possibly lead to more, if more orders came in. The decision was greeted by the Secretary of State for Defence, George Robertson, as a boost for the European defence industry, which had been (and still is) under governmental pressure to consolidate in the face of US competition. The contract could provide a focal point for the consolidation of the industry. Certainly the MRAV was, at the time, Europe's largest ever collaborative procurement programme for armoured vehicles, and numbers could have topped 7,000 if other European states had decided to join. It was one of the first projects to be overseen by OCCAR.

There was however, some confusion as to its precise value. GKN had stated that the MRAV project would have been worth some £800m to the company, if it ran to the projected 5,000 vehicles. This number was somewhat higher than the figures that had been used by the UK MoD. The initial contract for 600 vehicles was estimated to be worth around £500m. The French had been the sleeping partner, but objected to the plan to announce a major defence programme without French industrial participation, even though there was some doubt as to the final number required by the French Army.

GKN was also under the impression that it was going to be a mainly Anglo-German project until the French objected. Defence industry officials in the UK were also unhappy about the possibility of a deal that excluded France as a major participant, and were not sure about the final numbers that Britain would require as it was still working through the implications of its Strategic Defence Review. The losing consortium was still bitter about losing to what it called a last minute change in preference from a 6 x 6 configuration to an 8 x 8 one, and announced their intention to develop their own MRAV prototype.

Additionally, given that the final figure for the British Army had yet to be finalised, it was unclear whether the UK MoD could have funded it, as well as all the new projects that were planned for the first decade of the 21st Century. These included the Challenger 2 MBT, WAH-64 Longbow Apache attack helicopter and the Bowman communications system, but also potentially MRAV (M1P1 and M2P2 variants), TRACER and FRES (Future Rapid Effects System), Warrior mid-life improvement, the Terrier engineer vehicle and Future Engineer Tank Programme.

An AH-64D Longbow Apache (Source: Tech. Sgt. Andy Dunaway, US Army via Wikimedia Commons)

Two Steps Forward, One Step Back

The rationalisation process seemed to have finally started in the last few months of 1998 and the first few months of 1999. The merger of the defence businesses of GKN and Alvis was announced in September 1998 (Alvis had acquired Hagglunds AB in 1997), while the merger of the GKN owned Westland Helicopters with Agusta of Italy occurred in July 2000 (to form Agusta Westland). In addition, Vickers bought Ulstein Holding, a marine engineering group, while GKN bought Interlake Corporation, a US powder, metallurgy, aerospace components and industrial services company. Vickers was acquired by Rolls-Royce PLC in 1999 which then sold the defence arm (renamed Vickers Defence Systems) to Alvis, which became Alvis Vickers in 2002. BAE Systems eventually bought out Alvis Vickers in June 2004 with a £355m bid, beating US giant General Dynamics and ensuring that British armoured vehicle production would stay in the UK. Soon after it became part of the new BAE Systems Land Systems division.

The MRAV contract was finally placed in November 1999. On 31 January 2001 the Dutch Parliament gave clearance for their MoD to join the MRAV programme, effectively ignoring the efforts by the indigenous contractor, RDM Technology BV, and its Swiss partner MOWAG to promote a solution based on that company's Piranha IV vehicle. This committed the Dutch to invest $100m (NLG245m) in the programme, their requirement being for 384 vehicles with the prime contractor being Stork. Along with the GKN-Alvis merger, and the merger in 1999 of Krauss-Maffei Wehrtechnik and Wegmann GmbH & Co. as well as the acquisition of MaK, KUKA and Henschel by Rheinmetall (to form its Land Systems division in 2000) this meant that the ARTEC Consortium now consisted of Krauss-Maffei Wegmann, Rheinmetall Landsysteme, Stork NV and Alvis Vehicles, a significant proportion of which was the former TEAM International consortium. France had pulled out in 1996 to pursue its national Vehicule Blinde de Combat d'Infantrie (VBCI) programme, which eventually saw Giat team up with Renault.

A French VBCI wheeled IFV (Source: Selvejp via Wikimedia Commons)

While German and Dutch commitment remained strong, British interest in the project started to wane and change to the proposed FRES vehicle. Part of the reason was that the final design, at a combat weight of thirty-three tonnes (eight tons of which would be payload), a length of 7.88m, a width of 2.99m and a height of 2.37m (without armament), would be too big and heavy to fit into a C-130 and therefore unsuitable for rapid deployment missions that the British Army was restructuring to undertake. The British decision to withdraw from the programme was made in July 2003 with the then Defence Procurement Minister, Lord Bach, stating that MRAV was too heavy to fulfil the British Army's need for a lighter armoured vehicle, capable of being transported quickly by air to a trouble spot. The decision, however, while being couched in terms of a requirements mismatch, is open to question as the RAF had taken delivery of its first C-17A Globemaster transport aircraft on 17 May 2001, over two years before the decision to withdraw was made. The RAF now flies eight such aircraft, each of which has a 77,000kg payload capability, and can carry one M1 Abrams Main Battle Tank, three Strykers or six M1117 Armoured Security Vehicles. Carrying three (empty) or two fully-laden MRAVs would not have presented any problems. The A400-M transport aircraft should also be able to lift a single MRAV. Of course, one of the more frustrating developments for the UK MoD is that due to the need for heavier armour on the FRES Utility Vehicle (UV), the weight of the baseline FRES UV has increased from around seventeen tonnes to almost thirty tonnes negating the ability of the C-130 Hercules to transport it.

By the time of the UK's withdrawal from the project, the vehicle had been renamed 'Boxer' and prototypes were gradually being rolled out. Rheinmetall Landsysteme and Krauss-Maffei Wegmann provided the Boxer's diesel power pack, drive train and electronics, Stork PV supplied the subsystems, while Alvis Vickers provided the chassis and mission module. With the withdrawal of the UK from the programme, production of the chassis moved to Germany while the Dutch took on some of the mission modules. All twelve prototypes had been completed by mid-2005 and were undergoing an intensive trials programme which highlighted the need for a number of improvements, especially in light of experience from the fighting in Afghanistan. These included additional belly protection from explosive attack and side protection from rocket-propelled grenade attack.

A GTK Boxer (MRAV) prototype (Source: Heldt via Wikimedia Commons)

The German and Dutch armed forces agreed to buy a total of 472 Boxer MRAVs (272 for Germany, 200 for the Netherlands) in late 2006, with the Dutch version being armed with a 12.7mm (.50 cal) machinegun and the German version with either a 12.7mm machinegun or a 40mm grenade launcher. The first production vehicles were handed over to the Bundesheer in late 2009, which planned to operate five variants – ambulance, APC, cargo, command post vehicle and engineer vehicle. Some were subsequently deployed to Afghanistan in 2011 and upgraded to the A1 standard which included additional armour protection. The Netherlands is expected to take delivery of its first production Boxer vehicles this year (2013). Both Krauss-Maffei Wegmann and Rheinmetall have marketed an IFV version of the Boxer, the former having a remote controlled turret armed with a 30mm cannon and 7.62mm machinegun, the latter having a Lance Modular Turret System fitted, equipped similarly to the Krauss-Maffei Wegmann version.

Conclusion

The MRAV programme started off as an ambitious collaborative programme between, initially, two countries (Germany and France), then three (Germany, France and the UK then Germany, Netherlands and the UK) and finally two (Germany and the Netherlands), with interest shown by several others. As seems to happen in multinational collaborative schemes, a great deal of time is taken over setting requirements, negotiating workshare arrangements (something that OCCAR tries to mitigate by doing it over a portfolio of programmes), organising the competitive tendering process, waiting for industry to respond and if necessary form consortia, analysing the bids and awarding the contract. More time is consumed in the building of prototypes, trials, carrying out demonstration and development, as well as production, and finally getting the product into service. The Dutch, who joined the programme in early 2001, will only take delivery of their first Boxer vehicles this year (2013). The Germans only took delivery of their first vehicles in 2009 after being involved with the programme since the start. It is curious to note, however, that things did start to move somewhat quicker once the number of partners had been reduced to two, effectively becoming a bilateral programme. Perhaps this indeed supports the recent UK stance of looking to support bilateral defence relations and acquisition projects, in particular with the USA and France.

Issues

- What wider political purposes, beyond the acquisition of a new piece of equipment, were being served by the launch of the MRAV / GTK / VBM project?

- Does the MRAV experience demonstrate the utility and value of using competition in collaborative projects?
- Did the pursuit of MRAV via the multinational collaboration route affect the programme's risk?
- Does the MRAV experience demonstrate that collaborative projects can drive forward defence industrial restructuring?
- What could explain the decline in the French interest and involvement in the MRAV / GTK / VBM programme?
- What, apart for the alleged mismatch with requirements, could have caused the British to pull out of the programme?
- Was the British decision to pull out of the project a wise one, given that the acquisition of both the C-17 and the planned acquisition of the A400-M would have provided a means by which to airlift MRAVs?
- With MRAV seemingly ending up as a bilateral acquisition programme, is this the way forward for UK defence acquisition, as the 'National Security Through Technology' paper is suggesting? What other projects can be highlighted that support this contention?

Bibliography

BBC. (2000) 'Westland merger confirmed' on *BBC News* website, dated 26 July 2000, at http://news.bbc.co.uk/1/hi/business/852612.stm. Accessed: 8 August 2013.

Beaver, P. (1998) 'Eurokonsortium wins $2.4bn MRAV award' in *Jane's Defence Weekly*, 29 April 1998, p. 4.

Beaver, P. (1996) 'UK knocks on the door of Franco-German agency' in *Jane's Defence Weekly*, 28 February 1996, p. 11.

Bennett, N. (1998) 'GKN faces rival bid for Alvis' in *The Sunday Telegraph*, 20 September 1998 in *Defence News*, 21 September 1998.

Editorial. (1998) 'GKN pays £335m for US metal components firm' in *The Independent*, 8 December 1998 in *Defence News*, 8 December 1998.

Editorial. (1998) 'Vickers buys Oslo marine firm for £380m' in *The Independent*, 1 December 1998 in *Defence News*, 1 December 1998.

EuropeanVoice.com. (1998) '24-25 October Informal European Summit, Pörtschach', at http://www.europeanvoice.com/article/imported/24-25-october-informal-european-summit-pvrtschach/37283.aspx, dated 29 October 1998. Accessed: 7 August 2013.

Fagan, M. (1998) 'Fight to the death for the battlefield taxi' in *The Sunday Telegraph*, 1 March 1998 in *Defence News*, 2 March 1998.

Fagan, M. (1998) 'Vickers plans French tanks link' in *The Sunday Telegraph*, 12 April 1998 in *Defence News*, 15 April 1998.

Federation of American Scientists. (1999) *MRAV* webpage, at http://www.fas.org/man/dod-101/sys/land/row/mrav.htm as of 14 August 2013.

Foss. C F. (2013) 'Boxer comes out fighting as production ramps up' in *International Defence Review*, posted 7 February 2013 at ihm.janes.com. Accessed: 8 August 2013.

Foss, C F. (2011) 'Briefing: Wheels of Fortune' in *Jane's Defence Weekly*, posted 15 September 2011 at ihm.janes.com. Accessed: 8 August 2013.

Foss, C F. (1997) 'Foreword' in *Jane's Armour and Artillery 1997 - 8*, Jane's Information Group, 4 December 1997.

Foss, C F. (1998) 'European wheeled AFV decision due in March' in *Jane's Defence Weekly*, 4 February 1998, p. 5.

Foss, C F. (1998) 'Late offer adds impetus to Europe's AFV contest' in *Jane's Defence Weekly*, 11 March 1998, p. 3.

Foss, C F. (1995) 'UK is courting Germans for AFV Joint Venture' in *Jane's International Defence Review*, 16 September 1995, p. 11.

Foss, C F. (1998) 'Will France keep with Eurokonsortium?' in *Jane's Defence Weekly - Defence Industry Report*, June 1998, pp. 1 - 2.

Foss, C F. (1997) 'Wheeled AFVs for infantry in new era' in *Jane's Defence Weekly*, 22 January 1997, p. 20.

Gow, D and Bannister, N. (1998) 'GKN hails 'taxi' contract' in *The Guardian*, 23 April 1998 in *Defence News*, 23 April 1998.

Gribben, R. (1998) 'Vickers fights on for 'battlefield taxi' order' in *The Daily Telegraph*, 23 April 1998 in *Defence News*, 23 April 1998.

Jane's Information Group. (1999) 'Armoured Vehicles' in *Jane's Defence Industry*, posted 1 March 1999 at ihm.janes.com. Accessed: 8 August 2013.

Jane's Information Group. (1998) 'Bonn makes MRAV official' in *Jane's Defence Weekly*, 27 May 1998, p. 4.

Jane's Information Group. (2002) 'Boxer armoured personnel carrier finally rolled out' in *Jane's Defence Weekly*, posted 13 December 2002 at ihm.janes.com. Accessed: 8 August 2013.

Jane's Information Group. (2005) 'Boxer bid due by end of year' in *Jane's Defence Weekly*, posted 10 August 2005 at ihm.janes.com. Accessed: 8 August 2013.

Jane's Information Group. (2001) 'Dutch join German-UK armoured vehicle project' in *Jane's Defence Weekly*, posted 2 February 2002 at ihm.janes.com. Accessed: 7 August 2013.

Jane's Information Group. (1998) 'Eurokonsotium wins European AFV programme' in *Jane's Armour and Artillery 1997 - 8 - UPDATE*, Volume 4, Issue 5, 26 May 1998.

Jane's Information Group. (2003) 'Europe's Boxer: down but not out as UK quits' in *Jane's Defence Weekly*, posted 18 July 2003 at ihm.janes.com. Accessed: 8 August 2013.

Jane's Information Group. (2007) 'First Boxer vehicles on schedule for 2009 delivery' in *Jane's Defence Weekly*, posted 23 May 2007 at ihm.janes.com. Accessed: 8 August 2013.

Jane's Information Group. (2006) 'German and Dutch armies sign up for Boxer MRAVs' in *Jane's Defence Industry*, posted 13 December 2006 at ihm.janes.com. Accessed: 8 August 2013.

Jane's Information Group. (2002) 'Germany wants to expedite MRAV' in *Jane's Defence Weekly*, posted 28 February 2002 at ihm.janes.com. Accessed: 8 August 2013.

Jane's Information Group. (2013) 'GTK/MRAV/PWV (Boxer) wheeled armoured vehicle programme' in *Land Warfare Platforms – Armoured Fighting Vehicles*, posted 1 February 2013 at ihm.janes.com. Accessed: 8 August 2013.

Jane's Information Group. (1997) "Multi Role Armoured Vehicle (MRAV)" in *Jane's Armour and Artillery 1997 - 8*, 4 December 1997, p. 541.

Jane's Information Group. (1997) 'Rivals asked to rebid for trinational programme' in *Jane's Defence Weekly*, 10 September 1997, p. 18.

Jane's Information Group. (1995) 'UK considers joining Franco-German AFV Program' in *Jane's International Defence Review*, 1 April 1995, p. 18.

Jane's Information Group. (1997) 'VBM / GTK MRAV wheeled armoured vehicle programme' in *Jane's Armour and Artillery 1997 - 8*, 4 December 1997, p. 538.

Kemp, D. (1997) 'OCCAR to spread wings with more programmes' in *Jane's Defence Weekly*, 5 February 1997, p. 11.

Lok, J J. (1997) 'Dutch on road to OCCAR via new vehicle project' in *Jane's Defence Weekly*, 30 April 1997, p. 11.

Ministry of Defence. (2012) *National Security Through Technology: Technology, Equipment and Support for UK Defence and Security*, Cm8278, London: TSO, February 2012.

Missiroli, A. (1999) 'Life after the Blair 'initiative'' in *Newsletter*, Number 25, February 1999, by The Institute for Security Studies, Western European Union, p. 1.

Nicoll, A. (1997) 'Defence rivals imagine a life without Vickers' in *The Financial Times*, 7 November 1997 in *Defence News*, 7 November 1997.

Nicoll, A. (1997) 'Vickers hopeful of acquisitions for defence side' in *The Financial Times*, 29 October 1997 in *Defence News*, 29 October 1997.

Nicoll, A. (1997) 'War of words over 'battlefield taxis' contract intensifies' in *The Financial Times*, 12th March 1998.

Orlebar, E. (1998) 'Vickers fears for £3bn bid: A specification change could lose an armoured car contract to a rival' in *The Independent on Sunday*, 8 February 1998 in *Defence News*, 9 February 1998.

Paloczi-Horvath, G. (1998) 'Varying objectives spell MRAV minefield', The Engineer, 1 May 1998 in *Defence News*, 6 May 1998.

Pohling-Brown, P. (1997) 'Calling the shots on arms purchases: NATO reviews procedures, and Europe aims for increased joint procurement' in *Jane's Defence Contracts*, Jane's Information Group, 1 May 1997, p. 4.

PSI Logistics. (Unknown) *Krauss-Maffei Wegmann: Warehouse Management System*, at http://www.psilogistics.com/uploads/tx_referenceslist/Referenzblatt_KMW_06_02_en.pdf. Accessed: 8 August 2013.

Rogers, M. (1998) 'IDENTITY CRISIS' in *Jane's Defence Weekly*, 3rd June 1998.

Schulte, H. (1998) 'MRAV contract may spark industry restructuring' in *Jane's Defence Weekly*, 13 May 1998, p. 19.

Schulte, H. (1998) 'New German government threatens MRAV delay' in *Jane's Defence Weekly*, 4 November 1998.

Smy, L and Nicoll, A. (1998) 'Battle taxi deal agreed' in *The Financial Times*, 22 April 1998 in *Defence News*, 22 April 1998.

Stevenson, R. (2004) 'BAE trumps US bid for Alvis with £355m deal' in *The Independent*, dated 4 June 2004 at http://www.independent.co.uk/news/business/news/bae-trumps-us-bid-for-alvis-with-acircpound355m-deal-6168479.html. Accessed: 8 August 2013.

Swann, C and Edgecliffe-Johnson, A. (1998) 'Alvis makes tracks as it engineers a way around Vickers' in *The Financial Times*, 16 September 1998 in *Defence News*, 16 September 1998.

Tringham, M. (1998) 'Alvis - GKN alliance puts pressure on Vickers' in *The Independent*, 15 September 1998 in *Defence News*, 15 September 1998.

Wachman, R and Murphy, P. (1998) 'United Defence targets Alvis' in *The Sunday Business*, 20 September 1998 in *Defence News*, 21 September 1998.

Wikipedia. (2013) 'C-17 Globemaster III' webpage, currently located at http://en.wikipedia.org/wiki/Boeing_C-17_Globemaster_III#Royal_Air_Force. Accessed: 8 August 2013.

The author would like to thank Jeremy C. D. Smith for his help in putting this case study together.

Part Three // Logistics Challenges

The Options for Change Defence Review: Twenty-Five Years On

Dr Jeffrey P. Bradford

Defence and National Security Consultant

Introduction

Amongst other events such as the fall of the Berlin Wall signalling the end of the Cold War, the year 2014 represents the quarter century anniversary of the UK Ministry of Defence review known as 'Options for Change'. The purpose of this chapter is to examine the British government's Options for Change defence review initiated some twenty-five years ago, in 1989 and trace the evolution of this strategy led policy into the resource driven defence cost studies underpinning the policy known as 'Front Line First'. It could be suggested that from the perspective of defence procurement and acquisition practice this review process signalled a generational shift in thinking and understanding it has relevance to the continuing evolution of defence management practice.

To undertake this task the author has chosen to use four alternate and complimentary strategic decision-making models to offer distinct analysis and insight into the dynamics surrounding the review. Given issues of classification of documentation this chapter has drawn on secondary data sources to avoid issues of confidentiality and given that many documents still remain classified this analysis seeks to present the evolution of the policy process from four distinct perspectives.

The first perspective draws upon the author's doctoral research considering policy making as a process involving what game theorists term 'repetitive games' i.e. the behaviour of actors is conditioned by the fact that they will be involved in bargaining on a regular future basis (e.g. for a share of the defence budget). The next three slices draw on a landmark piece of research into the Cuban Missile Crisis of 1962 starting from a historical perspective and deepening the analysis by looking successively at the impact of organisational processes and lastly the power of individuals encompassed in the bureaucratic politics model.

Options for Change: Intra-Governmental Decision Model

This first section is concerned with the application of this model to governmental decision-making. It aims to identify the central players relevant to the defence environment, their characteristics and their interactions. This should in turn yield insights as to the policy-making process and explain the nature of the Options for Change process. The application of the model does not explicitly utilise hypotheses regarding the dominating causes underlying an individual decision. Rather it seeks to observe decision outputs through the continuum of time and cultural interactions.

In terms of viewing Options for Change through the Intra-Governmental decision model it is first necessary to identify the polyarchic environment (i.e. the central intra-governmental cultures) under examination. Those cultures relevant to this particular analysis are those of the Foreign Office, Government (that is referring to the political party in office), the Ministry of Defence (two major cultures – 'Management' & 'Security' - in addition to the individual armed services), and HM Treasury which we shall now consider in turn.

The Foreign Office has been characterised as having, "strong inherited likes and dislikes."[1] It has preferences for the countries it favours dealing with and likewise a set of those of whom it disapproves. The Foreign Office is relevant to understanding the defence decision-making environment as it can set the agenda as to what Britain's interests should be and whom its allies are at present. This Department of State represents the historical legacy of Britain's foreign policy and is a cultural trust retaining the sum of British experience. This is clearly important as the matching of scarce defence resources to potentially limitless international commitments has long been a challenge for policy-makers.

The Foreign and Commonwealth Office (Source: Adrian Pingstone via Wikimedia Commons)

In Britain the Government culture is examined as that of the party in power. Because of the historical development of the parliamentary process, the governing party has substantial control over information flows. Further, despite recent electoral results, the ruling Party is generally able to execute policy due to its inherent majority by virtue of the electoral system. The Government drawn from the Conservative party enjoyed uninterrupted rule from 1979 through until 1997 with one change of Prime Minister, a Conservative successor continuing throughout the Options for Change exercise. In its preparations for the election victory it had committed itself to offering a manifesto including, "freedom and free markets, limited government and a strong national defence."[2] In terms of succeeding with this agenda it was noted that everything had to fit in with a strategy to reverse economic decline.[3]

In government the Conservatives pursued twin policies of de-nationalisation of state companies with tight fiscal control of government expenditure. Experts from industry were brought in to pursue value for money initiatives within government.[4] Public expenditure was constantly reviewed with an aim of reducing the overall costs of government.[5]

The Ministry of Defence consists of two distinct cultures with respect to decision-making. On the one hand there is the budget minded culture of peace time accounting, audit and management of limited resources for potentially limitless ends. On the other exists the culture regarding the management mission of the Ministry, to provide for the security of the nation.[6] However impinging upon these two main cultures are the four distinct players, the three services and the civil service.

Due to the environments in which they operate and their historical experiences the Army, Royal Navy and Royal Air Force possess distinct views on how defence should be provided. Further they all possess distinctive styles of decision-making. The fourth player, the civil service element is a player due to its continuity of service as opposed to military officers that are seconded on limited postings to the Ministry of Defence.

The plaque outside the South Door of the Ministry of Defence Main Building in Whitehall, London. (Source: Harland Quarrington / MOD via Wikimedia Commons)

Finally, HM Treasury, due to its responsibility for public expenditure has interests in the activities of all government departments. Because of its small size it could be suggested that its interest is limited to critiquing the funding of various policies leading to the criticism that the Treasury understands 'the cost of everything and the value of nothing'.

Furthermore the influence which the Treasury exerts over policy plans by departmental ministers means that the Treasury is often viewed by Departments as an obstacle. This is highly relevant when considering the resource issue of defence and its constant struggle for resources.

HM Treasury viewed from St James Park (Source: Photograph supplied by author)

The 1989 Statement on the Defence Estimates published prior to the start of the Options study provides a starting point for understanding the subsequent decision-making activity. The Defence (Security) culture within the Ministry of Defence saw the Soviet Union as its main adversary despite recent arms control initiatives such as the INF Treaty.[7] The White paper noted, "We should be under no illusion about this new sense of realism; it is designed to serve Soviet interests, not those of the West."[8]

The annual appraisal of the White Paper by the House of Commons Defence Committee saw different issues being asked of Ministry officials.[9] The Defence (Management) culture was engaged regarding Treasury inflation estimates and the likelihood of defence spending falling as a percentage of GDP.[10]

The Foreign Office culture arguably saw the Soviet Union a little differently due to its representation at negotiations and summits. On author noted also the changing view of the government toward the Soviet Union, as for "the first time [since 1979], Soviet leaders appear to be genuinely able to influence the defence and foreign affairs debates within Britain."[11]

The divergence of the two main cultures within the Ministry of Defence and their relationship with the Treasury, the Foreign Office and Government is fundamental to the decision to undertake the review of policy known as Options for Change. The Government and Treasury cultures were in alignment viewing public expenditure as something to be reduced in size. However, against them were the alignment of the Foreign Office and the Defence cultures incrementally seeking to continue along the same trajectory as they had for the past several years.

The shift by the Foreign Office culture toward conceiving of a new form of relationship with the Soviet Union left the Defence (Security) culture out of step with developments broadly in the UK Government. Financial problems related to defence procurement throughout the late 1980s were being dealt with in an incremental manner rather than provoking a review within the organisation.

This effective breakdown in what might be termed the operational cultures of British defence policy enabled the more powerful axis of the Treasury and Government to intervene with a view to establishing resource savings in the Ministry of Defence programme during 1989.[12] From the analytical model's perspective both of these cultural groups had evolved in an incremental manner responding to the Cold War environment. However the responses to radical change were occurring at different velocities. The Foreign Office's proximity to the ending of the Cold War enabled it to move faster than Defence. The centrality of the Treasury to the Government's efforts throughout the 1980s to minimise expenditure meant that defence was drifting away from general thinking in government about resource allocation and political priorities.

Within the Ministry how did the three distinct service cultures and the civil service react to this event? The 1990 Statement on the Defence Estimates focused upon the Warsaw Pact and the negotiations over the Conventional Forces in Europe Treaty.[13] This Treaty would have deleterious effects to the ability of the services to argue against reductions. The focus of the CFE Treaty upon land and air forces whilst excluding naval forces meant that the services under immediate threat were the British Army and Royal Air Force.

The Defence (Management) culture meanwhile was grappling with the Treasury which had reneged upon a commitment allowing the Ministry of Defence to carry forward savings up to the value of 5%.[14] Further, the implementation of a new management regime was further soaking up their energies.

By early summer the House of Commons Defence Committee completed a major report on the changing security environment. Given the rumours regarding the nature of defence reductions the Committee sought to consider the possibilities. In considering the characteristics of future armed forces it is noted that they would be expensive.[15] In order to make this transition in a resource thin environment clearly the Government culture would have to ensure that the services responded to this vision.

The best example of this can be seen by examination of the House of Commons Defence Committee reports on Options for Change for each of the services. The documents for the Air Force and Navy are slender compared to those of the Army and reserve forces.[16] This is an indication of the battle mounted by the army to mitigate its position as the service due to bear the brunt of reductions. Evidence from a highly experienced former Secretary of State for Defence highlighted the problem of delegating change to the services;

"If you put this [Options for Change] entirely into the hands of people whose interests are to keep things as they are and who will look for new things for the services to do - I think the Navy's latest defence is controlling the drug traffic in the Caribbean."[17]

A former senior civil servant at the ministry noted of the services that, "when push comes to shove, sailors will want ships, airmen planes, and soldiers regiments - and secondarily tanks."[18] The July 1990 statement regarding the outcome of the Options review was only six pages in length.[19]

The Navy and Air Force as capital intensive organisations and technical cultures were able to reshape themselves by the removal of equipment approaching obsolescence. This reaction would have rapid impact on the balance sheet and also protected investment in future generations of their 'decisive weapons'. It could be suggested that in the early 1990s these were nuclear powered submarines for the Royal Navy and the Eurofighter Typhoon multi-role combat aircraft for the Royal Air Force. From a cultural perspective these weapons represented structures, procedures and values which had been inculcated to generations of service personnel. Therefore these were both symbols of differentiation between them as well as key indicators of the evolutionary nature of their response to the security environment.

For the Army the challenge was to maintain its core, that of the regimental system. Personnel reduction associated with reducing the BAOR commitment to Germany would inevitably threaten regiments. This in turn meant that service energies which might have been directed toward protecting its share of the defence budget were absorbed in protecting secular interests.[20]

The House of Commons Defence Committee noted from their assessment that at best there was, "no coherent overall [security] strategy."[21] and at its extreme;

"even worse would be for the Treasury to dictate the size of the surface fleet... Nothing we have heard in evidence... has dispelled our impression that this is a reasonable description of the methods used."[22]

In the context of Options for Change it is apparent which symbols hold distinct value for the three services. By definition, these provide the bargaining chips and vulnerabilities when competing with each other and external forces such as the Treasury. In the context of the model the issue of trust can be seen in terms that none of the cultures threatened the symbols of the other directly. It would appear that the decision-making process of Options for Change was driven by a Government and Treasury culture able to exploit the divisions within the Ministry to reduce capabilities quantitatively rather than eliminating them entirely.

Having completed the decision-making relevant to the Options review how effective were the services in curbing its implementation? Clearly the service cultures would seek to prevent a further haemorrhaging of their budget if not reverse elements of the reductions. The 1992 Statement on the Defence Estimates was in part concerned with the lessons of Britain's success as part of the United Nations coalition which reversed Iraq's 1990 invasion of Kuwait.[23]

A British Army convoy during Operation Granby / Desert Storm, 1991 (Source: PHC Holmes via Wikimedia Commons)

The 1993 Statement on the Defence Estimates introduced a new methodology demonstrating the roles and missions to which force elements were assigned.[24] The 1993 White Paper is important in demonstrating the reconciliation between the Management and Security cultures within the Ministry as well as the three services. The capabilities of the three services were matched to tasks across three tables.

The Army, Navy and Air Force sought to make their position increasingly secure by ensuring that their capabilities were assigned to as many tasks as possible in each role. This act in itself made further action by the Treasury and Government operationally as well as culturally more difficult. In terms of the analytical model this activity demonstrates how politically aware the service cultures are in protecting their position.

However, the Government began to face increasing criticism that the Options for Change review had gone too far and had left the defence establishment exposed.[25] This made further action in conjunction with the Treasury problematic, especially due to the high profile image enjoyed by the armed forces in the context of the Gulf and the emerging peacekeeping commitment in the former Yugoslavia. The House of Commons Defence Committee recommendations following examination of the 1993 White Paper noted, "the armed forces desperately need a period of financial calm."[26]

These pressures assisted in enabling a financial settlement for the Ministry for the remainder of the Parliament. However, in order to reach these expenditure targets whilst not incurring further criticism the Government had to arbitrate between the requirement to avoid criticism from MPs, the Treasury and the Ministry. 'Front Line First: The Defence Cost Study' can be seen as a clear compromise in this direction thus ending the Options review.[27]

In conclusion, it could be suggested that the failure of the Defence (Security) culture to adapt to the changing environment left it vulnerable to financial review. The incremental nature of the Cold War security policy can be traced through successive years of Statements on the Defence Estimates.

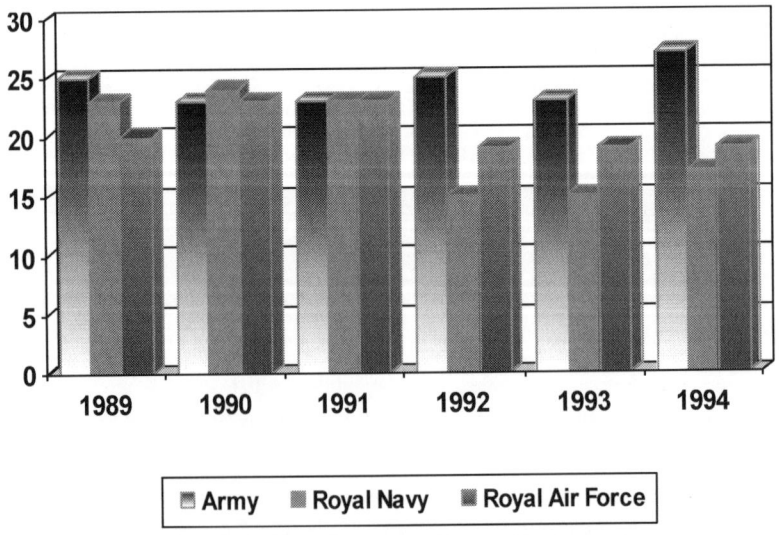

Figure 1. Percentage share of the Defence budget by service, 1989-94.

However, the armed services proved highly resilient in defending their fundamental interests. By the publication of the Defence Costs Study all three services were committed to acquiring new generations of decisive weaponry.[28] Furthermore, whilst the overall budget for defence contracted between 1989 and 1994 the percentage share by service showed interesting changes as depicted below in Figure 1. 1992 saw the effective implementation of the Options decisions for the Royal Navy and Royal Air Force. However, the Army was able to maintain their share of the budget and at times extend it.

The Treasury culture favouring reduced public expenditure was able to exploit very effectively Ministry confusion in 1989. However, once the Security and Management cultures within the Ministry of Defence demonstrated coherence it became subsequently harder to apply extra-ordinary pressure to achiee cost savings.

Having considered the Options for Change process using the Intra-governmental decision model the second part of the chapter shall consider this policy shift through the Allison framework using the Rational actor, Organisational process and Governmental (bureaucratic) politics lenses.

The Intra-Governmental Decision model focus upon culture and repeated interactions it could be suggested facilitates an appreciation of the constraints governing the principal actors' behaviour. Therefore in situations where data is scarce i.e. in considering recent policy decisions the model offers a greater level of specificity in terms of gauging the parameters for action. The model illustrated the response through time to the challenge of resource scarcity by the service cultures in assigning forces to mission types in order to justify their existence. Further the activities of the Navy and Air Force in dropping many types of combat weaponry in order to protect their core function offer further evidence of their political awareness.

Options for Change Viewed Through the Allison Lens

Having considered the Options for Change review through the Intra-governmental model, this examination of Options for Change using Allison's framework seeks in the first instance to introduce two hypotheses concerning the decision-making environment which led to a reassessment of Britain's defence needs in 1989. The choice of only two hypotheses reflects the importance of what was articulated at the time as being the central reasons underlining the policy-shift.[29]

Allison in his own work utilised hypotheses only for the application of the Rational Actor model in considering the Cuban Missile Crisis.

Options for Change: The Rational Actor Model

The rational actor lens introduces the perspective of a unitary British government making choices regarding its defence requirements on the basis of selecting the optimal course among competing choices.[30]

The first hypothesis 'international security' considers the review as the resultant of perceptions that a radical transformation of the international environment was occurring. Many official publications suggested that the increased warning time for Western Europe derived from arms control agreements enabled defence rationalisation. The second 'economic necessity' posits the alternate view that rather than security needs it was economic considerations that drove the decision process.

Hypothesis One: 'International Security'

In the period following the Second World War, British security concerns have fluctuated between what Darby had described as "the old beats of Empire rather than the gray realities of Germany and the Rhine."[31] With commitments ranging from supporting NATO to ensuring the orderly transition of power in colonial possessions, British security policy has, it could be suggested, been of an essentially reactive nature. These commitments were reflected in the force structures maintained by the armed forces to meet any contingency ranging from low intensity operations such as those in the Malayan 'emergency' to high intensity conflicts like Korea.

The mechanism by which Britain maintained this capability was a system of bases to which troops and materials could be flown or shipped in time of crisis. One of its largest and most important strategic bases was that in Egypt. This protected the Suez Canal. This base facilitated control of both shipping in transit to India, and oil from the Middle East. It also secured air transport to the Far East.[32]

The 1956 débâcle in Egypt following the nationalisation of the Suez Canal, and subsequent Anglo-French efforts to depose the Egyptian regime under President Nasser, resulted in a crisis of confidence for the British political system. The subsequent loss of Egypt hastened the British retreat from an imperial role. Subsequent governments sought to redefine Britain's security policy so as to orientate it away from colonial adventures towards the NATO alliance and Europe. The 1968 annual Statement on Defence declared that efforts would "in future be concentrated mainly in Europe and the North Atlantic area."[33] This followed a rational review of defence options detailed in Chapter three.

Once the shift towards a European defence posture emerged, with the basing system

British aircraft carriers during the Suez Crisis of 1956 – HMS Eagle leads HMS Bulwark and then HMS Albion (Source: Royal Navy / Imperial War Museum via Wikimedia Commons)

largely disbanded, force structures of the armed services were altered. The 1960s saw the cancellation of the Royal Navy project to build a new generation of large carriers. The Royal Air Force lost half its air transportation fleet in the next decade. It could be suggested that given the Royal Air Force view of air transportation being a second order concern, the loss would not have had the traumatic effect which the CVA-01 cancellation had upon the Royal Navy. Both of these capabilities were essential to maintain a global intervention strategy.[34]

The 1970s were characterised by civil disturbances and low intensity crises in Northern Ireland, Cyprus and the Arabian Peninsula. The tempo of withdrawal from the Persian Gulf was hastened. This, despite the wishes of the United States, who would have preferred to see British forces deployed in the Middle East against the communist threat.

The most demanding test for the armed forces post-1945 arose in the decision to reverse the Argentinean invasion of the Falkland Islands. Political moves to reduce the Royal Navy's surface fleet had been planned but not fully implemented before this conflict. The British Army of the Rhine continued its sedate garrison role against a threat that had not yet materialised. The government continued its policy of maintaining a nuclear deterrent force, composed mainly of submarine based missiles despite pressure from the opposition and domestic pressure groups.[35]

Rather than losing a major conventional conflict, it could be suggested that the 1990 review of British defence policy stemmed from the willingness of the Soviet Union to de-militarise its Cold War competition with the Western world. To best consider this critical factor the hypothesis will consider in turn nuclear and conventional arms control developments which influenced the shift in British policy.

In the field of nuclear arms control there had been levels of tacit co-operation between parties in the past, for example, although the United States never ratified the SALT II accord, it did stand by its provisions for strategic arms.[36] However, the significant changes to the security environment were the Intermediate Nuclear Forces Agreement (INF) and the successor to the Mutual and Balanced Force Reduction (MBFR) talks, the Conventional Forces in Europe Treaty (CFE).

The INF Treaty[37] addressed a problem which had resulted from a previous arms control agreement known as SALT. Its provisions both enabled and proved a catalyst for the development of a new generation of nuclear weaponry. The Soviet deployment of mobile, highly accurate missiles proved of considerable concern to the NATO alliance. NATO members feared that this deployment undermined deterrence. At worst it left them vulnerable to a surprise decapitation strike aimed at their political leadership.

The United States, keen to allay these fears planned to deploy the neutron bomb.[38] However, these weapons caused great public anxiety in Europe. Their withdrawal was forced both by public concerns, and from political leaders, who realised these weapons undermined rather than reinforced deterrence.

In response NATO adopted a two-track approach, whereby it would develop the next generation INF, the Ground Launched Cruise Missile, whilst simultaneously negotiating limits of such future weapons, in return for reductions in the current Soviet holdings of INF missiles. If the talks preceded beyond December 1983 then the US would deploy these new INF weapons.[39]

The European governments attempt to generate positive public opinion for the deployment of these weapons led to a period of political turmoil. The depiction of the SS-20 threat had a perverse effect in raising public anxiety about all nuclear weapons not only Soviet ones. In 1981, President Reagan announced the zero-option. NATO would not deploy any new INF if the USSR eliminated all its older and some newer theater missiles. US Secretary of State Haig noted that this proposal was intended to "take the high ground in propaganda, without real expectation that the Soviet Union would ever accept this outcome."[40] A week later the

USSR made a counter-proposal suggesting staged reductions west of the Ural mountains.

The rational actor model as applied here illuminates the issue of states as unitary actors making choices regarding arms control postures aiming to maximise their individual security.

The negotiations commenced with significant reluctance on the part of the United States. They were against cancellation of the deployment of Pershing II which caused great concern to the Soviet Union. This fact alone was enough to reduce the chances of any positive outcome. However, it could be suggested that one key event changed the attitude of the US, making it more willing to negotiate constructively.

Once European states had gained enough support for the stationing of the new INF forces, the superpower summit at Reykjavik, Iceland saw two superpowers come close to an accord without the United States consulting its NATO allies. The USSR had come to Iceland with concrete proposals to eliminate INF motivated it seems by a wish to reduce the burden of the arms race on the Soviet economy.

The US was surprised by this. The Soviet moves towards the United States position virtually bargained away INF without European input. The British were apparently furious to hear this, having endured substantial domestic opposition to facilitate the cruise missile deployment, and updating the strategic deterrent.

The INF Treaty was unique. It was the first accord which actively involved the dismantling of nuclear weapons. Verification procedures were settled, and future production of such weapons was banned. However the INF process resulted in a rift in transatlantic relations. NATO publications attempted to limit this by reinterpreting the culture of the USA and explaining the nature of the American psyche.[41]

President Reagan and General Secretary Gorbachev sign the INF Treaty, 8 December 1987 (Source: NARA via Wikimedia Commons)

From the rational actor perspective the early difficulties and failures of nuclear arms control can be traced to the individual state based cost-benefit calculus. Unilateral disarmament from any individual state's point of view did not enhance their security. Choosing a level of arms to which all could agree was not possible either until the mid-1980s. At this point changes in the security environment enabled the rational consideration of the broad costs of the nuclear posture enabled states to successfully negotiate Treaties such as INF which combined reductions in weapons with confidence building measures.

The speed with which this nuclear armaments treaty was concluded can be seen in sharp contrast to the much thornier issue of conventional arms control. In 1968, the NATO ministerial conference proposed negotiations on conventional force levels with the USSR. Three key factors drove this effort. Firstly, there was a perception that a reduction in military confrontation could allow a reduction in defence expenditure.

The 1967 Harmel report for NATO expressly forbade further cuts in forces by members pending the start of MBFR. Unilateral reductions adversely affected the chances of reaching a common negotiation position. Secondly the West wished to regain the initiative from the USSR who had recently proposed the formation of the CSCE.[42] Third, the talks were seen as a way of relieving domestic pressure in the US to unilaterally reduce forces. The negotiations acted as a brake on any timetable for disengagement. In 1971, a member of the US Congress proposed an amendment to the draft laws. The Mansfield amendment was defeated in part because the USSR announced its intention to participate in the MBFR talks. This served as a catalyst to the commencement of MBFR negotiations.

Problems became apparent shortly after negotiations opened. The UK and West Germany wanted Soviet nuclear forces included but not NATO ones. The Soviet Union disagreed. It wanted ground and air forces included. Whereas NATO only wanted army manpower to be considered. In the context of the Rational Actor model this indicates the value maximising aspirations of all parties. The Soviet Union wanted an agreement which protected their advantage, numbers of soldiers. NATO states sought to protect their superiority in quality of combat aircraft.

The ceilings issue was resolved by setting manpower limits of 900,000 on NATO ground and air forces and 700,000 ceiling on Soviet ground forces. Another problem was that of definition. What did "balanced" in MBFR actually mean? Did it refer to quantity or quality?

The Soviet Union introduced another proposal. In this foreign forces would be included under the ceilings. Excess numbers would be gradually returned to their home state. This created obvious problems for NATO e.g. the difference in distance between the West German border and the USSR, and the West German Border and North America was 4,300 miles in the Soviet Union's favour. Other problems emerged such as the nature of verification, especially difficult in the case of mobile nuclear missile forces as compared to static silos, was noted by one observer;

"Counting troops and arms in the territory of the other party can become a charade – as was the case in summer 1980, when allied intelligence staffs lost track of the Soviet 6th armoured division - which had been declared withdrawn from the Wittenberg region of East Germany to the Soviet Union since October 1979."[43]

Also problematic was how should the geography of the area be related to force balances, put simply does the terrain favour attack or defence? Should the manpower ceilings be altered accordingly? In sum should the reductions be symmetrical (equal) or asymmetrical? When the talks began to stagnate over technical issues, NATO played its trump negotiating card. This "option 3" involved the direct offer to have NATO withdraw 1,000 US nuclear weapons in return for the withdrawal of one Soviet tank army.

In effect NATO broke its own negotiation rules, by including nuclear weapons. The talks degenerated from this point into various proposals and counter-proposals. However several one-off withdrawals were made before the talks lapsed into mediocrity with the end of détente and the start of the second Cold War with the invasion of Afghanistan. It could be suggested that the Soviet Union, mindful of its conventional superiority could not rationally contemplate its reduction for fear of jeopardising its own security.

In summary, the MBFR talks were a failure. Although neither party achieved tangible results they did facilitate contact and exchanges of position for both sides. They also established a basis for the CFE process. The process highlighted the difficulty that verification posed in the realm of conventional arms control. As summed up by Ambassador Blackwill of the US delegation, "the good news is that we now have permanent check-points; the bad news is that nobody goes through them."[44]

A by-product was the quelling of demands in the US for force reductions. As noted by one writer, defeat of the Mansfield amendment eased pressure for unilateral withdrawals of US servicemen and "significantly decreased the likelihood of an accord."[45]

The key difference in assessing the CFE and MBFR was it could be suggested in the intentions of the participants. The NATO call for negotiations at Halifax, Canada and the USSR's Budapest address, coupled with the distinct thaw in superpower confrontation, engendered a climate for meaningful discussions to take place. The guiding aims of the CFE talks were to "eliminate disparities prejudiced to stability and security, and to eliminate as a matter of priority the capability to launch surprise attack and to initiate large-scale offensive action."[46]

Further, the talks avoided the problem which had dogged the MBFR process, that of manpower, deciding instead to focus upon key forms of equipment which could be monitored, and counted more easily, within four zones comprising the Atlantic-to-the-Urals. CFE talks also took place at a time of general progress in arms control. The CSCE Stockholm Accord was nearing fruition, placing tighter controls on military movements, and the INF Treaty was in its final stages.[47]

This indicated a common interest between Europe, the US and the Soviet Union to curb the military excesses of East-West confrontation. From a technical standpoint, advanced satellites were available to both superpowers. This made the possibility of verification in both nuclear and conventional agreements more practical. From the Rational Actor perspective the environment enabled arms control in a situation in which all participants could benefit.

The negotiations were rapid in comparison to the MBFR process. The Soviet Union made early concessions. With the fall of the Berlin Wall in 1989 one writer noted that these concessions "dried up."[48] The Warsaw Treaty Organisation negotiating team became increasingly independently minded, leading to the Soviet military representatives taking over negotiations de facto. From the Rational Actor perspective the Soviet Union as a value-maximising state did not wish to see its negotiating power diluted.

Further the impending break-up of the Union was making CFE problematic for Russia. The sufficiency rules placing limits on equipment holdings per country were based on the Eastern Blocs continued existence and not a newly independent Russia.

The US were prepared to drop aircraft from the talks, as they had proven a sticking point due to definition problems in order to move the process on. The European members were not prepared to accept this. There were further problems concerning forces which the Soviet Union had re-designated as naval units thus they were not covered by CFE.

Rather than a malevolent move, this was perceived as being an attempt to squeeze every concession possible from the treaty. The Soviet Union as a rational value-maximising actor sought to maximise its own security in this bargaining situation.

By limiting equipment in geographical regions, along with stringent verification procedures, and an element of disarmament (the level of which has been a source of disagreement between observers/participants), the agreement provided for the security of all the participants. One observer noted that, "in many ways the CFE treaty is a combined peace treaty for WWII and for the cold war."[49] The previous quotation is of particular relevance to the international security hypothesis.

Having illustrated the security environment in which the UK has operated since the end of the Second World War - the gradual shift towards Europe as the focus of its security concerns, the arms control agreements coupled with the break-up (due to nationalist pressures) of the Warsaw Pact and Soviet Union, all facilitated a fundamental reassessment.

The 1990 Statement on the Defence Estimates was released some five months following the collapse of the Berlin Wall.[50] Given the lag time in its annual preparation the one-page introduction provides the greatest amount of information regarding the new environment. The key concerns noted were that the CFE accord was not at this time signed, and of course the fact that the Soviet Union still possessed all of its equipment, although the Warsaw Treaty Organisation was falling into obsolescence.

The day of the Secretary of State for Defence's statement initiating formally the Options for Change review coincided with the release of the House of Commons Defence Committee report assessing the state of the international security environment, bearing the acronym DIRE.[51]

In its compilation the Committee conducted visits throughout Europe calling upon several expert witnesses including current and former Defence Secretary's King and Healey, senior service heads, and members of the academic community. The report summarised the arms control events of the late 1980s succinctly, and considered possible future threats. However its impact can be summed up by its key sentence, "As a military alliance the Warsaw Pact is effectively defunct [original emphasis]."[52]

The same day, the Secretary of State for Defence delivered a statement on Options for Change.[53] The statement was an interim report prior to the autumn statement on defence, and therefore was not specific in its intent insofar as many of the questions fielded to the Minister were from Members of Parliament whose constituencies had a stake in particular defence contracts and establishments.

Within a week, a brief interlude occurred as Iraq annexed Kuwait, leading to an international response in which Britain sent a force of some 40,000 personnel to the Middle East who eventually fought to liberate Kuwait. In November, a Heads of State meeting of the CSCE set out a plan to assist the newly independent states of Central Europe carry out democratic elections, noting in their communiqué that, "the era of confrontation and division of Europe has ended. We declare that henceforth our relations will be founded on respect and co-operation."[54]

In July 1991, following completion of CFE, the Minister for Defence noted, "The key international developments on which Options for Change were founded have been generally fulfilled... The government has a clear strategy for future defence policy."[55]

To summarise, the first argument concerning the emergence of the Options for Change review, has been as a result of the drastic changes wrought in the international environment at the end of the 1980s. Changing international security considerations viewed from the rational actor perspective were fundamental in facilitating a shift in the United Kingdom's defence posture.

The thaw in relations between East and West resulted in arms control agreements which could be practically verified and were of equal value to both parties. Given that Britain had gravitated towards a continental strategy defending Europe, as it relinquished control over its dominions, the arms controls efforts culminating in INF and CFE, allied with the demise of the Soviet Union facilitated a government re-think as to how it should organise its defence. The second hypothesis, economic necessity shall look at the need for options for change as resulting from a differing set of circumstances.

Hypothesis Two: 'Economic Necessity'

The second hypothesis concerning the decision to embark on the Options for Change review in 1989 can be summed up by the writings of Cicero a little over two thousand years ago in his statement, "the sinews of war are infinite money."[56] It could be suggested that little has changed since that time. From this hypothesis we will use the Rational Actor model to assess the Options for Change review as being the outcome of economic priorities rather than environmental changes in international security.

The international system as we know it today, is founded on the right of sovereignty as recognised by other states, giving each absolute jurisdiction within its recognised boundaries. The raising of armed forces has guaranteed both the maintenance of those boundaries against external threats, but in some countries also acted in a manner to preserve the state from domestic challenges.

However, the armed forces have an opportunity cost. By having skilled people removed from the economy, scientists engaged in defence research, and monies spent on military hardware, these assets cannot be used elsewhere. In time of clear security threats this is, by and large, accepted by society. It could be suggested however that in periods of peace, when threats are of a distant nature and economic needs are pressing, there arises a temptation to reduce the size of one of the largest sectors of government expenditure. This is indicative of the Rational Actor seeking to maximise value from the resources of the State in order to maximise their security.

The United States during the Suez crisis of 1956 engineered a crash in the value of Sterling through international financial markets. This was done to pressure the British to cease their activities in Egypt.[57] The series of defence reviews during the mid-1960s resulted from various economic crises which forced the government of the day to reconsider spending.[58] As noted by Keohane, "The devaluation of the pound sterling in 1967 obliged the government to accept that Britain was no longer a world power."[59] Further, the OPEC decision to rise oil prices influenced the public expenditure round and the defence review of 1974, with the Chancellor seeking a 4.5% reduction in GNP as a whole within twelve months.[60]

For Britain, the government of the early 1980s faced an international security environment which posed many challenges. The Cold War confrontation between the superpowers entered a second phase. Following the Soviet invasion of Afghanistan the Reagan administration entered office committed to a major build-up of US defences to protect both itself and its allies. NATO members were committed to increasing their defence budgets by three percent a year in real terms (i.e. above the rate of inflation).

Troops from the Soviet 350th Airborne Regiment get ready to board Mil Mi-8 'Hip' helicopters in Afghanistan (Source: Anatoly315 via Wikimedia Commons)

The Secretary of State for Defence John Nott, was recruited to government from merchant banking. His 1981 review noted that it was "incumbent upon the government to ensure that resources are spent to the very best effect in terms of security."[61] Greenwood rationalised Nott's skills learnt as a merchant banker to the outputs of the review.[62]

He [Greenwood] saw the decision to withdraw from service one quarter of the Royal Navy's surface fleet as removing a strategic anomaly. Given Britain's focus upon Europe this seemed logical and would lower the amount of capital tied in assets. Greenwood noted that the aim of the review "was for rationalisation of the business."[63] This measure was however, overtaken by events in the South Atlantic, following the Argentine invasion of the Falklands.

The mid 1980s saw a consumer led boom in the domestic economy which took political pressure off of the Ministry of Defence. Nott's successor Michael Heseltine pushed for efficiency savings in the ministry. He especially targeted defence equipment procurement by recruiting Peter Levine from industry. Further, the Ministry sought to stretch procurement programmes, and delay deploying new equipment to keep the costs low within the overall budget.

Greenwood suggests that, "what they were doing at the Ministry of Defence was muddling through and calling it management."[64] Further, although the three percent target was not met in real terms there was a gradual increase in the budget, which coupled to the governments pursuit of low inflation saw more money available than a decade earlier in 1975 when the defence budget of a little over five percent of GNP was eroded by inflation of over twenty percent.

However there were problems. The government's economic strategy involved keeping control of public expenditure, and gradually in the years following the Falklands conflict, a series of optimistic forecasts from the Treasury for inflation started to create a funding gap, between the resources allocated to defence, and those needed. This was identified by Greenwood and indeed he presented in testimony to the House of Commons Defence Committee.[65] His figures areillustrated in the Figure 2 below:

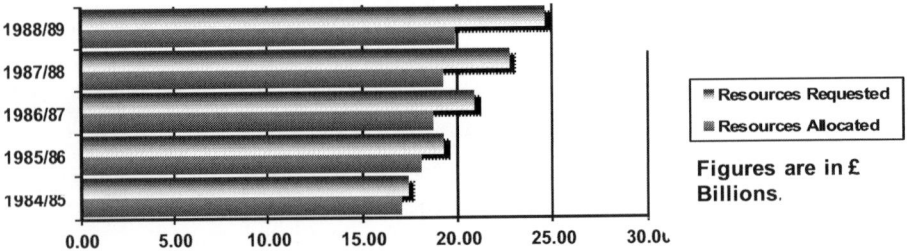

Figure 2. Illustration of the Ministry of Defence funding gap 1984 - 1989.

Towards the end of the decade the British economy started to enter recession. The first warning came from the stock market crash in autumn 1987. Following this economic growth began to slow, with full economic recession commencing in the first quarter of 1990.[66] The Treasury noted that the cause rather than external, "followed a period of unsustainably fast growth during the late 1980s."[67]

The problems with managing the defence budget could be characterised as the growing disparity between defence needs and funding. This was exacerbated by the onset of an economic down turn. In terms of the Rational Actor it could be suggested that a re-assessment of defence needs was well over-due due to solely economic reasons. Reductions in defence could free resources for the private sector to stimulate the economy.

At the beginning of 1990, the funding gap issue was addressed in a report to the Commons Committee on Public Accounts. The report identified the slippage of nine projects that were now over two years behind schedule, further it identified five projects whose costs had increased over 25% those projected, one of which by 183%.[68]

The annual Defence Committee examination of the Defence Estimates saw the Secretary of State defending the inflation planning figures which had eroded the defence budget in the previous year.[69] August 1990 saw an inflation figure of ten percent – presenting a serious erosion of the defence budget, which would have to have been addressed by some form of review.[70]

Several commentators posited that a review of defence requirements for financial reasons was overdue thereby validating the 'economic necessity' hypothesis. Baylis writing on the economic challenges for British defence policy in 1989 noted that;

> "major cuts in defence will become necessary unless there are increases in defence spending... One of the key questions for the future, therefore, is whether the Defence Secretary will undertake a major review before the next election in 1991 or 1992."[71]

Sabin noted that, "Even if high inflation had not put paid to the plan to stabilise British defence spending at its 1988 level, a financially driven defence review could not have been avoided much longer."[72]

This second hypothesis has posited that the decision to engage in a review of defence requirements was the resultant of economic demands. From a Rational Actor perspective the value-maximising state sought to reduce expenditure on defence to support economic development. Specifically this was attributable to the funding gap which had emerged in the Ministry of Defence on the one hand, and the performance of the British economy on the other.

The problems with procurement projects identified by the Commons in early 1990 demonstrated rationally that there had to be some re-evaluation of defence needs. Given the increasing cost of each new generation of military equipment it was inevitable that the cost of re-equipping the armed services would come at the expense of numbers of personnel.

This first part of the analysis of Options for Change using Allison's framework has considered the decision-making during Options for Change as resulting from the rational choice made by the United Kingdom, reacting to the environment.

The analysis will now turn to the second lens through which the decision to embark on a defence review emerged, that of the organisational process model. This perspective shall examine the decision to start the options for change review as the result of governmental activity.

Options for Change: The Organisational Process Model

The second of Allison's three lenses seeks to explain decisions as the outcome of inter-departmental activity within government.[73] Simply put, how are major decisions regarding the shape of defence policy influenced by organisational structure and processes? This analysis of the period preceding the 'Options' review aims to identify the relevant Ministry's, specialist departments and the political oversight bodies behind the various reports as well the standard operating procedures which lead to the policy outputs.

Given the secrecy surrounding British defence processes and the recent nature of the Options exercise the analysis will be limited in scope due to the availability of materials. Rather than offering hypotheses this analysis will seek to define the procedures which would lead to organisational outputs which we recognise as policy it intends to concentrate on the public expenditure process and those documents available.

In December 1989, the senior civil servant wrote of the Ministry of Defence in its 25th year of existence as being, "a large and complex organisation. It spends £20 billion a year, employs half a million people, and is one of the largest landowners in the country."[74] It describes its role as being, "a Department of State responsible for the formulation and execution of defence policy."[75] Further, it is a unique organisation insofar as it comprises both military staff on secondment, dedicated civil servants, and its political masters.

In order that these disparate interest groups can be understood by one another the Ministry publishes charts showing the comparisons between rank structure in the forces and the civil service, in order that everyone is aware of their position in the hierarchy.[76] The political leadership of the Ministry encompasses five posts, the Secretary of State for Defence, Ministers of State, and Parliamentary Under Secretaries of State for the Armed Forces and Procurement.[77]

The Ministry is, as indicated previously, responsible for planning defence needs, and executing policy. It must however justify its expenditure both to the Treasury (in order to obtain its yearly budget) and to parliamentary scrutiny.

In order to plan defence requirements information is required. At the time, the Ministry of Defence had its Defence Intelligence Staff. This organisation's staff provided the Ministry with a threat assessment from which to allocate resources on the basis of political need. The assessment itself generated a certain amount of controversy as it looked beyond the ten year long term costing cycle to consider the environment in the long term. McIntosh cites discussions with on the one hand the Chief of Defence Intelligence who "can think of one case where capabilities were exaggerated" and a Permanent Under Secretary who perceived threat assessment "to be over-estimated most of the time."[78]

The threat assessment, and therefore the Defence Intelligence Staff, held a powerful organisational niche in the defence planning environment. The assessment could not be challenged due to their expertise, which is not possessed anywhere else. An excerpt from a television interview with a former director of the Defence Intelligence Staff, Sir Richard Armitage provides an insight into the primacy of the Staff;

Interviewer: "Surely, a Minister has a right to challenge a threat assessment if he sees fit, and indeed if he has sufficient knowledge to be able to do so?"

Sir Richard: "I think you've hit the nail on the head. The Ministers don't have access to the detailed research that goes on, for example in the DIS, and it would be a very bold Minister indeed who ignored the advice of people like myself on expert matters like that."[79]

McIntosh concludes, "DIS is a secret world in a secretive Ministry."[80] Another department within the ministry of note is the Office of Management and Budget, created by reforms in the mid-1980s. This office is responsible for the allocation of resources as well as financial matters, and is therefore of relevance to the policy makers.[81]

Her Majesty's Treasury possesses one of the smallest staffs of a Whitehall Ministry, and among the oldest. It describes its function as "to help ministers formulate and implement their economic policies."[82] Its central authority is derived from its position as guardian of the finances from spending requirements. This responsibility in turn profoundly defines the culture of the Treasury, as noted by Pliatzky, "The Treasury sees itself as a small beleaguered citadel of financial prudence, surrounded by spendthrift predators and surviving only by its wits and by tireless vigilance."[83]

This responsibility is exercised in the annual public expenditure round commences in July each year, with a statement from the Treasury Secretary on the state of the economy. Departments such as the Ministry of Defence, having already prepared well ahead of time, submit their requests for the following year's funding.[84] A period of bargaining follows, with any outstanding problems dealt with in a 'star chamber' that autumn prior to the autumn statement in the House of Commons.[85] Early the following year, the Government would publish its expenditure plans for the next two years, for example, in January 1989 the plans for 1989-1990, 1990-1991, and 1991-1992 were published.[86]

Assuming that the defence budget survived the public expenditure round relatively intact, the finishing touches could be placed to the annual Statement on the Defence Estimates. This document was also known as the Defence White Paper. It provided the House of Commons with statistical information on the Ministry's activities as well as the unclassified summary of the threat assessment, and details concerning the composition of the armed forces, and procurement projects underway.

This document provided the basis (in part) for the House of Commons Defence Committee (established in 1979) to exercise its function as an over-sight body, with its annual response to that year's defence white paper. The Committee is composed on the basis of the result of the previous election; therefore the government will always have a majority on the Committee.

Its aim is to engender a sense of accountability in its home department, as the Committee can call the Minister or civil servants before it to give evidence. The effectiveness of the Defence Committee was demonstrated in its inquiry into the Westland affair, where the emphasis upon impartial analysis rather than adversarial politics transferred to another forum led to some valuable insights.

However, the Committee suffers from an Achilles heel in terms of access to information. Classified information of a certain level is made available only with permission of the Secretary of State - however, how does one request access to information that one cannot know about? The Committee is to an extent hostage to the Ministry which feeds it with witnesses and papers to work from.

However there is a perception that the Committee provides a greater measure of accountability, the Chairman noting, "that we have got their attention."[87] A contrary view however is provided by a former special advisor to the Secretary of State for Defence, "I think its own perception of its influence is at times exaggerated."[88]

A further legislative barrier for the Ministry is the Public Accounts Committee. This Committee is significant due to the fact that it receives reports from the National Audit Office and is responsible financially for the body rather than the Treasury. It is to all intents and purposes independent, although staffed by civil servants. Further as McIntosh notes, the Chairman of the Public Accounts Committee is virtually always a former senior minister, which assists in lending the committee a certain gravitas.[89]

Having described the major organisations that would be involved in defence planning, the Ministry of Defence and the Treasury, the bodies within that have influence upon policy such as the Defence Intelligence Staff, and Parliamentary oversight bodies such as the Public Accounts and Defence committees, and the National Audit Office, the study will suggest the impact which these bodies operating routines have had on the decision to pursue Options for Change.

The National Audit Office on Buckingham Palace Road, London (Source: Thomas Nugent via the Geograph website)

Given that governmental organisations often have their roles duplicated, or delegated in a manner which whilst perfectly nonsensical administratively, is perfectly understandable politically, conflicts are bound to arise in examining organisational outputs. Bruce-Gardyne observed, "British civil servants are territorial animals, and nothing arouses such passions round the [Whitehall] village as trespass."[90]

In the late 1980s as the public finances tightened due to the impending recession, and the Soviet threat began to diminish in stature, a certain amount of evidence can be observed of departmental politicking between the Ministry of Defence and its 'rivals'.

McDonald cites a situation where the Defence and Public Accounts Committee were both examining problems with procurement in 1989. The Defence Committee wanted access to the Accounts Committees evidence to assist their own investigation, but were denied.[91] As an example of organisational process both committees were following their own procedures without regard for activities conducted by the other, thus duplicating effort.

The Ministry of Defence involvement in an international naval programme was curtailed in 1989, though sources the following year observed, "The participation in the NATO frigate replacement 90 was axed last year by the Treasury, not the defence ministry."[92]

Clearly, given the identification of the funding gap in the mid-1980s, and the changing international environment, plus domestic economic retrenchment, it seems that the Ministry of Defence was facing a series of challenges to its budget, given the management problems of its major projects. Simpson noted that the Ministry could in the past point to the Soviet threat, as perceived by the Defence Intelligence Staff, and justify projects through the Treasury. The fall of the Berlin Wall however, had removed this certainty.[93]

The Treasury, by the start of 1990, was already advancing plans for the public expenditure through until 1992-93.[94] Given the start of the recession, the government had added to public spending £2.2, £7.9, and £11.6 billion respectively for the years 1991, 1992, and 1993. Clearly there were problems which needed to be addressed.

To consider the organisational process paradigm as the key influence behind the Options for Change review, what can be said tentatively, given the release of few documents, about its impact? It has been demonstrated that the planning cycles of both the Ministry and the Treasury, particularly with regard to factoring in a projected figure for inflationary pressures, can lead to severe difficulties as were experienced throughout the 1980s.

Departmental politics offered the Treasury an opportunity to seek reductions in the defence budget given the poor project management exercised by the Ministry, coupled with the changing environment in Central and Eastern Europe. The parliamentary oversight committees facilitated reports which highlighted the Ministry's problems, exposing the organisation to the budgetary predators.

One issue which whilst hypothetical, given the lack of evidence, but of interest to this analysis, is the role of the political figures in the Ministry. Was initiating the review, a means for individuals to wrest the initiative from the Ministry of Defence? In order to consider this it is appropriate to consider the final analytical lens, that of governmental (bureaucratic) politics.

Options for Change: The Bureaucratic Politics Model

This final examination of the decision making process leading to the Options for Change review considers the bargaining process between the political figures, astride the administrative departments of state. It could be suggested that there are difficulties in applying this framework.[95] Memoirs of the principal participants are both few and brief in their discussion of relatively recent government business and tend to focus more on the role of the individual than the policy process.[96]

Essentially there are two elements to consider in this analysis of the decision making process which led to the review - interactions between political figures within the Ministry of Defence, and broader interaction with the cabinet and Prime Minister.

An important part of this process is the manner in which factions within the organisations represented by Ministers make their views heard. These action channels, because of a lack of public information are not considered within the confines of this report.

A Ministerial reshuffle on the 24th July 1989 saw the appointment of a new team of ministers to the Ministry of Defence. Tom King, (the Secretary of State), had worked previously with Alan Clark (Minister for Defence Procurement) during the 1980s at the Department of Employment. Alan Clark suggested in his Diaries that his relationship with King was somewhat less than satisfactory.[97] A journalist friend of Clark's noted that, "Mixing Alan Clark and Tom King could be the only mistake of the reshuffle."[98]

The previous Secretary of State for Defence, George Younger, had enjoyed very good relations with the Prime Minister.[99] He had been able to broker a deal with the Treasury to obtain clarity as to the budget for defence in the late 1980s and establish a carry-over for funds saved through cost cutting. It could be suggested that possibly his replacement by a weaker figure lacking Younger's presence enabled the Chancellor to strip away the carry-over facility bringing forward the requirement for a review of defence policy.

George Younger MP who was Secretary of State for Defence from 1986 to 1989 (Source: US Government via Wikimedia Commons)

Given Clark's role in procurement, the area in which resource decisions are typically made first when considering change in defence expenditure, his participation in a review would be inevitable. Already he had authored a twenty-year projection of defence requirements as early as 1984.[100] This coupled with his own impression that his position in Procurement at the Ministry of Defence would be his last chance to succeed in politics, by obtaining a senior ministerial post, suggested a willingness to take risks.

His opportunity came, according to his recollections at a seminar at the Government retreat at Chequers concerning developments in the CFE conventional forces negotiations. Apparently, by breaking precedents he requested in September 1989 that he be able to write a paper on "equipment requirements over the next five years."[101] There then followed a series of political manoeuvres. The Treasury team of Chancellor Lawson and Secretary Lamont were keen on cuts in defence expenditure (which would assist them in their goal of lowering overall public expenditure).

However, why did the Prime Minister not charge the Secretary of State for Defence with the task of writing a review as political leader of the Department? It could be suggested that it is a well-known fact that Prime Ministers regardless of their political persuasion enjoy creating creative tension between their ministers.

Margaret Thatcher (Baroness Thatcher), who was Prime Minister at the time (Source: Chris Collins via Wikimedia Commons)

Furthermore the Prime Minister was in her third term as leader with a commanding majority in the House of Commons. This dominance led to a leadership style which was suggested by her Chancellor Lawson, "as disagreeably strident, excessively authoritarian, and unbearably bossy."[102] The 1986 Westland affair had caused the Prime Minister to believe that, "her colleagues were troublesome and her courtiers were loyal."[103] These characteristics possibly led the Prime Minister to come to a conclusion on policy issues based on instinct, and then support people who supported those issues. This it could be suggested was the motivation behind the Prime Minister formally sanctioning Clark's 'shadow study'.

Having completed the shadow study by December, the official study prepared by the senior civil servant at the Ministry of Defence was completed shortly after. At a Departmental meeting Clark recollects that the shadow study received much attention by the Secretary of State noting that, "we have all got to ensure that this does not get into the hands of the Prime Minister."[104] Fortunately or unfortunately for Clark he had already passed it onto the Prime Minister's offices at No. 10 Downing Street.

Throughout 1990 Clark's memoirs suggest that his report was smothered by the Secretary of State who sought to take control over proceedings. The Ministry of Defence official review effort was led by two staffs, one under the leadership of Sir David Craig, Chief of the Defence Staff. The second, a team from the Office of Management and Budget led by the Second Permanent under Secretary. Both teams reported directly to the Secretary of State with the two staffs providing respectively a strategic analysis, and economic assessment.[105]

The Secretary of State for Defence in turn, reported to a Cabinet Committee (one of the Misc. series) consisting of the Prime Minister, and the Secretaries of State for Defence, Foreign Affairs, and the Chancellor of the Exchequer. The small numbers involved highlighted the fact that the government had been embarrassed during the 1981 review and wanted no repeat of the event.[106]

The invasion of Kuwait by Iraq in August 1990 and the British commitment to Kuwait and Saudi Arabia gave, in Clark's words, "the AF [Armed Forces] side of the department a renewed raison d'être."[107] This meant that procurement issues would take second place to the task at hand, ending albeit temporarily the pressure on resources. In the meanwhile a leadership challenge from within the Conservative party led to a change of Prime Minister.

What can be inferred from this case study about government activity? Clearly the personalities and their aspirations (Alan Clark for example), plus belief systems (the Prime Ministers) all impact on decision-making, shattering the myth of the cool, rationalised debate over policy options within the framework of collective responsibility. In the case of the commencement of the Options for Change process personalities were key in the breakdown within and between the Ministry of Defence and HM Treasury.

The Governmental (Bureaucratic) Politics model has limited utility other than as an organising device for material in this instance. The nature of collective responsibility in the British Cabinet system means that the only events we can observe are those released in biographies or press reports. Compared to the Intra-Governmental Decision model it is not possible, without dynamic trust and reputation issues, to adequately interpret the Options for Change process.

Conclusion

In summary, this study has sought to show the utility of the Intra-Governmental Decision model vis-à-vis the Allison framework in a contemporary situation. The primary advantage of the Allison framework appears to be as a mechanism for organising a wealth of information into readily assimilated parts within a coherent whole.

The Rational Actor Model facilitates an examination of defence policy making as arising from the state considering courses of action, their costs and alternatives.

The Organisational Process Model hints at the interaction between organisations which both adds a second layer of richness to the picture, and simultaneously demonstrating the operation of government.

The Governmental (Bureaucratic) Politics model shows the process of bargaining between the figures at the pinnacle of their respective agencies in government.

The three models are complimentary, as having read an interpretation of each, when applied to the 1989-1990 defence review, the reader is left with a sophisticated understanding of the situation. This may have not been possible using merely the traditional classical model.

The four models provide the reader with different perspectives from which to consider not only a historical case study but also as a magnifying lens through which to see how decision-making bodies are responding to the challenges of implementing the Strategic Defence Review against a background of rapid change in the strategic environment.

Endnotes

[1] Bruce-Gardyne, J. (1986) *Ministers and Mandarins: Inside the Whitehall Village*, London: Sidgwick & Jackson, p. 57.

[2] Thatcher, M. (1993) *The Downing Street Years*, London: HarperCollins, p. 15.

[3] *Ibid.*

[4] *Ibid.* pp. 30 - 31.

[5] Lawson, N. (1992) *The View from No. 11: Memoirs of a Tory Radical*, London: Bantam, esp. (1981) pp. 103 – 104, (1988) pp. 299 – 301 and Ch. 58.

[6] These cultures were formally recognised in the 1970s. For a typical commentary of their interaction see *The Guardian*. 'An officer and a management man' (9 March 1990).

[7] For more details regarding the Intermediate Nuclear Forces or INF Treaty see as a starting-point http://www.state.gov/www/global/arms/treaties/inf1.html.

[8] Ministry of Defence. (1989) *Statement on the Defence Estimates 1989, Volume 1*, Cm675-I, London: HMSO, p. 1, para. 105.

[9] House of Commons Defence Committee. (1989) *Statement on the Defence Estimates 1989*, HC383, London: HMSO.

[10] *Ibid.* pp. 1 – 2, para. 6.

[11] Clarke, M. 'The Soviet Union and Eastern Europe' in Byrd, P (ed.). (1991) *British*

Foreign Policy under Thatcher, New York: St. Martin's Press, p. 74.

[12] The memoirs of Alan Clark suggest the process as being started formally after a meeting at Chequers on Saturday 30th September 1989. One of the earliest indications of this cultural rift can be seen in *The Times* (23/03/90). 'MoD faces White Paper dilemma on East bloc changes'.

[13] Ministry of Defence. (1990) *Statement on the Defence Estimates 1990, Volume 1*, Cm1022-I, London: HMSO, esp. Ch. 1.

[14] House of Commons Defence Committee. (1990) *Statement on the Defence Estimates 1990*, HC388, London: HMSO, pp. 16 – 17, paras. 94 – 103.

[15] House of Commons Defence Committee. (1990) *Defence Implications of Recent Events*, HC320, London: HMSO, p. x1, para. 99.

[16] See House of Commons Defence Committee. (1991) *Options for Change: Royal Navy*, HC266, London: HMSO, pp. 25. Also (1991) *Options for Change: Royal Air Force*, HC393, London: HMSO, pp. 27. Further (1992) *Options for Change: Army - Review of the White Paper, Britain's Army for the 90s, CM1595*, HC45, London: HMSO, pp. 95. Lastly (1992) *Options for Change: Reserve Forces*, HC163, London: HMSO, pp. 68.

[17] *Op Cit.* HCDC, HC320, p. 78, para. 343. Evidence from Lord Healey.

[18] *Interview.* Sir Michael Quinlan (Shrivenham: Royal Military College of Science 07/10/98).

[19] *Jane's Defence Weekly* 14 (5) (04/08/90). 'UK forces face 18% reduction'. p. 152.

[20] For details of the political battle to preserve regiments see *Op. Cit.* HCDC, HC45. pp. 80 – 95. Also *Jane's Defence Weekly* 14 (6) (11/08/90). 'Britain's Army: building a new structure'. p. 194. Further Strachan, H. (1997) *The Politics of the British Army*, Oxford: Oxford University Press, pp. 195 – 233. esp. 225 – 233.

[21] *Op. Cit.* HCDC, HC45, pp. vi – vii, para. 7 – 8.

[22] *Op. Cit.* HCDC, HC266, p. xii, para. 20.

[23] Ministry of Defence. (1992) *Statement on the Defence Estimates 1992*, Cm1981, London: HMSO, pp. 68 – 79. The White Paper introduced three Defence Roles, 1: Protection of the United Kingdom and dependent territories, 2: Defence of the United Kingdom against a major external threat, and 3: The United Kingdom's wider security interests. Within these roles were a number of military tasks against which force elements were assigned.

[24] Ministry of Defence. (1993) *Defending our Future: Statement on the Defence Estimates 1993*, Cm2270, London: HMSO, pp. 19 - 60.

[25] House of Commons Defence Committee. (1993) *Britain's Army for the 90s: Commitments and Resources*, HC306, London: HMSO, pp. 6 – 7, paras. 671 – 673 and

written evidence. pp. 32 - 35. The evidence articulates the over-stretch faced by the army and inability to train effectively.

[26] *Ibid.* p. ix, para. 10.

[27] Ministry of Defence. (1994) *Front Line First: The Defence Costs Study*, London: HMSO.

[28] Ministry of Defence. (1994) Statement on the Defence Estimates 1994, Cm2550, London: HMSO, pp. 53 - 66. The White Paper indicated tendering for new nuclear submarines, Army plans to acquire helicopter gunships and new tanks, and the continuing development of Eurofighter for the RAF.

[29] *Op. Cit.* MoD, Cm1022-I, p. 44, para. 404. This statement was indicative of the economic hypothesis as being the central determinant of policy. The international security hypothesis gains credence from government citation in *Ibid.* p. 9, para. 110.

[30] Allison, G. (1971). *Essence of Decision – Explaining the Cuban Missile Crisis*, London: Longman, pp. 9 – 38.

[31] Darby, P. (1973) *British Defence Policy East of Suez*, Oxford: Oxford University Press, p. 268.

[32] Ovendale, R. (1994) *British Defence Policy since 1945*, Manchester: Manchester University Press, p. 18. Ovendale cites Public Record Office, London, CAB 128/11, fos 7-8, CM6(47)3, Confidential annex, 15 January 1947.

[33] Ministry of Defence. (1968) *Statement on the Defence Estimates 1968*, Cm3540, London: HMSO, p. 2.

[34] The CVA-01 aircraft carrier project was deleted in the 1966 Defence White Paper. For a detailed discussion see chapter 2.

[35] The British nuclear deterrent was carried first by the V-bomber force in the 1950s. Following the 1962 Nassau agreement with the United States, Britain received the *Polaris* submarine based missile. The 1980s saw an agreement which led to the purchase of the *Trident* missile currently in service with the Royal Navy

[36] SALT and its successor SALT II were nuclear arms control acronyms standing for Strategic Arms Limitation Talks.

[37] Its full title is The Treaty between the United States of America and the Union of Soviet Socialist Republics on the elimination of their intermediate range and short range missiles.

[38] The neutron bomb was a US developed enhanced radiation weapon which had much greater effects upon people with reduced, albeit still significant, destructive potential.

[39] The deployment involved 572 weapons, including 108 Pershing II, and 464 cruise missiles.

[40] SIPRI (1988) *World Armaments and Disarmament Yearbook 1988*, SIPRI: Stockholm, p. 381.

[41] Feifenberg, J. (1986) 'Transatlantic relations - a case of continental drift' in *NATO Review*, Vol. 34, No. 5. The article discussed the 'Rambo' element of American culture.

[42] The CSCE was the Conference on Security and Co-operation in Europe. Its recent successor is the OSCE or Organisation for Security and Co-operation in Europe.

[43] Ruehl, L. (1982) *MBFR: Lessons and Problems,* London: International Institute for Strategic Studies, Adelphi Paper No. 176, p. 2.

[44] Alexander, M. (1986) 'MBFR - Verification is the key' in *NATO Review*, Vol. 34, No. 3, p. 10.

[45] Blacker, C D. 'Negotiating security: The MBFR experience' in *Arms Control* Vol. 7. p. 215.

[46] Sharp, J M O. (1990) 'Conventional arms control in Europe' in *SIPRI World Armaments and Disarmament Yearbook 1990*, p. 478.

[47] The Conference on Security and Co-operation in Europe (CSCE) became the Organisation for Security and Co-operation in Europe (OSCE) in January 1995.

[48] Dean, J. (1990) 'The CFE negotiations, present and future' in *Survival*, Vol. 32. No. 4. (Jul. - Aug. 1990), pp. 313 – 324.

[49] *ibid.* p. 93.

[50] *Op. Cit.* MoD, Cm1022-I.

[51] *Op. Cit.* HCDC, HC320. The Committee Chairman, Michael Mates attributed the title of the report to one of his clerks in an address to the Royal United Services Institute. See the *RUSI Journal*, Vol. 35. No. 3. (Autumn 1990) p. 72.

[52] *Ibid.* p. x. Para. 13.

[53] Houses of Parliament. (1990) *Hansard*, 25th July 1990, pp. 468 - 486. The phrase 'Options for Change' was first used officially by Secretary of State for Defence Tom King on the 6th February 1990.

[54] Foreign & Commonwealth Office. (1990) *Charter of Paris for a New Europe*, Cm1464, London: HMSO, p. 1.

[55] Ministry of Defence (1991) *Statement on the Defence Estimates 1991, Volume One*, Cm1559-I, London: HMSO, p. 6.

[56] Heinl, R D Jr. (1966) *Dictionary of Military and Naval Quotations*, Annapolis: Naval Institute Press, p. 115.

[57] Keohane, D. (1993) *Labour Party Defence Policy since 1945*, Leicester: Leicester University Press, p. 20.

[58] Browning, P. (1986) *The Treasury and Economic Policy 1964 – 1985*, London:

Longman 1986, pp. 13 – 14.

[59] *Op. Cit.* Keohane. 1993, p. 21.

[60] Carver, M. (1992) *Tightrope Walking, British Defence Policy since 1945*, London: Hutchinson, p. 104.

[61] *Op. Cit.* Ovendale, 1994, p. 162. Citation originates from Ministry of Defence. (1981) *The United Kingdom Defence Programme: The Way Forward*, Cm8288, London: HMSO.

[62] Greenwood, D. 'Expenditure and Management' in *Op. Cit.* Byrd, 1991, pp. 36 – 66.

[63] *Ibid.* p. 45.

[64] *Ibid.* p. 56.

[65] Centre for Defence Studies. (1992) *United Kingdom Defence Policy in the 1990s*, London: Centre for Defence Studies, pp. 10 – 18.

[66] HM Treasury. (1994) *Economic Briefing* No. 6 (February 1994), pp. 1 – 5.

[67] *Ibid.* p. 1.

[68] House of Commons Committee of Public Accounts. (1990) *Ministry of Defence: The Annual Statement on Major Defence Projects*, HC295, London: HMSO, p. 23.

[69] *Op Cit* . HCDC, HC388, pp. 1 – 2.

[70] Sabin, P A G. (1990) *British Strategic Priorities in the 1990s*, Adelphi Paper 254, London: Brassey's (IISS), p. 12.

[71] Baylis, J. (1989) *British Defence Policy: Striking the Right Balance*, London: Macmillan, pp. 78 – 79.

[72] *Op. Cit.* Sabin, p. 12.

[73] *Op. Cit.* Allison, pp. 11 – 14 and pp. 67 – 100.

[74] Ministry of Defence. (1990) *The Ministry of Defence*, London: HMSO, p. 1.

[75] *Ibid.* p. 3.

[76] Ministry of Defence. (1996) *Ministry of Defence Staff Handbook: A Guide for Civilians in the Ministry of Defence*, London: HMSO, December 1996, 4.5 Table of civilian and service equivalents.

[77] In January 1990, these posts were held by the Rt. Hon Tom King MP, Hon. Archibald Hamilton, the Earl of Arran, the Hon. Alan Clark MP, and Michael Neubert MP.

[78] McIntosh, M. (1990) *Managing Britain's Defence*, London: Palgrave Macmillan, p. 92. In 1992, Dr. McIntosh was Chief of Defence Procurement, Ministry of Defence.

[79] Taylor, D. (1986) *Ministry of Defence: Keepers of the Threat*, London: BBC, 9th April 1986.

[80] *Op Cit.* McIntosh, 1990, p. 93.

[81] *Ibid.* p. 153.

[82] HM Treasury (1990) *Economic Briefing No. 1*, December 1990, p. 1.

[83] Pliatzky, L. (1989) *The Treasury under Mrs Thatcher*, Oxford: Basil Blackwell, p. 160.

[84] *Op. Cit.* Browning, p. 220. The Public Expenditure Survey "spans more than twelve months, because one round begins before the previous round is brought to a conclusion".

[85] *Op Cit* . Lawson, pp. 289 – 293. The Star Chamber was formally known as Misc. Committee 62.

[86] HM Treasury. (1989) *The Government's Expenditure Plans 1989 - 90 to 1991 - 92*, Cm601, London: HMSO, p. 1.

[87] Mates, M. (1990) 'The Role of the House of Commons Defence Committee: Relationships and Prospects' in *RUSI Journal*, Vol. 135, No. 3 (Autumn 1990), p. 72. At this point, Michael Mates MP was Chairman of the Defence Committee. See also Hockaday, A. (1990) 'Parliamentary Control of Defence: The Role of Select Committees' in *RUSI Journal*, Vol. 135, No. 1 (Spring 1990), pp. 7 – 10; and McDonald, O. (1993) *The Defence Select Committee 1979-92*, London: Brassey's, Centre for Defence Studies. Further George, B MP & Morgan, J D. *The Defence select committee: Presented to a symposium on "The Whitehall Machine"*, Royal United Services Institute for Defence Studies, 6th November 1997.

[88] Simpson, K. (1992) 'Frock Coats, Mandarins, and Brass Hats: The Relationship between Politicians, Civil Servants and the Military' in *RUSI Journal*, Vol. 137, No. 1 (Feb. 1992), p. 62.

[89] *Op. Cit* . McIntosh. pp. 55 – 56. In 1990 the Chairman was the Rt. Hon. Robert Sheldon MP.

[90] *Op. Cit* . Bruce-Gardyne, p. 62. Bruce-Gardyne was formerly an Economic Secretary to the Treasury from 1981 to 1983.

[91] *Op. Cit* . McDonald, p. 16.

[92] Cook, N. (1990) 'Changing Winds of Fortune' in *Jane's Defence Weekly*, 14 (9) (1st September 1990), p. 326.

[93] *Op. Cit.* Simpson, p. 62.

[94] *Op Cit* . Centre for Defence Studies, p. 10.

[95] A description and analysis of the Governmental (bureaucratic) politics model are contained in *Op Cit.* Allison, 1971, Ch. 1. pp. 14 – 15. See also *Op. Cit.* Allison, 1971, pp. 144 – 184.

[96] *Op. Cit* . Thatcher. p. 812.

[97] Clark, A. (1993) *Diaries*, London: Weidenfield & Nicholson. Upon King's promotion to Secretary of State for Northern Ireland Clark noted, "He always loses in Cabinet... This, and his testy manner with officials, has eroded his support in Whitehall". 1985, p. 109.

[98] *Ibid.* 1989, p. 253.

[99] *Op. Cit* . Thatcher, p. 756. Upon his leaving the PM noted that, "George's departure was something of a blow. I valued his common sense, trusted his judgement and relied on his loyalty".

[100] *Op. Cit* . Clark, 1984, p.100.

[101] *Ibid.* 1989, p. 258.

[102] *Op. Cit* . Lawson, p. 1001.

[103] *Ibid.* p. 680. This Defence Industry controversy led to the resignation of the then Secretary of State for Defence, Michael Heseltine, who had a pivotal role in the effort to remove the Prime Minister, Margaret Thatcher, in 1990.

[104] *Op. Cit* . Clark, 1993, pp. 263 - 264.

[105] Editorial. (1990) 'MoD Faces White Paper Dilemma on East Bloc Changes' in *The Times*, 23rd March 1990. See also *Op. Cit.* HCDC. HC45. p. 31. para. 1331.

[106] Editorial. (1990), 'Secret Defence Review to Consider Forces Cuts after E Europe Upheaval' in *Daily Telegraph*, 22 March 1990.

[107] *Op. Cit.* Clark. 1990, p. 335.

A New Entente Cordiale or Business as Usual? The UK – France Defence Relationship[1]

Pete Ito, Peter D. Antill and Steve Robinson

Centre for Defence Acquisition, Cranfield University, Defence Academy of the UK.

From the UK TV series "Yes Minister", an exchange between senior civil servant Sir Humphrey Appleby and Minister James Hacker on fallout shelters:

> Appleby: Well, you have the weapons; you must have the shelters.
>
> Hacker: I sometimes wonder why we need the weapons.
>
> Appleby: Minister! You're not a unilateralist?
>
> Hacker: I sometimes wonder, you know.
>
> Appleby: Well, then, you must resign from the government!
>
> Hacker: Ah, no, no, no, no, no. I'm not that unilateralist!
>
> Anyway, the Americans will always protect us from the Russians, won't they?
>
> Appleby: Russians? Who's talking about the Russians?
>
> Hacker: Well, the independent deterrent.
>
> Appleby: It's to protect us against the French!
>
> Hacker: The French?!! But they're our allies!
>
> Appleby: Well, they might be now; but they were our mortal enemies for centuries, and old leopards don't change their spots.

France has no friends, only interests. – Charles de Gaulle

We have no eternal allies, and we have no perpetual enemies. Our interests are eternal and perpetual. – Lord Palmerston

Introduction

On 2 November 2010, UK Prime Minister David Cameron and French President Nicolas Sarkozy signed the Anglo-French Defence Co-Operation Treaty. It is comprised of an overarching treaty on defence cooperation as well as a subordinate treaty related to joint nuclear facilities. The Letter of Intent signed by the Defence Ministers and Chiefs of

Defence Staff of both countries noted increasing interoperability between the armed forces of the UK and France as a major goal, as well as a number of separate joint initiatives.

As noted by the UK Ministry of Defence at the signing of the Treaty, the measures agreed between the UK and France included work in the following areas: jointly developing a Combined Joint Expeditionary Force as a non-standing bilateral capability; developing the ability to deploy a UK-French integrated carrier strike group incorporating assets owned by both countries (building primarily on maritime task group cooperation centred on the French carrier Charles de Gaulle); developing joint military doctrine and training programmes; extending bilateral cooperation on the acquisition of equipment and technologies; aligning (wherever possible) logistics arrangements; developing a stronger defence industrial and technology base, and enhancing joint working to defend against emerging security concerns such as cyber security. Overall, the MoD noted that the Treaty is intended to enable the strengthening of operational linkages between the UK and French Armed Forces, sharing and pooling of materials and equipment, building of joint facilities, mutual access to defence markets, and increased industrial and technological cooperation.[2]

The French aircraft carrier Charles de Gaulle
(Source: US Navy via Wikimedia Commons)

It would be fair to say that previous attempts at Anglo-French cooperation, most recently the St. Malo declaration of December 1998, did not achieve the level of bilateral cooperation that was initially anticipated by many observers, or indeed London and Paris. Nor, as will be discussed later, did St. Malo serve as the foundation for a larger European effort to generate defence capabilities, as had been anticipated by then-Prime Minister Tony Blair.

In the case of the 2010 treaty, it is apparent that pressures on both countries' military budgets have driven a shift in policy toward greater bilateral cooperation, particularly in the area of defence acquisition. Subsequently, the 2011 cooperation between London and Paris on military operations in Libya and the recent support afford by the British to the French operations in Mali provided further indication of the benefits of greater bilateral coordination in the security area. On the other hand, the political dispute at the end of 2011 regarding the reluctance of the UK to fully support Franco-German proposals to save the Euro led to concerns that a weakened overall Anglo-French political relationship would have an impact on future defence cooperation. However, the outcome of the February 2012 Anglo-French Summit indicates that, despite the clash over the Euro, there appears to be continued determination to proceed with strengthened bilateral military cooperation.

This paper seeks to assess, from a predominantly UK perspective, the potential implications for both the U.S. and Europe of such enhanced Anglo-French defence cooperation, recognising that future problems in non-defence areas could put a brake on such efforts. The paper will mainly focus on defence cooperation and not the subordinate agreement regarding limited cooperation on nuclear weapons, although a brief examination of that document is necessary. The agreement addresses cooperation on the safety and security of nuclear weapons, stockpile certification and countering nuclear and radiological terrorism. The immediate focus is the construction of joint radiographic-hydrodynamic facilities[3] and the initiatives were possible due to "long-term strategic shifts"[4], but appear to be driven by "acute financial pressures, symptomatic of severe structural deficiencies".[5]

Past Successes and Failures

As noted by Jones[6], enhanced defence cooperation between the UK and France would appear to be a natural fit. In 2010, the UK defence budget was around €43.4bn (£36.4 bn)[7] and the French budget around €39.2 bn[8]. Defence spending was between 3.5 – 5% of total government spending in both countries. The two combined defence budgets were just under half of all European defence spending (€82.6bn compared to €193.5bn) and accounted for around 75% of research and development spending (€6.48bn compared to €8.56bn).[9] Jones added that RAND has estimated that by 2015, combined UK and French defence budgets could be around 65% of EU defence spending.[10]

There has been a long-standing record of Anglo-French defence coordination. The two established a High-Level Working Group in 2006 to promote closer cooperation in armaments programmes. They had already established a Franco-British European Air Group (1994), completed a Letter of Intent on naval cooperation (1996), as well as a Letter of Intent on cooperation between the two armies (1997) and established a Joint Commission on Peacekeeping (1996) to harmonise peacekeeping procedures and doctrine.

A German Boxer (MRAV) prototype from GTK (Source: Heldt via Wikimedia Commons)

On the other hand, the history of Anglo-French defence acquisition cooperation has been mixed. There were successful programs in the 1960s and 1970s (including the Puma and Gazelle helicopters and the Jaguar strike aircraft) and the establishment of MBDA, Europe's leading manufacturer of guided weapons, in 2001, is a significant Anglo-French creation. However, there have been notable failures. For example, the UK dropped out of the agreement with France and Germany for production of the TRIGAT anti-tank missile and the Trimilsatcom communications satellite programme. It also dropped out of the Horizon Common New Generation Frigate project which included France and Italy.[11] Both countries also dropped out of the Multi-Role Armoured Vehicle (MRAV) programme, although at different times, which eventually became a joint German-Dutch effort.[12]

Following on from the success of the MILAN anti-tank missile project, the UK, France and Germany (with the Netherlands and Belgium as associate partners) signed a trilateral requirement to develop and produce its successor. However, whereas the MILAN project had been essentially a bilateral project with other countries signing up to provide economies of scale in production, the TRIGAT programme began with requirements that were more quantitative rather than qualitative due to the slightly differing requirements of all three lead countries. In addition, the contract was signed under French law which did not tie industry to performance measurement.[13] The UK eventually withdrew from the TRIGAT production phase in 2000 due to unacceptable delays and uncertainty in a programme which at the time was already ten years later than originally planned. The UK withdrew from Project Horizon in 1999 to pursue a national Type 45 Destroyer programme. The UK concluded that "Overall, the absence of an industrially robust – as distinct from a specially formed – prime contractor encompassing responsibility for the platform and the weapons fit spelled the end of what had looked at least like a very promising project".[14] However, it is impossible to identify whether this was the only key reason for withdrawal. Alternatives might have been pressure from the national shipbuilding industry and the Armed Forces to undertake a national project, ministers wanting flexibility to reduce its orders (the order for the Type 45s was eventually cut from twelve to eight and then to six) or the delays caused by the three partners being unable to reconcile their differing requirements – the UK had primarily wanted a ship that was a true ocean-going vessel, the Italians wanted a ship to primarily operate in the littoral and the French wanted something that lay between the two.

Continued Commitment

At the February 17, 2012 UK-France Summit, the two leaders reemphasized their commitment to do more in the area of defence cooperation. They noted that the 2010 agreement has led to expansion of cooperation "in every major field: capabilities, industry, operations and intelligence".[15] After analysing the Libya operation, the two countries "have decided to prioritise our joint work in the key areas of: command and control; information systems; intelligence, surveillance, targeting and reconnaissance; and precision munitions".[16] They also noted that the Libya experience reinforced the desire to set up the Combined Joint Expeditionary Force[17] and the two nations will establish a Combined Joint Forces Headquarters by 2016[18], a move that will surely be reinforced by the British support to French operations in Mali, aimed at expelling the fundamentalist Islamic rebels from the country[19] and underlined by the increasing number of joint exercises.[20]

It was notable that the most concrete results cited by the two leaders were in specific areas of defence equipment. The desire for cooperation on unmanned aerial vehicles (UAVs) was made manifest with specific projects. With regard to the Medium Altitude Long Endurance (MALE) drone, the two leaders announced they would soon "place with BAE Systems and Dassault a jointly funded contract to study the technical risks associated with the MALE UAV".[21] France also confirmed its "interest for the (British) Watchkeeper system" with an evaluation by France to begin this year.[22]

A Royal Air Force C-17 Globemaster. Two of these aircraft supported the French intervention in Mali during 2013 – Operation Serval. (Source: Airman 1st Class Tiffany Deuel, US Air Force via Wikimedia Commons)

There was also a reaffirmation of the pledge "to undertake in 2013 a joint Future Combat Air System Demonstration Programme that will set up a co-operation of strategic importance for the future of the European Combat Air Sector." The document highlighted the contract let to MBDA in December 2011 for two initial studies on a future cruise and an anti-ship weapon.[23] And it noted the intention to sign a contract in coming months for development and manufacture of the Future Anti-ship Guided Weapon.

Rationale - Policy Concurrence

To determine what the Anglo-French Treaty may mean for the U.S., it is important to assess the driving forces behind this renewed effort at Anglo-French defence cooperation. The question, as formulated by Lindley-French[24], is whether the Anglo-French Treaty is "a new departure or simply the latest twist in the centuries-old Anglo-French tussle for power? It is probably a bit of both." As he adds, "if Britain and France are to remain European powers with global reach they will need to share a vision of the big picture and stick to it".[25] Put even more bluntly, but in terms that will probably resonate in Washington:

> "Defence cooperation between Britain and France is and must always be about power. The alternative is the decline of both countries, along with the rest of a Europe that seems to accept weakness as strength, equating an inability to act as meaning no need to act in the hope that danger simply bypasses a continent too weak to matter any longer."[26]

James Arbuthnot, the Chairman of the UK House of Commons Defence Select Committee, provided a similarly frank assessment in providing an overarching view of Anglo-French cooperation.[27] Arbuthnot stated that the opportunity to cooperate with France is one which the UK cannot pass up. Certainly, he added, there are suspicions between the UK and France. The UK is always suspicious of what France can do or wishes to do. But Arbuthnot suggested that it may be best to view the UK and France like two brothers: while they quarrel, what unites them is more than what divides them.

General Sir Kevin O'Donoghue, Chief of Defence Materiel at the UK Ministry of Defence until 2011, concurred that the UK and France have roughly the same capabilities and policy views.[28] Bilateral cooperation is clearly logical for the UK. And assessing the agreement from the French perspective, he believed that it makes sense for Paris to collaborate with London.

Rationale - Shortage of Money

The impact of budget cuts for the UK and France in spurring a desire for defence cooperation cannot be overstated. Arbuthnot conceded that scarce resources are a key driving force for increased cooperation. But referring back to the earlier point on policy, he emphasized that there are also shared threats and responses which makes Anglo-French defence cooperation easier to develop.

Indeed, the argument has been made that the focus of the bilateral effort is not even to preserve defence capabilities, but "it is apparent that the strong aspiration will be to achieve a specific quantum of savings".[29] In the UK, the Strategic Defence and Security Review (SDSR) mandated a cut of around 8% in UK defence spending in real terms over four years.[30] As a result, Bickerton comments that "there is a chance that the budgetary crisis in the UK will push the government to recognise that potential savings can be made to the defence budget by cooperating more closely with France on armaments."[31]

With regard to France, one writer notes that "a senior French military officer believes that the defence cuts in France in future are likely to be 'unprecedented' with 'big decisions' on major programmes necessary".[32] Stevens agrees that France is facing the same problem, noting that the then Defence Minister Morin announced a reduction of 3% out of the defence budget, which cut across a range of capabilities. Perhaps more important, Stevens adds that there is speculation that even without a change of government, there could be a further 4-5% reduction.[33] Such tight budgets necessitate a focus on how best to generate military capability from scarce resources. Bickerton notes that "the French Government has also been interested above all in capabilities and force effectiveness."[34]

However, some analysts warn against placing too much emphasis on funding problems as the motivator behind the Anglo-French Treaty, arguing that there are more fundamental issues involved. Jones argues that "it would be wrong to see Franco-British defence cooperation as driven purely by a short-term need to balance the books", outlining three long-term trends that challenge traditional thinking in London and Paris.[35] First, "defence budgets have not been funded to compensate for the rising cost of military capability." Second, the security environment makes it "all but impossible to make the political case for more defence spending." Finally, "flat or lower spending combined with increasingly expensive technology undermines the viability of national, and even multinational, industries." Jones asserts that these factors threaten British and French national defence industrial capabilities and potentially, operational autonomy.[36]

If the Anglo-French treaty is indeed driven purely by immediate budgetary considerations, this raises questions regarding the long term prospects of this partnership. As noted by Gomis:

"The Franco-British treaties, although signed for a 50-year period, focus on the short-term need for capabilities. A number of crucial questions therefore remain. What will happen when the British and French economies recover? Will the two countries' strategic differences re-emerge? Will they return to old habits of more protectionism and nationalism in the defence realm? Will both governments gradually abandon the increased financial imperative in defence spending recently induced by budgetary austerity?"[37]

As a partial response, Jones cites the overarching political, military and industrial considerations which are critical to London and Paris, commenting

"For now, Franco-British defence cooperation is driven primarily by an aspiration in both countries to retain access to a full spectrum of military capabilities, sufficient to contribute strategic effect and retain credibility in the eyes of the United States, and therefore NATO. A secondary motive is to sustain their national defence capabilities for core sovereign obligations. A third is to contribute to bilateral and European missions, as well as to sustain general European military capabilities for an uncertain future."[38]

Rationale – Practical Defence Cooperation

It also can be argued that the intentions behind this latest Anglo-French effort are quite practical, and are focused on the need to simply maintain credible military capabilities. Jones states that the motivation

"is to maintain French and British aspirations to power projection and to military credibility in the eyes of the United States. The many similarities and shared vital interests of France and the UK underpin, but do not drive, the initiative. The end-goal is to retain access to military capability, whether that is through mutual dependence on each other's industrial base and armed forces, or through pooling and sharing capability".[39]

Reinforcing the point that there are practical aspects to the cooperation, Jones asserts that while London and Paris want to be seen as credible partners by Washington, national sovereignty is also a key consideration. The UK and France are driven by the motivation of retaining access "to a full range of capabilities to pursue independent foreign policies".[40]

Echoing the point of practical areas for developing capabilities, one UK official[41] commented that there is potential with regard to better Anglo-French cooperation in areas such as joint support and training. There could be more use of simulators, for example, as well as opportunities for sharing facilities. With regard to practical examples of defence cooperation, the International Institute for Strategic Studies[42] notes that the UK and France have an agreement to develop a common support plan for the A400-M transport and there is discussion of an arrangement whereby France could use some of the extra capacity in the UK Future Strategic Tanker Aircraft.

An A400-M transport aircraft (Source: Dval027 via Wikimedia Commons)

Political Leadership is Key

There appears to be widespread agreement that political leadership in London and Paris is essential to making bilateral cooperation work. That certainly was the case in previous agreements, such as St. Malo, which also highlighted the significance of the rationale (at least from the UK perspective) behind pursuing greater Anglo-French defence cooperation. With regard to St. Malo, Bickerton notes that "the wars in Yugoslavia and rising tensions in Kosovo had pushed Tony Blair towards a Franco-British defence agreement in order to enhance the EU's capabilities for intervention."[43] Shearer concurs that the Bosnia crisis was a "major challenge to Britain's defence identity" and strengthened "Britain's sense of belonging to a European political community."[44] Later, the Kosovo crisis was a key factor for Blair as it made apparent "Europe's relative military impotence".[45]

The St. Malo example highlights two issues. The first issue is whether Anglo-French defence cooperation can survive if bilateral relations are strained over other issues. As noted by one writer, the St. Malo spirit was dashed by the sharp policy divisions regarding Iraq and reflected the divergent political views in London and Paris.[46] The results of the initial test for the 2010 agreement would seem to provide grounds for optimism. Even after the critical dispute over the package to support the Euro, the results of the 2012 Anglo-French Summit were quite positive.

The second issue is the extent to which this bilateral push is a creation of the political leadership. For if that is indeed the case, that raises the two questions of 1) whether bilateral cooperation has become embedded as "business as usual" in the two bureaucracies and 2) whether it can survive a change in leadership. The mixed views on the first question are provided later. On the second question, from the UK perspective this relates to the extent to which French enthusiasm would continue if Sarkozy did not stay on as President. As it turns out, Francois Hollande won the May 2012 election and while it is still relatively early in his administration, seems to be enthusiastic about the relationship. Writing about the French return to the NATO integrated military command, Bickerton notes that from the UK perspective, there is a question whether the French attitude regarding the U.S. and NATO "goes much further than the President himself and much will depend on whether or not Sarkozy is able to win a second term".[47]

Addressing these issues, Arbuthnot stressed that the high-level political push on Anglo-French cooperation is essential, particularly with regard to bilateral commercial success. At summits, there is a drive to get deliverables and action. That has a direct impact on efforts which lead to industry taking concrete steps. That would certainly appear to be apparent in the various defence industrial initiatives announced in 2012.

Arbuthnot conceded that the difficulties regarding the Euro could well remain a critical factor, which leads to questions regarding the personal relationship between Cameron and Sarkozy. He emphasized however, that the press always seizes on personal relationships as the decisive factor, while he believes the drive for bilateral cooperation goes deeper than that. Arbuthnot noted that when he and the Deputy Chair of the Defence Select Committee went to Paris soon after the dispute on the Euro, UK and French officials were very clearly determined to ensure that bilateral defence cooperation would continue.

On the question of the level of support for bilateral cooperation below the political leadership, O'Donoghue commented that there are lots of challenges and mistrust which must be overcome. He asserted that the MOD leadership has bought into Anglo-French cooperation. But with regard to farther down in the UK bureaucracies, the level of support is mixed, as some individuals are pro-U.S. and some are pro-Europe. O'Donoghue stressed that the point is that these are not mutually exclusive, but acknowledged that these differing views exist.

Taking a different perspective on the issue, the UK official noted that Anglo-French defence cooperation will work as well as the politicians want it to work. As an example, the establishment of OCCAR (Organisation Conjointe de Cooperation en matiere d'Armement) was cited, which was set up to handle the through-life management of collaborative European defence equipment programmes. OCCAR has six European members, including the UK and France. The UK official noted that there was a big political push to establish OCCAR and a lot of support at that time. The intention was to change European defence acquisition, and steps were taken quickly to achieve that goal. It had impressive results, and a treaty was concluded.

But then, noted the UK official, the politicians walked away and left it to the bureaucrats to manage and in the absence of political leadership, the result was an ethos of 'not' making decisions. Each country wanted to make things work in its own way while no-one was there "to bang heads together." The UK official commented that this would apply to any effort, and the key is whether there is real political support in London and Paris to make Anglo-French defence cooperation work.

And in the view of this UK official, this is still an open question. This could still be a case of just good words, and not following up. Below the political level, there is a lot of scepticism in the UK MoD and UK defence industry about big ticket items, especially due to doubts about whether the Anglo-French initiative will be enduring. In addition, the point was reiterated that defence cooperation is subject to developments in non-defence areas, such as the Euro and elections.

On that count, Jones notes that "if bureaucratic and industrial obstacles can be overcome, there is a clear path to substantial cost savings and interoperability gains".[48] However, he appears to agree with O'Donoghue and the UK official that there is a risk that the Anglo-French effort could founder due to simple bureaucratic inertia.

"Ministries of Defence in both London and Paris have highly effective 'immune systems', notorious for rejecting new ideas. It can be challenging enough to embed change within the confines of a single department, never mind across different departments in two different countries. It is only natural that such a process will meet resistance from those who will tend to protect their functions and be cautious of different ways of working".[49]

Impact of Libya

It is apparent that the Anglo-French efforts in the Libyan campaign have been a shot in the arm for bilateral defence cooperation. Nick Harvey, UK Minister for the Armed Forces, told a UK Parliamentary Committee that Anglo-French cooperation on Libya was "undoubtedly ... a significant success".[50] He went on to note that "we are pleased to have demonstrated the ability of the UK and France to act together in a leading role in the way that we have, which is encouraging for the future."

Certainly, there were positive aspects of the Libya experience. For example, there was solid UK-French air and maritime cooperation. However, commentators noted that the

Libya campaign exposed the problems which remain in bilateral military cooperation. There were difficulties in communications, different concepts of operation, gaps in intelligence sharing and a problem with aligning political ambition and military capabilities. Perhaps most important were the problems in sharing classified information. Whether that particular issue can be resolved can come down to the question of whether the UK can expand its exchanges with Paris while not risking its arrangements with Washington.[51] Jones notes that there are agreements in place between the UK and France to share intelligence, but they are "lower-key"[52] and Lindley-French noted that "enhanced intelligence-sharing will be critical" to enhanced bilateral cooperation, and was noticeable by its absence in the 2010 agreement.[53]

Taking a larger perspective on the lessons from the Libya experience, Arbuthnot noted that the U.S. took a positive step by giving Europeans the opportunity to take the lead. Ultimately, the U.S. provided assistance when that became necessary to address European shortfalls. But the Libya operation, stressed Arbuthnot, reminded Europeans of their obligations, highlighted the gaps in their military capabilities, and subsequently allowed the U.S. to press Europe to fill those gaps.

Practical Impediments

The commentary on weaknesses in intelligence sharing during Libya operations highlights some of the practical difficulties with enhancing defence cooperation. For example, there continue to be comments about the extent to which the UK and France might be able to work together with regard to their aircraft carriers. One area cited by the 2010 agreement is development of an integrated carrier strike group. The UK decided in its SDSR that it would continue with the construction of two carriers, but potentially only bring one into service. Some commentators have noted that the UK decision in the SDSR to acquire the F-35C carrier version of the Joint Strike Fighter might allow the UK's F-35Cs to land on the French Charles de Gaulle.[54] Such cooperation has however, been thrown into serious doubt[55] with the decision by the UK to revert to the F-35B STOVL variant[56] (due to the cost of converting the carriers to operate 'cats and traps').

Assessing such an idea, O'Donoghue asked what kind of Anglo-French cooperation on aircraft carriers was really possible. He asked as a practical matter whether there is enough room on the carriers for combined crews. O'Donoghue noted that when he saw how the U.S. carrier George Washington operated, it appeared to be chaos, but it worked due to years of training. With any combination of Anglo-French planes and carriers, there would be the same kind of chaos, but without the years of training. A French carrier alongside a UK carrier would be a separate issue, added O'Donoghue.

F-35B landing on the USS Wasp (Source: Mass Communication Specialist Seaman Andrew Rivard via Wikimedia Commons)

Continuing on with the issue of practical impediments and addressing it at a higher level, O'Donoghue noted that the French budget and financial system is different from the UK. While the larger goal may be to come together, the two processes are different, and that has an impact. The key, stressed O'Donoghue, is to find the common ground that allows possible solutions and cooperation to go forward.

Multinational Defence Cooperation in General

Before turning from the area of practical defence cooperation to defence industrial cooperation, it is worthwhile to assess the general UK experience with regard to multinational defence industrial cooperation. In general, the UK record on multinational defence acquisition has been beneficial to the UK. A 2001 report from the National Audit Office (NAO), cited by the UK official as still the best assessment on benefits to the UK of multinational defence cooperation, noted that

> "Cooperation in defence research offers economic and technology benefits, generating a 5:1 return on the Department's £40 million annual investment on joint research programmes and providing knowledge with an annual value of approximately £280 million at minimal cost through information exchange programmes."[57]

In general terms, the NAO assessed that cooperative defence acquisition can bring economic benefits due to cost-sharing and economies of scale. Moreover, it can enhance interoperability with Allies as well as develop technological competence and influence industrial restructuring.[58] With regard to OCCAR, the NAO noted that it offers "the opportunity for significant improvements in the efficiency and effectiveness of European cooperative procurement".[59] It commented that OCCAR was intended to serve as the body that would place contracts, manage cooperative European acquisition programs and generate European cooperative military programmes.

However, it is notable that the overall conclusions by the NAO on multinational defence cooperation are that

"Cooperation adds another layer of complexity to the challenge of procuring equipments within time, cost and performance parameters and subsequently supporting them in-service. The track record of defence equipment cooperation to date has been mixed. Whilst there have been economic, political, military and industrial benefits, on significant numbers of cooperative procurement programmes, not all of the potential benefits have been secured."[60]

Industrial Cooperation is Key

As noted previously, the 2012 Summit declaration placed great emphasis on bilateral defence industrial cooperation and the case can be made that industrial cooperation may, over the long haul, be more valuable than practical military cooperation. For that reason, it is notable that "the treaties have been warmly received by the defence industries of both countries".[61]

One of the goals of expanded bilateral cooperation was to provide some support for defence industries in both countries which are facing reduced defence spending. As noted by some commentators, "by moving closer to commonly set equipment requirements, the treaty was intended to promote stepped-up cross-channel industrial ties between the two nations' defence-aerospace sectors".[62]

At the lower level, noted the UK official, there have been successful bilateral projects. However, they do not get much attention, citing marine engines as a good example. They are not high-profile items, but they are built on an existing relationship and there is a solid commercial basis for the work. Cooperation works, emphasized the official, but because of that commercial logic. Critically, this removes the bureaucracy as a hindrance. Citing another example, the UK official asserted that MBDA is a good and more prominent example of a result of Anglo-French political commitment.

The question arises whether Anglo-French industrial cooperation actually is possible across the board, or might have to be limited to smaller, non-controversial areas such as marine engines and if it has broader applicability, how would the UK and France establish "red lines" to protect national interests? Is it a case of deciding the items which are appropriate for cooperation? Or is it a case of establishing processes to limit activities, such as information sharing? O'Donoghue came down strongly in favour of deciding the specific items, emphasizing that "if you select the right equipment, there are no red lines. If there are red lines, you have pushed the wrong equipment."

Impediments to Industrial Cooperation

But if the critical long-term aspect of Anglo-French cooperation is on defence procurement, there are numerous obstacles noted by commentators. One wrote soon after St. Malo that

> "sensible defence procurement between Britain and France means that those two proud and sometimes arrogant nations have to concede political, technical and manufacturing grounds to one another and accept some form of loss of independence, concessions on foreign policy, intrusions in the shaping of industry, and last but not least the inevitable jobs casualties, a price that fewer and fewer politicians are prepared to pay".[63]

There are clear differences in views on defence procurement. France has "traditionally retained a protectionist attitude towards its defence sector, which is in large part owned by the state, in line with the country's tradition of Colbertian economic policies in which the central government retains a central role".[64] The UK approach has been to allow for the defence market to be free. Moreover, while France's industrial relations "are more oriented towards Europe" UK industries retain strong ties with the U.S. market.[65]

As noted by Carre, UK defence procurement is "a clear means to a clear end - that is to equip the defence forces".[66] On the other hand, Carre notes the French policy aim is

> "being pro-active in contributing to the building of a European defence base with a strong French footprint. This is mainly to be able to compete and/or establish partnerships with U.S. companies, on an equal foothold. The means to achieve this goal remains a direct interventionist policy, enforced by an elite administration. Thus, French defence procurement has been and remains an element to achieve this ultimate political goal of creating a European defence force equipped with, at worst,

inter-operable systems and, at best, the same weapons... In such an environment, economic rationale, efficiency and defence companies' profits have been, for some years, the least of the concerns for the French State."[67]

Moreover, there are fundamental conflicts between the behaviours of the two countries regarding defence acquisition. A UK official noted that there are differences in the way the two countries approach efforts at defence cooperation. The UK declares its intention for cooperation early. In contrast, the French declare it late when they frankly have a solution they want others to buy into.

There are many practical hurdles to be overcome in obtaining greater defence industrial cooperation. Lindley-French noted that then-UK Defence Secretary Fox highlighted the need for UK firms to have better access to French military procurement projects. For their part, the French "regard the British as unreliable partners, too subject to political whim and the sudden cancellation of or adjustment to programmes".[68] Having said that, Lindley-French reinforces the point that

"even a cursory analysis of the defence economics and costs of production in Britain and France suggests that it is only through greater synergy between their defence industries that any modicum of affordability and security of supply and re-supply will be assured."[69]

Arbuthnot concurred with many of the points noted above. France has a directed industrial strategy, and the French government owns a good chunk of French defence industry. The UK does not have that kind of ownership pattern, and the UK defence market is open. But Arbuthnot emphasized that these are not insurmountable obstacles, and the value of the bilateral defence cooperation should be considerable and can overcome those obstacles, stressing that there is a fundamental logic for Anglo-French cooperation.

Taking a different perspective, O'Donoghue commented that industry has to change, and the MoDs in London and Paris need to work to smooth the path. He noted that government cannot change the goals of industry, but it can influence how industry's goals evolve. For example, the UK does not necessarily want the ability to cut steel for future armoured vehicles. What it needs is the ability to integrate complex systems and sub-systems. If that is a clear government policy, industry will then change its perspective.

O'Donoghue also noted that this is even more important regarding larger policy issues. If the UK gives up a logistical capability, it cannot get it back, so the UK has to be clear about what it wants to do. Industry faces a similar situation. O'Donoghue stressed that a big request is being made of the UK defence industry. Will it get rid of fifty percent of its engineers? Will it actually rely on the French over the long haul?

Returning to the importance of leadership, the UK official emphasized that big political statements and commitments are critical to make better Anglo-French commercial relationships. If the political commitment is weakened, there can be work on minor, lower-level items, but the big ticket projects will not happen and this is precisely the area where Europe has expertise, perhaps even a comparative advantage, and needs to focus its attention.

Cutting Edge Defence Technology

The 2012 Summit declaration had a particular focus on Anglo-French high-tech defence cooperation. One of the areas in which there is particular emphasis is UAVs. On MALE UAVs, commentators have noted there is a business logic to the arrangement, as BAE Systems and Dassault have capabilities in the area, and their domestic markets would only generate a market of some forty to fifty MALE UAVs.[70] Indeed, should MALE work, there is the possibility of more collaboration on unmanned combat air vehicles, and such work would probably be important to maintaining the skills of European industry.[71] Returning to the practical considerations noted above, what will be interesting to observe is whether this cooperation will be possible in light of competition in other areas, for example, after India selected the Rafale from Dassault over the Eurofighter from BAE Systems as its preferred choice for its new fighter in late 2011.

An example of the current generation of drones – a Boeing MQ-9 Reaper at Creech Air Force Base, Nevada. (Source: Senior Airman Larry E. Reid via Wikimedia Commons)

Certainly, the argument could be made that the French approach to long-term planning with regard to defence technology could be appealing to the UK. As Carre notes, the French MOD has upwards of a thirty-year prospective plan which is updated annually.[72] In the case of the UK, the government reconfirmed through its White Paper "National Security Through Technology"[73] that it would maintain its baseline of spending 1.2% of its defence budget on science and technology (around £400 million annually).

In addition, Lindley-French highlights the agreement concerning a 10-year strategic plan for the UK and French Complex Weapons sector, commenting that it "makes sense if it does lead to the creation of a single European prime contractor (and realizes 30% savings as envisaged)".[74] The UK official noted that the UAV area is one in which France is trying to bring the UK into a joint venture and where there is potentially substantial growth. But harkening back to the point noted above, the broader cost to the UK has to be considered and a clear policy decision must be made.

Arbuthnot asserted that work in this high-tech area is important in a broader Western context. Large U.S. firms clearly have an advantage over European companies. But high-quality defence research is broadly needed and that cannot be obtained just with small UK and French firms. Thus, there is logic to UK-French cooperation in this expensive, high-tech area. However, he conceded, while there are benefits of scale, there is also a natural suspicion. There is a mutual concern in France and the UK that the other is stealing intellectual property. Those suspicions have to be overcome by openness, noted Arbuthnot and both a top-down and bottom-up approach for further bilateral cooperation is needed to spur progress and generate that transparency. In that regard, Libya served as practical experience to increase that level of trust and obtain more openness by both sides.

O'Donoghue commented that three years ago, it was clear to officials in the UK and France that more industrial cooperation, in general, would be mutually beneficial. Citing complex weapons specifically, he said there are clear options, and it is far too expensive for each country to work in this area separately. True, he noted, the UK could simply have bought high-tech U.S. equipment. But the other option was to have an arrangement between Paris and London with each spending as much as possible to generate an Anglo-French complex weapons capability.

It took a long time for defence industries in the UK and France to recognise the benefits of such collaboration, admitted O'Donoghue. He concurred with the point made by Arbuthnot about obstacles due to attitudes and behaviours. But he asserted that a lot of the problem may have been due to media hype about potential conflicts. Addressing practical problems, O'Donoghue cited intellectual property rights and third party sales, commenting that London and Paris have to generate arrangements to smooth obstacles in these and other areas for industry.

Perhaps most important, up to this point, noted O'Donoghue, industry has not put its weight behind Anglo-French cooperation. It will be interesting to see if they are ready to do so from now on. In short, asserted O'Donoghue, it is not clear if industry has "crossed the Rubicon" and is ready to embrace bilateral cooperation, but in his view, they certainly need to do so. Industry, he asserted flatly, has to get that message.

Reaction of Other Europeans

The Anglo-French agreement has not been met with universal approval, especially as it involves the two largest defence budgets in Europe seeking to cooperate more with each other, rather than working to develop European capabilities. Gomis notes that "reactions in Berlin have demonstrated Germany's unease over an exclusive Franco-British agreement."[75] A UK official agreed that Anglo-French cooperation has generated tensions within the rest of Europe. Italy and others are "incensed." But the question to be asked of the other Europeans is simple: who has the money?

Consideration has now turned to the question of whether the bilateral efforts could potentially provide an impetus to a larger European effort to generate defence capabilities. One writer commented that "given the difficulties encountered in defence procurement in the past decade, the Franco-British treaties can nonetheless be seen as a first salutary step towards more joint action in European defence procurement".[76] Lindley-French argues that

> "Anglo-French defence cooperation would be a pioneer group par excellence for the rest of Europe. Thus permanent structured cooperation and reinforced cooperation, as stipulated in the 2009 Lisbon Treaty, would assist Britain and France to create a European strategic culture worthy of the name."[77]

One commentator noted that "the enhancement of Franco-British common efforts will benefit the EU by stemming the deterioration of British and French military capabilities, on which EU deployments rely".[78] The effort has significance as London is "particularly exasperated by its European partners inertia; but even in Paris frustrations are mounting" regarding the absence of effort in the rest of Europe to maintain defence capabilities.[79]

Arriving at a similar destination through a different route, Jones asserts that the primary motivation for the Anglo-French initiative is "not to produce a greater or more effective

'European 'military capability".[80] He notes that it could possibly "cause divisions among European states if the Franco-British relationship is seen as too exclusive and not sufficiently concerned with wider European security".[81] However, Jones also notes that Anglo-French cooperation could indeed be "a road-map to more effective European defence cooperation, based on deeper capability planning and mutual dependency".[82] Indeed, taking the point further, he notes that unless Europe ascertains "how, and, indeed, whether, the initiatives that France and the UK embark on can work in practice, wider European defence cooperation has little hope of delivering anything".[83]

It is notable that there is speculation that the request for proposals for the MALE UAV could be open to other European (as well as possibly U.S.) firms and there is the possibility that broader cooperation could be expanded. However, other commentators note that the UK has been burned by multinational European projects like the A-400M and will not be enthusiastic about such expanded projects.[84]

Indeed, it appears that the UK has had enough of projects involving a number of European partners. A comment from the IISS states "Having tired of the delays and haggling that often accompany multilateral European procurements, the UK now firmly prefers collaborative procurement on a bilateral basis."[85] Jones notes that there is "a pragmatic assumption that bilateralism between 'natural partners' ought to work more effectively than a multilateral approach".[86] He adds that the UK "now prefers bilateral programmes as a matter of policy, on the grounds that they are more 'straightforward'".[87]

The trend of UK reluctance to participate in Europe-wide defence efforts, which had already begun under the previous Labour Government, has continued. While there are many factors, it has been argued that the principal motivating force is

"the belief, widely held in government and military circles, that efforts in this direction are an inefficient use of Britain's limited resources -- a belief resulting from years of frustrations at the lack of serious commitment to defence on the part of many European countries."[88]

Then-UK Defence Secretary Fox stated in September 2011 that the Anglo-French arrangement will not be copied between the UK and other Europeans stating, "The UK-French agreement is not a prototype for wider European defence, but I do think it might be useful in setting an example to other European nations who want to work closely together".[89] That view reflects the fact that the SDSR only specifically cited France[90] along with the U.S. as countries with which the UK would be working assiduously to strengthen bilateral efforts.

In line with the points above, Arbuthnot commented that it is too early to say if there would be more European initiatives as a result of the Anglo-French agreement. He thought that European efforts would probably expand a little as a result, but emphasized that the extent of the expansion depends on how others are willing to go along with the Anglo-French framework. Arbuthnot firmly noted that it is definitely not desirable to have a new framework which destroys the UK-French arrangement.

The main idea, stressed Arbuthnot, is to get the two big European countries to work together. If bringing in others means the dilution of Anglo-French cooperation, this would not be acceptable. Other European states should decide whether to join the existing arrangement. As it stands, he noted, Italy is "cross" about Anglo-French cooperation, Spain is not happy, and Germany would like to be involved. With regard to defence industrial cooperation, it must be based on an arrangement between the UK and France, or British and French firms, with other European states or firms then joining.

O'Donoghue concurred strongly with Arbuthnot, stating that he dislikes multinational projects, but supports bilateral programs.

This had also been stressed in the White Paper: "we will favour bilateral collaboration on technology, equipment, and support issues, as we believe this offers the best balance of advantages and disadvantages".[91] Mistakes in past efforts on joint cooperation could and should be fixed. But with regard to future European efforts in defence cooperation, the Anglo-French path is the one and only road that should be followed.

It is important to note that other analysts who share that view believe this means the death of any European efforts to maintain a defence capability and acknowledgment that only bilateral efforts will work. O'Donnell argues that the agreement "could come to symbolize the demise of EU defence efforts" as "the summit took place against the backdrop of a loss of interest in the CSDP within Paris and, to an even greater extent, London".[92]

It appears for that very reason to be in the interest of the U.S. that Anglo-French defence cooperation proceed. It is arguably the only way in which European defence capabilities can be maintained. O'Donnell notes that "little demonstration is required of the hollowness of EU defence cooperation without the full support of Britain and France"[93] and flatly states that

"EU defence efforts are doomed to flounder if there is no enthusiasm from the only two EU countries with extensive experience in expeditionary warfare and global ambitions in security, and which between them account for nearly half of Europe's defence spending".[94]

US Interest

Therein lies the reason for the U.S. to support the Anglo-French efforts and hope that they will succeed. The implications for the U.S. of Anglo-French cooperation are quite clear: they constitute the best hope of providing a vehicle or framework for European Allies to develop defence capabilities. With European defence budgets having shrunk over the last decade and economic difficulties making it unlikely that there will be any major increases in the near future and an absence of political will to spend large sums on defence, one hope for the U.S. of getting more defence capabilities out of its European Allies is that others will join an effort driven by London and Paris.

Commentators have noted that one of the key conditions for success for the Anglo-French treaty includes the "support of the United States, based on the understanding that the Franco-British treaties do not clash with its global role but will rather reinforce it".[95] Gomis adds later that "Washington may be tempted to view this partnership as competition, but it is very unlikely to be the case" and asserts that "the Franco-British treaties are useful for European defence and should not be opposed".[96] Indeed, the argument is made that the U.S. "has a crucial role to play in making the case for the treaties and other examples of bilateral cooperation that would benefit both NATO and the EU".[97]

Indeed, PM Cameron emphasized the benefit of the treaty to U.S. interests when he stated that "they want European countries like France and Britain to come together and share defence resources so that we actually have greater capabilities (...) So I think this will get a very warm welcome in Washington".[98] One commentator asserts that "it is generally recognized that Washington perceives the Anglo-French Defence Treaty as a potential catalyst for creating the greater cooperation on conventional capabilities in Europe".[99]

Those who are particularly critical about European capabilities focus on the possibilities in the Anglo-French treaty. Lindley-French notes that "the central challenge for both Britain and France is that much of the European continent remains on strategic vacation".[100] Continuing on, he argues that "at the very least, Anglo-French defence cooperation will need to regenerate a European strategic culture".[101] He also makes the point that the Anglo-French Treaty "only makes political sense if it is seen as an attempt to kick-start Europe as a whole into considering its strategic future; and that will require a degree of political solidarity and consistency for which neither London nor Paris are renowned".[102] He bluntly states that "Franco-British defence cooperation is thus not just vital for London and Paris but for a Europe that is dangerously and strategically adrift".[103]

Arbuthnot also asserted that the U.S. should encourage Anglo-French cooperation, noting that it is likely to maximise defence output for the UK and France, which would benefit the U.S. And it could increase the defence output of other European countries if others are willing to sign on to the Anglo-French framework. Arbuthnot commented that his hope is that the U.S. will welcome the idea that Allies are working together to increase military capabilities. As for what concrete steps it should take with regard to Anglo-French cooperation, Arbuthnot stated that the U.S. could simply take "a benign watching brief."

O'Donoghue echoed the point that Anglo-French cooperation is not an either/or situation vis-a-vis the U.S. If Europe "gets its act together," it would be better for the U.S. Indeed, O'Donoghue said that his message to the U.S. would be that both the UK and France will both be better allies for the U.S. if they engaged in more robust defence cooperation. Without collaboration, they will just lose capabilities and it will be harder to generate more efficient use of resources.

He went on to posit that it may be better for the West to have different capabilities. O'Donoghue stressed that the UK and France have superb engineers. Indeed, some UK equipment and technology is better than that produced in the U.S. And in some capability areas, noted O'Donoghue, "made in the U.S.A." is not necessarily the best label, and a European label might be better. An Anglo-French military-industry capability, posited O'Donoghue, should be welcomed by the U.S. Europe is not big enough to have national defence industrial competition. But pan-European competition is possible. An Anglo-French effort could compete on complex weapons, and other areas. The U.S. government ought to welcome this cooperation as strengthening Allied capabilities, even if U.S. industry is not enthused.

Conclusion

From the literature, public statements, interviews, and, above all, actions, it is clear that the U.S. has little, if any, reason for concern regarding enhanced Anglo-French defence cooperation. Any fears that this would signal a weakening of attention by the UK towards the U.S. appear groundless. This latest initiative is driven by practical considerations: reduced defence budgets require London and Paris to find new ways to get more "bang for the buck." There are policy factors which promote enhanced cooperation. The French return to the NATO integrated military command and the policies generally pursued by the Sarkozy government (and seemingly the Hollande government) have made it easier for London to seek greater bilateral efforts and it should be noted that the clearly stated U.S. shift in emphasis towards Asia has also prompted the UK to re-evaluate the extent to which it needs to focus more on European Allies which could really assist in generating defence capabilities.

It would appear that the primary U.S. concern lies in how to ensure that the Anglo-French initiative succeeds. If it does indeed meet the goals that have been set forth, it would assist London and Paris in becoming more capable Allies and moving beyond that goal, it would be in the interest of the U.S. if the Anglo-French cooperation could be the foundation for other European states to also participate and develop their military capabilities. U.S. dissatisfaction with the overall European effort in the Libyan campaign was apparent across Europe. However, there is no indication that European governments are ready to do more on defence, especially with continued economic problems in the Eurozone.

From a U.S. policy perspective, the recommendation from Arbuthnot is relatively straightforward and worth consideration: Washington should simply watch the developments. It is hard to imagine active U.S. support for more Anglo-French cooperation, particularly as such work on the industrial side might generate negative commentary from U.S. defence industry. Moreover, it is hard to imagine such U.S. support having much effect, particularly in view of the lack of response in European capitals to the constant U.S. requests for European Allies to do more in developing military capabilities.

However, if the U.S. is genuinely concerned about the level of European military spending and, more important, the extent of the military capabilities that Allies can bring to any future operations, it has a vested interest in seeing Anglo-French cooperation succeed and serve as a vehicle for other Europeans to develop their military forces. Criticism from Washington will have a difficult time overcoming the lack of political will and financial resources in European capitals for effective national action. The Anglo-French efforts may at least provide a vehicle for channelling scarce resources into more effective defence spending. While that may yet turn out to be more of a hope than a reality, it is certainly in line with U.S. defence and security policy interests and worthy of support.

Endnotes

[1] A highly condensed version of this paper was published in RUSI Defence Systems 2013.

[2] Ministry of Defence (MoD). (2010) 'UK France Defence Co-operation Treaty Announced', dated 2 November 2010, retrieved 29 February 2012 from http://www.MoD.uk/DefenceInternet/DefenceNews/DefencePolicyAndBusiness/UkfranceDefenceCooperationTreatyAnnounced.htm .

[3] Harries, M. (2012) 'Britain and France as Nuclear Partners' in *Survival*, Vol. 54, No. 1 (February – March 2012, pp. 7 – 30), p. 13.

[4] *Ibid*. p. 21.

[5] *Ibid*. p. 15.

[6] Jones, B. (2011) *Franco-British Military Cooperation: A New Engine for European Defence?*, Paris: European Union Institute for Security Studies, February 2011, p. 12.

[7] On February 29, 2012, £1 equalled $1.59 or 1.194 Euros.

[8] On February 29, 2012, 1 Euro equalled $1.33.

[9] Pires, M. L. (2012) *Defence Data: EDA Participating Member States in 2010*, European Defence Agency, Brussels, 18 January 2012, available at http://www.eda.europa.eu/ Libraries/Documents/National_Defence_Data_2010_3.sflb.ashx as of 1 March 2012.

[10] *Op Cit*. Jones, 2012, p. 12.

[11] Antill, P. (2011) 'European Collaborative Procurement – The Horizon Common New Generation Frigate' in Moore, D. *Case Studies in Defence Procurement and Logistics – Volume 1: From World War II to the Post-Cold War World*, Cambridge: Cambridge Academic Press, pp. 155 – 176.

[12] Jane's Information Group. (2013) 'GTK/MRAV/PWV (Boxer) wheeled armoured vehicle programme' in *Land Warfare Platforms – Armoured Fighting Vehicles*, posted 1 February 2013 at ihm.janes.com, as of 8 August 2013.

[13] Poole, P. (2013) 'The Realities of Collaboration on Land Systems: A Historical Perspective' in Moore, D. and Antill, P. (Eds) (2013) *Case Studies in Defence Acquisition: Malaysia*, Cranfield: Cranfield University Press, pp. 45-73.

[14] National Audit Office (NAO). (2001) *Maximising the Benefits of Defence Equipment Co-operation*, HC 300, Session 2000-2001, London: The Stationary Office, 16 March 2001, p. 54.

[15] Prime Minister's Office. (2012) *UK-France Declaration on Security and Defence*, dated 17 February 2012, located at http://www.number10.gov.uk/news/uk-france-declaration-security/ , as of 23 February 2013, paragraph 2.

[16] *Ibid*. paragraph 7.

[17] *Ibid*. paragraph 9.

[18] *Ibid*. paragraph 14.

[19] Inside Government. (2013) 'UK-France relationship strong in Mali operation', published 1 February 2013, located at https://www.gov.uk/government/news/uk-france-relationship-strong-in-mali-operation as of 26 February 2013.

[20] Inside Government. (2013) 'British and French forces work together on artillery exercise', published 25 February 2013, located at https://www.gov.uk/government/news/ british-and-french-forces-work-together-on-artillery-exercise, as of 26 February 2013.

[21] *Op Cit*. Prime Minister's Office, 2012, paragraph 16.

[22] Chuter, A. (2012) 'UK-France move closer to joint UCAS development' in *Defense News*, February 27 2012, p. 6.

[23] *Op Cit*. Prime Minister's Office, 2012, paragraph 23.

[24] Lindley-French, J. (2010) *Britain and France: A Dialogue of Decline?* Programme Paper: ISP PP 2010/02, London: Chatham House, December 2010, p. 20.

[25] *Ibid*.

[26] *Ibid*.

[27] Interview with James Arbuthnot MP, Chairman of the House of Commons Select Committee on Defence, on 31 January 2012 at Portcullis House, London. All further references to what he said in the text refer to this interview.

[28] Interview with General Sir Kevin O'Donoghue, former Chief of Defence Materiel on 17 January 2012 in the Centre for Defence Acquisition. All further references to what he said in the text refer to this interview.

[29] Stevens, J. (2011) *Some Remarks on the Anglo-French Defence Treaty*, Strategic Update 11.4, London: London School of Economics and Political Science, November 2011, p. 6.

[30] HM Government. (2010) *Securing Britain in and Age of Uncertainty: The Strategic Defence and Security Review*, Cm 7948, London: The Stationary Office, October 2010; International Institute of Strategic Studies (IISS). (2010a) 'UK cost-cutting review shrinks military capability', *IISS Strategic Comments*, Vol. 16, Comment 39, November 2010.

[31] Bickerton, C. (2010) 'Oh Bugger, They're in the Tent: British Responses to French Reintegration into NATO' in *European Security*, Vol. 19, No. 1 (March 2010, pp. 113 – 122), p. 121.

[32] *Op Cit*. Jones, 2011, p. 16.

[33] *Op Cit*. Stevens, 2011, p. 3.

[34] *Op Cit*. Bickerton, 2010, p. 115.

[35] *Op Cit*. Jones, 2011, p. 7.

[36] *Ibid*.

[37] Gomis, B. (2011) *Franco-British Defence and Security Treaties: Entente While it Lasts?*, Programme Paper: ISP PP 2001/01, London: Chatham House, March 2011, p. 18.

[38] *Op Cit*. Jones, 2011, p. 21.

[39] *Ibid*. p. 5.

[40] *Ibid*. p. 8.

[41] Interview with an official from the National Audit Office on 31 January 2012 who wished to remain anonymous. All further references to what he said in the text refer to this interview.

[42] International Institute of Strategic Studies (IISS) (2010b).'The Ambitious UK-France

Defence Accord', *IISS Strategic Comments*, Vol. 16, Comment 41, November 2010.

[43] *Op Cit*. Bickerton, 2010, p. 120.

[44] Shearer, A. (2000) 'Britain, France and the Saint-Malo Declaration: Tactical Rapprochement or Strategic Entente?' in *Cambridge Review of International Affairs*, Vol. XIII, No. 2 (Spring – Summer 2000, pp. 283 – 298), p. 288.

[45] *Ibid*. p. 293.

[46] Howorth, J. (2004) 'France, Britain and the Euro-Atlantic Crisis' in *Survival*, Vol. 45, No. 4 (Winter 2003-04, pp. 173 – 192), p. 188.

[47] *Op Cit*. Bickerton, p. 117.

[48] *Op Cit*. Jones, 2011, p. 35.

[49] *Ibid*. p. 33.

[50] International Institute of Strategic Studies (IISS). (2011a) 'Anglo-French Defence: Entente Frugale Plus', *IISS Strategic Comments*, Vol. 17, Comment 47, December 2011.

[51] *Ibid*.

[52] *Op Cit*. Jones, 2011, p. 13.

[53] *Op Cit*. Lindley-French, 2010, p. 16.

[54] *Op Cit*. IISS, 2010a.

[55] Hoyos, C. (2012) 'UK fighter choice risks French entente', *Financial Times*, 20 March 2012, located at http://www.ft.com/cms/s/0/1ae3aaa0-72b6-11e1-9be9-00144feab49a.html#axzz2LS7xvOXy as of 20 February 2013.

[56] Kirkup, J. 'About-turn on new variant of carriers' fighter plane' in *The Daily Telegraph*, 9 May 2012, located at http://www.telegraph.co.uk/news/uknews/defence/9253377/About-turn-on-new-variant-of-carriers-fighter-plane.html as of 26 February 2013.

[57] *Op Cit*. NAO, 2001, p. 1.

[58] *Ibid*.

[59] *Ibid*. p. 35.

[60] *Ibid*. p. 5.

[61] *Op Cit*. Gomis, 2011, p. 16.

[62] *Op Cit*. IISS, 2011a.

[63] Carre, B. (2001) 'The Recent Opening of the French Defence Market and Anglo-French Defence Relationships' in *RUSI Journal*, Vol. 146, Issue 4 (August 2001, pp. 6 – 11), p. 6.

[64] *Op Cit*. Gomis, 2011, p. 17.

[65] *Ibid*.

[66] *Op Cit*. Carre, 2001, p. 7.

[67] *Ibid.*

[68] *Op Cit.* Lindley-French, 2010, p. 17.

[69] *Ibid.*

[70] *Op Cit.* IISS, 2010b.

[71] *Op Cit.* IISS, 2011a.

[72] *Op Cit.* Carre, 2001, p. 9.

[73] Ministry of Defence. (2012) *National Security through Technology: Technology, Equipment, and Support for UK Defence and Security*, Cm 8278, London: The Stationary Office, February 2012, p. 9.

[74] *Op Cit.* Lindley-French, 2010, p. 17.

[75] *Op Cit.* Gomis, 2011, p. 14.

[76] *Ibid.*

[77] *Op Cit.* Lindley-French, 2010, p. 14.

[78] O'Donnell, C. (2011) 'Britain's Coalition Government and EU Defence Cooperation: Undermining British Interests' in *International Affairs*, Vol. 87, No. 2 (March 2011, pp. 419 – 433), p. 428.

[79] *Ibid.*

[80] *Op Cit.* Jones, 2011, p. 5.

[81] *Ibid.*

[82] *Ibid.*

[83] *Ibid.* pp. 5 – 6.

[84] *Op Cit.* IISS, 2011a.

[85] International Institute of Strategic Studies (IISS). (2011b) 'Unmanned future: the next era of European aerospace?', *IISS Strategic Comments*, Vol. 17, Comment 24, June 2011.

[86] *Op Cit.* Jones, 2011, p. 8.

[87] *Ibid.* p. 15.

[88] *Op Cit.* O'Donnell, 2011, p. 420.

[89] Bell, M. (2011) 'Fox underlines importance of Anglo-French co-operation and growing efforts with Australia' in *Jane's Defence Industry*, posted 28 September 2011.

[90] HM Government. (2010) *Securing Britain in and Age of Uncertainty: The Strategic Defence and Security Review*, Cm 7948, London: The Stationary Office, October 2010, p. 60.

[91] *Op Cit.* Ministry of Defence, 2012, p. 8.

[92] *Op Cit.* O'Donnell, 2011, p. 433.

[93] *Ibid.* p. 428.

[94] *Ibid.* p. 429.

[95] *Op Cit*. Gomis, 2011, p. 4.

[96] *Ibid*. p. 12.

[97] *Ibid*. p. 19.

[98] *Ibid*. p. 11.

[99] *Op Cit*. Stevens, 2011, p. 4.

[100] *Op Cit*. Lindley-French, 2010, p. 9.

[101] *Ibid*.

[102] *Ibid*. p. 4.

[103] *Ibid*. p. 5.

Future Small Arms

Anthony G. Williams

Centre for Defence Acquisition, Cranfield University, Defence Academy of the UK.

Introduction

Combat experience in Afghanistan has prompted some rapid changes in the small arms carried by ISAF foot soldiers; and most especially by the British Army and Royal Marines and the US Army and USMC. The purpose of this article is to outline these changes, determine the lessons learned, and look ahead to examine the extent to which the growing variety of rifles (including DMRs: Designated Marksman Rifles), carbines, IARs (Infantry Automatic Rifles) and LMGs (light machine guns) might be replaced in the future by a smaller number of weapons without losing any capability.

Developments to Date

Before the Afghan conflict began, it was assumed that most small-arms engagements would continue to take place within the traditional 300 metre limit, as they had in Iraq, and ISAF forces were equipped accordingly. The rifles and LMGs carried by the infantry on foot patrols were overwhelmingly in the relatively short-range 5.56mm calibre, using the NATO standard (SS109) ammunition. The British patrols used the 5.56mm L85A2 rifle, L86A2 Light Support Weapon and the L110 LMG (FN Minimi Para). The L85A2 and L86A2 are the principal members of the SA80 family, which has had a controversial history. The 7.62mm L7A2 GPMG (FN MAG) was available in support, and bolt-action 7.62mm sniper rifles were also in service. The US forces used three principal weapons: the M16 rifle (favoured by the USMC), short-barrelled M4 Carbine (favoured by the US Army because its compactness makes it more suitable for urban fighting, the typical scenario in Iraq) and the M249 development of the FN Minimi LMG. As with the British forces, some long-range weapons in 7.62×51 NATO calibre, most notably the M240 GPMG (FN MAG variant) and also some sniper rifles and DMRs, were available for use in a support role when required.

The 7.62x54R PKM LMG (Source: US DOD via Wikimedia Commons)

These arrangements were thrown into disarray when faced with the very different circumstances of Afghanistan, where the Taliban noted the range limitation of the 5.56mm weapons and, wherever circumstances permitted, opted to engage ISAF troops from longer distances. They could do this because as well as the ubiquitous but short-ranged AK family of assault rifles in 7.62×39 calibre, they have weapons chambered in the powerful Russian 7.62×54R round, equivalent in performance to the NATO 7.62×51. The principal weapons using this cartridge are the lightweight PKM belt-fed LMG and the SVD semi-automatic sniper rifle. Both the British and US forces have reported that more than half of Taliban small-arms attacks are launched from ranges greater than 300 metres, out to as far as 900 metres. While the 5.56mm NATO weapons were previously claimed to be effective out to 450-600 metres, experience has shown that their performance falls off sharply beyond 300m - or even less, when used in short-barrelled weapons.

The adoption by US forces of replacements for the M855, in the form of the M855A1 EPR (Enhanced Performance Round) for the US Army and MK318 Mod 0 (USMC), should resolve some other problems with the existing 5.56mm ammunition concerning erratic terminal effectiveness and poor barrier penetration. However, these are unlikely to help the UK and other NATO nations whose lawyers tend to adopt a very literal interpretation of the Hague Convention prohibition of bullets "with a hard envelope which does not entirely cover the core" – which describes both of the new US bullets. In any case, no 5.56mm developments could achieve enough of an improvement to eliminate the need for a larger calibre to cover the longer small-arms ranges.

The L129A1 'sharpshooter' rifle (Source: Steve Johnson via Wikimedia Commons)

The immediate – and indeed, only immediately available – response of the UK and US forces was to redistribute existing 7.62mm weapons to the foot patrols, despite their unsuitability in terms of weight (FN MAG) or low rate of fire (bolt-action sniper rifles).

The next stage was to launch urgent requirements for new 7.62mm weapons. In machine guns, both the UK and USA have been developing lightened versions of the FN MAG (although the British effort doesn't seem to have been followed up) and also adopting new lightweight MGs, comparable in weight and performance to the Taliban's PKM. The US already has the MK48, its designation for the 7.62mm version of the FN Minimi, which the British also selected in mid-2011, apparently for Special Forces, at least initially.

A Mk. 48 Mod 0/1 LMG – a variant of the FN Herstal Minimi in 7.62mm NATO (Source: US DOD via Wikimedia Commons)

New rifles have been acquired; the British have purchased a limited quantity of a 7.62mm self-loading "Sharpshooter" rifle from the USA, the L129A1, which has been enthusiastically received. The US had the advantage of already having selected the 7.62mm M110 SASS (Semi-Automatic Sniper System) and have also refurbished several thousand of the old 7.62mm M14 rifles as the M14 EBR (Enhanced Battle Rifle) with modern furniture and accessories. These are also proving very popular. In contrast, the USMC has kept one eye on the needs of urban fighting and has rather controversially acquired a new, compact 5.56mm IAR to replace many of the M249s at section level; the HK 416-based M27.

The Case for Change

So we now have the following rifles and MGs in service or in prospect, all intended to be carried by dismounted soldiers on patrol:

- The UK forces have the 5.56mm L85A2, L86A2 (effectively an IAR) and L110, plus the 7.62mm L129A1, L7A2 GPMG, and 7.62mm FN Minimi: a total of six weapons, with three in each calibre. There are also bolt-action sniper rifles in use, and special forces use other rifles in 5.56mm and 7.62mm calibres.

- The USA uses the 5.56mm M4, M16, M27 and M249, plus the 7.62mm M14EBR, M110, MK48 and M240. That's a total of eight weapons, four in each calibre. In addition they have heavier sniper rifles, plus special forces use other weapons, most notably the MK17 (FN SCAR-H) 7.62mm rifle.

The M27 Infantry Automatic Rifle (Source: Sergeant B L Saunders, USMC via Wikimedia Commons)

Such a variety of weapons has self-evident drawbacks in complicating and increasing the cost of acquisition, logistics, maintenance and training. Less obviously, there may also be penalties in combat. Those troops armed with 7.62mm weapons will be penalised by the weight of the guns and particularly the ammunition (7.62mm cartridges weigh twice as much as 5.56mm), plus the much heavier recoil in rifles which slows down aimed semi-auto fire and makes automatic fire impractical. The bigger and less wieldy weapons are also less suited to urban fighting. On the other hand, those with 5.56mm weapons will be able to make little or no contribution to long-range engagements - not even in supplying their ammunition to other members of their section. When combat ranges may fluctuate rapidly it is necessary to carry weapons in both calibres to cover the tactical demands but this reduces the potential firepower of a section in both short-range and long-range engagements.

The urgent need to plug gaps in weapon capability has made the current proliferation of firearms inevitable for the time being, but this situation raises an obvious issue: when planning the next generation of weapons, is it possible to provide a similar range of capabilities with a smaller number of guns, each effective at all normal small-arms ranges?

The key question is: what capabilities do we need from infantry rifles and portable MGs? The answer to this will determine the characteristics of the ammunition, the guns and the weapon sights. These characteristics will also be influenced by new developments in all three fields.

Some pointers to this were included in a document called Soldier Battlefield Effectiveness, produced in 2011 by the US Army's Program Executive Office, Soldier. Some of the most relevant quotes concerning future infantry rifles include:

A Soldier must be able to engage the threat he's faced with – whether it's at eight meters or 800.

Weapons....must be accurate and capable of engaging the enemy at overmatch distances.

To be effective in all scenarios, a Soldier needs to have true "general purpose" rounds in his weapon magazine that are accurate and effective against a wide range of targets.

Army service rifles must be general purpose in nature and embody a series of tradeoffs that balance optimum performance for a wide range of possible missions in a range of operating environments. With global missions taking Soldiers from islands to mountains and jungles to deserts, the Army can't buy 1.1 million new service rifles every time it's called upon to operate in a different environment.

Following on from this appeal for general-purpose rifles firing general-purpose ammunition, I suggest that the following capabilities should be sought in new small arms, beyond the obvious ones of reliability, robustness, reliability, good ergonomics, reliability, easy maintenance, reliability, ability to accept a wide range of accessories, and of course reliability in extended combat conditions:

- The rifle should be effective out to the maximum feasible range for small-arms engagements; at least 800 metres. The definition of effectiveness to include hit probability, barrier penetration and rapid incapacitation of personnel.

- The rifle should be as compact as possible, so that it is handy for urban warfare and for carrying in cramped vehicles and helos.

- The rifle's recoil should be light enough to facilitate training, rapid and accurate semi-automatic fire, and controllable burst fire.

- The rifle should be capable of maintaining a high rate of fire for several minutes.

- The LMG should use the same ammunition as the rifle, be belt-fed and be capable of accurate and sustained automatic fire out to at least 1,000 metres.

- The guns and their ammunition should be as light as they can be without compromising any of the above requirements.

I will now consider the three elements – ammunition, guns and sights – to examine the implications of these requirements.

Ammunition

In this section I will be considering ammunition performance; essentially, ballistics. I don't intend to consider advanced cartridge technologies such as the caseless-telescoped and plastic-cased-telescoped rounds being developed as a part of the US Lightweight Small Arms Technologies programme. If one of these is eventually selected for production it will bring the considerable benefits of a substantial weight reduction, but it won't alter such matters as the choice of calibre, bullet weight and type, external and terminal ballistics.

To summarise a complex argument: it is both possible and desirable to develop one round which could replace both the 5.56mm and the 7.62mm in portable infantry guns. This would halve the number of different weapons and would also ensure that each weapon has a much wider range of capabilities. It would significantly reduce the weight and recoil compared with 7.62mm ammunition, while improving the range, barrier penetration and terminal effectiveness compared with 5.56mm.

If the ammunition is to be effective at long range, it must match the standard 7.62mm NATO ball round in its trajectory, retained energy and barrier penetration at 1,000 metres from the same length barrels. However, if it is to reduce the ammunition weight and recoil compared with 7.62mm, it must be smaller and less powerful. This conflict can be resolved by selecting a calibre intermediate between the 5.56mm and 7.62mm, with a low-drag bullet which will lose velocity (and therefore energy) more slowly than the 7.62mm ball.

Other things being equal, low-drag bullets are heavier than usual, so to keep recoil in check need to be fired at a lower velocity. Muzzle energy will be lower than the 7.62mm (but appreciably higher than the 5.56mm) but the right specification of low-drag bullet will eventually catch up with and even surpass the 7.62mm at long range.

In practical terms, the smallest calibre likely to deliver a performance comparable with the 7.62mm is unlikely to be less than 6.5mm, while the largest which would enable recoil and weight to be kept in check is, at the most, 7mm. Exactly which calibre proves to be the best compromise should be determined by more detailed analysis, comprehensive testing and preferably combat experience. Initial calculations indicate that a muzzle energy in the region of 2,500 joules, compared with 1,700 J for the 5.56mm and 3,200 J for the 7.62mm, will be required. Experience of existing cartridges in this class indicates that the weight will be mid-way between the 5.56mm and 7.62mm, but the perceived recoil will be much closer to 5.56mm, thereby maintaining good controllability.

The US Army's ARDEC Small Caliber Munitions Technology Branch recently conducted an analysis of calibres for future infantry weapons, with the results emerging in March 2011. A wide range of criteria were examined including: penetration; terminal effectiveness; accuracy; initial, retained and striking energy; wind drift; stowed kills; and recoil. The existing 5.56mm and 7.62mm rounds were tested at various ranges in comparison with 6.0mm, 6.35mm and 6.8mm, in all cases when loaded with similar lead-free copper+steel bullets (representative of the EPR). The conclusion of the study was that the 6.8mm calibre offered the best overall compromise between ballistic and terminal performance on the one hand, and weight and recoil on the other. It was closely followed by the 6.35mm calibre, with the others being well behind. The AMU (US Army Marksmanship Unit) has since researched the issue of ideal rifle calibres and settled on the 6.5mm calibre as offering the optimum compromise.

Gun Design

The need for good long-range performance combined with a short overall length for handiness in urban fighting and in vehicles causes problems for traditional rifles, since the first requires a long barrel and the second a short one. A folding stock can resolve the carrying problem (where that is possible: which it isn't with the M16 and M4, for instance, as the action extends into the stock) but doesn't help in urban fighting when the stock must be extended to provide controllability.

One option is to have barrels of different lengths which can be changed depending on the circumstances, but that may not be convenient, particularly if the ranges keep changing during a patrol (for example, a section might be searching a village but then be attacked from long range as they leave). Another option is to select a compromise barrel length, but this will result in a gun which is longer than is desirable in urban fighting and which will have a reduced long-range performance - unless the power of the cartridge is increased to deliver the same performance from a shorter barrel, in which case the ammunition weight, recoil, muzzle flash and blast will be increased. The obvious solution to this dilemma is to adopt a bullpup configuration, with the action and magazine located at the back of the gun, behind the pistol grip.

The proposal of a bullpup is controversial, since the British Army has been put off them by the long and painful saga of the SA80 while the US Army has never used them, so requires some further justification.

There are three principal objections to a bullpup:

- Poor ergonomics: the location of the action and magazine well to the rear of the pistol grip often makes operating the controls and changing magazines more difficult. This is particularly an issue with the SA80.

- Lack of ambidexterity: most bullpups (although not the SA80) can be converted to left-hand use, but that takes some time to achieve so can't be done in the heat of battle. This means that users can't switch shoulders to aim round the corner of a building, for instance, without being hit in the face by their own ejected cases.

- Lack of ability to adjust the stock length to allow for the wearing of body armour: again, a particular problem with the SA80 which has quite a long stock.

The Israeli Tavor assault rifle (Source: Israeli Weapon Industries, via Flickr)

Apart from these practical concerns, some users dislike the rearward weight balance of the bullpup and the proximity of the action to the firer's head in case of a chamber explosion.

There are responses to all of these objections:

- The ergonomics do not have to be as poor as the SA80's: the latest version of the Israeli Tavor, for instance, has controls which match those of the M16 and M4 in location and operation, since it was designed to replace them.

- There are various ways of achieving ambidexterity. The FN F2000 uses a forward ejection tube, which carries the spent cases to the front of the gun before they are expelled. The new Beretta ARX-160, although not a bullpup, has a mechanism which changes the case ejection side at the flick of a switch. The STK SAR-21 from Singapore has a simpler solution for emergency left-hand use: a large and effective case deflector. The latest version of the Chinese 5.8mm bullpup rifle, the QBZ95-1, also features a case deflector to throw the cases forwards.

- An adjustable stock could be provided if the gun action behind the magazine were designed to be shorter: something which hasn't happened so far since there has been no call for it. However, that should not be difficult to achieve in a new design.

- Gun balance is, to a great extent, a matter of what you are used to. Some bullpup users prefer the rearwards weight balance, arguing that it is easier to hold one-handed or for extended periods, and makes the rifle quicker to change aim. What is undoubtedly true is that a bullpup is far more evenly balanced once an under-barrel grenade launcher, large electro-optical sights and other tactical kit such as torches start being added: a traditional rifle then becomes massively front-heavy.

- The firer's head can be shielded from the action by using a tough kevlar cheek-piece, as with the STK SAR-21; this could be designed to flip quickly from one side to the other in conjunction with a switchable-side ejection system like the ARX-160's.

It is worth emphasising the key argument in favour of the bullpup: the design reduces the overall gun length by some 200-250mm for the same barrel length, which is a huge reduction. This is not just an advantage in urban fighting; it also facilitates fitting a suppressor, which is increasingly popular to reduce muzzle blast and flash and make firers more difficult to locate (it also protects the firer from long-term hearing damage). With barrels of the same length, a bullpup with an effective suppressor may still be no longer than a traditional rifle without one.

In addition, the adoption of a general-purpose intermediate round as proposed here would strengthen the case for the bullpup. At the moment, it is possible to argue that 5.56mm rifles can have short barrels because they are now principally seen as short-range weapons. On the other hand, 7.62mm rifles are being introduced for the long-range role and therefore don't need to be very compact for urban warfare. However, a single general-purpose infantry rifle in a general-purpose calibre must be well suited to both urban fighting and the long-range role. As previously mentioned, this combination can be achieved with a modular traditional design with quick-change barrels of different lengths (as most recent designs offer), especially if the action design also allows the stock to be fully telescoped. However, the bullpup layout does not require any such changes, and it is effectively two existing weapons - a rifle and a carbine - in one.

One issue which often receives little attention is recoil control, which as already observed is important in a rifle in order to facilitate training, rapid and accurate semi-automatic fire and controllable automatic fire. In guns of similar type, recoil is largely a function of the gun weight and the cartridge power (specifically, the momentum - mass × velocity - as opposed to energy - mass × velocity squared). However, the gun action can also have a significant effect, with advantages being demonstrated by soft-recoil mechanisms or even opposed-piston types like the AK-107. The US Army has recently been researching this and achieved reductions in the peak recoil force of up to 90% by using a counter-mass principle; but this would inevitably add weight. Controllability in automatic fire can also be enhanced simply by reducing the rate of fire. The very high cyclic rate common in modern 5.56mm small arms has little if any practical benefit and leads to more rapid ammunition exhaustion and barrel heating as well as greater cumulative recoil.

To achieve a large volume of automatic fire, as may be involved in fighting off a close-range attack, usually requires a heavier barrel to delay overheating. However, the US HPAWA project (High Performance Alloys for Weapon Applications) aims to result in barrels which will withstand far heavier rates of sustained fire, so that MGs can be issued with only one barrel. Good progress has since been reported by ARDEC in the development of highly temperature-resistant cobalt alloys. If such alloys reach production, this should enable a standard rifle to offer volumes of fire comparable with an IAR without any increase in barrel weight. The problem of cook-off after an intense engagement could be addressed, if need be, by arranging for the gun to fire from an open bolt in automatic mode (although the USMC has not required this of their new IAR). In other words, we could replace three weapons (carbine, rifle and IAR) with one.

The design of the belt-fed LMG to accompany this rifle has not been discussed here, since the same design problems do not apply and existing designs could be adapted well enough to a new cartridge. The adoption of a general-purpose intermediate cartridge developing significantly less recoil than the 7.62mm would however obviously allow the weight of the gun to be reduced without compromising reliability, which with the significantly lighter ammunition would deliver a substantial reduction in the weight currently carried by GPMG gunners and ammunition carriers.

Sights

Rifle and MG sights are currently making great advances in capability. Variable magnification has been available on the specialist market for a very long time, and has now been joined by dual-magnification military sights, initially from Elcan (with 1-4× and 1.5-6× versions currently available), equipping the infantry with a sight suitable for both short and long-range use. The addition of electronics is bringing even more dramatic advances, most obviously in night-vision capability. In 2010 the US military stated a requirement for a 1-4× day/night sight, merging thermal and light intensifying images, with a built-in rangefinder (and possibly a laser pointer), with a 3 lb (1.36 kg) weight, low power consumption and a price of $3-5,000. With this kind of technology, such issues as air pressure, weapon cant and the effects of firing up or down hill can also be taken into account in providing an aiming solution.

The Elcan C79 sight (Source: en:User:Milofficer via Wikimedia Commons)

Even more remarkable is the LIDAR (Laser Identification Detection And Ranging) unit developed by the Israeli Soreq Nuclear Research Center. This works by firing a laser beam at the target, the reflection being captured by an array of photodiodes. Fluctuations in the signals received by the photodiodes are used to detect the direction and velocity of any cross wind, which can have a major effect on hit probability at long range. Something like this may well have an application in the DARPA One Shot next-generation sniper scope programme. The One Shot programme is intended to enable snipers to be on target with the first round, under crosswind conditions, up to the maximum effective range of the weapon: a target of 65% probability of a first-round hit at up to 1,500 metres has been set when using long-range sniper rifles.

What all of this means is that we are soon likely to see practical day/night variable magnification sights which can take into account all of the usual factors which affect bullet trajectory. All the soldier will have to do is to lase the target and the sights will automatically indicate the correct aiming mark to put the bullets into the target area.

Initially, such sights will be bulky, heavy and expensive and thereby restricted to snipers, but it is safe to predict that within the foreseeable future they will become smaller, lighter and eventually cheap enough for general issue. This is enormously important because it means that the main objection to providing rifles with a long-range capability - that most soldiers will never be well-enough trained to hit anything at such ranges - is removed. In conjunction with a long-barrelled standard rifle and long-range intermediate ammunition (and assuming a fundamentally accurate weapon and ammunition combination), this also means that a separate DMR or sharpshooter rifle may no longer be required. Potentially we could therefore replace four existing guns (carbine, rifle, IAR, DMR) with one.

The same sights and ammunition will of course also transform the long-range effectiveness of the belt-fed LMG, although the sustained-fire capability of a rifle with an advanced-alloy barrel may mean that fewer MGs will be needed.

Conclusion

So we have reduced our two cartridges to one, and our six or eight different guns to two - the general-purpose infantry rifle and the belt-fed LMG - without any loss in capability. The practical and financial advantages of such a simplification would be huge, as would the boost to the capability of the infantry sections in whatever tactical circumstances may arise.

There is an interesting parallel with the situation immediately after World War 2, when the British Army had accumulated a variety of small arms in different calibres and was faced with rationalising them. Their solution, after much deliberation and analysis of wartime experience? Just two weapons: the EM-2 bullpup selective-fire rifle and the TADEN belt-fed

MG, both in the long-range intermediate 7×43 calibre. Sadly, international politics prevented these promising weapons (or more specifically the ammunition they were designed around) from reaching service status.

All of the technologies which have been mentioned are either available now or are very likely to be available by the time the next generation of small arms has been developed. If one of the lightweight ammunition projects succeeds, then a significant weight reduction can be added to the other advantages; it would mean that an intermediate round using such technologies could weigh little more than the current brass-cased 5.56mm.

Now all that is needed are the people in the right places with the vision to see and drive towards what is possible, rather than simply going down the same old road because that's what has always been done. It is time for small arms to leave the 20th century.

Cartridges (from left to right): 5.56x45 NATO, 6.5x38 Grendel, 7x43 EM-2, 7.62x51 NATO, 7.62x54R Russian (PKM), 7.62x39 Russian (AK). The 6.5mm Grendel and 7mm EM-2 are not current military cartridges, but represent the top and bottom of the calibre and power range judged to be suitable for a general-purpose military small-arms cartridge. (Source: Author)

Naval Procurement in Emerging Markets – Asia

Peter D. Antill and Stuart Young

Centre for Defence Acquisition, Cranfield University, Defence Academy of the UK.

Introduction

The last few years have seen the majority of Asian states increasing their defence budgets and expanding their capabilities, in contrast to what has been happening in the West. The Financial Crisis of 2008 and subsequent economic recession brought about serious economic difficulties that forced many states in both Europe and North America to cut Government spending (including defence spending) to deal with budget deficit and sovereign debt problems.[1] Asia however, has seen a general trend upwards since 2000, which has continued between 2008 and 2012 despite the global recession.[2] Given the strategic geography of the region, a significant proportion of defence spending goes on naval procurement. This case study looks at what is driving the current trends in naval procurement, the policy implications of those trends and what implications this will have for future force structures.[3]

Current Requirements: Drivers

"The Asia-Pacific region's status as the world's most populous and dynamic economic zone is tempered by the fact that it is riven with unresolved territorial disputes. These – as well as continued concerns over China's military development – are driving defence spending across the region. This has been characterised by some as an arms race, although it may be better viewed as a region-wide material upgrade propelled by resource competition, rising government revenues, and declining markets elsewhere in the world."[4]

As indicated above, the increases in defence spending and build-up of naval power seen in the region has largely been a result of several complex and inter-related factors.

Economic Performance

Unlike the West, the region has seen a continued growth in Gross Domestic Product (GDP) figures despite the wider global economic recession. GDP around the region "grew by 15 per cent between 2008 and 2011, and is forecast – despite some headwinds – to climb by a further 18 per cent to 2015."[5] This economic performance has in turn, allowed Asian defence spending to increase accordingly. Specific drivers vary between states, but all have seen improvements in social and economic conditions and have used military procurement in conjunction with offsets, industrial participation and technology transfer to increase indigenous skills, employment and diversification into high technology fields. Indeed, "offset demands have proliferated across the world in recent years, although the trend towards ever-greater requests has been notable in the Asia-Pacific region."[6] Defence spending (at late 2013 prices and exchange rates) rose from US$257.42bn in 2010 to US$293.85bn in 2011 (an increase of just over 14 per cent) and to US$314.81bn in 2012 (an increase of just over 7 per cent). After taking into account exchange rate and inflationary effects, defence spending in Asia rose by 3.76 per cent in 2011 and 4.94 per cent in 2012 (at constant 2010 prices and exchange rates). A breakdown of defence spending by area shows that East Asia accounted for the largest proportion of the total at 63.9 per cent, which equated to US$201.26bn, a rise of 4.43 per cent in 2012. Over 90 per cent of the increase was due to the rise in Chinese defence spending, which officially exceeded US$100bn for the first time and accounted for about 32.5 per cent of all Asian defence spending. In East Asia, defence spending rose by 3.74 percent in 2012 to US$49.6bn, around 15.8 per cent of the total, with India accounting for over three-quarters of the region's spending. Southeast Asian defence spending totalled US$36.41bn in 2012, a rise of 6.89 per cent in 2012 and accounted for 11.6 per cent of the total. Large increases were seen from Vietnam (a rise of 16.9 per cent in real terms in 2012), Cambodia (8.14 per cent in 2012) and the Philippines (37.1 per cent in 2011 and 5.1 per cent in 2012). Australasia saw defence spending cuts in Australia while New Zealand increased defence spending by 2.7 per cent in real terms during 2012.[7]

Royal Malaysian Navy and US Navy ships on exercise (Source: Chief Mass Communication Specialist Steve Vasquez, US Navy via Wikimedia Commons)

Geo-Strategic Imperatives

At the heart of this is the uncertainty as to where exactly the regional distribution of power will lie in the coming years. This suspicion, allied to what could be perfectly innocent preparations to deal with other security concerns (some of which are listed below), has led to increases in tension between a number of regional states, which in turn has led to evidence of "action-reaction dynamics taking hold and influencing regional states' military programmes."[8] As if this wasn't complex enough, three additional factors have come into play. The first was three of the major powers in the region all underwent changes of leadership in a relatively short period of time (China, Japan and South Korea), all of which was preceded by a change of leadership in North Korea in December 2011, when Kim Jong-un succeeded his father. He immediately set about following his 'military first' policy with launching a long-range rocket and testing a nuclear device, in contravention of UN Security Council mandates. In China, the carefully prepared changeover to Xi Jinping was preceded by a sizeable amount of political infighting and manoeuvring by different factions within the Chinese Communist Party. In Japan, the Liberal Democratic Party returned to power after an absence of three years, headed by Prime Minister Shinzo Abe, who immediately embarked on an ambitious programme to revive Japan's stalled economy. In South Korea, a conservative leader and the county's first female President, Park Geun-hye, was elected and quickly subjected to a torrent of abuse from its northern neighbour.[9]

The second additional factor is the expanding power and ambition of China, whose "maritime agencies continued to send paramilitary vessels to promote and defend its extensive but ill-defined claims in the South China Sea."[10] Such vessels include unarmed ships from China Marine Surveillance (CMS) and the Fisheries Law Enforcement Command (FLEC). CMS vessels confronted the Filipino flagship *Gregorio del Pilar* near Scarborough Shoal in April 2012, an incident which started a standoff that lasted months. Although tensions eventually eased, China's stance and its willingness to use coercive economic and maritime diplomacy (via import quotas and the use of paramilitaries) underscore its growing assertiveness over its maritime interests.[11] A much more recent example was the declaration in late November 2013 of an air defence identification zone over the disputed Senkaku Islands in the East China Sea[12], a move that some worry could be repeated over other disputed territories, such as the Spratly and Paracel Islands in the South China Sea.[13]

The Chinese aircraft carrier Liaoning – in a former life the Soviet aircraft carrier Varyag (Source: US Navy via Wikimedia Commons)

The third factor is the heightened interest of the world's one remaining superpower, the United States, which starting in 2011, has refocused its attention on the region, partly as a result of Chinese moves. While this can be considered a significant shift in US policy, it is not a matter of US disengagement is Asia followed by US re-engagement in Asia, but a shift in emphasis and focus, building on the elaborate relations the US already has in the region. The United States has had wide-ranging interests in the region since the end of World War II, which has lasted through the Cold War (despite the Vietnam experience) and beyond. The current administration's policy has evolved through two distinct phases – the first in 2011 and 2012 which emphasised military initiatives (and which provoked Chinese disapproval and various responses) while in late 2012, a second phase began which downplayed military initiatives and emphasised economic and diplomatic policy actions, as well as a closer relationship with China. While some analysis has suggested these actions are a new form of 'containment' aimed at China, it is too simplistic to suppose that the new policy has just a single cause. The USA is of course aware of the growing economic and military power of China but the policy shift has been driven by a wide range of issues and concerns. Firstly, after more than a decade of conflict in both Iraq and Afghanistan, the US needs to refocus its attention of the rest of Asia, an area of the world which will be of increasing economic and political importance as the 21st Century progresses. Secondly, it reflects the need to give the rest of Asia and in particular US allies, some form of strategic reassurance vis-à-vis an increasingly powerful China – that the United States has not been weakened by years of war and by economic problems at home and that it is not going to disengage from the region. Thirdly, the US wants to expand the areas of cooperation beneficial to its interests, with both individual states (for example, China, Indonesia and India) and regional institutions. As such, the change in policy emphasis is a region-wide, multi-dimensional initiative which consists of security, economic and diplomatic elements. The US is moving substantial military capability from other theatres and restructuring its regional security arrangements while also promoting economic initiatives that expand bilateral and multilateral economic cooperation and intensifying diplomatic activity towards new and existing partners, as well as China.[14]

The USS John F Kennedy – the aircraft carrier remains at the centre of the US Navy's force structure (Source: Photographer's Mate 3rd Class Joshua Karsten, US Navy via Wikimedia Commons)

Territorial and Border Disputes

The region is rife with border and territorial disputes, many going back decades. Examples include the already mentioned Senkaku Islands in the East China Sea (which involves Japan, China and to a lesser extent South Korea and Taiwan)[15] and the Spratly and Paracel Islands in the South China Sea (which involves China, Taiwan, Vietnam, Philippines, Malaysia and Brunei).[16] Other disputes include the Kurile Islands (between Russia and Japan), the Arunachal Pradesh / Tibet border and Aksai Chin (India and China), the Takeshima Islands (Japan and South Korea), Kashmir (India and Pakistan), North Borneo (Malaysia and the Philippines), the Korean Peninsula (North and South Korea) and Scarborough Shoal (China, Taiwan and the Philippines).[17] While some of the impetus behind the recent naval procurement activity seen in the area is related to a number of the territorial disputes that are on-going, it is also very likely that some of these are related purely to the fact that an upgrade of many naval platforms is overdue, with a large number of states continuing to hold aging equipment stocks (for example, the Philippines still has World War Two-era ships in its fleet).[18]

To focus on one particular dispute, the area around the Spratly Islands is important to the economies of the states surrounding them, due to the natural resources both in terms of fish and the potential for oil and gas. This bonanza has fed various over-sized claims, which have led to a number of confrontations, both diplomatic and military. The area also sees a substantial flow of maritime commerce, which is important to both the regional and global economy with whoever is occupying the islands being able to dictate what happens with regard to the region's maritime traffic, security and economic exploitation. Such is the importance of these islands, they currently hold around fifty isolated garrisons from the claiming states and and a long history of clashes, which increases the risk of conflict in the region. All states use customary law and the United Nations Convention on the Law of the Sea (UNCLOS) to a greater or lesser degree, with parties to the dispute having to answer three legal questions – sovereignty over the islets, the nature of a claimed land feature and the delimitation of maritime jurisdiction. China, Taiwan and Vietnam use historic doctrine to claim the whole of the South China Sea as well as the doctrine of occupation to claim a variety of land features, something the Philippines and Malaysia also use. Many of the claims have counterclaims from other states with no single state holding an effective sovereignty over everything. If sovereignty for each feature type could be determined, then zones of authority could be established, taking into account freedom of navigation and access by all the concerned parties. It is this freedom of navigation which is of very real concern to the United States. The current policy of China, Vietnam and Malaysia is to restrict foreign naval activity in their zones beyond that which is normally associated with UNCLOS. If the US were to conclude an 'Incidents at Sea Agreement' with China, it would clarify the roles and responsibilities of the two powers and along with other forms of inter-government communication, could help build confidence and trust, as would US ratification of UNCLOS. Another area of concern for the US is open economic access to the South China Sea maritime commons, but one which might clash with freedom of navigation. Access to the resources of the high seas is extremely important to the US, one which has effectively held up the ratification of UNCLOS for almost twenty years. So long as the US remains outside the treaty, it remains at a disadvantage as to how maritime law evolves and is interpreted as well as shaping events, such as whether the South China Sea is completely divided up among the claiming states or becomes a 'Joint Management Zone' run for the benefit of all.[19] To

". . . contribute to overall stability and prosperity in the region, the United States must delicately play the roles of conciliator and balancer as circumstances require. The United States is an honest broker because it shares goals in common with the states around the South China Sea. Although the United States may not be truly neutral, it has less direct demands in the disputes, garnered more trust than most other states, and possesses resources to bear on these issues, making it a useful interlocutor in resolving problems."[20]

Protection of Offshore Territory / Installations

Closely linked to the above, the geography of much of the region means that many states have territory (or at least claim territory) that is geographically separate from the mainland or the main islands. The distances involved mean that the only effective way of patrolling / protecting this territory are, in many cases, naval forces. As air power is critical to naval and amphibious operations, this explains the drive by several regional powers to build up their expeditionary and naval aviation capabilities.

Defence Diplomacy, 'Showing the Flag' and Deterrence

In much of the world, but especially the West, the direct impact of war touches fewer and fewer people. In the past, the first call on taxation was always the protection of the country, its citizens and its national security. It has gradually become a generally held assumption that this 'good order' is a natural condition and can be taken for granted because 'nothing happens'. But 'nothing happens' is not by accident. In the world we live in, 'nothing happens' because of either pre-emption or deterrence, which is not, as it has come to mean, purely the prerogative of strategic nuclear forces. The term 'deterrence' can equally be applied to every day scenarios, such as having a policeman on a beat, a cyber-warfare specialist patrolling cyberspace or a warship making regular visits around a coastline. When terrorist activity does not happen (for example, bombs do not go off in city centres) there is some recognition that the state has foiled plots or that it has simply deterred a plot in the first place.[21] However, few people associate "the full supermarket shelves, the availability of a range of other goods and the supply of fuels to power our homes, cars and industry with the free flow of sea trade. But there is no natural law that assures this flow and restricts interruptions; nor is there any natural law which protects and regulates the use of the sea for the extraction of resources or inhibits territorial disputes at sea. The free flow that makes globalised trade and the creation of prosperity possible depends prominently upon the presence of naval units at sea, unseen and silent and therefore easily forgotten. This is the classic operation of deterrence and is an essential part of the reason why things do not happen."[22]

But pre-emption can also be looked at as a much wider activity. In many instances, it means developing relationships in areas of strategic importance, which can include bi-lateral or multi-lateral agreements or treaties, conducting joint exercises, undertaking joint training, port visits, providing assistance to local forces on operations, intelligence sharing or harmonising patrol schedules. In fact

"a navy serves as a diplomatic instrument. The transnational 'visibility' of a state's military might bring forth many dividends, especially if accompanied by assistance or reassurance to foreign countries. Along with showcasing the nation, 'naval diplomacy' also brings about a better appreciation of its security concerns and contributes towards building political trust."[23]

Criminal and Terrorist Activity

"Piracy is an ancient, persistent, and elusive phenomenon in the South China Sea. In the past two decades it has increased substantially, leading to a renewed interest in piracy and its possible nexus with maritime terrorism".[24] With around 90 per cent of the world's trade travelling by sea, it is no wonder there is a growing concern about this age-old phenomenon and it's link to the so-called 'ungoverned maritime space'. It is in these areas of the sea, which are often sparsely populated and rarely patrolled by government forces, that human and drug trafficking, piracy and occasionally maritime terrorism occurs. While it is true that criminal and terrorist organisations cannot sustain themselves at sea in the long-term and thus need some form of land-based support network, this does not diminish the importance the sea holds for these groups as a transport, communication and supply network, as well as a way to hide from detection. In the context of South and Southeast Asia, the main area of concern is off the coast of Sumatra, in the waters east of Singapore and off the eastern coast of Kalimantan.[25] However, it is not only direct action against shipping that is a threat. In March 2000 and May 2001 from resorts in Sipadan, Malaysia and Palawan, Philippines respectively, the Abu Sayyaff Group kidnapped Western tourists using amphibious tactics. Following the terrorist attacks in New York on 11 September 2001, Singaporean intelligence discovered a number of Al Qa'ida plots to attack several international targets, including visiting warships. There was also the bombing of the ferry *Kalifornia*, which was transporting Christians along Indonesia's Maluku Archipelago, in December 2001.[26] Indeed since 2000 "al-Qa'ida, the Moro Islamic Liberation Front, the Abu Sayyaff Group, Jemaah Islamiyah, the Kumpulan Militan Malaysia, the Gerakan Aceh Merdeka and Laskar Jihad have all been suspected of planning or executing maritime attacks."[27]

The USS Cole after being damaged by a suspected terrorist attack on 12 October 2000 (Source: US DOD via Wikimedia Commons)

Humanitarian Aid and Disaster Relief

Maritime forces are "uniquely equipped to provide international aid and rapid response to natural and man-made disasters. While these roles are not a direct response to a 'threat' to the country or international community to which the naval or maritime force belongs, by carrying out these roles navies nevertheless make a proactive and positive, if not absolutely imperative, contribution to security."[28]

437

Current Requirements: Policy Implications

The above drivers necessarily have policy implications for the states in the region, including for defence procurement itself. As with the build-up of any military capability, questions have to be asked about exactly what sort of capability a country should seek to acquire and how much. Much of this will revolve around what exactly the country wants its navy to do. In the broadest sense, navies are there to provide 'maritime security' and many would argue that this is something that they've always done but therein lies the difficulty, especially in an increasingly complex maritime environment. Many of the drivers listed above fall into what could be called the low-to-medium end of the conflict spectrum (see Figure 1 below[29]) but the requirements to engage in these sorts of operations differ from those required to engage in conventional warfare against opponents with similar capabilities and technology. As such, they demand relatively large numbers of unsophisticated ships, something than runs counter to the procurement policies practised by almost every major navy since the end of World War II, which involves a steadily shrinking number of high-quality, high-technology platforms. This then involves a major dilemma – vessels in the low-to-medium sophistication bracket will be at a real disadvantage if asked to fight a sophisticated enemy. Engaging in expeditionary warfare against a capable opponent (which is what has happened since 1990) demands a high-quality, sophisticated fleet with a full-range of capabilities. While many navies have taken the stance that these ships can be used for lesser tasks, is that really sustainable? Firstly, by definition, there can never be enough of them. Secondly, their very cost makes their potential loss undertaking such tasks an expensive risk. Thirdly, their full capability may simply prove to be too destructive to use on such missions (risking accusations of 'overkill') and fourthly, being engaged in such tasks could harm a crew's proficiency with regard to fighting a more sophisticated opponent, a mission that needs to be trained for regularly.[30]

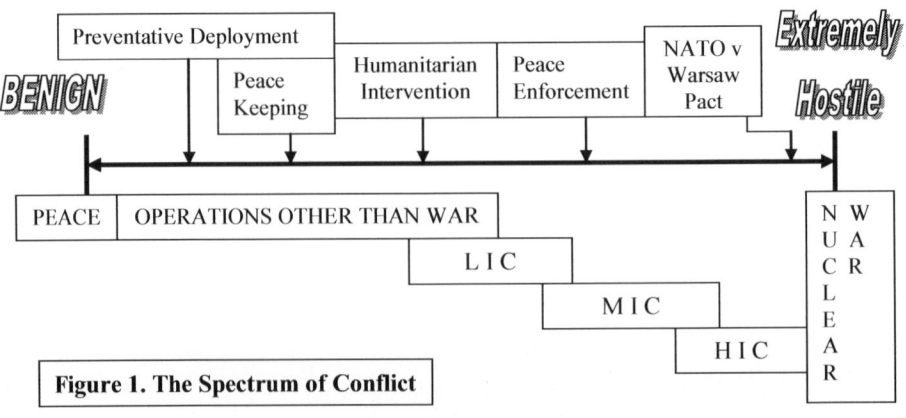

Figure 1. The Spectrum of Conflict

It should also be remembered that the actual combat forces acquired are only the tip of the iceberg. In order to carry out their duties effectively, there will be a need for additional resources committed to creating or expanding combat support and combat service support assets, infrastructure and personnel. Such additional capability includes:

Maritime Surveillance

An important component of maritime power is the ability to locate and track targets of interest, identify them, determine their status and to feed that information back to the relevant decision-makers as quickly as possible. This is made all the more critical given the vast distances involved within this region and the still (relatively) small number of naval vessels and aircraft operated by the states involved. As an attempt to try and mitigate this problem, Australia started the Pacific Patrol Boat Programme in 1983 and by 1997 had donated twenty-two vessels to twelve Pacific island nations to help with maritime surveillance, governance and to counter illegal fishing.[31]

Inter-Operability

With the rebalancing of US strategic priorities towards the Pacific and the likelihood of increasing amounts US naval combat power being based in the region, one important factor for states to consider will be their degree of inter-operability with not only US forces, but other regional forces too. This latter point is important in light of the build-up of Chinese naval power, something that no regional actor can hope to counter on its own.

Network-Centric Warfare

Linked to both the above concepts is the idea of Network Centric Warfare (NSW) which involves the use of Information Technology (IT), high-speed data links and networking software to link widely separate personnel, assets and combat units into integrated local- and wide-area networks. This will enable all those who are linked to the network to share critical information on a continuous basis in real-time and lead to improvements in both combat capability and efficiency[32]

The Royal Australian Navy auxiliary oiler replenishment ship HMAS Success attending to both the USS Kitty Hawk (CV63) and USS Cowpens (CG63) in the Coral Sea in 2005 (Source: Photographer's Mate 2nd Class William H. Ramsey, US Navy via Wikimedia Commons)

Logistic Support

Any military force, as part of its overall capability needs to have an effective, sustainable and resilient logistic support system in place so it can carry out its operational tasks. This includes a supply chain anchored in the home base (and is linked to industry) but is flexible enough to be projected across the sea using underway replenishment. An alternative to this would be to establish foreign basing rights.

Current Requirements: Force Structure Implications

Both India and China are building up large blue water naval forces with a carrier strike capability, as well as nuclear submarines. Such assets represent capabilities that are generally associated with the generation of balanced task forces for expeditionary operations and power projection. This will be important in terms of both countries' ambitions and their involvement in disputes over territory in the region. But for China, a major justification for this will be to counter US operations in the area, its perceived encirclement and the continued involvement (both militarily and politically) with states in the region, which China sees as a form of 'containment'. As such, the South and East China Seas will be a potential flashpoint for what could become an informal 'G3' (USA, China and India) in the coming decades.[33] The other states of the region will have to decide what this trend means in terms of their force structures, weighing the possible requirement to fight a conventional naval campaign against the very real requirement to deal with piracy, drug trafficking, terrorism and disaster relief operations.

One interesting trend that differentiates South and Southeast Asia from that of North America and Europe and has implications for future force structures is the ratio of defence expenditure to the number of personnel in the armed forces. This can be used as an approximate indicator of troop quality, as it's a measure of the total resources made available for recruiting, training, compensating, equipping and sustaining an individual soldier. The marked difference (with the exception of Japan) is due to the larger overall force structures retained by many countries, when compared to their overall defence spending. The relatively low per-soldier defence spending seen in four of the top five defence spenders indicates that the current priority is quantity, rather than quality. This is in diametric opposition to the trends seen in North America and Europe where force structures have been cut considerably in favour of generating higher quality forces. For example, China, India, South Korea and Taiwan all spent between $28,200 and $43,600 per service member in 2011, which was significantly less than Japan ($238,100), Europe as a whole ($140,400) and the USA ($504,800). This however disguises the fact that per-soldier defence spending has generally been on the rise, as defence budgets have increased while force structures have remained relatively stable.[34]

Current and Future Programmes

The region's naval procurement programmes include:[35]

- Australia – with government plans to implement austerity measures that include cutting Au$4bn from the defence budget by 2016, new procurement is thin on the ground. Work began on the Navy's new *Hobart*-class air warfare destroyer in April 2012 and delivery of the Canberra-class landing helicopter dock (LHD) vessels looks to be on schedule. The Navy is also considering the conversion of a number of F/A-18 Super Hornets to EA-18G Growler configuration and still expects twelve new submarines to be built in-country.

- Bangladesh – plans exist to expand the navy's capabilities with the acquisition of submarines, frigates and maritime patrol aircraft, with China as a major supplier. For example, in 2012 both the Wuchang and Khulna Shipyards launched large patrol craft, built under a May 2010 technology transfer agreement.

- Brunei – Following the failure of the Nakhoda Ragam Offshore Patrol Vessel (OPV) programme, Brunei procured four forty-one metre *Ijtihad*-class fast patrol boats in 2010 and three eighty metre *Darussalam*-class OPVs from Germany's Lurssen, in 2011. A fourth *Darussalam*-class OPV is currently being built.

- China – continues to expand its power projection capabilities. In September 2012, China launched its first aircraft carrier, the 50,000-tonne *Liaoning*, which is based on the uncompleted Soviet carrier *Varyag*. This was followed a month later by arrested landings and take-offs of Su-33 derived Shenyang J-15 fighters, as well as Z-8 airborne early warning (AEW) helicopter operations. A fixed-wing AEW aircraft, the JZY-01 is known to be under development. Since mid-2012, three further Type-052D destroyers have been built, production continued on the Type-054 frigates, two *Fuchi*-class replenishment ships launched and six Type-056 corvettes completed.

The two Indian aircraft carriers – INS Vikramaditya (foreground) and the INS Viraat (background). The INS Viraat was formerly HMS Hermes (Source: Indian Navy via Wikimedia Commons)

- India – the navy accounts for eighteen per cent of the defence budget and has several major procurement programmes underway. It has adopted a capability-based approach rather than a threat-based to try and guide modernisation and ensure a fleet with adequate balance, reach and combat power. The Indian Navy has received two *Talwar*-class frigates and commissioned the *Akula*-class nuclear-powered attack submarine INS *Chakra* (Project 971). The delays and problems surrounding this programme has been symptomatic of India's continued struggle with defence programme project management, as has the continued delays to the aircraft carrier *Vikramaditya* (the ex-Soviet *Admiral Korshkov*) and its own indigenous 37,500 tonne carrier. Six *Scorpene*-class submarines are under construction at Mazagon Dock in Mumbai and the Navy continues to move towards trialling the *Arihant*-class nuclear-powered ballistic missile submarine, due to enter service in around 2015.

- Indonesia – is looking to acquire at least three, and possibly as many as ten *Cang Bogo* submarines (based on the German Type 209) which will be partially built by local industry, as well as at least two, and perhaps as many as twenty *Sigma*-class frigates. Additional programmes include the C-235 maritime patrol aircraft (the first of which was handed over in October 2013[36]), Bell 212EP helicopters and naval trimarans with stealth characteristics.

- Japan – Despite stringent austerity measures brought in to tackle Japan's huge public debt, the Maritime Self-Defense Force (MSDF) has asked for funding to acquire a new 5000-tonne anti-submarine destroyer, two Aegis destroyers, an extra submarine and the Kawasaki P-1 maritime patrol aircraft, while the Ground SDF is looking to buy four amphibious assault vehicles.

- Malaysia – force modernisation seems to taking place at a slower rate than many of its neighbours, with two *Scorpene*-class submarines being acquired in 2010 and six 'Littoral Combat Ships' based on the based on the DCNS 'Gowind' design having been ordered in 2011, a follow-up to the procurement of six *Kadeh*-class Next Generation Patrol Vessels..

- Philippines – With the improvement in the US-Philippines relationship, Manila agreed to allow the US military to establish a semi-permanent forward base at Subic Bay (formerly the USA's largest overseas naval installation). Added to that much better economic conditions and a confrontation between Chinese and Philippine vessels at

Scarborough Shoal in April 2012, the Philippines is looking to acquire a range of new equipment including frigates and naval helicopters from Italy, light attack helicopters from France and multipurpose assault craft.

- Singapore – the central programme underway at the moment is the replacement of the twelve *Fearless*-class patrol vessels although the Defence Minister Dr Ng Eng Hen indicated that Singapore would be looking to replace its *Challenger*-class submarines in the near future.

- South Korea – while Seoul's main priority is to counter the North's growing ballistic missile and long-range artillery threats, the navy plans to introduce greater integrated surface, submarine and naval aviation capabilities by 2020. It also plans to acquire an additional six KDX-IIA and three KDX-III destroyers and the Type 214 submarine.

- Taiwan – has plans to improve naval surveillance with P-3C *Orion* maritime patrol aircraft and E-2K *Hawkeye* early-warning aircraft. In keeping with a move towards an asymmetric strategy for countering any Chinese aggression, it has deployed thirty-one *Kuang Hua* VI seventy-tonne fast-attack missile boats, upgraded its 500-tonne *Jinn Chiang*-class patrol boats and started development on a 450-tonne fast-attack corvette and a medium-sized submarine, to complement its two *Hai Lung* submarines, which are being upgraded to take *Harpoon*.

- Thailand – the Royal Thai Navy has a requirement for two frigates, for which US$1bn has been allocated by the government. In April 2013, it was announced that South Korea's DSME was chosen to provide two 3,000 to 4,000-tonne frigates by 2015. It is also upgrading its two *Naresuan*-class frigates but the plans for its submarine fleet are in limbo with the deal to buy six surplus Type 206A class submarines from Germany falling through.

- Vietnam – Russia remains the country's chief supplier. In recent years the Navy has acquired two *Gepard*-class guided missile frigates, with another two on order. Future acquisitions include six *Kilo*-class attack submarines, *Svetlyak*-class fast attack craft, *Tarantul*-class missile corvettes, HQ-272 (Project TT400TP) patrol craft and four Dutch *Sigma*-class corvettes, two of which are expected to be built in-country. Hanoi also launched two indigenous vessels, a fifty-four metre, 400-tonne fast patrol boat and a seventy-two metre transport vessel.[37]

Conclusion

Naval procurement in South and Southeast Asia has seen steadily increasing levels of expenditure as the economies of the region grow. The current and future size of these budgets and how these budgets have been and will be spent, hinge of a number of complex, yet inter-dependent variables that include geographic considerations, foreign and defence policies, strategic aspirations, relations between individual states, border and territorial disputes as well as local, regional and global security concerns tied up with such activity as piracy, the trafficking of people and drugs and terrorism. What complicates an already complex picture will be the interaction of the region's three major players, China, India and the USA and the great power political manoeuvring that will develop between them.

Endnotes

[1] International Institute for Strategic Studies. (2013) *The Military Balance 2013*, Routledge: London, 14 March 2013, located at http://dx.doi.org/10.1080/04597222.2013. 756999, pp. 59-66 and 92-94, as of 28 November 2013.

[2] Hofbauer, J., Hermann, P. and Raghavan, S. (2012) *Asian Defense Spending 2000-2011*, October 2012, Center for Strategic & International Studies, currently located at http://csis.org/files/publication/121005_Berteau_AsianDefenseSpending_Web.pdf, as of 28 November 2013; *Op Cit*. IISS, 2013, p. 249.

[3] This case study is based on an article first published in *Defence Procurement International*, Winter 2013, pp. 28-35.

[4] Hardy, J. (2013) 'Annual Defence Report 2013: Asia-Pacific' in *Jane's Defence Weekly*, posted 4 December 2013, at www.janes.ihs.com, as of 4 December 2013.

[5] Anderson, G. (2012) 'Briefing: Asia-Pacific Emerging Markets – Growing and Evolving' in *Jane's Defence Weekly*, posted 3 July 2012, at www.janes.ihs.com, as of 3 December 2013.

[6] *Ibid*.

[7] *Op Cit*. IISS, March 2013, pp. 249-251.

[8] *Ibid*. p. 245.

[9] International Institute for Strategic Studies. (2013) *Strategic Survey 2013*, Routledge: London, 13 September 2013, located at http://dx.doi.org/10.1080/04597230.2013.830467 , pp. 309 and 333, as of 7 January 2014,

[10] *Ibid*.

[11] *Op Cit*. IISS, March 2013, p. 253.

[12] Branigan, T. (2013) 'Airlines 'Must Warn China' of Flight Plans Over Disputed Islands' in *The Guardian*, posted 25 November 2013, at http://www.theguardian.com/world/2013/nov/25/china-air-defence-zone-japan-islands-diaoyu-senkaku, as of 3 December 2013.

[13] Lewis, P. and Ackerman, S. (2013) 'US Calls on China to Rescind Air Defence Zone to Avoid Japanese Confrontation' in *The Guardian*, posted 3 December 2013 at http://www.theguardian.com/world/2013/dec/02/us-china-rescind-air-defence-zone-confrontation-japan, as of 3 December 2013.

[14] Sutter, R. et al. (2013) *Balancing Acts: The U.S. Rebalance and Asia-Pacific Stability*, August 2013, at http://www.gwu.edu/~sigur/assets/docs/BalancingActs_Compiled1.pdf, as of 3 December 2013.

[15] BBC. (2013) 'Q&A: China-Japan Islands Row' webpage, dated 27 November 2013, located at http://www.bbc.co.uk/news/world-asia-pacific-11341139, as of 3 December 2013.

[16] BBC. (2013) 'Q&A: South China Sea Dispute' webpage, dated 15 May 2013, located at http://www.bbc.co.uk/news/world-asia-pacific-13748349, as of 3 December 2013.

[17] Le Mière, C. and Raine, S. (2013) 'Water Pollution – South China Sea Dispute Taints the Region' in *Jane's Intelligence Review*, posted 17 January 2013, at www.janes.ihs.com, as of 3 December 2013; Moss, T. (2013) 'History's Long Wars: A Long View of Asia's Territorial Disputes', the diplomat.com, dated 15 September 2013, located at http://thediplomat.com/2013/09/history-wars-a-long-view-of-asias-territorial-disputes/, as of 3 December 2013; Dolvin, B., Kan, S. and Manyin, M. (2013) *Maritime Territorial Disputes in East Asia – Issues for Congress*, Congressional Research Service, 30 January 2013, located at http://www.fas.org/sgp/crs/row/R42930.pdf, as of 3 December 2013.

[18] Grevatt, J. (2013) 'Briefing: Powering Up' in *Jane's Defence Weekly*, posted 16 July 2013 at www.janes.ihs.com, as of 3 December 2013.

[19] Bouchat, C. (2013) *Dangerous Ground: The Spratly Islands and US Interests and Approaches*, Strategic Studies Institute, US Army War College, December 2013, located at http://www.strategicstudiesinstitute.army.mil/pubs/display.cfm?pubID=1187, as of 9 January 2014.

[20] *Ibid*. p. xi.

[21] Blackham, J and Prins, G. (2010) 'Why Things Don't Happen: Silent Principles of National Security' in *The RUSI Journal*, Vol. 155, No. 4, pp. 14-22.

[22] *Ibid*. p. 16.

[23] Khurana, G. (2005) 'Cooperation Among Maritime Security Forces: Imperatives for

India and Southeast Asia' in *Strategic Analysis*, Vol. 29, No. 2 (April-June 2005, pp. 295-316), pp. 308-309.

[24] Rosenberg, D. (2009) 'The Political Economy of Piracy in the South China Sea' in the *Naval War College Review*, Vol. 62, No. 3, pp. 43-58, available at http://community.middlebury.edu/~scs/docs/Rosenberg%20NWCR%20SU09.pdf, as of 14 January 2014, p. 43.

[25] Le Mière, C. (2013) 'All at Sea – Illicit Activity Thrives in Ungoverned Maritime Areas' in *Jane's Intelligence Review*, posted 9 October 2013, at www.janes.ihs.com, as of 4 December 2013.

[26] Bradford, Lt J. (2005) 'The Growing Prospects for Maritime Security Cooperation in Southeast Asia' in *Naval War College Review*, Vol. 58, No. 3 (Summer 2005), pp. 63-86.

[27] *Ibid.* p. 70.

[28] Bellamy, C. (2013) 'Naval Power: Strategic Relevance in the 21st Century' in *Jane's Navy International*, posted 2 December 2013, at www.janes.ihs.com, as of 4 December 2013.

[29] Moore, D and Antill, P. (2011) 'Swords, Ploughshares and Supply Chains: NGO and Military Integration in Disaster Relief Operations' in Moore, D. (Ed) (2011) *Case Studies in Defence Procurement and Logistics – Volume I: From World War II to the Post-Cold War World*, Cambridge: Cambridge Academic Press, p. 329.

[30] Murphy, M. (2007) 'Suppression of Piracy and Maritime Terrorism' in *Naval War College Review*, Volume 60, No. 3, pp. 23-45, available at http://www.mtholyoke.edu/~dewar20e/International%20Security%20Research/murphy.pdf, as of 14 January 2014.

[31] *Op Cit.* Le Mière, 9 October 2013.

[32] O'Rourke, R. (2005) *Navy Network-Centric Warfare Concept: Key Programs and Issues for Congress*, Congressional Research Service, dated 31 May 2005, currently located at http://www.history.navy.mil/library/online/navy_network.htm, as of 4 December 2013.

[33] Ministry of Defence. (2012) *Regional Survey – South Asia out to 2040*, Strategic Trends Programme, Defence Concepts and Doctrine Centre, October 2012, currently located at https://www.gov.uk/government/uploads/system/uploads/attachment_data/file/49954/20121129_dcdc_gst_regions_sasia.pdf, as of 4 December 2013.

[34] *Op Cit.* Hofbauer, Hermann and Raghavan, 2012, p. vii and pp. 45-46.

[35] *Op Cit.* IISS, 2013, pp. 245-277; Hardy, J. et al. 'JDW 2012 Annual Defence Report: Asia-Pacific' in *Jane's Defence Weekly*, posted 14 December 2012, at www.janes.ihs.com as of 28 November 2013; Mahadzir, D. (2013) 'Briefing: Building Capabilities' in

Jane's Defence Weekly, posted 26 April 2013, at www.janes.ihs.com, as of 3 December 2013; *Op Cit*. Hardy, 4 December 2013.

[36] Taylor, E. (2013) 'IAe hands over maritime patrol C-235 to Indonesia's navy', *Flight International*, dated 4 October 2013, at http://www.flightglobal.com/news/articles/iae-hands-over-maritime-patrol-cn235-to-indonesias-navy-391310/, as of 29 November 2013.

[37] *Op Cit*. Grevatt, 16 July 2013.

Index

Printed in Great Britain
by Amazon.co.uk, Ltd.,
Marston Gate.